国家级一流专业建设点（英语专业）项目成果
南京航空航天大学"十四五"规划教材
南京航空航天大学研究生教育教学改革专项项目成果

跨学科英语文学阅读与欣赏

主　编　姜礼福

副主编　孟庆粉　白雪花

编　委　信慧敏　邵　珊　刘世红

南京大学出版社

图书在版编目(CIP)数据

跨学科英语文学阅读与欣赏 / 姜礼福主编. —南京：南京大学出版社，2022.11
ISBN 978-7-305-26256-2

Ⅰ.①跨… Ⅱ.①姜… Ⅲ.①英语-阅读教学-高等学校-教材 Ⅳ.①H319.37

中国版本图书馆 CIP 数据核字(2022)第 213383 号

出版发行	南京大学出版社
社　　址	南京市汉口路 22 号　　邮　编　210093
出 版 人	金鑫荣

书　　名	跨学科英语文学阅读与欣赏
主　　编	姜礼福
责任编辑	孙　辉　　　　　　编辑热线　025-83592409
照　　排	南京开卷文化传媒有限公司
印　　刷	徐州绪权印刷有限公司
开　　本	787 mm×1092 mm　1/16　印张 20.75　字数 505 千
版　　次	2022 年 11 月第 1 版　2022 年 11 月第 1 次印刷
ISBN	978-7-305-26256-2
定　　价	66.00 元

网　　址：http://www.njupco.com
官方微博：http://weibo.com/njupco
官方微信号：njupress
销售咨询热线：(025)83594756

＊版权所有，侵权必究
＊凡购买南大版图书，如有印装质量问题，请与所购
　图书销售部门联系调换

前　言

匆匆流年，不知不觉中，我已从事英语文学教学十余载。我讲授的课程包括英国文学、美国文学、英语文学等，教学对象涵盖英语专业高年级本科生、非英语专业辅修班、文科强化班、英语专业研究生等。随着对教学的认知不断深化，我萌生了编写教材的想法。文学教学和研究是一个不断修炼的过程，而一本好的教材可以让教师教得得心应手、如虎添翼，使学生如沐春风，学得酣畅淋漓。于是，我与几位同仁合作，一起编写了这本教材。

文学教材应当面向学生并具有明确的目标。该教材主要面向有一定文学史基础知识的高年级英语专业本科生、英语专业研究生，突破了传统的文学史编写模式，可优化学生的知识结构，从新的视角实现知识重构，提供的译文使该教材亦适用于非英语专业本研学生。文学教学绝非仅仅是学习语言、汲取知识、赏析技巧、了解文化，更重要的是，透过文学作品了解社会现实、追溯历史真实，而最可贵的是可以引领学生品味人生、认识自我、形塑品格、铸造灵魂，牢固树立正确的世界观、人生观和价值观。

文学教材应具有鲜明特色和独特气质。该教材未采用传统的文学史编写模式，而是以专题为纲。人与自然之间的关系、两性关系、人与自我之间的关系、种族关系等四个专题皆紧紧围绕知识传授、能力培养和价值引领，并融入诸多中国文化元素，实现由文学教学到文学教育的提升。通过四个专题，分别开展全球视野/世界公民责任教育、幸福情感教育、心理健康教育、家国情怀/文明互鉴教育，倡导人与自然之间的"天人合一"、两性关系的"琴瑟和鸣"、人与自我的"身心和谐"、民族/种族之间的文明互鉴和"和而不同"精神。

跨学科性是该教材的灵魂所在，这也体现了该教材在"新文科"建设方面的探索。本教材将文学鉴赏根植于整个人文社科乃至自然科学领域，借鉴哲学、心理学、社会学、人类学、和平学、政治学、历史学、地质学等领域的相关概念,助力作品分析和鉴赏,体现了鲜明的跨学科性。教材还注重研究性,通过跨学科概念的使用,实现高度、深度和温度的统一。该教材通过思维导图板块训练学生的"思维肌",探索并呈现了"三维思辨法",引导学生形成三维思考习惯,促进学生逻辑推理、批判思维、研究能力的提升,强化学生对作品理解的深度,达到固化新思维的效果,从而实现真正的思维训练和创新。更重要的是,该教材有一个"中国魂",体现了国家意识。通过专题的形式将传统文化中的"天人合一"、新时代文化中的"人类命运共同体"等理念融入其中。

本教材所选取的文本体裁多样,涉及小说、诗歌、散文、戏剧等,既有文坛巨擘的经典之作,也有文学新秀的作品,同时注重作家国别的多样性,涉及的国别包括英国、美国、加拿大、新西兰、南非等,充分体现了该教材英语文学的定位。无论何种题材和选题,都历经多轮教学实践,凡是经典作品都尝试采用新的视角进行重读,新的作品则同学术前沿相交融,力图使学生学有所思、学有所获、学有所成,达到丰富知识、开拓视野、提升能力、启迪智慧之效果。

姜礼福

2022年10月于南京月牙湖畔

CONTENTS

Section One Tianren Heyi: Human-Nature Relationship

    Unit 1   Michael McCarthy: From *The Moth Snowstorm: Nature and Joy* ······ 3

    Unit 2   Stephen King: *The Cat from Hell* ·· 18

    Unit 3   Paolo Bacigalupi: *The Tamarisk Hunter* ······································· 34

Section Two Male-Female Affinity: Gender Relationship

    Unit 4   Edgar Allan Poe: *The Black Cat* ··· 51

    Unit 5   Doris Lessing: *Our Friend Judith* ··· 62

    Unit 6   Joyce Carol Oates: *The White Cat* ··· 80

    Unit 7   Alice Munro: *Runaway* ·· 102

Section Three Body-Mind Harmony: Self-Relationship

    Unit 8   William Faulkner: *A Rose for Emily* ·· 135

    Unit 9   Theodore Dreiser: From *An American Tragedy* ···························· 146

    Unit 10 Katherine Mansfield: *The Fly* ·· 158

    Unit 11 Edward Albee: From *The Goat, or Who is Sylvia?* ···················· 167

Section Four Diversity and Respect: Ethnic/Racial Relationship

    Unit 12 Langston Hughes: *My People* ·· 197

    Unit 13 Ralph Ellison: *Flying Home* ·· 201

    Unit 14 Maya Angelou: *Still I Rise* ·· 221

    Unit 15 J. M. Coetzee: From *Waiting for the Barbarians* ······················ 226

Appendix Chinese Translation of Some Selected Texts

目　录

第一部分　天人合——人与自然的关系
第一讲　迈克尔·麦卡锡：《飞蛾茫茫——自然与欢愉》节选 …… 3
第二讲　斯蒂芬·金：《夺命灵猫》 …… 18
第三讲　保罗·巴奇加卢皮：《柽柳猎人》 …… 34

第二部分　琴瑟和鸣——两性间的情感关系
第四讲　埃德加·爱伦·坡：《黑猫》 …… 51
第五讲　多丽丝·莱辛：《我们的朋友朱迪斯》 …… 62
第六讲　乔伊斯·卡罗尔·欧茨：《白猫米兰达》 …… 80
第七讲　爱丽丝·门罗：《逃离》 …… 102

第三部分　身心和谐——人与自我之间的关系
第八讲　威廉·福克纳：《献给艾米丽的一朵玫瑰》 …… 135
第九讲　西奥多·德莱赛：《美国的悲剧》节选 …… 146
第十讲　凯瑟琳·曼斯菲尔德：《苍蝇》 …… 158
第十一讲　爱德华·阿尔比：《山羊或谁是西尔维亚？》节选 …… 167

第四部分　和而不同——种族/民族之间的关系
第十二讲　兰斯顿·休斯：《同胞》 …… 197
第十三讲　拉尔夫·埃里森：《归航》 …… 201
第十四讲　玛雅·安吉罗：《我仍将崛起》 …… 221
第十五讲　约翰·库切：《等待野蛮人》节选 …… 226

附录　部分文本译文

Section One

Tianren Heyi: Human-Nature Relationship

The invention of the steam engine in 1784 heralded a new era of the industrial revolution and Western modernity characterized by the rejection of tradition, belief in social progress and scientific development, and faith in the benefits of rationalism. Modernity is based on the dichotomy between nature and humanity. Human beings have benefited so much from exploiting nature and are dependent on it, which is leading to severe environmental problems. Nowadays climate change has emerged as one of the biggest challenges facing the world. It is a "wicked problem" that makes many people feel so helpless and powerless that they tend to ignore it, rather than solve it.

The current predicament human beings are plunged into rings the alarm bell that for generations human beings have not been taught an important lesson: nature should be taken seriously and be appropriately respected. On an individual basis, people have not been taught these lessons during childhood. Now it is high time people learned a lesson, and it can never be too late.

There is no question that ecological education should be taught, which can not be stressed enough. There is a very long history of ecological tradition in China, and the Confucian concept of "Tianren Heyi", or "heaven-and-human oneness", is the most essential and offers an invaluable source for people to re-conceptualize and reflect upon the relationship between human beings and nature. The notion of "Tianren Heyi" resonates with the exploration into a new mode of modern civilization.

Currently, China is sparing no effort to enhance ecological civilization. Through ensuring greater harmony between humanity and nature while pursuing development, China is committed to addressing pollution, protecting and restoring ecosystems. China has increased the treatment of solid waste and new pollutants and implemented measures to sort and reduce waste, and boost recycling. Furthermore, China is working hard to reduce the use of fossil fuels and replace them with alternative energy to achieve a carbon emissions peak by 2030 and carbon neutrality by 2060. In the new era, it is necessary to promote "the creative development and innovative transformation of fine traditional Chinese culture" to confront the problem the epoch of the Anthropocene triggers.

Unit 1
From *The Moth Snowstorm: Nature and Joy*

Michael McCarthy

Introduction to the Author

Michael McCarthy (1947—) is an environmentalist, naturalist, newspaper journalist and one of the leading writers on the environment in Britain. McCarthy studied modern languages at the University of Liverpool. He was a longtime environment editor of *The Independent* and environment correspondent of *The Times*. He is the recipient of the RSPB Medal from the Royal Society for the Protection of Birds and the Silver Medal from the Zoological Society of London.

His books include *Say Goodbye to the Cuckoo* in 2009 and *The Moth Snowstorm* in 2015, and *The Consolation of Nature: Spring in the Time of Coronavirus* (2020).

Introduction to the Work

Drawing on a wealth of memorable experiences from a lifetime of watching and thinking about wildlife and natural landscapes, *The Moth Snowstorm* not only presents a new way of looking at the world around us, but effortlessly blends with it a remarkable and moving memoir of childhood trauma from which love of the natural world emerged. It is a powerful, timely, and wholly original book which comes at a time when nature has never needed it more. McCarthy offers the world a galvanizing call by suggesting that a more effective way of helping people connect with nature—and take up the cause of protecting it—is by focusing on our joy in nature as our reason for defending it.

Text

The Moth Snowstorm: Nature and Joy
(Excerpt)

The twenty-first century will be terrible for the natural world to which as a young boy I became so bound.

I am a baby boomer; I am of that generation born in the rich West in the aftermath of the Second World War, the generation which came to adulthood in the explosion of new freedoms of the 1960s and thought it had inherited the mastery of the universe simply by being young. And perhaps it had. So heady were its early years that my generation has been wholly defined by them, till now; we were as sharply marked by rock and roll as our parents and grandparents were by the two world wars. But as we come to the end of our time a different way of categorizing us is beginning to manifest itself: we were the generation who, over the long course of our lives, saw the shadow fall across the face of the earth.

Let us set it out. Our world is under threat, as it has never been before, from a malady previous generations did not anticipate: the scale of the human enterprise ... This is the sudden headlong rush of exponential growth. It took us all by surprise. After the long unfolding of the human story, after all the millennia of history of prehistory, it happened in a mere four decades, well within a single human lifetime, indeed within my own: between my teenage years and my middle years, between 1960 and 2000, the world's population doubled, from 3 to 6 billion. (Then it added another billion in the next decade, and will grow by a further 3 billion in the four decades to come.) And not only did the numbers mushroom, in the poorer countries especially; consumption exploded in the richer nations as they grew richer still and the baby boomers, the luckiest generation who ever lived, lapped it up; and while population doubled, the world economy in the same period grew more than six times bigger. Looking back, this now seems much the most consequential historical event of the second half of the twentieth century, of more fundamental import even than the development and spread of nuclear weapons or retreat from empires, or the Arab-Israeli conflict, or the failure of the socialist project.

When did humans, creatures of the genus *Homo*, first begin to modify the world in a measurable way? Almost certainly when anatomically and behaviourally modern people, that is, members of the species *Homo sapiens*, emerged out of Africa some time perhaps around sixty thousand years ago, and began to spread eastwards across the world, to Asia, then down to Australasia, then back north-westwards into Europe, and finally over the Bering Strait land bridge from Siberia into the Americas. Formidably advanced through their possession of language, they—we—displaced and almost certainly annihilated the earlier species of humans which had spread out of Africa long before them, *Homo erectus* in Asia and the Neanderthals in Europe (who may not have possessed fully developed speech); and while they were at it, they visited a similar fate on the enormous animals which, over millions of years, had everywhere evolved as the top layer of the mammal and marsupial fauna which we still possess today. We do not accord much imagining to these vanished behemoths. We should. It was a massacre unparalleled. By the end of the Pleistocene, the long epoch of the ice ages, whole continental guilds of great beasts had been extirpated by humans, by the hunter-gatherers, such as the Australian megafauna with its two-tonne wombat, diprotodon, or the megafauna of South America with its colossal ground sloths whose fossils Darwin found, or the megafauna of Eurasia with its giant Irish elk whose ten-feet wide and ten-feet high antlers make you gasp in surprise when you encounter them in the atrium of the biological sciences department at the University of Durham.

No one really knows what happened, of course, and some paleontologists believe changes in climate may have been responsible, but the most persuasive arguments strongly suggest that humans took them out; we did it. Twenty thousand, thirty, even forty thousand years ago, we were already transforming the world around us, we were destroying on a grand scale; and our populations were minuscule. What must be the effect, then, when not only has the technology for earth modification advanced, in our stirring journey upwards, from the hand-axe to the chainsaw, from the deer shoulder-blade to the bulldozer, from the fish-hook to the mile-long driftnet and from the throwing spear to the automatic rifle, but when we ourselves have undergone an upsurge in numbers which can only be described as gargantuan?

It is extraordinary: we are wrecking the earth, as burglars will sometimes wantonly wreck a house. It is a strange and terrible moment in history. We who ourselves depend upon it utterly are laying waste to the biosphere, the thin, planet-encircling envelope of life, rushing to degrade the atmosphere above and the ocean below and the soil at the centre and everything it supports; grabbing it, ripping it, scattering it, tearing at it, torching it, slashing at it, shitting on it. Already more than half the rainforests are gone, pesticide use has decimated wild flowers and the insect populations of farmland and rivers, the beds of the seas are deeply degraded and most of the fish stocks are at danger levels, the acidity of the ocean steadily rising, coral reefs are under multiple assault, 40 billion tonnes of climate-changing carbon are loading the atmosphere every year and currently one-fifth, and rising, of all vertebrates—mammals, birds, fish, reptiles, and amphibians—are threatened with extinction... Loss is everywhere, and the defining characteristic of the natural world in the twenty-first century is no longer beauty, nor riches, nor abundance, nor, if you like, life force, but has vulnerability.

It cannot be stressed enough: these losses are not caused by natural events, such as tsunamis or volcanic eruptions. They are the work of people—of us—and as we continue to grow, and our needs continue to expand, so will the devastation. The proximate causes can be easily enumerated—we can see that they are habitat destruction, pollution, over-exploitation or overhunting, the havoc caused by invasive species and increasingly, a changing climate—but the ultimate cause of the great spreading ruination remains *Homo sapiens*: just one of the earth's great array of millions of radiated life forms, whose numbers, having exploded beyond the planet's ability to carry them, are now firmly on course to wreck it.

In a curious historical coincidence, at the very time when the explosion in numbers was beginning, a new vision of the earth it was so direly to affect was vouchsafed to us. We can put a precise date on it: Christmas Eve 1968. The person directly responsible was William Anders, an American astronaut, one of the crew of Apollo 8, the first manned spacecraft to leave the earth's orbit and circle the moon. When, on 24 December, he and fellow crewmen Frank Borman and Jim Lovell emerged in their craft from behind the moon's dark side, they saw in front of them an astounding sight: an exquisite blue sphere hanging in the blackness of space. The photograph Anders took of it is known as *Earthrise*, and its taking was without doubt one of the profoundest events in the history of human culture, for at this moment, for the first time, we saw ourselves from a distance, and the earth in its surrounding dark emptiness not only seemed impossibly beautiful but also impossibly fragile. Most of all, we could see clearly that it was finite. This does not appear to us on the earth's surface; the land or the sea stretches to the horizon, but there is always something beyond. However many horizons we cross, there's always another one waiting. Yet on

glimpsing the planet from deep space, we saw not only the true wonder of its shimmering blue beauty, but also the true nature of its limits. Seen in the round, not really very big at all—the Apollo 8 astronauts could cover it with a thumbnail—and most assuredly, isolated. Only the one. Nowhere else for us to decamp to, in the never-ending blackness. Thanks to *Earthrise*, we now understand it in the intuitive way, in our souls: what we are wrecking is our home.

The idea that something might be done about this, that a way might be found to hold back the tide of human destruction across the globe has been one of the great moral and intellectual challenges of the last quarter of a century given that the pressures involved are intractable and problem itself is fully acknowledged by relatively few. They are usually classed as environmentalists or conservationists. They are in every country, and they are often loud and sound influential, but their small number in global terms. Most ordinary individuals do not care, because the consequences are not yet visited upon them (although they will be) and also because people are quite naturally focused on their own concerns, which often seem harmless enough, and do not grasp that the essence of the trouble to come is their own individual choices, multiplied seven billion times.

Furthermore, the destruction of humanity's home by humanity's own actions is not something that can be coped with adequately—and that means, confronted—by our current belief system which we might term liberal secular humanism. This creed, which has held sway since the Second World welfare. It wants people everywhere to be free from hunger and fear and disease, and in so far as is possible, to be happy and to live fulfilled lives. It is principled and upright. It is admirable. But there is a gap at its core: the failure to acknowledge that humans are not necessarily good. Still less does it admit that, more, there may be something intrinsically troubling about humans as a species: admit that more about humans as a species that *Homo sapiens* may be the earth's problem child.

Many, indeed, would be outraged by the suggestion, for poverty and hunger and disease are terrible enough without proposing that people as a whole are in some way flawed. Yet for the Greeks, the founders of our culture, this idea was central to their morality. There was a continual problem with man. Man was glorious, almost godlike, and continually striving upwards; yet only the gods were actually up there, and if man tried to get too high, as he often did, the gods would destroy him. The gods represented man's limits. We think of Icarus, of course, but there are deeper lessons to be learned. The principal fault of Oedipus in Sophocles' *Oedipus Rex*, remember, was not that he murdered his father and married his mother; those were the incidentals of his fate. His real fault was that he thought he *knew* everything, he had answered the riddle of the Sphinx, he was beyond peradventure wise. The gods showed him he was not.

In the modern consensus, in liberal secular humanism, this spiritual view of man has having limits, as not being able to do everything he chooses, and of potentially being a problem creature-for what else is a species which destroys its own home?—is missing entirely. There is no trace of it whatsoever. To suggest it, is absolute anathema. With the dying of religion and vanishing of spirituality we have become our own moral yardstick: at the heart of our notions of good and bad lies human suffering and what we can do to avoid it. This is so deep-rooted in us now, so instinctive, that it has been internalised in the language: one of our most prized virtues is humanity, one of our deepest tributes to another person, that they are humane. He, or she, is a humane human. It's only one letter, one squiggle away from saying he, or she, is a human human. Our morality now is entirely anthropocentric: we automatically define objective good by what is best for ourselves. So where humanity's interests clash with other interests, the other they are likely to get short shrift from us, even when thy involve the proper functioning of the planet, which is the only place we have to live …

Here we are at a peculiar moment in history, when the natural world is mortally threatened as never before, and those who love it are crying out for a defence. Yet while a new defence is being offered—one which is far more realistic and hard-headed than previous defences, one which must stand a better chance of succeeding—as we examine it, we realise that it too is deeply, crucially, fatally flawed.

What are we to do?

In a famous preface to one of his short novels, Joseph Conrad pointed out that the enterprise of the scientist or the intellectual may have more immediate impact, but that of the artist is more enduring because it goes far deeper; the statement of fact, however powerful, does not take hold like the image does …

The idea that wild places, those which remain wholly untouched by people, might be of value to us and even cherished and protected, rather than just being thought of as waste land or worse, is relatively recent, in historical terms. Once, of course, there were no wild places as such; during the fifty thousand generations and more we spent evolving through the Pleistocene, the epoch of the ice ages, as hunter-gatherers, when we ourselves were an organic part of the natural world, all places were by definition wild; but then, in the greatest of all human revolutions, as the last of the ice disappeared about twelve thousand years ago, farming was invented. With the cultivation of crops and the domestication of animals, agriculture for the first time permitted stable settlements, it allowed for villages to be created, then towns, then cities and the rise of everything we call civilisation; but even more than that, it fundamentally altered our relationship with nature, from one of partnership, more or less—for even as hunter-gatherers we could be demanding partners—to one of formalized mastery and domination. We have spent most of the five hundred generations since, the Holocene epoch, breaking the sod and hacking the forest down and proclaiming our God-given right to do so, God-given quite literally—the Old Testament spelt out bluntly the farmers' ascendancy over nature, and their entitlement to do whatever they damn well liked with it, in the famous lines of Genesis, 1:28: "and God said unto them, be fruitful, and multiply, and replenish the earth, and subdue it: and have dominion over the fish of the sea, and over the fowl of the air, and over every living thing that moveth upon the earth". Thus we long regarded wild places and wilderness, the bits we hadn't managed to subdue or have dominion over, with near universal disapproval, indeed with a revulsion sometimes verging on horror. It was against wild places, after all, that the civilizing struggle was being waged, to clear the forest and grow corn in its stead; the forest was the enemy, it held deadly wild beasts, and sometimes deadly wild men, as deserts did, or mountains. The civilised looked to the cities. What was there in wilderness other than the absence of everything that made life worth living? For aeons it was hated and feared and despised.

The shift in opinion that started to change this attitude, in the early 1700s, was fairly shallowly based: it was aesthetic. But it was effective, nonetheless. It began when English gentlemen started taking the Grand Tour of Europe, in the course of which they survived the vetiginous crossing of the Alps, and enjoyed having been terrified. So arose the influential concept of the Sublime, the appreciation of the awe-inspiring side to nature, something which was not quite the same as beauty but which prompted admiration just as powerfully. It became an influential literary and artistic fashion, and in the second half of the eighteenth century it was joined by another, slightly tamer vogue for viewing the natural world, wild places and all, in a positive artistic light, the concept of the Picturesque. Their combined influence meant that by the 1780s, especially as turnpike roads were built and public transport improved, Britain's once-despised wild scenery, on the River Wye in Wales and in the Lake District in England in particular, was attracting an increasing number of tourists, while in continental Europe, Jean-Jacques Rousseau had sung the praises of the Alps and insisted on the innate goodness of the natural world and of man himself; all of these streams of thought fed into the swelling river that was Romanticism, until as the nineteenth century began, William Wordsworth could proclaim himself, from first to last, a follower of nature, and he himself was followed by many more.

So nature finally found its champions; but they were not specifically champions of wilderness, of what we might call wholly untouched, *unhumanised* land. Much of Wordsworth's Lake District, mountainous and awe-inspiring though it might be, was a farmed landscape, one way or another; it had people in it. It had Michael. It had Lucy. It could not really be called a wilderness. The champions of wilderness proper began to emerge fifty years later, in America.

It was only natural. In the United States, in this new-found world, the extent of completely untouched land was colossal, especially in the centre and west of the continent, which had never been settled. Wilderness was virtually the country's defining landscape. Yet despite its magnitude, it began to come under mortal threat as the nineteenth century progressed and the young country stormed headlong into the swiftest and most extensive mastering of nature the world had ever seen, breaking the sod and hacking the forest down on a continent-wide scale in just a few decades, as part of the westward expansion of the Frontier, and enterprise regarded by Americans themselves as so heroic that it came to symbolise for them their national character, with its virtues of individualism, self-reliance and independence. Year after year, the pioneers pushed further westwards and built their log cabins; the untouched prairies were ploughed; the ancient trees were toppled in their thousands; the indigenous inhabitants, the Native Americans, were evicted from their ancestral lands; and cattle replaced the buffalo herds, and the bear and the lynx and the wolf, all to the approbation of the citizenry as a whole.

And yet ... even as this was all going on, doubts about the wisdom of so forcibly taming, often in effect destroying, the extraordinary wild landscapes which were being discovered in the west, many of them more freshly magnificent than anything in Europe, were growing in the minds of young America's own nature writers, led by Ralph Waldo Emerson and Henry David Thoreau, both of whom, as Transcendentalists, saw the unspoiled natural world as a way to spiritual truth. Thoreau went further and—perhaps the first person to do so—specifically championed the concept of *wildness/wilderness*. Although best-known for *Walden*, an account of two years living in a cabin in the woods, his forceful views on wildness are set out in *Walking*, a lecture given several times and published after his death in 1862, which contains the famous line 'In Wildness is the preservation of the World.' Thoreau saw man as being a part of nature, and he saw wild places not only as essential to human well-being, but also as a source of primitive strength; it was "not a meaningless fable", he said, that Romulus and Remus, the founders of Rome, had been suckled by a she-wolf.

His support for wilderness was soon echoed by one of the nineteenth-century America's most noteworthy public men, George Perkins Marsh, who is barely known in Britain, an omission that needs to be rectified. A lawyer, politician, diplomat, and outstanding linguist, successively US envoy to the Ottoman Empire and to Italy, a polymath and universal man who was almost the Victorian-era equivalent of Thomas Jefferson, Marsh was also an ecologist *avant la lettre*; and in 1864 he produced a book which is the first-ever summary of the *ecological* consequences of doing what Genesis urged us to do and of dominating the subduing the earth. American critics not infrequently link it with Darwin's *The Origin of Species*, published just five years earlier, and while Marsh does not, like Darwin, overturn all previous conceptions of what humanity is and cannot be made the Englishman's intellectual twin, there is no doubt that in challenging another enormous assumption which people had always made about the world, his originality is of a comparable order.

The assumption was that doing things to the earth had no cost. It followed on inevitably from the Bible's declaration that the planet's resources were put there by God for our use, and thus by implication were boundless. That was woven inextricably into the Christian mindset. It is hard to overstate how fundamental, in a still Christian world, was Marsh's contesting of it. But in *Man and Nature*, he did that at length, highlighting the early Mediterranean societies, which, he said, had collapsed because the deforestation in which they had engaged had destroyed their water supplies. He bolstered his case with own vast travel experience and mammoth erudition—*Man and Nature* is a dense read—and moved inexorably to his point, which was that in its headlong conquest of the Frontier, America was in grave danger of repeating the mistakes that these earlier societies had made, and ruining itself.

His was the first voice to enunciate these insights, now commonplace amongst us. And he went further. Such was the sweep of his learning and the depth of his vision that he felt able to generalise about the baleful influence of the human species on nature as a whole, as he perceived it, and he did so in words as darkly memorable about us as Adam Smith's hard-headed remark as to why the butcher, the brewer and the baker provide us with our dinner. "Man is everywhere a disturbing agent." Marsh wrote, "Wherever he plants his foot, the harmonies of nature are turned to discords."

There, was the true value of wilderness, of unhumanised land: it was where the harmonies of nature, the balance and beauty of the natural world, remained. This was a far profounder assessment of its worth than the fact that it could give a gentleman a fright, and it became the intellectual underpinning of the devotion to wilderness which began to gain an increasing foothold in American thinking about the natural world. But it was not Marsh who orchestrated it. That was a torch taken up by John Muir, the Scots-born writer who emigrated to the United States aged eleven, in 1849. Muir spent his adolescence on his father's farm in the wilds of the Wisconsin frontier, and after an accident in which he nearly lost his sight, he realised that the wilds were where he wanted to spend his life. In 1868 he moved to California and discovered the mountains of the Sierra Nevada, a wilderness supreme, and for the next forty years and more he informed a growing audience of their transcendental qualities and why they mattered, in lyrical and sometimes quasi-mystical terms: undisturbed nature, he said, was "a window opening into heaven, a mirror reflecting the Creator". By the end of the nineteenth century, then, the value of wilderness, something barely recognized in any other society, was in America formally and widely acknowledged, and the word itself, for long in use disparagingly—think of Jesus in the wilderness—was for the first time being used in a positive way. Thoreau, Marsh, and Muir had all seen something in wholly wild land which made the most powerful appeal to the human spirit, and their perception was increasingly shared. Muir became a national celebrity, not only for his writings but also for his wilderness activism, helping to bring about the creation of California's Yosemite National Park in 1890 and becoming the founding president of the United States' first major conservation body, the Sierra Club. By the time of his death, in 1914, the love of wilderness was becoming ineradicably established in the American mind, and as the new century went on it only grew, supported by thinkers such as the lyrical forester-philosopher Aldo Leopold, who called for a new "land ethic" of ecological responsibility. It reached its climax in 1964 when President Lyndon Johnson signed the Wilderness Act, a piece of legislation establishing a National Wilderness Preservation System for America, a gigantic protection scheme for vast areas of untouched, unhumanised country, quite unlike anything else in the world.

...

So many powerful minds have addressed it, the unrelenting destruction of nature around the globe, so many experts have looked at the economics and the ecology and tried to reconcile them, so many thousands of detailed policies have been worked out and applied, so much intellectual effort and so much idealistic concern have been thrown at the problem, year after year after year, that the question presents itself at once: how on earth might it be the basis of a better defence, a better defence of the natural world, the fact that one autumn afternoon, more than half a century ago, a teenager sat looking down an estuary and suddenly felt happy?

We think of ourselves, especially since the decline of Christianity in the West, and its replacement by our current creed, liberal secular humanism, as rational beings entirely; we pride ourselves that, faced with a Problem, with a capital P, we may employ Reason, with a capital R, and naturally find a Solution, with a capital S. We believe that this will deliver every time. Rationality is ingrained in a million mindsets. Yet the world does not always work like that. And there is another way of going about things, in dealing with the mortal threats that our planet now faces, which is to consider, not what we do, but who we are.

Most of us probably think we know. We do not give it a second thought. But in the last thirty years or so, a new understanding, by no means yet widespread or popularized, has began to dawn of what it means to be human, based on a simple but monumental perception: the fifty thousand generations through which we evolved as hunter-gatherer are more important to our psychological make-up, even today, than the five hundred generations we have spent since agriculture began and with it, civilisation ...

Terrible, though, is the word for it, the century that is coming for nature, and it is well under way. In fact, the destruction and losses are already proceeding so rapidly and their scale is so colossal that a new problem arises: it is becoming difficult to describe them adequately, to do real justice to do what its loss means, to expound them in other than the most generalized terms. You end up using statistics. I have done it here myself. *One in five vertebrates is threatened with extinction* ... And perhaps it is worth considering that something vital can be missed, as the subject of environmental loss daily becomes more theoretical, abstract, and academic.

A prime example of this is the creation of two new metaphors to describe what is taking place. One is the Sixth Great Extinction. In the geological record researchers recognise five cataclysmic, life-extinguishing events in the earth's prehistory, beginning at the end of the Ordovician period 440 million years ago, when each time, the majority of species on the planet died out. Some of these events may have been caused by drastic changes in climate; others by the impacts of asteroids or comets, such as the object which hit what is now the Yucatan peninsula of Mexico at the end of the Cretaceous period, 65 million years ago, and wiped out the dinosaurs, in the most recent of the five. But such is the rate at which species are presently disappearing that many biologists consider we are today going through yet another major extinction, a sixth, which is comparable in scale to the rest—with the difference, of course, that this one has been caused by us.

The other metaphor is also inspired by the geological record, specifically by the idea of the geological timescale; it consists of a new label, the Anthropocene, to designate the epoch in which we are currently living. This is still formally considered to be the Holocene, from the Greek for "wholly recent", covering the period since the end of the last glaciation in which agriculture began and civilisation took off; but so overwhelming has the human impact on the planet now become, above all on the atmosphere, whose composition we are so rapidly altering with such potentially disastrous results, that a growing number of scientists accept that the present times has a decisive character of its own and ought to be renamed as such. So welcome to the Anthropocene: the epoch when humans changed the planet.

They are very suggestive, these large-scale conceptions. Far-reaching images, such as the Anthropocene and the Sixth Great Extinction are, help us register the true degree of the planet's predicament and the real magnitude of the processes we have set in train which may bring about our ruin. They are of enormous value. They are talked about daily. Indeed, they are generating an academic industry on their own …

There are about 200,000 moth species in the world, as a ballpark figure, but only about 20,000 butterflies: butterflies are just a branch, halfway down, on the moth evolutionary tree, a group of moths which split off and evolved to fly by day, and developed bright colours to recognise each other. This disparity in species numbers is even more pronounced in Britain, where there are a mere 58 regularly breeding butterfly species, but about 900 larger moths and another 1,600 or so smaller or micro-moths, for a total of about 2,500. Thus, in the world as a whole, there may be ten times as many moth species as butterfly species; but in Britain, it is approaching fifty times as many.

This means, of course, that in the dark there are far, far more moths out and about than ever there are butterflies during the daytime; it's just that we don't see them. Or at least, we didn't, until the invention of the automobile. The headlight beams of a speeding car on a muggy summer's night in the countryside, turning the moths into snowflakes and crowding them together the faster you went, in the manner of a telephoto lens, meant that the true startling scale of their numbers was suddenly apparent, not least as they plastered the headlights and the windscreen until driving became impossible, and you had to stop the car to wipe the glass surfaces clean. Of all the myriad displays of abundance in the natural world in Britain, the moth snowstorm was the most extraordinary, as it only became perceptible in the age of the internal combustion engine. Yet now, after but a short century of existence, it has gone.

In recent years I have often talked to people about it, and I am surprised, not just at how many of those over fifty (and especially over sixty) remember it, but at how animated they become once the memory is triggered. It's as if it were locked away in a corner of their minds, and in recalling it and realising that it has disappeared, they can recognise what an exceptional phenomenon it was, whereas at the time, it just seemed part of the way things were …

It was in the millennium year, 2000, that I myself began to realise that the moth snowstorm had disappeared, and I began to write about it as part of the issue of insect decline as a whole, which seemed to me to be wide-ranging and extremely serious …

For the most important of the many important aspects of this new understanding is of course its context: this innovative sense of what nature really means to us, of what its value is, has come along at the very moment when we are tearing it to pieces. Just as *Earthrise*, the photo from space, showed us for the first time the planet's fragility and beauty, its uniqueness and isolation, so the insights of psychology and of evolutionary biology are showing us for the first time how we as humans are hound to it, bound to it in our souls inextricably, and how if we destroy it, we are destroying not only our home, which is dreadful enough, but also a fundamental part of ourselves which we cannot afford to lose …

That the natural world can bring us peace; that natural world can give us joy: these are the confirmations of what many people may instinctively feel but have not been able to articulate; that nature is not an extra, a luxury, but on the contrary is indispensable, part of our essence.

Topics for Discussion

1) What does the author mean when he says "[o]ur world is under threat, as it has never been before, from a malady previous generations did not anticipate"?

2) According to the author, what is the "most consequential historical event of the second half of the twentieth century"?

3) When did Homo sapiens begin to walk out of Africa?

4) What's the relationship between Homo sapiens, Homo erectus, and the Neanderthals?

5) What does the author mean by "we are wrecking the earth, as burglars will

sometimes wantonly wreck a house"?

6) What is the fact that "cannot be stressed enough" and why?

7) According to the excerpt, what event is "one of the profoundest events in the history of human culture"?

8) According to the author, what is currently the predominant belief system in the West, and what is its essence?

9) What is the gist of modern human morality?

10) Which important figures mentioned can be regarded as ecologists?

Interdisciplinary Concepts for Further Thinking

1. Modernity

Modernity, a topic in the humanities and social sciences, is both a historical period, as well as an ensemble of particular socio-cultural norms, attitudes, and practices that arose in the wake of the Renaissance, the Age of Reason, or the Age of Enlightenment. Modernity can be characterized by a belief in the benefits of progress in science, technology, and rationality. Madan argues that modernity is seen as an "enlargement of human freedoms" and an "enhancement of the range of choices" as people began to "take charge" of themselves. Foucault emphasizes, modernity "refers to a period marked by a questioning or rejection of tradition; the prioritization of individualism, freedom and formal equality; faith in inevitable social, scientific, and technological progress [...] a movement from feudalism towards capitalism and the market economy." Thus, modernism came with a set of principles that center upon the full liberation of the human being.

We all benefit from the process of modernity, yet, we can't neglect that modernity has also resulted in severe environmental problems such as pervasive pollution and climate change.

1) How is modernity evaluated in the excerpt of *The Moth Snowstorm*?

2) What is the relationship between modernity and liberal secular humanism depicted in *The Moth Snowstorm*?

2. The Anthropocene

The "Anthropocene" （人类世） is a concept in geology, coined in the 1980s and then popularized in 2000 by atmospheric chemist, Nobel Laureate Paul J. Crutzen.

The word "Anthropocene" comes from the Greek terms for human ("anthropo") and new ("cene"). Crutzen thinks our species, Homo sapiens, has had such a significant impact on the Earth and its inhabitants that we will have a lasting—and potentially irreversible—influence on its systems, environment, processes, and biodiversity. Therefore, he proposes the Anthropocene to indicate that we are living in a new geological epoch. To Crutzen, the Anthropocene could have started in the latter part of the eighteenth century, when analyses of air trapped in polar ice showed the beginning of growing global concentrations of carbon dioxide and methane; this date also happens to coincide with James Watt's design of the steam engine in 1784. Since the 1950s in particular, the impacts of human beings have unfolded at an unprecedented rate and scale.

There are mainly three symptoms of the Anthropocene: global climate change, the loss of biodiversity, and the presence of pervasive toxins, among which climate change is the defining factor. Essentially, the Anthropocene makes people rethink, reconsider and reflect on their relationship with and attitude to nature.

 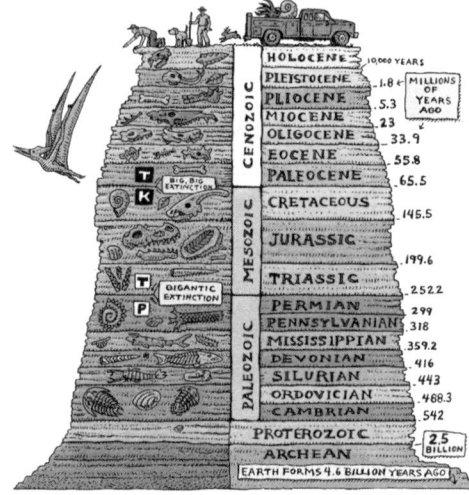

1) How does the writer understand the Anthropocene in the excerpt?

2) What is the significance of the Anthropocene for literary appreciation and analysis?

3. Pastoral, Picturesque, and Sublime

The "Pastoral," the "Picturesque," and the "Sublime" are three aesthetic concepts.

These aesthetic concepts established during the Romantic era divided the natural world into 3 categories. The first two represent Nature as a comforting source of physical and spiritual sustenance. The last, as proposed by Edmund Burke in his *Philosophical Enquiry into the Origin of Our Ideas of the Sublime and Beautiful* (1757), refers to the thrill and danger of confronting untamed Nature and its overwhelming forces, such as tsunamis, hurricanes and deep chasms. Whereas the Pastoral and Picturesque refer to mankind's confidence before the natural world, the Sublime is a humbling reminder that humanity is not all-powerful.

Pastoral landscapes celebrate the dominion of mankind over nature. The scenes are peaceful, often depicting ripe harvests, lovely gardens, and manicured lawns with fattened livestock. Man has developed and tamed the landscape—it yields the necessities we need to live on, as well as beauty and safety. The Picturesque refers to the charm of discovering the landscape in its natural state. These scenes are uplifting, but not frightening. Sublime images, on the other hand, show Nature at its most fearsome; in fact, Burke believed that "terror is in all cases ... the ruling principle of the sublime." For him, humanity is small and impotent in front of raging rivers, dizzying cliffs and canyons, ferocious animals, and violent storms. These works can also be uplifting, but in a deeply spiritual way. The Sublime emphasizes God's dominion over humanity and considers the possible folly in mankind's overriding confidence.

1) Why does the author mention these three terms in the excerpt?
2) What is the value of the three aesthetic concepts in the epoch of the Anthropocene?

Thinking in Numbers

Thinking in numbers is an effective way to make one's ideas and self-expression more coherent, logical and well-knit. In *The Moth Snowstorm* the writer proposes one core problem from the phenomenon of the disappearance of the moth snowstorm, mentions three aesthetic concepts which shed light on people's understanding of the human-nature relationship, and five important well-known nature-lovers. Clarify the "One", "Three", "Five" respectively to have a deeper understanding of the excerpt.

Visual Thinking with Mind Mapping

The moth snowstorm is an essential natural phenomenon the writer depicts to put forward his sound argument in the seemingly loose form in *The Moth Snowstorm*. Reorganize the main idea of the excerpt following the writer's logic of proposing a problem, analyzing the problem and solving the problem with the method of mind mapping.

Critical Thinking for Reality

According to the concept of the Anthropocene, humanity has become a geological force. Human beings have become dramatically powerful and human impact and role on the Earth are very much like that of God. In the meantime, one point should be realized to confront the Anthropocene. That is, human-centeredness should be reflected, questioned, and subverted. What do you think of the status of human beings and what role should humans play in the epoch of the Anthropocene? Can we get inspiration from traditional Chinese culture regarding the human-nature relationship?

Unit 2
The Cat from Hell

Stephen King

Introduction to the Author

Stephen Edwin King (1947—) is an American writer of horror, supernatural fiction, suspense, crime, and fantasy novels. He graduated from the University of Maine in 1970 with a bachelor's degree in English. Regarded as the "King of Horror", his name has become synonymous with the genre. His books have sold more than 350 million copies, many of which have been adapted into films, television series and miniseries. King has published 64 novels and has also written approximately 200 short stories. And his important works include *The Shining* in 1977 and the novella *Rita Hayworth and Shawshank Redemption* in 1982.

To date, King is the only author in history to have had more than 30 books which become No. 1 best-sellers. In 2003, the National Book Foundation awarded him the Medal for Distinguished Contribution to American Letters. In 2015, he was awarded with a National Medal of Arts from the U.S. National Endowment for the Arts for his contributions to literature.

Introduction to the Work

"The Cat from Hell" is a horror short story by Stephen King. King initially published the first 500 words of the story in March 1977 in *Cavalier*, and the magazine held a contest for readers to finish the story. King's complete story was published in the magazine in June of the same year. King revised the story and it was reprinted in *Tales of Unknown Horror* (1978), in *Year's Finest Fantasy* (1978), in *Magicats!* (1984), and again in *Twists of the Tale: An Anthology of Cat Horror* (1996). This story was also adapted into film in the anthology film *Tales from the Darkside: The Movie* (1990).

Halston, a professional hitman, is offered $12,000 to take out an unusual target—a cat. He accepts, despite being told that the cat was implicated in the murders of three people. He soon discovers that the cat is much more than it seems—the employer reveals that his company tortured and destroyed thousands of cats in the name of research, and he believes this cat is a feline emissary of revenge. While the hitman is driving toward a desolate place to kill it, the cat escapes confinement and eventually attacks him—crawling inside his body to finish the job—after he is temporarily paralyzed in the resulting accident. After killing the hitman, the cat leaves on "unfinished business" to go after the hitman's employer.

Text

The Cat from Hell

Halston thought the old man in the wheelchair looked sick, terrified, and ready to die. He had experience in seeing such things. Death was Halston's business; he had brought it to eighteen men and six women in his career as an independent hitter. He knew the death look.

The house—mansion, actually—was cold and quiet. The only sounds were the low snap of the fire on the big stone hearth and the low whine of the November wind outside.

"I want you to make a kill," the old man said. His voice was quavery and high, peevish. "I understand that is what you do."

"Who did you talk to?" Halston asked.

"With a man named Saul Loggia. He says you know him."

Halston nodded. If Loggia was the go-between, it was all right. And if there was a bug in the room, anything the old man—Drogan—said was entrapment.

"Who do you want hit?"

Drogan pressed a button on the console built into the arm of his wheelchair and it buzzed forward. Closeup, Halston could smell the yellow odors of fear, age, and urine all mixed.

They disgusted him, but he made no sign. His face was still and smooth. "Your victim is right behind you," Drogan said softly.

Halston moved quickly. His reflexes were his life and they were always set on a filed pin. He was off the couch, falling to one knee, turning, hand inside his specially tailored sport coat, gripping the handle of the short-barreled .45 hybrid that hung below his armpit in a spring-loaded holster that laid it in his palm at a touch. A moment later it was out and pointed at . . . a cat.

For a moment Halston and the cat stared at each other. It was a strange moment for Halston, who was an unimaginative man with no superstitions. For that one moment as he knelt on the floor with the gun pointed, he felt that he knew this cat, although if he had ever seen one with such unusual markings he surely would have remembered.

Its face was an even split: half black, half white. The dividing line ran from the top of its flat skull and down its nose to its mouth, straight-arrow. Its eyes were huge in the gloom, and caught in each nearly circular black pupil was a prism of firelight, like a sullen coal of hate.

And the thought echoed back to Halston: *We know each other, you and I*. Then it passed. He put the gun away and stood up. "I ought to kill you for that, old man. I don't take a joke."

"And I don't make them," Drogan said. "Sit down. Look in here." He had taken a fat envelope out from beneath the blanket that covered his legs.

Halston sat. The cat, which had been crouched on the back of the sofa, jumped lightly down into his lap. It looked up at Halston for a moment with those huge dark eyes, the pupils surrounded by thin green-gold rings, and then it settled down and began to purr.

Halston looked at Drogan questioningly.

"He's very friendly," Drogan said. "At first. Nice friendly pussy has killed three people in this household. That leaves only me. I am old, I am sick . . . but I prefer to die in my own time."

"I can't believe this," Halston said. "You hired me to hit a cat?"

"Look in the envelope, please."

Halston did. It was filled with hundreds and fifties, all of them old.

"How much is it?"

"Six thousand dollars. There will be another six when you bring me proof that the cat is dead. Mr. Loggia said twelve thousand was your usual fee?"

Halston nodded, his hand automatically stroking the cat in his lap. It was asleep, still purring. Halston liked cats. They were the only animals he did like, as a matter of fact. They got along on their own. God—if there was one—had made them into perfect, aloof killing machines. Cats were the hitters of the animal world, and Halston gave them his respect.

"I need not explain anything, but I will," Drogan said. "Forewarned is forearmed, they say, and I would not want you to go into this lightly. And I seem to need to justify myself. So you'll not think I'm insane."

Halston nodded again. He had already decided to make this peculiar hit, and no further talk was needed. But if Drogan wanted to talk, he would listen. "First of all, you know who I am? Where the money comes from?"

"Drogan Pharmaceuticals."

"Yes. One of the biggest drug companies in the world. And the cornerstone of our financial success has been this." From the pocket of his robe he handed Halston a small, unmarked vial of pills. "Tri-Dormal-phenobarbin, compound G. Prescribed almost exclusively for the terminally ill. It's extremely habit-forming, you see. It's a combination painkiller, tranquilizer, and mild hallucinogen. It is remarkably helpful in helping the terminally ill face their conditions and adjust to them."

"Do you take it?" Halston asked.

Drogan ignored the question. "It is widely prescribed throughout the world. It's a synthetic, was developed in the fifties at our New Jersey labs. Our testing was confined almost solely to cats, because of the unique quality of the feline nervous system."

"How many did you wipe out?"

Drogan stiffened. "That is an unfair and prejudicial way to put it."

Halston shrugged.

"In the four-year testing period which led to FDA approval of Tri-Dormal-G, about fifteen thousand cats ... uh, expired."

Halston whistled. About four thousand cats a year. "And now you think this one's back to get you, huh?" ·

"I don't feel guilty in the slightest," Drogan said, but that quavering, petulant note was back in his voice. "Fifteen thousand test animals died so that hundreds of thousands of human beings "

"Never mind that," Halston said. Justifications bored him.

"That cat came here seven months ago. I've never liked cats. Nasty, disease-bearing animals ... always out in the fields ... crawling around in barns ... picking up God knows what germs in their fur ... always trying to bring something with its insides falling out into the house for you to look at ... it was my sister who wanted to take it in. She found out. She paid." He looked at the cat sleeping on Halston's lap with dead hate.

"You said the cat killed three people."

Drogan began to speak. The cat dozed and purred on Halston's lap under the soft, scratching strokes of Halston's strong and expert killer's fingers.

Occasionally a pine knot would explode on the hearth, making it tense like a series of steel springs covered with hide and muscle. Outside the wind whined around the big stone house far out in the Connecticut countryside. There was winter in that wind's throat. The old man's voice droned on and on.

Seven months ago there had been four of them here-Drogan, his sister Amanda, who at seventy-four was two years Drogan's elder, her lifelong friend Carolyn Broadmoor ("of the Westchester Broadmoors," Drogan said), who was badly afflicted with emphysema, and Dick Gage, a hired man who had been with the Drogan family for twenty years. Gage, who was past sixty himself, drove the big Lincoln Mark IV, cooked, served the evening sherry. A day maid came in. The four of them had lived this way for nearly two years, a dull collection of old people and their family retainer. Their only pleasures were *The Hollywood Squares* and waiting to see who would outlive whom.

Then the cat had come.

"It was Gage who saw it first, whining and skulking around the house. He tried to drive it away He threw sticks and small rocks at it, and hit it several times. But it wouldn't go. It smelled the food, of course. It was little more than a bag of bones. People put them out beside the road to die at the end of the summer season, you know. A terrible, inhumane thing."

"Better to fry their nerves?" Halston asked.

Drogan ignored that and went on. He hated cats. He always had. When the cat refused to be driven away, he had instructed Gage to put out poisoned food. Large, tempting dishes of Calo cat food spiked with Tri-Dormal-G, as a matter of fact. The cat ignored the food. At that point Amanda Drogan had noticed the cat and had insisted they take it in. Drogan had protested vehemently, but Amanda—had gotten her way. She always did, apparently.

"But she found out," Drogan said. "She brought it inside herself, in her arms. It was purring, just as it is now. But it wouldn't come near me. It never has . . . yet. She poured it a saucer of milk. 'Oh, look at the poor thing, it's starving,' she cooed. She and Carolyn both cooed over it. Disgusting. It was their way of getting back at me, of course. They knew the way I've felt about felines ever since the Tri-Dormal-G testing program twenty years ago. They enjoyed teasing me, baiting me with it." He looked at Halston grimly. "But they paid."

In mid-May, Gage had gotten up to set breakfast and found Amanda Drogan lying at the foot of the main stairs in a litter of broken crockery and Little Friskies. Her eyes bulged sightlessly up at the ceiling. She had bled a great deal from the mouth and nose. Her back was broken, both legs were broken, and her neck had been literally shattered like glass.

"It slept in her room," Drogan said. "She treated it like a baby . . . 'Is oo hungry, darling? Does oo need to go out and do poopoos!' Obscene, coming from an old baffle-ax like my sister. I think it woke her up, meowing. She got his dish. She used to say that Sam didn't really like his Friskies unless they were wetted down with a little milk. So she was planning to go downstairs. The cat was rubbing against her legs. She

Unit 2　*The Cat from Hell*

was old, not too steady on her feet. Half asleep. They got to the head of the stairs and the cat got in front of her … tripped her …"

Yes, it could have happened that way, Halston thought. In his mind's eye he saw the old woman falling forward and outward, too shocked to scream. The Friskies spraying out as she tumbled head over heels to the bottom, the bowl smashing. At last she comes to rest at the bottom, the old bones shattered, the eyes glaring, the nose and ears trickling blood. And the purring cat begins to work its way down the stairs, contentedly munching Little Friskies …

"What did the coroner say?" he asked Drogan. "Death by accident, of course. But I knew."

"Why didn't you get rid of the cat then? With Amanda gone?"

Because Carolyn Broadmoor had threatened to leave if he did, apparently. She was hysterical, obsessed with the subject. She was a sick woman, and she was nutty on the subject of spiritualism. A Hartford medium had told her (for a mere twenty dollars) that Amanda's soul had entered Sam's feline body. Sam had been Amanda's, she told Drogan, and if Sam went, she went.

Halston, who had become something of an expert at reading between the lines of human lives, suspected that Drogan and the old Broadmoor bird had been lovers long ago, and the old dude was reluctant to let her go over a cat.

"It would have been the same as suicide," Drogan said. "In her mind she was still a wealthy woman, perfectly capable of packing up that cat and going to New York or London or even Monte Carlo with it. In fact she was the last of a great family, living on a pittance as a result of a number of bad investments in the sixties. She lived on the second floor here in a specially controlled, superhumidified room. The woman was seventy, Mr. Halston. She was a heavy smoker until the last two years of her life, and the emphysema was very bad. I wanted her here, and if the cat had to stay …"

Halston nodded and then glanced meaningfully at his watch.

"Near the end of June, she died in the night. The doctor seemed to take it as a matter of course … just came and wrote out the death certificate and that was the end of it. But the cat was in the room. Gage told me."

"We all have to go sometime, man," Halston said.

"Of course. That's what the doctor said. But I knew. I remembered. Cats like to get babies and old people when they're asleep. And steal their breath."

"An old wives' tale."

"Based on fact, like most so-called old wives' tales," Drogan replied.

"Cats like to knead soft things with their paws, you see. A pillow, a thick shag rug … or a blanket. A crib blanket or an old person's blanket. The extra weight on a person who's weak to start with …"

Drogan trailed off, and Halston thought about it. Carolyn Broadmoor asleep in her bedroom, the breath rasping in and out of her damaged lungs, the sound nearly lost in the whisper of special humidifiers and air conditioners. The cat with the queer black-and-white markings leaps silently onto her spinster's bed and stares at her old and wrinkle-grooved face with those lambent, black-and-green eyes. It creeps onto her thin chest and settles its weight there, purring . . . , and the breathing slows . . . slows . . . and the cat purrs as the old woman slowly smothers beneath its weight on her chest.

He was not an imaginative man, but Halston shivered a little.

"Drogan," he said, continuing to stroke the purring cat. "Why don't you just have it put away? A vet would give it the gas for twenty dollars."

Drogan said, "The funeral was on the first day of July, I had Carolyn buried in our cemetery plot next to my sister. The way she would have wanted it. On July third I called Gage to this room and handed him a wicker basket, a picnic hamper sort of thing. Do you know what I mean?"

Halston nodded.

"I told him to put the cat in it and take it to a vet in Milford and have it put to sleep. He said, 'Yes, sir,' took the basket, and went out. Very like him. I never saw him alive again. There was an accident on the turnpike. The Lincoln was driven into a bridge abutment at better than sixty miles an hour. Dick Gage was killed instantly. When they found him there were scratches on his face."

Halston was silent as the picture of how it might have been formed in his brain again. No sound in the room but the peaceful crackle of the fire and the peaceful purr of the cat in his lap. He and the cat together before the fire would make a good illustration for that Edgar Guest poem, the one that goes: "The cat on my lap, the hearth's good fire/ . . . A happy man, should you enquire."

Dick Gage moving the Lincoln down the turnpike toward Milford, beating the speed limit by maybe five miles an hour. The wicker basket beside him—a picnic hamper sort of thing. The chauffeur is watching traffic, maybe he's passing a big cab-over Jimmy and he doesn't notice the peculiar black-on-one-side, white-on-the-other face that pokes out of one side of the basket. Out of the driver's side. He doesn't notice because he's passing the big trailer truck and that's when the cat jumps onto his face, spitting and clawing, its talons raking into one eye, puncturing it, deflating it, blinding it. Sixty and the hum of the Lincoln's big motor and the other paw is hooked over the bridge of the nose, digging in with exquisite, damning pain—maybe the Lincoln starts to veer right, into the path of the Jimmy, and its airhorn blares ear-shatteringly, but Gage can't hear it because the cat is yowling, the cat is spread-eagled over his face like some huge furry black spider, ears laid back, green eyes glaring like spotlights from hell, back legs jittering and digging into the soft flesh of the old man's neck. The car veers wildly back the other way. The bridge abutment looms. The cat jumps down and the Lincoln, a shiny black torpedo, hits the cement and goes up like a bomb.

Halston swallowed hard and heard a dry click in his throat. "And the cat came back?"

Drogan nodded. "A week later. On the day Dick Gage was buried, as a matter of fact. Just like the old song says. The cat came back."

"It survived a car crash at sixty? Hard to believe."

"They say each one has nine lives. When it comes back ... that's when I started to wonder if it might not be a ... a ..."

"Hellcat?" Halston suggested softly.

"For want of a better word, yes. A sort of demon sent ..."

"To punish you."

"I don't know. But I'm afraid of it. I feed it, or rather, the woman who comes in to do for me feeds it. She doesn't like it either. She says that face is a curse of God. Of course, she's local." The old man tried to smile and failed. "I want you to kill it. I've lived with it for the last four months. It skulks around in the shadows. It looks at me. It seems to be ... waiting. I lock myself in my room every night and still I wonder if I'm going to wake up one early and find it ... curled up on my chest ... and purring."

The wind whined lonesomely outside and made a strange hooting noise in the stone chimney.

"At last I got in touch with Saul Loggia. He recommended you. He called you a stick, I believe."

"A one-stick. That means I work on my own."

"Yes. He said you'd never been busted, or even suspected. He said you always seem to land on your feel ... like a cat."

Halston looked at the old man in the wheelchair. And his long-fingered, muscular hands were lingering above the cat's neck.

"I'll do it now, if you want me to," he said softly. "I'll snap its neck. It won't even know—"

"No!" Drogan cried. He drew in a long, shuddering breath. Color had come up in his sallow cheeks. "Not ... not here. Take it away."

Halston smiled humorlessly. He began to stroke the sleeping cat's head and shoulders and back very gently again. "All right," he said. "I accept the contract. Do you want the body?"

"No. Kill it. Bury it." He paused. He hunched forward in the wheelchair like some ancient buzzard. "Bring me the tail," he said. "So I can throw it in the fire and watch it burn."

Halston drove a 1973 Plymouth with a custom Cyclone Spoiler engine. The car was jacked and blocked, and rode with the hood pointing down at the road at a twenty degree angle. He had rebuilt the differential and the rear end himself. The shift was a

Pensy, the linkage was Hearst. It sat on huge Bobby Unser Wide Ovals and had a top end of a little past one-sixty.

He left the Drogan house at a little past 9:30. A cold rind of crescent moon rode overhead through the tattering November clouds. He rode with all the windows open, because that yellow stench of age and terror seemed to have settled into his clothes and he didn't like it. The cold was hard and sharp, eventually numbing, but it was good. It was blowing that yellow stench away. He got off the turnpike at Placer's Glen and drove through the silent town, which was guarded by a single yellow blinker at the intersection, at a thoroughly respectable thirty-five. Out of town, moving up S. R. 35, he opened the Plymouth up a little, letting her walk. The tuned Spoiler engine purred like the cat had purred on his lap earlier this evening. Halston grinned at the simile. They moved between frost-white November fields full of skeleton cornstalks at a little over seventy.

The cat was in a double-thickness shopping bag, tied at the top with heavy twine. The bag was in the passenger bucket seat. The cat had been sleepy and purring when Halston put it in, and it had purred through the entire ride. It sensed, perhaps, that Halston liked it and felt at home with it. Like himself, the cat was a one-stick.

Strange hit, Halston thought, and was surprised to find that he was taking it seriously *as* a hit. Maybe the strangest thing about it was that he actually liked the cat, felt a kinship with it. If it had managed to get rid of those three old crocks, more power to it … especially Gage, who had been taking it to Milford for a terminal date with a crew-cut veterinarian who would have been more than happy to bundle it into a ceramic-lined gas chamber the size of a microwave oven. He felt a kinship but no urge to renege on the hit. He would do it the courtesy of killing it quickly and well. He would park off the road beside one of those November-barren fields and take it out of the bag and stroke it and then snap its neck and sever its tail with his pocketknife. And, he thought, the body I'll bury honorably, saving it from the scavengers. I can't save it from the worms, but I can save it from the maggots.

He was thinking these things as the car moved through the night like a dark blue ghost and that was when the cat walked in front of his eyes, up on the dashboard, tail raised arrogantly, its black-and-white face turned toward him, its mouth seeming to grin at him.

"Sssssshhhh—" Halston hissed. He glanced to his right and caught a glimpse of the double-thickness shopping bag, a hole chewed—or clawed—in its side. Looked ahead again, and the cat lifted a paw and batted playfully at him. The paw skidded across Halston's forehead. He jerked away from it and the Plymouth's big tires wailed on the road as it swung erratically from one side of the narrow blacktop to the other.

Halston batted at the cat on the dashboard with his fist. It was blocking his field of vision. It spat at him, arching its back, but it didn't move. Halston swung again, and instead of shrinking away, it leaped at him.

Gage, he thought. *Just like Gage—*

He stamped the brake. The cat was on his head, blocking his vision with its furry belly, clawing at him, gouging at him. Halston held the wheel grimly. He struck the cat once, twice, a third time. And suddenly the road was gone, the Plymouth was running down into the ditch, thudding up and down on its shocks. Then, impact, throwing him forward against his seat belt, and the last sound he heard was the cat yowling inhumanly, the voice of a woman in pain or in the throes of sexual climax.

He struck it with his closed fists and felt only the springy, yielding flex of its muscles.

Then, second impact. And darkness.

The moon was down. It was an hour before dawn.

The Plymouth lay in a ravine curdled with groundmist. Tangled in its grille was a snarled length of barbed wire. The hood had come unlatched, and tendrils of steam from the breached radiator drifted out of the opening to mingle with the mist.

No feeling in his legs.

He looked down and saw that the Plymouth's firewall had caved in with the impact. The back of that big Cyclone Spoiler engine block had smashed into his legs, pinning them.

Outside, in the distance, the predatory squawk of an owl dropping onto some small, scurrying animal.

Inside, close, the steady purr of the cat.

It seemed to be grinning, like Alice's Cheshire had in Wonderland.

As Halston watched it stood up, arched its back, and stretched. In a sudden limber movement like rippled silk, it leaped to his shoulder. Halston tried to lift his hands to push it off.

His arms wouldn't move.

Spinal shock, he thought. *Paralyzed. Maybe temporary. More likely permanent.*

The cat purred in his ear like thunder.

"Get off me," Halston said. His voice was hoarse and dry. The cat tensed for a moment and then settled back. Suddenly its paw batted Halston's cheek, and the claws were out this time. Hot lines of pain down to his throat.

And the warm trickle of blood.

Pain.

Feeling.

He ordered his head to move to the right, and it complied. For a moment his face was buried in smooth, dry fur. Halston snapped at the cat. It made a startled, disgruntled sound in its throat—*yowk*!—and leaped onto the seat. It stared up at him angrily, ears laid back.

"Wasn't supposed to do that, was I?" Halston croaked. The cat opened its mouth and hissed at him. Looking at that strange, schizophrenic face, Halston could understand how Drogan might have thought it was a hellcat. It—

His thoughts broke off as he became aware of a dull, tingling feeling in both hands and forearms.

Feeling. Coming back. Pins and needles.

The cat leaped at his face, claws out, spitting.

Halston shut his eyes and opened his mouth. He bit at the cat's belly and got nothing but fur. The cat's front claws were clasped on his ears, digging in. The pain was enormous, brightly excruciating. Halston tried to raise his hands.

They twitched but would not quite come out of his lap.

He bent his head forward and began to shake it back and forth, like a man shaking soap out of his eyes. Hissing and squalling, the cat held on. Halston could feel blood trickling down his cheeks. It was hard to get his breath. The cat's chest was pressed over his nose. It was possible to get some air in by mouth, but not much. What he did get came through fur. His ears felt as if they had been doused with lighter fluid and then set on fire.

He snapped his head back and cried out in agony—he must have sustained a whiplash when the Plymouth hit. But the cat hadn't been expecting the reverse and it flew off. Halston heard it thud down in the back seat.

A trickle of blood ran in his eye. He tried again to move his hands, to raise one of them and wipe the blood away.

They trembled in his lap, but he was still unable to actually move them. He thought of the .45 special in its holster under his left arm.

If I can get to my piece, kitty, the rest of your nine lives are going in a lump sum.

More tingles now. Dull throbs of pain from his feet, buried and surely shattered under the engine block, zips and tingles from his legs—it felt exactly the way a limb that you've slept on does when it's starting to wake up. At that moment Halston didn't care about his feet. It was enough to know that his spine wasn't severed, that he wasn't going to finish out his life as a dead lump of body attached to a talking head.

Maybe I had a few lives left myself.

Take care of the cat. That was the first thing. *Then get out of the wreck*—maybe someone would come along, that would solve both problems at once. Not likely at 4:30 in the morning on a back road like this one, but barely possible. And—

And what was the cat doing back there?

He didn't like having it on his face, but he didn't like having it behind him and out of sight, either. He tried the rearview mirror, but that was useless. The crash had knocked it awry and all it reflected was the grassy ravine he had finished up in.

A sound from behind him, like low, ripping cloth.

Purring.

Hellcat my ass. It's gone to sleep back there.

And even if it hadn't, even if it was somehow planning murder, what could it do? It was a skinny little thing, probably weighed all of four pounds soaking wet. And soon ... soon he would be able to move his hands enough to get his gun. He was sure of it.

Halston sat and waited. Feeling continued to flood back into his body in a series of pins-and-needles incursions. Absurdly (or maybe in instinctive reaction to his close brush with death) he got an erection for a minute or so. *Be kind of hard to beat off under present circumstances*, he thought.

A dawn-line was appearing in the eastern sky. Somewhere a bird sang.

Halston tried his hands again and got them to move an eighth of an inch before they fell back.

Not yet. But soon.

A soft thud on the seatback beside him. Halston turned his head and looked into the black-white face, the glowing eyes with their huge dark pupils.

Halston spoke to it.

"I have never blown a hit once I took it on, kitty. This could be a first. I'm getting my hands back. Five minutes, ten at most. You want my advice? Go out the window. They're all open. Go out and take your tail with you."

The cat stared at him.

Halston tried his hands again. They came up, trembling wildly. Half an inch. An inch. He let them fall back limply. They slipped off his lap and thudded to the Plymouth's seat. They glimmered there palely, like large tropical spiders.

The cat was grinning at him.

Did I make a mistake? He wondered confusedly. He was a creature of hunch, and the feeling that he had made one was suddenly overwhelming. Then the cat's body tensed, and even as it leaped, Halston knew what it was going to do and he opened his mouth to scream.

The cat landed on Halston's crotch, claws out, digging.

At that moment, Halston wished he *had* been paralyzed. The pain was gigantic, terrible. He had never suspected that there could be such pain in the world. The cat was a spitting coiled spring of fury, clawing at his balls.

Halston *did* scream, his mouth yawning open, and that was when the cat changed direction and leaped at his face, leaped at his mouth. And at that moment Halston knew that it was something more than a cat. It was something possessed of a malign, murderous intent.

He caught one last glimpse of that black-and-white face below the flattened ears, its eyes enormous and filled with lunatic hate. It had gotten rid of the three old people and now it was going to get rid of John Halston.

It rammed into his mouth, a furry projectile. He gagged on it. Its front claws pinwheeled, tattering his tongue like a piece of liver. His stomach recoiled and he vomited. The vomit ran down into his windpipe, clogging it, and he began to choke.

In this extremity, his will to survive overcame the last of the impact paralysis. He brought his hands up slowly to grasp the cat. *Oh my God*, he thought.

The cat was forcing its way into his mouth, flattening its body, squirming, working itself farther and farther in. He could feel his jaws creaking wider and wider to admit it.

He reached to grab it, yank it out, destroy it ... and his hands clasped only the cat's tail.

Somehow it had gotten its entire body into his mouth. Its strange, black-and-white face must be crammed into his very throat.

A terrible thick gagging sound came from Halston's throat, which was swelling like a flexible length of garden hose.

His body twitched. His hands fell back into his lap and the fingers drummed senselessly on his thighs. His eyes sheened over, then glazed. They stared out through the Plymouth's windshield blankly at the coming dawn.

Protruding from his open mouth was two inches of bushy tail ... half black, half white. It switched lazily back and forth.

It disappeared.

A bird cried somewhere again. Dawn came in breathless silence then, over the frost-rimmed fields of rural Connecticut.

The farmer's name was Will Reuss.

He was on his way to Placer's Glen to get the inspection sticker renewed on his farm truck when he saw the late-morning sun twinkle on something in the ravine beside the road. He pulled over and saw the Plymouth lying at a drunken, canted angle in the ditch, barbed wire tangled in its grille like a snarl of steel knitting.

He worked his way down and then sucked in his breath sharply. "Holy moley," he muttered to the bright November day. There was a guy sitting bolt upright behind the wheel, eyes open and glaring emptily into eternity. The Roper organization was never going to include him in its presidential poll again. His face was smeared with blood. He was still wearing his seat belt.

The driver's door had been crimped shut, but Reuss managed to get it open by yanking with both hands. He leaned in and unstrapped the seat belt, planning to check for ID. He was reaching for the coat when he noticed that the dead guy's shirt was rippling, just above the belt buckle. Rippling ... and bulging. Splotches of blood began to bloom there like sinister roses.

"What the Christ?" He reached out, grasped the dead man's shirt, and pulled it up.

Will Reuss looked—and screamed.

Above Halston's navel, a ragged hole had been clawed in his flesh. Looking out was the gore-streaked black-and-white face of a cat, its eyes huge and glaring.

Reuss staggered back, shrieking, hands clapped to his face. A score of crows took cawing wing from a nearby field.

The cat forced its body out and stretched in obscene languor.

Then it leaped out the open window. Reuss caught sight of it moving through the high dead grass and then it was gone.

It seemed to be in a hurry, he later told a reporter from the local paper.

As if it had unfinished business.

Topics for Discussion

1) What is the plot of the story?
2) Who are the main characters in the story and what is their relationship?
3) When and where does the story happen?
4) How much do you know about Halston?
5) How many people die in the story in total?
6) Why does the cat kill people in the story?
7) Why is the person who appears to be most guilty not punished?
8) Can the cat kill people as depicted in the story?
9) Why does the novelist design such an implausible and illogical plot?
10) What is the key to understanding the story?

Interdisciplinary Concepts for Further Thinking

1. Anthropocentrism

Anthropocentrism is a major concept in the field of environmental ethics and environmental philosophy.

"Anthropos" in Greek is the same as "Homo" in Latin, which means human being.

The term "anthropocentric" was first coined in the 1860s to mean that humans are the center of the universe and the most important life form. In its most relevant philosophical form, anthropocentrism is the ethical belief that humans are separate from and superior to nature. Further, anthropocentrism asserts that human life has intrinsic value while other entities (including animals, plants, mineral resources, and so on) are resources that may be justifiably exploited for the benefit of humanity. For these reasons, it is believed that anthropocentrism is the root of modern environmental problems.

1) What is the main idea of the term anthropocentrism?
2) How is anthropocentrism manifested in "The Cat from Hell"?

2. Speciesism

Speciesism is a term used in philosophy regarding the treatment of individuals of different species.

It refers to the practice of treating members of one species as morally more important than members of other species. As a term, speciesism was introduced by the English philosopher Richard Ryder in the 1970s and subsequently popularized by the Australian philosopher Peter Singer. Ryder, Singer, and other opponents of speciesism have claimed that it is exactly analogous to racism, sexism, and other forms of irrational discrimination and prejudice.

An influential argument against speciesism, advanced by Singer, rests on what he calls the principle of equal consideration of interests. This is the claim that one should give equal weight in one's moral decision-making to the interests of all those affected by one's actions. In his groundbreaking book *Animal Liberation*, Singer defines speciesism as "a prejudice or attitude of bias in favor of the interests of members of one's own species and against those of members of other species." According to him, animals as well as humans have interests though not all of their interests are the same. Because both animals and humans are capable of feeling pain, for example, both have an interest in avoiding it. Indeed, Singer holds that the capacity to feel pain is the condition of having any interests at all.

1) What does the term speciesism mean?
2) Is the idea of speciesism reflected in "The Cat from Hell"?

Thinking in Numbers

Numbers influence our cognition and are important means for us to understand others and the world. In "The Cat from Hell", there are many important numbers mentioned such as the number of people who are killed by Halston, his charge for a hit, the number of cats that are killed in Drogan's development of the medicine, etc. Highlight as many numbers as possible and analyze their functions in the story.

Visual Thinking with Mind Mapping

Death is an important theme in "The Cat from Hell". In the story, the writer focuses on four people's death. What the writer really intends to disclose is the impending death of Drogan. Some clues can be found in the first and last paragraphs of the story. Create a mind map to disclose the cause-effect relationship between the cat and the fate of Drogan.

Critical Thinking for Reality

The story of "The Cat from Hell" is "unnatural" considering the slim possibility of the fictional events happening in real life. Why does Stephen King write such a kind of story?

In *The Moth Snowstorm*, Michael McCarthy employs the term "liberal secular humanism" to express people's creed since the Second World welfare. It wants people to be free from hunger and fear and disease, which is also the essence of modernity. The medicine Drogan develops in "The Cat from Hell" is to help people be free from disease or alleviate people's suffering. This seems to resonate with the "three passions" of Bertrand Russell in "What I have lived for", that is, the longing for love, the search for knowledge, and unbearable pity for the suffering of mankind. In the story, hundreds of thousands of cats are killed during tests in the name of decreasing the suffering of mankind. Surely, the use of animals in research remains essential to the discovery of the causes, diagnoses, and treatment of disease and suffering of humans. But is there anything wrong with it? Think critically about animal testing by referring to the historical context in which the story was published.

Unit 3
The Tamarisk Hunter

Paolo Bacigalupi

Introduction to the Author

Born in Western Colorado and raised on a fifteen-acre farm, Paolo Bacigalupi (1972—) attended Oberlin College, where he decided to major in Chinese—a choice that enabled him to teach in China and visit such countries and regions as India, Laos, Thailand, Malaysia, Singapore, Hong Kong, and Japan. He drew upon his experiences in the Far East, as well as writing environmental columns for *High Country News*, to write short stories that were eventually collected in *Pump Six and Other Stories* (2008). Although his early stories were influential, Bacigalupi first became widely recognized as a central writer of the early twenty-first century with his first novel, *The Windup Girl* (2009), which won Hugo, Nebula and Locus Awards.

Introduction to the Work

This is a short story by Paolo Bacigalupi and published by *First Country News*. The short story gave the possibility of the future with global warming effects. It describes a land controlled by the government, where water is the scarce liquid gold that everyone needed to survive. It deals with a "tamarisk hunter", a person who wins money and bounty by eradicating tamarisk trees in the Colorado River basin to reduce their water consumption.

Text

The Tamarisk Hunter

A big tamarisk can suck 73,000 gallons of river water a year. For $2.88 a day, plus water bounty, Lolo rips tamarisk all winter long.

Ten years ago, it was a good living. Back then, tamarisk shouldered up against every riverbank in the Colorado River Basin, along with cottonwoods, Russian olives, and elms. Ten years ago, towns like Grand Junction and Moab thought they could still squeeze life from a river.

Lolo stands on the edge of a canyon, Maggie the camel his only companion. He stares down into the deeps. It's an hour's scramble to the bottom. He ties Maggie to a juniper and starts down, boot-skiing a gully. A few blades of green grass sprout neon around him, piercing juniper-tagged snow clods. In the late winter, there is just a beginning surge of water down in the deeps; the ice is off the river edges. Up high, the mountains still wear their ragged snow mantles. Lolo smears through mud and hits a channel of scree, sliding and scattering rocks. His jugs of tamarisk poison gurgle and slosh on his back. His shovel and rockbar snag on occasional junipers as he skids by. It will be a long hike out. But then, that's what makes this patch so perfect. It's a long way down, and the riverbanks are largely hidden.

It's a living; where other people have dried out and blown away, he has remained: a tamarisk hunter, a water tick, a stubborn bit of weed. Everyone else has been blown off the land as surely as dandelion seeds, set free to fly south or east, or most of all north where watersheds sometimes still run deep and where even if there are no more lush ferns or deep cold fish runs, at least there is still water for people.

Eventually, Lolo reaches the canyon bottom. Down in the cold shadows, his breath steams.

He pulls out a digital camera and starts shooting his proof. The Bureau of Reclamation has gotten uptight about proof. They want different angles on the offending tamarisk, they want each one photographed before and after, the whole process documented, GPS'd, and uploaded directly by the camera. They want it done on-site. And then they still sometimes come out to spot check before they calibrate his headgate for water bounty.

But all their due diligence can't protect them from the likes of Lolo. Lolo has found the secret to eternal life as a tamarisk hunter. Unknown to the Interior Department and its BuRec subsidiary, he has been seeding new patches of tamarisk, encouraging vigorous brushy groves in previously cleared areas. He has hauled and planted healthy root balls up and down the river system in strategically hidden and inaccessible corridors, all in a bid for security against the swarms of other tamarisk hunters that scour these same tributaries. Lolo is crafty. Stands like this one, a quarter-mile long and thick with salt-laden tamarisk, are his insurance policy.

Documentation finished, he unstraps a folding saw, along with his rockbar and shovel, and sets his poison jugs on the dead salt bank. He starts cutting, slicing into the roots of the tamarisk, pausing every 30 seconds to spread Garlon 4 on the cuts, poisoning the tamarisk wounds faster than they can heal. But some of the best tamarisk, the most vigorous, he uproots and sets aside, for later use.

$2.88 a day, plus water bounty.

It takes Maggie's rolling bleating camel stride a week to make it back to Lolo's homestead. They follow the river, occasionally climbing above it onto cold mesas or wandering off into the open desert in a bid to avoid the skeleton sprawl of emptied towns. Guardie choppers buzz up and down the river like swarms of angry yellowjackets, hunting for porto-pumpers and wildcat diversions. They rush overhead in a wash of beaten air and gleaming National Guard logos. Lolo remembers a time when the guardies traded potshots with people down on the river banks, tracer-fire and machine-gun chatter echoing in the canyons. He remembers the glorious hiss and arc of a Stinger missile as it flashed across redrock desert and blue sky and burned a chopper where it hovered.

But that's long in the past. Now, guardie patrols skim up the river unmolested.

Lolo tops another mesa and stares down at the familiar landscape of an eviscerated town, its curving streets and subdivision cul-de-sacs all sitting silent in the sun. At the very edge of the empty town, one-acre ranchettes and snazzy five-thousand-square-foot houses with dead-stick trees and dust-hill landscaping fringe a brown tumbleweed golf course. The sandtraps don't even show any more.

When California put its first calls on the river, no one really worried. A couple of towns went begging for water. Some idiot newcomers with bad water rights stopped grazing their horses, and that was it. A few years later, people started showering real fast. And a few after that, they showered once a week. And then people started using the buckets. By then, everyone had stopped joking about how "hot" it was. It didn't really matter how "hot" it was. The problem wasn't lack of water or an excess of heat, not really. The problem was that 4.4 million acre-feet of water were supposed to go down the river to California. There was water; they just couldn't touch it.

They were supposed to stand there like dumb monkeys and watch it flow on by.

"Lolo?"

The voice catches him by surprise. Maggie startles and groans and lunges for the mesa edge before Lolo can rein her around. The camel's great padded feet scuffle dust and Lolo flails for his shotgun where it nestles in a scabbard at the camel's side. He forces Maggie to turn, shotgun half-drawn, holding barely to his seat and swearing.

A familiar face, tucked amongst juniper tangle.

"Goddamnit!" Lolo lets the shotgun drop back into its scabbard. "Jesus Christ, Travis. You scared the hell out of me."

Travis grins. He emerges from amongst the junipers' silver bark rags, one hand on his gray fedora, the other on the reins as he guides his mule out of the trees. "Surprised?"

"I could've shot you!"

"Don't be so jittery. There's no one out here' cept us water ticks."

"That's what I thought the last time I went shopping down there. I had a whole set of new dishes for Annie and I broke them all when I ran into an ultralight parked right in the middle of the main drag."

"Meth flyers?"

"Beats the hell out of me. I didn't stick around to ask."

"Shit. I'll bet they were as surprised as you were."

"They almost killed me."

"I guess they didn't."

Lolo shakes his head and swears again, this time without anger. Despite the ambush, he's happy to run into Travis. It's lonely country, and Lolo's been out long enough to notice the silence of talking to Maggie. They trade ritual sips of water from their canteens and make camp together. They swap stories about BuRec and avoid discussing where they've been ripping tamarisk and enjoy the view of the empty town far below, with its serpentine streets and quiet houses and shining untouched river.

It isn't until the sun is setting and they've finished roasting a magpie that Lolo finally asks the question that's been on his mind ever since Travis's sun-baked face came out of the tangle. It goes against etiquette, but he can't help himself. He picks magpie out of his teeth and says, "I thought you were working downriver."

Travis glances sidelong at Lolo and in that one suspicious uncertain look, Lolo sees that Travis has hit a lean patch. He's not smart like Lolo. He hasn't been reseeding. He's got no insurance. He hasn't been thinking ahead about all the competition, and what the tamarisk endgame looks like, and now he's feeling the pinch. Lolo feels a twinge of pity. He likes Travis. A part of him wants to tell Travis the secret, but he stifles the urge. The stakes are too high. Water crimes are serious now, so serious Lolo hasn't even told his wife, Annie, for fear of what she'll say. Like all of the most shameful crimes, water theft is a private business, and at the scale Lolo works, forced labor on the Straw is the best punishment he can hope for.

Travis gets his hackles down over Lolo's invasion of his privacy and says, "I had a couple cows I was running up here, but I lost 'em. I think something got 'em."

"Long way to graze cows."

"Yeah, well, down my way even the sagebrush is dead. Big Daddy Drought's doing a real number on my patch." He pinches his lip, thoughtful. "Wish I could find those cows."

"They probably went down to the river."

Travis sighs. "Then the guardies probably got 'em."

"Probably shot 'em from a chopper and roasted 'em."

"Californians."

They both spit at the word. The sun continues to sink. Shadows fall across the town's silent structures. The rooftops gleam red, a ruby cluster decorating the blue river necklace.

"You think there's any stands worth pulling down there?" Travis asks.

"You can go down and look. But I think I got it all last year. And someone had already been through before me, so I doubt much is coming up."

"Shit. Well, maybe I'll go shopping. Might as well get something out of this trip."

"There sure isn't anyone to stop you."

As if to emphasize the fact, the thud-thwap of a guardie chopper breaks the evening silence. The black-fly dot of its movement barely shows against the darkening sky. Soon it's out of sight and cricket chirps swallow the last evidence of its passing.

Travis laughs. "Remember when the guardies said they'd keep out looters? I saw them on TV with all their choppers and Humvees and them all saying they were going to protect everything until the situation improved." He laughs again. "You remember that? All of them driving up and down the streets?"

"I remember."

"Sometimes I wonder if we shouldn't have fought them more."

"Annie was in Lake Havasu City when they fought there. You saw what happened." Lolo shivers. "Anyway, there's not much to fight for once they blow up your water treatment plant. If nothing's coming out of your faucet, you might as well move on."

"Yeah, well, sometimes I think you still got to fight. Even if it's just for pride." Travis gestures at the town below, a shadow movement. "I remember when all that land down there was selling like hotcakes and they were building shit as fast as they could ship in the lumber. Shopping malls and parking lots and subdivisions, anywhere they could scrape a flat spot."

"We weren't calling it Big Daddy Drought, back then."

"Forty-five thousand people. And none of us had a clue. And I was a real estate agent." Travis laughs, a self-mocking sound that ends quickly. It sounds too much like self-pity for Lolo's taste. They're quiet again, looking down at the town wreckage.

"I think I might be heading north," Travis says finally.

Lolo glances over, surprised. Again he has the urge to let Travis in on his secret, but he stifles it. "And do what?"

"Pick fruit, maybe. Maybe something else. Anyway, there's water up there."

Lolo points down at the river. "There's water."

"Not for us." Travis pauses. "I got to level with you, Lolo. I went down to the Straw."

For a second, Lolo is confused by the non sequitur. The statement is too outrageous. And yet Travis's face is serious. "The Straw? No kidding? All the way there?"

"All the way there." He shrugs defensively. "I wasn't finding any tamarisk, anyway. And it didn't actually take that long. It's a lot closer than it used to be. A week out to the train tracks, and then I hopped a coal train, and rode it right to the interstate, and then I hitched."

"What's it like out there?"

"Empty. A trucker told me that California and the Interior Department drew up all these plans to decide which cities they'd turn off when." He looks at Lolo significantly. "That was after Lake Havasu. They figured out they had to do it slow. They worked out some kind of formula: how many cities, how many people they could evaporate at a time without making too much unrest. Anyway, it looks like they're pretty much done with it. There's nothing moving out there except highway trucks and coal trains and a couple truck stops."

"And you saw the Straw?"

"Oh sure, I saw it. Out toward the border. Big old mother. So big you couldn't climb on top of it, flopped out on the desert like a damn silver snake. All the way to California." He spits reflexively. "They're spraying with concrete to keep water from seeping into the ground and they've got some kind of carbon-fiber stuff over the top to stop the evaporation. And the river just disappears inside. Nothing but an empty canyon below it. Bone-dry. And choppers and Humvees everywhere, like a damn hornet's nest. They wouldn't let me get any closer than a half mile on account of the eco-crazies trying to blow it up. They weren't nice about it, either."

"What did you expect?"

"I dunno. It sure depressed me, though: They work us out here and toss us a little water bounty and then all that water next year goes right down into that big old pipe. Some Californian's probably filling his swimming pool with last year's water bounty right now."

Cricket-song pulses in the darkness. Off in the distance, a pack of coyotes starts yipping. The two of them are quiet for a while. Finally, Lolo chucks his friend on the shoulder. "Hell, Travis, it's probably for the best. A desert's a stupid place to put a river, anyway."

Lolo's homestead runs across a couple acres of semi-alkaline soil, conveniently close to the river's edge. Annie is out in the field when he crests the low hills that overlook his patch. She waves, but keeps digging, planting for whatever water he can collect in bounty.

Lolo pauses, watching Annie work. Hot wind kicks up, carrying with it the scents of sage and clay. A dust devil swirls around Annie, whipping her bandana off her head. Lolo smiles as she snags it; she sees him still watching her and waves at him to quit loafing.

He grins to himself and starts Maggie down the hill, but he doesn't stop watching Annie work. He's grateful for her. Grateful that every time he comes back from tamarisk hunting she is still here. She's steady. Steadier than the people like Travis who give up when times get dry. Steadier than anyone Lolo knows, really. And if she has nightmares sometimes, and can't stand being in towns or crowds and wakes up in the middle of the night calling out for family she'll never see again, well, then it's all the more reason to seed more tamarisk and make sure they never get pushed off their patch like she was pushed.

Lolo gets Maggie to kneel down so he can dismount, then leads her over to a water trough, half-full of slime and water skippers. He gets a bucket and heads for the river while Maggie groans and complains behind him. The patch used to have a well and running water, but like everyone else, they lost their pumping rights and BuRec stuffed the well with Quickcrete when the water table dropped below the Minimum Allowable Reserve. Now he and Annie steal buckets from the river, or, when the Interior Department isn't watching, they jump up and down on a footpump and dump water into a hidden underground cistern he built when the Resource Conservation and Allowable Use Guidelines went into effect.

Annie calls the guidelines "RaCAUG" and it sounds like she's hawking spit when she says it, but even with their filled-in well, they're lucky. They aren't like Spanish Oaks or Antelope Valley or River Reaches: expensive places that had rotten water rights and turned to dust, money or no, when Vegas and L. A. put in their calls. And they didn't have to bail out of Phoenix Metro when the Central Arizona Project got turned off and then had its aqueducts blown to smithereens when Arizona wouldn't stop pumping out of Lake Mead.

Pouring water into Maggie's water trough, and looking around at his dusty patch with Annie out in the fields, Lolo reminds himself how lucky he is. He hasn't blown away. He and Annie are dug in. Calies may call them water ticks, but fuck them. If it weren't for people like him and Annie, they'd dry up and blow away the same as everyone else. And if Lolo moves a little bit of tamarisk around, well, the Calies deserve it, considering what they've done to everyone else.

Finished with Maggie, Lolo goes into the house and gets a drink of his own out of the filter urn. The water is cool in the shadows of the adobe house. Juniper beams hang low overhead. He sits down and connects his BuRec camera to the solar panel they've got scabbed onto the roof. Its charge light blinks amber. Lolo goes and gets some more water. He's used to being thirsty, but for some reason he can't get enough today. Big Daddy Drought's got his hands around Lolo's neck today.

Annie comes in, wiping her forehead with a tanned arm. "Don't drink too much water," she says. "I haven't been able to pump. Bunch of guardies around."

"What the hell are they doing around? We haven't even opened our headgates yet."

"They said they were looking for you."

Lolo almost drops his cup.

They know.

They know about his tamarisk reseeding. They know he's been splitting and planting root-clusters. That he's been dragging big healthy chunks of tamarisk up and down the river. A week ago he uploaded his claim on the canyon tamarisk—his biggest stand yet—almost worth an acre-foot in itself in water bounty. And now the guardies are knocking on his door.

Lolo forces his hand not to shake as he puts his cup down. "They say what they want?" He's surprised his voice doesn't crack.

"Just that they wanted to talk to you." She pauses. "They had one of those Humvees. With the guns."

Lolo closes his eyes. Forces himself to take a deep breath. "They've always got guns. It's probably nothing."

"It reminded me of Lake Havasu. When they cleared us out. When they shut down the water treatment plant and everyone tried to burn down the BLM office."

"It's probably nothing." Suddenly he's glad he never told her about his tamarisk hijinks. They can't punish her the same. How many acre-feet is he liable for? It must be hundreds. They'll want him, all right. Put him on a Straw work crew and make him work for life, repay his water debt forever. He's replanted hundreds, maybe thousands of tamarisk, shuffling them around like a cardsharp on a poker table, moving them from one bank to another, killing them again and again and again, and always happily sending in his "evidence."

"It's probably nothing," he says again.

"That's what people said in Havasu."

Lolo waves out at their newly tilled patch. The sun shines down hot and hard on the small plot. "We're not worth that kind of effort." He forces a grin. "It probably has to do with those enviro crazies who tried to blow up the Straw. Some of them supposedly ran this way. It's probably that."

Annie shakes her head, unconvinced. "I don't know. They could have asked me the same as you."

"Yeah, but I cover a lot of ground. See a lot of things. I'll bet that's why they want to talk to me. They're just looking for eco-freaks."

"Yeah, maybe you're right. It's probably that." She nods slowly, trying to make herself believe. "Those enviros, they don't make any sense at all. Not enough water for people, and they want to give the river to a bunch of fish and birds."

Lolo nods emphatically and grins wider. "Yeah. Stupid." But suddenly he views the eco-crazies with something approaching brotherly affection. The Californians are after him, too.

Lolo doesn't sleep all night. His instincts tell him to run, but he doesn't have the heart to tell Annie, or to leave her. He goes out in the morning hunting tamarisk and fails at that as well. He doesn't cut a single stand all day. He considers shooting himself with his shotgun, but chickens out when he gets the barrels in his mouth. Better alive and on the run than dead. Finally, as he stares into the twin barrels, he knows that he has to tell Annie, tell her he's been a water thief for years and that he's got to run north. Maybe she'll come with him. Maybe she'll see reason. They'll run together. At least they have that. For sure, he's not going to let those bastards take him off to a labor camp for the rest of his life.

But the guardies are already waiting when Lolo gets back. They're squatting in the shade of their Humvee, talking. When Lolo comes over the crest of the hill, one of them taps the other and points. They both stand. Annie is out in the field again, turning over dirt, unaware of what's about to happen. Lolo reins in and studies the guardies. They lean against their Humvee and watch him back.

Suddenly Lolo sees his future. It plays out in his mind the way it does in a movie, as clear as the blue sky above. He puts his hand on his shotgun. Where it sits on Maggie's far side, the guardies can't see it. He keeps Maggie angled away from them and lets the camel start down the hill.

The guardies saunter toward him. They've got their Humvee with a .50 caliber on the back and they've both got M-16s slung over their shoulders. They're in full bulletproof gear and they look flushed and hot. Lolo rides down slowly. He'll have to hit them both in the face. Sweat trickles between his shoulder blades. His hand is slick on the shotgun's stock.

The guardies are playing it cool. They've still got their rifles slung, and they let Lolo keep approaching. One of them has a wide smile. He's maybe 40 years old, and tanned. He's been out for a while, picking up a tan like that. The other raises a hand and says, "Hey there, Lolo." Lolo's so surprised he takes his hand off his shotgun. "Hale?" He recognizes the guardie. He grew up with him. They played football together a million years ago, when football fields still had green grass and sprinklers sprayed their water straight into the air. Hale. Hale Perkins. Lolo scowls. He can't shoot Hale.

Hale says. "You're still out here, huh?"

"What the hell are you doing in that uniform? You with the Calies now?"

Hale grimaces and points to his uniform patches: Utah National Guard.

Lolo scowls. Utah National Guard. Colorado National Guard. Arizona National Guard. They're all the same. There's hardly a single member of the "National Guard" that isn't an out-of-state mercenary. Most of the local guardies quit a long time ago, sick to death of goose-stepping family and friends off their properties and sick to death of trading potshots with people who just wanted to stay in their homes. So even if there's still a Colorado National Guard, or an Arizona or a Utah, inside those uniforms with all their expensive nightsight gear and their brand-new choppers flying the river bends, it's pure California.

And then there are a few like Hale.

Lolo remembers Hale as being an OK guy. Remembers stealing a keg of beer from behind the Elks Club one night with him. Lolo eyes him. "How you liking that Supplementary Assistance Program?" He glances at the other guardie. "That working real well for you? The Calies a big help?"

Hale's eyes plead for understanding. "Come on, Lolo. I'm not like you. I got a family to look after. If I do another year of duty, they let Shannon and the kids base out of California."

"They give you a swimming pool in your backyard, too?"

"You know it's not like that. Water's scarce there, too."

Lolo wants to taunt him, but his heart isn't in it. A part of him wonders if Hale is just smart. At first, when California started winning its water lawsuits and shutting off cities, the displaced people just followed the water—right to California. It took a little while before the bureaucrats realized what was going on, but finally someone with a sharp pencil did the math and realized that taking in people along with their water didn't solve a water shortage. So the immigration fences went up.

But people like Hale can still get in.

"So what do you two want?" Inside, Lolo's wondering why they haven't already pulled him off Maggie and hauled him away, but he's willing to play this out.

The other guardie grins. "Maybe we're just out here seeing how the water ticks live."

Lolo eyes him. This one, he could shoot. He lets his hand fall to his shotgun again.

"BuRec sets my headgate. No reason for you to be out here."

The Calie says, "There were some marks on it. Big ones."

Lolo smiles tightly. He knows which marks the Calie is talking about. He made them with five different wrenches when he tried to dismember the entire headgate apparatus in a fit of obsession. Finally he gave up trying to open the bolts and just beat on the thing, banging the steel of the gate, smashing at it, while on the other side he had plants withering. After that, he gave up and just carried buckets of water to his plants and left it at that. But the dents and nicks are still there, reminding him of a period of madness. "It still works, don't it?"

Hale holds up a hand to his partner, quieting him. "Yeah, it still works. That's not why we're here."

"So what do you two want? You didn't drive all the way out here with your machine gun just to talk about dents in my headgate."

Hale sighs, put-upon, trying to be reasonable. "You mind getting down off that damn camel so we can talk?"

Lolo studies the two guardies, figuring his chances on the ground. "Shit." He spits. "Yeah, OK. You got me." He urges Maggie to kneel and climbs off her hump. "Annie didn't know anything about this. Don't get her involved. It was all me."

Hale's brow wrinkles, puzzled. "What are you talking about?"

"You're not arresting me?"

The Calie with Hale laughs. "Why? Cause you take a couple buckets of water from the river? Cause you probably got an illegal cistern around here somewhere?" He laughs again. "You ticks are all the same. You think we don't know about all that crap?"

Hale scowls at the Calie, then turns back to Lolo. "No, we're not here to arrest you. You know about the Straw?"

"Yeah." Lolo says it slowly, but inside, he's grinning. A great weight is suddenly off him. They don't know. They don't know shit. It was a good plan when he started it, and it's a good plan still. Lolo schools his face to keep the glee off, and tries to listen to what Hale's saying, but he can't, he's jumping up and down and gibbering like a monkey. They don't know—

"Wait." Lolo holds up his hand. "What did you just say?"

Hale repeats himself. "California's ending the water bounty. They've got enough Straw sections built up now that they don't need the program. They've got half the river enclosed. They got an agreement from the Department of Interior to focus their budget on seep and evaporation control. That's where all the big benefits are. They're shutting down the water bounty payout program." He pauses. "I'm sorry, Lolo."

Lolo frowns. "But a tamarisk is still a tamarisk. Why should one of those damn plants get the water? If I knock out a tamarisk, even if Cali doesn't want the water, I could still take it. Lots of people could use the water."

Hale looks pityingly at Lolo. "We don't make the regulations, we just enforce them. I'm supposed to tell you that your headgate won't get opened next year. If you keep hunting tamarisk, it won't do any good." He looks around the patch, then shrugs. "Anyway, in another couple years they were going to pipe this whole stretch. There won't be any tamarisk at all after that."

"What am I supposed to do, then?"

"California and BuRec is offering early buyout money." Hale pulls a booklet out of his bulletproof vest and flips it open. "Sort of to soften the blow." The pages of the booklet flap in the hot breeze. Hale pins the pages with a thumb and pulls a pen out of another vest pocket. He marks something on the booklet, then tears off a perforated check. "It's not a bad deal." Lolo takes the check. Stares at it. "Five hundred dollars?"

Hale shrugs sadly. "It's what they're offering. That's just the paper codes. You confirm it online. Use your BuRec camera phone, and they'll deposit it in whatever bank you want. Or they can hold it in trust until you get into a town and want to withdraw it. Any place with a BLM office, you can do that. But you need to confirm before April 15. Then BuRec'll send out a guy to shut down your headgate before this season gets going."

"Five hundred dollars?"

"It's enough to get you north. That's more than they're offering next year."

"But this is my patch."

"Not as long as we've got Big Daddy Drought. I'm sorry, Lolo."

"The drought could break any time. Why can't they give us a couple more years? It could break any time." But even as he says it, Lolo doesn't believe. Ten years ago, he might have. But not now. Big Daddy Drought's here to stay. He clutches the check and its keycodes to his chest.

A hundred yards away, the river flows on to California.

Topics for Discussion

1) What is the story "The Tamarisk Hunter" about?
2) What is the background of the story?
3) What does the town look like in the story?
4) How does Lolo make a living?
5) What does "the Straw" refer to?
6) What is the relationship between Lolo and Hale?
7) What does the Calie refer to?
8) What are two guardies coming for at the end of the story?
9) What might be the fate of Lolo?
10) What is the theme of the story?

Interdisciplinary Concepts for Further Thinking

1. Climate Change Justice

Climate change justice is a branch of philosophical inquiry concerned with fair terms of cooperation for addressing global climate change.

"Climate justice" is a term that acknowledges that climate change can have social, economic, and other adverse impacts on underprivileged people or communities. Advocates of climate justice are striving to have these inequities addressed through long-term mitigation and adaptation strategies.

There are two key aspects to consider while thinking about climate justice:

First, climate justice begins with recognizing that key groups are differently affected by climate change. Generally, many victims of climate change also bear disproportionately low responsibility for causing the emissions that give rise to climate change in the first place—particularly people in developing countries who produce fewer emissions per capita than those in developed countries. Simply put, those who emit the least are impacted the most.

Second, climate impacts can cause inequitable social conditions. Low-income communities, people of color, indigenous people, people with disabilities, older or very young people, and women—all can be more susceptible to risks posed by climate impacts like raging storms and floods, increasing wildfire, severe heat, poor air quality, insufficient access to food and water, and disappearing shorelines.

1) What is the implication of climate justice?
2) How is the theme of climate justice demonstrated in "The Tamarisk Hunter"?

2. Dystopia

A utopia is a paradise, a dystopia a paradise lost. In 1516, Thomas More published a fictional account of a sailor on one of Vespucci's ships to the island of Utopia, where he found a perfect republic. The word "dystopia", meaning "an unhappy country", was coined in the 1740s by the historian Gregory Claeys in "Dystopia: A Natural History". In its modern definition, a dystopia can be apocalyptic, or post-apocalyptic, or neither, but it has to be anti-utopian, a utopia turned upside down, a world in which people tried to build a republic of perfection only to find that they had created a republic of misery. "A Trip to the Island of Equality", a 1792 reply to Thomas Paine's "Rights of Man", is a dystopia (on the island, the pursuit of equality has reduced everyone to living in caves); it's merely apocalyptic. Utopians believe in progress; dystopians don't. They fight this argument out in competing visions of the future, utopians offering promises, and dystopians issuing warnings.

1) What is the difference between utopia and dystopia?
2) Is the society depicted in "The Tamarisk Hunter" a dystopia?

Thinking in Numbers

In the 21st century, with the growing scale and intensity of natural disasters, humanity's sustainability is severely threatened and the decades of people's existence on the Earth seem to be counted in numbers in a metaphorical sense. To make people realize the urgency of climate change, consider some influential numbers such as the emission of carbon dioxide or other important figures.

Visual Thinking with Mind Mapping

1) Create a mind map to demonstrate the "crisis" in "The Tamarisk Hunter" by referring to the triangle concepts of environmental crisis, social crisis and spiritual crisis.

2) All people on the Earth are equal in face of climate change. In the meantime, the effects of climate change on different groups of people are distributed differently, which leads to the problem of the environmental justice. Analyze the climate injustice shown in "The Tamarisk Hunter" and try to figure out the means to overcome the injustice with a mind map.

Critical Thinking for Reality

Heat waves, droughts, and extreme weather events have become the new normal throughout the world. Nowadays, the world is already $1.2°C$ warmer than in pre-industrial times, and every fraction of a degree counts. Research shows that with $2°C$ of global warming, we will have more intense droughts and more devastating floods, more wildfires, and more storms. Every one on the planet is responsible for global climate change, however, people tend to think that they can do nothing about it because no one wants to believe their daily activities—from switching on a light to checking their phones to washing their hair to going to work—are responsible for a global disaster that has already turned millions of people into climate refugees and killed scores of others. The term to describe this phenomenon is cognitive dissonance. Consider how cognitive dissonance can be overcome to deal with climate change.

Section Two

Male-Female Affinity: Gender Relationship

The relationship between the two genders is an eternal topic in literature. The famous lines "Guan! Guan! Cry the fish hawks/on sandbars in the river: /a mild-mannered good girl, /fine match for the gentleman" in *The Book of Songs* (《诗经》) indicate young men's yearning for sweet and romantic love. Regardless of their temporal and spatial boundaries, the tragic love stories of Liang Shanbo and Zhu Yingtai and Romeo and Juliet have been eulogized and passed on from generation to generation. The theme of love finds voice in these classic literary works and astoundingly resonates with people.

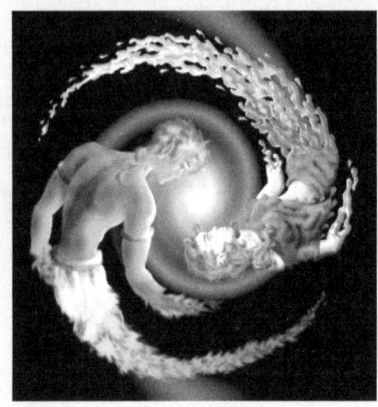

In modern society, the issue of the relationship between genders has been examined differently, depending on people's developing perception of gender. Owing to waves of feminism, women's status has been gradually elevated, the power balance between the two genders has also undergone a drastic change, and people's understanding of masculinity as well as femininity is also being constantly renewed. In this process, more diversified roles and identities of women emerge as women are not merely someone's wife or mother but can more fundamentally be themselves. Self-independence has become a label for a new woman. Women are beginning to rebuild their self-image and define themselves by taking control of their position in their relationships, family, and society.

Despite the change, there is something timeless when it comes to relationship between the genders. What remains unchanged is young people's beautiful wish of seeking true love, together with their confusion and self-growth in the process. Love, as well as life, is a kind of art that requires "strategies" and "techniques" to maintain and sustain a relationship. As the psychoanalyst and philosopher Erich Fromm (1900—1980) wrote in *The Art of Loving* (1956), "To love somebody is not just a strong feeling—it is a decision, it is a judgment, it is a promise." Love is not merely integrity, passion, or even fidelity; rather, love is effective mutual communication, interaction, understanding, and tolerance. Literature, as a representative form of artistic experience, can always offer us scenarios regarding different aspects of love, including both bright side and dark side, happiness and trauma, dominance and submission, hatred and forgiveness, etc. Through enduring literary classics about love, readers learn and explore a form of knowledge that transcends time.

Unit 4
The Black Cat

Edgar Allan Poe

Introduction to the Author

Edgar Allan Poe (1809—1849) was an important figure in the American Romantic movement. After his father's abandonment and mother's death, Poe was adopted by the Allan's of Richmond when he was three years old, from whom he got the name Allan. At 27, Poe married his 14-year-old niece Virginia Eliza Clemm. In 1847, Virginia died of tuberculosis, which directly caused Poe to become addicted to booze and drugs. The passing of his mother and wife was projected in a number of his writings. Accounts suggest that Poe was deeply scarred by his mother's premature death, carrying this trauma with him throughout his life. Roger Asselineau wrote in his biography of Poe, "He always remembered, more or less unconsciously, that his mother vomited blood and that she was taken away forever by sinister men dressed in black."

Poe is widely acknowledged as the father of Gothic horror, the inventor of the modern detective story and an innovator in the genre of science fiction. His work has also been described as mystery, macabre, and Gothic. His legacy today remains focused on his tales of terror and haunting lyric poetry. Death and darkness remained a strong and consistent theme throughout his published prose. In his famous poems "The Raven" (1845), "Annabelle Lee" (1849), death and beauty remained two consistent themes, as mentioned in his own literary criticism.

Introduction to the Work

Poe's short story, "The Black Cat" was published in 1843 in *The Saturday Evening Post*. It was popular with readers, but Poe did not receive instant success until he published his famous poem, "The Raven". Since its publication, elements of "The Black Cat" have inspired films, television episodes, paintings, plays, comics, and novels. The story is told from the perspective of a narrator who, in his own words, does not expect the reader to believe him. He tells the reader up front that he is scheduled to die the following day, but the reader doesn't find out why until the end of the story.

Text

The Black Cat

For the most wild, yet most homely narrative which I am about to pen, I neither expect nor solicit belief. Mad indeed would I be to expect it, in a case where my very senses reject their own evidence. Yet, mad am I not—and very surely do I not dream. But to-morrow I die, and to-day I would unburden my soul. My immediate purpose is to place before the world, plainly, succinctly, and without comment, a series of mere household events. In their consequences, these events have terrified—have tortured—have destroyed me. Yet I will not attempt to expound them. To me, they have presented little but Horror—to many they will seem less terrible than baroques. Hereafter, perhaps, some intellect may be found which will reduce my phantasm to the commonplace—some intellect more calm, more logical, and far less excitable than my own, which will perceive, in the circumstances I detail with awe, nothing more than an ordinary succession of very natural causes and effects.

From my infancy I was noted for the docility and humanity of my disposition. My tenderness of heart was even so conspicuous as to make me the jest of my companions. I was especially fond of animals, and was indulged by my parents with a great variety of pets. With these I spent most of my time, and never was so happy as when feeding and caressing them. This peculiar of character grew with my growth, and, in my manhood, I derived from it one of my principal sources of pleasure. To those who have cherished an affection for a faithful and sagacious dog, I need hardly be at the trouble of explaining the nature or the intensity of the gratification thus derivable. There is something in the unselfish and self-sacrificing love of a brute, which goes directly to the heart of him who has had frequent occasion to test the paltry friendship and gossamer fidelity of mere Man.

I married early, and was happy to find in my wife a disposition not uncongenial with my own. Observing my partiality for domestic pets, she lost no opportunity of procuring those of the most agreeable kind. We had birds, gold-fish, a fine dog, rabbits, a small monkey, and a cat.

This latter was a remarkably large and beautiful animal, entirely black, and sagacious to an astonishing degree. In speaking of his intelligence, my wife, who at heart was not a little tinctured with superstition, made frequent allusion to the ancient popular notion, which regarded all black cats as witches in disguise. Not that she was ever serious upon this point—and I mention the matter at all for no better reason than that it happens, just now, to be remembered.

Pluto—this was the cat's name—was my favorite pet and playmate. I alone fed him, and he attended me wherever I went about the house. It was even with difficulty that I could prevent him from following me through the streets.

Our friendship lasted, in this manner, for several years, during which my general temperament and character—through the instrumentality of the Fiend Intemperance— had (I blush to confess it) experienced a radical alteration for the worse. I grew, day by day, more moody, more irritable, more regardless of the feelings of others. I suffered myself to use intemperate language to my wife. At length, I even offered her personal violence. My pets, of course, were made to feel the change in my disposition. I not only neglected, but ill-used them. For Pluto, however, I still retained sufficient regard to restrain me from maltreating him, as I made no scruple of maltreating the rabbits, the monkey, or even the dog, when by, accident, or through affection, they came in my way. But my disease grew upon me—for what disease is like Alcohol!—and at length even Pluto, who was now becoming old, and consequently somewhat peevish—even Pluto began to experience the effects of my ill temper.

One night, returning home, much intoxicated, from one of my haunts about town, I fancied that the cat avoided my presence. I seized him; when, in his fright at my violence, he inflicted a slight wound upon my hand with his teeth. The fury of a demon instantly possessed me. I knew myself no longer. My original soul seemed, at once, to take its flight from my body; and a more than fiendish malevolence, gin-nurtured, thrilled every fibre of my frame. I took from my waistcoat-pocket a penknife, opened it, grasped the poor beast by the throat, and deliberately cut one of its eyes from the socket! I blush, I burn, I shudder, while I pen the damnable atrocity.

When reason returned with the morning—when I had slept off the fumes of the night's debauch—I experienced a sentiment half of horror, half of remorse, for the crime of which I had been guilty; but it was, at best, a feeble and equivocal feeling, and the soul remained untouched. I again plunged into excess, and soon drowned in wine all memory of the deed.

In the meantime the cat slowly recovered. The socket of the lost eye presented, it is true, a frightful appearance, but he no longer appeared to suffer any pain. He went about the house as usual, but, as might be expected, fled in extreme terror at my approach. I had so much of my old heart left, as to be at first grieved by this evident dislike on the part of a creature which had once so loved me. But this feeling soon gave place to irritation. And then came, as if to my final and irrevocable overthrow, the spirit of PERVERSENESS. Of this spirit philosophy takes no account. Yet I am not more sure that my soul lives, than I am that perverseness is one of the primitive impulses of the human heart—one of the indivisible primary faculties, or sentiments, which give direction to the character of Man. Who has not, a hundred times, found himself committing a vile or a stupid action, for no other reason than because he knows he should not? Have we not a perpetual inclination, in the teeth of our best judgment, to violate that which is Law, merely because we understand it to be such? This spirit of perverseness, I say, came to my final overthrow. It was this unfathomable longing of the soul to vex itself—to offer violence to its own nature—to do wrong for the wrong's sake only—that urged me to continue and finally to consummate the injury I had inflicted upon the unoffending brute. One morning, in cool blood, I slipped a noose about its neck and hung it to the limb of a tree;—hung it with the tears streaming from my eyes, and with the bitterest remorse at my heart;—hung it because I knew that it had loved me, and because I felt it had given me no reason of offence;—hung it because I knew that in so doing I was committing a sin—a deadly sin that would so jeopardize my immortal soul as to place it—if such a thing were possible—even beyond the reach of the infinite mercy of the Most Merciful and Most Terrible God.

On the night of the day on which this cruel deed was done, I was aroused from sleep by the cry of fire. The curtains of my bed were in flames. The whole house was blazing. It was with great difficulty that my wife, a servant, and myself, made our escape from the conflagration. The destruction was complete. My entire worldly wealth was swallowed up, and I resigned myself thenceforward to despair.

I am above the weakness of seeking to establish a sequence of cause and effect, between the disaster and the atrocity. But I am detailing a chain of facts—and wish not to leave even a possible link imperfect. On the day succeeding the fire, I visited the ruins. The walls, with one exception, had fallen in. This exception was found in a compartment wall, not very thick, which stood about the middle of the house, and against which had rested the head of my bed. The plastering had here, in great measure, resisted the action of the fire—a fact which I attributed to its having been recently spread. About this wall a dense crowd were collected, and many persons seemed to be examining a particular portion of it with every minute and eager attention. The words "strange!" "singular!" and other similar expressions, excited my curiosity. I approached and saw, as if graven in bas relief upon the white surface, the figure of a gigantic cat. The impression was given with an accuracy truly marvellous.

There was a rope about the animal's neck.

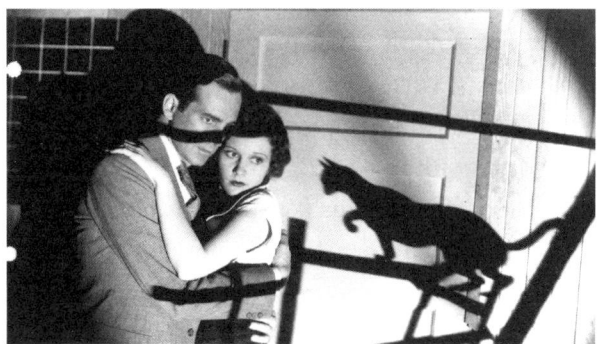

When I first beheld this apparition—for I could scarcely regard it as less—my wonder and my terror were extreme. But at length reflection came to my aid. The cat, I remembered, had been hung in a garden adjacent to the house. Upon the alarm of fire, this garden had been immediately filled by the crowd—by some one of whom the animal must have been cut from the tree and thrown, through an open window, into my chamber. This had probably been done with the view of arousing me from sleep. The falling of other walls had compressed the victim of my cruelty into the substance of the freshly-spread plaster; the lime of which, had then with the flames, and the ammonia from the carcass, accomplished the portraiture as I saw it.

Although I thus readily accounted to my reason, if not altogether to my conscience, for the startling fact just detailed, it did not the less fail to make a deep impression upon my fancy. For months I could not rid myself of the phantasm of the cat; and, during this period, there came back into my spirit a half-sentiment that seemed, but was not, remorse. I went so far as to regret the loss of the animal, and to look about me, among the vile haunts which I now habitually frequented, for another pet of the same species, and of somewhat similar appearance, with which to supply its place.

One night as I sat, half stupefied, in a den of more than infamy, my attention was suddenly drawn to some black object, reposing upon the head of one of the immense hogsheads of gin, or of rum, which constituted the chief furniture of the apartment. I had been looking steadily at the top of this hogshead for some minutes, and what now caused me surprise was the fact that I had not sooner perceived the object thereupon. I approached it, and touched it with my hand. It was a black cat—very large one—fully as large as Pluto, and closely resembling him in every respect but one. Pluto had not a white hair upon any portion of his body; but this cat had a large, although indefinite splotch of white, covering nearly the whole region of the breast.

Upon my touching him, he immediately arose, purred loudly, rubbed against my hand, and appeared delighted with my notice. This, then, was the very creature of which I was in search. I at once offered to purchase it of the landlord; but this person made no claim to it—knew nothing of it—had never seen it before.

I continued my caresses, and, when I prepared to go home, the animal evinced a disposition to accompany me. I permitted it to do so; occasionally stooping and patting it as I proceeded. When it reached the house it domesticated itself at once, and became immediately a great favorite with my wife.

For my own part, I soon found a dislike to it arising within me. This was just the reverse of what I had anticipated; but I know not how or why it was—its evident fondness for myself rather disgusted and annoyed me. By slow degrees, these feelings of disgust and annoyance rose into the bitterness of hatred. I avoided the creature; a certain sense of shame, and the remembrance of my former deed of cruelty, preventing me from physically abusing it. I did not, for some weeks, strike, or otherwise violently ill use it; but gradually—very gradually—I came to look upon it with unutterable loathing, and to flee silently from its odious presence, as from the breath of a pestilence.

What added, no doubt, to my hatred of the beast, was the discovery, on the morning after I brought it home, that, like Pluto, it also had been deprived of one of its eyes. This circumstance, however, only endeared it to my wife, who, as I have already said, possessed, in a high degree, that humanity of feeling which had once been my distinguishing trait, and the source of many of my simplest and purest pleasures.

With my aversion to this cat, however, its partiality for myself seemed to increase. It followed my footsteps with a pertinacity which it would be difficult to make the reader comprehend. Whenever I sat, it would crouch beneath my chair, or spring upon my knees, covering me with its loathsome caresses. If I arose to walk it would get between my feet and thus nearly throw me down, or, fastening its long and sharp claws in my dress, clamber, in this manner, to my breast. At such times, although I longed to destroy it with a blow, I was yet withheld from so doing, partly it at by a memory of my former crime, but chiefly—let me confess it at once—by absolute dread of the beast.

This dread was not exactly a dread of physical evil—and yet I should be at a loss how otherwise to define it. I am almost ashamed to own—yes, even in this felon's cell, I am almost ashamed to own—that the terror and horror with which the animal inspired me, had been heightened by one of the merest chimeras it would be possible to conceive. My wife had called my attention, more than once, to the character of the mark of white hair, of which I have spoken, and which constituted the sole visible difference between the strange beast and the one I had destroyed. The reader will remember that this mark, although large, had been originally very indefinite; but, by slow degrees—degrees nearly imperceptible, and which for a long time my reason struggled to reject as fanciful—it had, at length, assumed a rigorous distinctness of outline. It was now the representation of an object that I shudder to name—and for this, above all, I loathed, and dreaded, and would have rid myself of the monster had I dared—it was now, I say, the image of a hideous—of a ghastly thing—of the GALLOWS!—oh, mournful and terrible engine of Horror and of Crime—of Agony and of Death!

And now was I indeed wretched beyond the wretchedness of mere Humanity. And a brute beast—whose fellow I had contemptuously destroyed—a brute beast to work out for me—for me a man, fashioned in the image of the High God—so much of insufferable woe! Alas! neither by day nor by night knew I the blessing of rest any more! During the former the creature left me no moment alone; and, in the latter, I started hourly from dreams of unutterable fear, to find the hot breath of the thing upon my face, and its vast weight—an incarnate nightmare that I had no power to shake off—incumbent eternally upon my heart!

Beneath the pressure of torments such as these, the feeble remnant of the good within me succumbed. Evil thoughts became my sole intimates—the darkest and most evil of thoughts. The moodiness of my usual temper increased to hatred of all things and of all mankind; while, from the sudden, frequent, and ungovernable outbursts of a fury to which I now blindly abandoned myself, my uncomplaining wife, alas! was the most usual and the most patient of sufferers.

One day she accompanied me, upon some household errand, into the cellar of the old building which our poverty compelled us to inhabit. The cat followed me down the steep stairs, and, nearly throwing me headlong, exasperated me to madness. Uplifting an axe, and forgetting, in my wrath, the childish dread which had hitherto stayed my hand, I aimed a blow at the animal which, of course, would have proved instantly fatal had it descended as I wished. But this blow was arrested by the hand of my wife. Goaded, by the interference, into a rage more than demoniacal, I withdrew my arm from her grasp and buried the axe in her brain. She fell dead upon the spot, without a groan.

This hideous murder accomplished, I set myself forthwith, and with entire deliberation, to the task of concealing the body. I knew that I could not remove it from the house, either by day or by night, without the risk of being observed by the neighbors. Many projects entered my mind. At one period I thought of cutting the corpse into minute fragments, and destroying them by fire. At another, I resolved to dig a grave for it in the floor of the cellar. Again, I deliberated about casting it in the well in the yard—about packing it in a box, as if merchandize, with the usual arrangements, and so getting a porter to take it from the house. Finally I hit upon what I considered a far better expedient than either of these. I determined to wall it up in the cellar—as the monks of the Middle Ages are recorded to have walled up their victims.

For a purpose such as this the cellar was well adapted. Its walls were loosely constructed, and had lately been plastered throughout with a rough plaster, which the dampness of the atmosphere had prevented from hardening. Moreover, in one of the walls was a projection, caused by a false chimney, or fireplace, that had been filled up, and made to resemble the rest of the cellar. I made no doubt that I could readily displace the at this point, insert the corpse, and wall the whole up as before, so that no eye could detect anything suspicious.

And in this calculation I was not deceived. By means of a crowbar I easily dislodged the bricks, and, having carefully deposited the body against the inner wall, I propped it in that position, while with little trouble, I relaid the whole structure as it originally stood. Having procured mortar, sand, and hair, with every possible precaution, I prepared a plaster which could not be distinguished from the old, and with this I very carefully went over the new brick-work. When I had finished, I felt satisfied that all was right. The wall did not present the slightest appearance of having been disturbed. The rubbish on the floor was picked up with the minutest care. I looked around triumphantly, and said to myself—"Here at least, then, my labor has not been in vain."

My next step was to look for the beast which had been the cause of so much wretchedness; for I had, at length, firmly resolved to put it to death. Had I been able to meet with it, at the moment, there could have been no doubt of its fate; but it appeared that the crafty animal had been alarmed at the violence of my previous anger, and forebore to present itself in my present mood. It is impossible to describe or to imagine the deep, the blissful sense of relief which the absence of the detested creature occasioned in my bosom. It did not make its appearance during the night—and thus for one night at least, since its introduction into the house, I soundly and tranquilly slept; aye, slept even with the burden of murder upon my soul!

The second and the third day passed, and still my tormentor came not. Once again I breathed as a freeman. The monster, in terror, had fled the premises forever! I should behold it no more! My happiness was supreme! The guilt of my dark deed disturbed me but little. Some few inquiries had been made, but these had been readily answered. Even a search had been instituted—but of course nothing was to be discovered. I looked upon my future felicity as secured.

Upon the fourth day of the assassination, a party of the police came, very unexpectedly, into the house, and proceeded again to make rigorous investigation of the premises. Secure, however, in the inscrutability of my place of concealment, I felt no embarrassment whatever. The officers bade me accompany them in their search. They left no nook or corner unexplored. At length, for the third or fourth time, they descended into the cellar. I quivered not in a muscle. My heart beat calmly as that of one who slumbers in innocence. I walked the cellar from end to end. I folded my arms upon my bosom, and roamed easily to and fro. The police were thoroughly satisfied and prepared to depart. The glee at my heart was too strong to be restrained. I burned to say if but one word, by way of triumph, and to render doubly sure their assurance of my guiltlessness.

"Gentlemen," I said at last, as the party ascended the steps, "I delight to have allayed your suspicions. I wish you all health, and a little more courtesy. By the bye, gentlemen, this—this is a very well-constructed house," (In the rabid desire to say something easily, I scarcely knew what I uttered at all),—"I may say an excellently well-constructed house. These walls—are you going, gentlemen?—these walls are solidly put together"; and here, through the mere frenzy of bravado, I rapped heavily with a cane which I held in my hand, upon that very portion of the brick-work behind which stood the corpse of the wife of my bosom.

But may God shield and deliver me from the fangs of the Arch-Fiend! No sooner had the reverberation of my blows sunk into silence than I was answered by a voice from within the tomb!—by a cry, at first muffled and broken, like the sobbing of a child, and then quickly swelling into one long, loud, and continuous scream, utterly anomalous and inhuman—a howl—a wailing shriek, half of horror and half of triumph, such as might have arisen only out of hell, conjointly from the throats of the damned in their agony and of the demons that exult in the damnation.

Of my own thoughts it is folly to speak. Swooning, I staggered to the opposite wall. For one instant the party upon the stairs remained motionless, through extremity of terror and of awe. In the next, a dozen stout arms were tolling at the wall. It fell bodily. The corpse, already greatly decayed and clotted with gore, stood erect before the eyes of the spectators. Upon its head, with red extended mouth and solitary eye of fire, sat the hideous beast whose craft had seduced me into murder, and whose informing voice had consigned me to the hangman. I had walled the monster up within the tomb.

Topics for Discussion

1) Who is the narrator of the story?
2) What's the narrator's attitude towards animals?
3) Why does the narrator tell the story?
4) What are the important features of Pluto in the story?
5) Where is the narrator when he tells the story?
6) How is the first black cat killed?
7) How does the big fire happen?
8) How does the "second" cat come to the house of the narrator?

9) Why is the narrator intoxicated to alcohol?
10) What is the theme of the story?

Interdisciplinary Concepts for Further Thinking

1. Historicism

The term "historicism" is adopted in various disciplines of study, including philosophy, anthropology, and theology.

Historicism holds that there is an organic succession of developments, and that conditions and environments decisively influence the results. Hegelian Historicism is the position, adopted by Georg Hegel that all human societies and all human activities such as philosophy, art and science are defined by their history, and that their essence can be sought only through understanding that. That is to say, to understand why a person is a way he is, one must view that person within a societal context. Similarly, to understand a society, one must understand its history as well as the forces that shaped it.

1) What is the historical background of the short story?
2) Why is historicism helpful for us to understand "The Black Cat"?

2. New Historicism

New Historicism is a term used to refer to an intellectual movement that holds that each epoch has its own knowledge system within which individuals are inexorably entangled. Generally, new historicism is a literary theory based on the idea that literature should be studied and interpreted within the context of both the history of the author and the critic. Based on the literary criticism of Stephen Greenblatt and influenced by the philosophy of Michel Foucault, New Historicism acknowledges not only that a work of literature is influenced by its author's times and circumstances, but that the critic's response to that work is also influenced by his environment, beliefs, and prejudices. A New Historicist looks at literature in a wider historical context, examining both how the writer's times affected the work and how the work reflects the writer's times, in turn recognizing that current cultural contexts color that critic's conclusions.

1) What are the essential ideas of new historicism?
2) Is new historicism helpful for us to understand the fate of the wife and the narrator in "The Black Cat"?

Thinking in Numbers

1) One "eye", two cats and three characters are important markers of "The Black Cat". Explain what these three numbers indicate in your own words respectively.

2) The wife is a minor character in "The Black Cat". Read the story again and count how many times the wife is mentioned in the narration and explain the function of the wife in the plot.

Visual Thinking with Mind Mapping

"The Black Cat" is essentially a confession of a murderer. He told us his story, but apparently he did not tell us the whole story. The biggest secret of the narrator is what has led to the dramatic change in his temperament and character after several years of marriage, which is the root of all the consecutive violent events including the final death of his wife. Create a mind map to analyze the possible events that led to the narrator's personality change.

Critical Thinking for Reality

The narrator in "The Black Cat" is extremely gentle and kind-hearted when he is a little boy. But several years after marriage, he becomes moody, irritable, and finally a devil-like man. His wife does not complain or leave him even though she is the first and long-term victim of his violence. Why is she so tolerant of her husband? Imagine that your lover is a person who has violent tendencies. What will you do?

Unit 5
Our Friend Judith

Doris Lessing

Introduction to the Author

Doris Lessing (1919—2013) was born in Persia (modern Iran), where her British parents had moved following World War I. In 1925, the family immigrated to the British colony of Southern Rhodesia (modern Zimbabwe) in Africa, where, from an early age, she was both captivated by the wild beauty of the bush and disturbed by the pervasive racial oppression she witnessed. Her early experiences did, in a way, greatly influence the majority of her writings.

With her inventive and ground-breaking writing, Doris Lessing established herself as a major figure in 20th-century British and international literature. She was awarded the 2007 Nobel Prize for Literature and labeled as an "epicist of the female experience, who with scepticism, fire and visionary power has subjected a divided civilization to scrutiny" and regarded as the best female author since Virginia Woolf. She was the oldest person ever to receive the Nobel Prize in Literature. Her writings deal with a wide range of subjects, including racial tensions, gender roles, youth violence, and modern sociopolitical and economic structures. Her fiction mostly focuses on denouncing colonialism, supporting women's freedom, and predicting the fate of humanity. In 2008 *The Times* ranked her fifth on a list of "The 50 greatest British writers since 1945". She authored 27 novels, 17 collections of short stories, four memoirs, and a number of collections, the most well-known of which are *The Grass is Singing* (1950), *The Golden Notebook* (1962), *The Fifth Child* (1988) and *African Laughter: Four Visits to Zimbabwe* (1992).

Introduction to the Work

Our Friend Judith (1960) begins and ends in London, England between the 1950s and 60s. It later changes location to the Italian Riviera in Italy. The last bit of the story is back in London, England. The narrator, Betty, and Judith are long time friends with different lifestyles. While the narrator and Betty live what would be considered a normal lifestyle for the women of their time, housewives with children, Judith is different. She is a single, older women who lives alone in her one bedroom apartment, she is labeled as a "English spinster". The story consists of events the narrator sees as significant moments that help the narrator understand Judith and who she really is. The story examines and criticizes the gender roles constricting and controlling the lives of women in the 1960s. Thus, the story follows the life of Judith, a single woman in her 40's, who faces a great deal of condemnation and judgement for her liberal, independent lifestyle.

Text

Our Friend Judith

I stopped inviting Judith to meet people when a Canadian woman remarked, with the satisfied fervour of one who has at last pinned a label on a rare specimen: "She is, of course, one of your typical English spinsters."

This was a few weeks after an American sociologist, having elicited from Judith the facts that she was fortyish, unmarried, and living alone, had enquired of me: "I suppose she has given up?" "Given up what?" I asked; and the subsequent discussion was unrewarding.

Judith did not easily come to parties. She would come after pressure, not so much—one felt—to do one a favour, but in order to correct what she believed to be a defect in her character. "I really ought to enjoy meeting new people more than I do," she said once. We reverted to an earlier pattern of our friendship: odd evenings together, an occasional visit to the cinema, or she would telephone to say: "I'm on my way past you to the British Museum. Would you care for a cup of coffee with me? I have twenty minutes to spare."

It is characteristic of Judith that the word spinster, used of her, provoked fascinated speculation about other people. There are my aunts for instance: aged seventy-odd, both unmarried, one an ex-missionary from China, one a retired matron of a famous London hospital. These two old ladies live together under the shadow of the cathedral in a country town. They devote much time to the Church, to good causes, to letter writing with friends all over the world, to the grandchildren and the great-grandchildren of relatives. It would be a mistake, however, on entering a house in which nothing has been moved for fifty years, to diagnose a condition of fossilized late-Victorian integrity. They read every book reviewed in the *Observer* or *The Times*, so that I recently got a letter from Aunt Rose enquiring whether I did not think that the author of *On the Road* was not—perhaps?—exaggerating his difficulties. They know a good deal about music, and write letters of encouragement to young composers they feel are being neglected—"You must understand that anything new and original takes time to be understood." Well-informed and critical Tories, they are as likely to dispatch telegrams of protest to the Home Secretary as letters of support. These ladies, my aunts Emily and Rose, are surely what is meant by the phrase *English spinster*. And yet, once the connection has been pointed out, there is no doubt that Judith and they are spiritual cousins, if not sisters. Therefore it follows that one's pitying admiration for women who have supported manless and uncomforted lives needs a certain modification?

One will, of course, never know; and I feel now that it is entirely my fault that I shall never know. I had been Judith's friend for upwards of five years before the incident occurred which I involuntarily thought of—stupidly enough—as "the first time Judith's mask slipped."

A mutual friend, Betty, had been given a cast-off Dior dress. She was too short for it. Also she said: "It's not a dress for a married woman with three children and a talent for cooking. I don't know why not, but it isn't." Judith was the right build. Therefore one evening the three of us met by appointment in Judith's bedroom, with the dress. Neither Betty nor I were surprised at the renewed discovery that Judith was beautiful. We had both too often caught each other, and ourselves, in moments of envy when Judith's calm and severe face, her undemonstratively perfect body, succeeded in making everyone else in a room or a street look cheap.

Judith is tall, small-breasted, slender. Her light brown hair is parted in the centre and cut straight around her neck. A high straight forehead, straight nose, a full grave mouth are setting for her eyes, which are green, large and prominent. Her lids are very white, fringed with gold, and moulded close over the eyeball, so that in profile she has the look of a staring gilded mask. The dress was of dark green glistening stuff, cut straight, with a sort of loose tunic. It opened simply at the throat. In it Judith could of course evoke nothing but classical images. Diana, perhaps, back from the hunt, in a relaxed moment? A rather intellectual wood nymph who had opted for an afternoon in the British Museum reading room? Something like that. Neither Betty nor I said a word, since Judith was examining herself in a long mirror, and must know she looked magnificent.

Slowly she drew off the dress and laid it aside. Slowly she put on the old cord skirt and woollen blouse she had taken off. She must have surprised a resigned glance between us, for she then remarked, with the smallest of mocking smiles: "One surely ought to stay in character, wouldn't you say?" She added, reading the words out of some invisible book, written not by her, since it was a very vulgar book, but perhaps by one of us: "It does everything *for* me, I must admit."

"After seeing you in it," Betty cried out, defying her, "I can't bear for anyone else to have it. I shall simply put it away." Judith shrugged, rather irritated. In the shapeless skirt and blouse, and without makeup, she stood smiling at us, a woman at whom forty-nine out of fifty people would not look twice.

A second revelatory incident occurred soon after. Betty telephoned me to say that Judith had a kitten. Did I know that Judith adored cats? "No but of course she would," I said.

Betty lived in the same street as Judith and saw more of her than I did. I was kept posted about the growth and habits of the cat and its effect on Judith's life. She remarked for instance that she felt it was good for her to have a tie and some responsibility. But no sooner was the cat out of kittenhood than all the neighbours complained. It was a tomcat, ungelded, and making every night hideous. Finally the landlord said that either the cat or Judith must go, unless she was prepared to have the cat "fixed." Judith wore herself out trying to find some person, anywhere in Britain, who would be prepared to take the cat. This person would, however, have to sign a written statement not to have the cat "fixed." When Judith took the cat to the vet to be killed, Betty told me she cried for twenty-four hours.

"She didn't think of compromising? After all, perhaps the cat might have preferred to live, if given the choice?"

"Is it likely I'd have the nerve to say anything so sloppy to Judith? It's the nature of a male cat to rampage lustfully about, and therefore it would be morally wrong for Judith to have the cat fixed, simply to suit her own convenience."

"She said that?"

"She wouldn't have to *say* it, surely?"

A third incident was when she allowed a visiting young American, living in Paris, the friend of a friend and scarcely known to her, to use her flat while she visited her parents over Christmas. The young man and his friends lived it up for ten days of alcohol and sex and marijuana, and when Judith came back it took a week to get the place clean again and the furniture mended. She telephoned twice to Paris, the first time to say that he was a disgusting young thug and if he knew what was good for him he would keep out of her way in the future; the second time to apologise for losing her temper. "I had a choice either to let someone use my flat, or to leave it empty. But having chosen that you should have it, it was clearly an unwarrantable infringement of your liberty to make any conditions at all. I do most sincerely ask your pardon." The moral aspects of the matter having been made clear, she was irritated rather than not to receive letters of apology from him—fulsome, embarrassed, but above all, baffled.

It was the note of curiosity in the letters—he even suggested coming over to get to know her better—that irritated her most. "What do you suppose he means?" she said to me. "He lived in my flat for ten days. One would have thought that should be enough, wouldn't you?"

The facts about Judith, then, are all in the open, unconcealed, and plain to anyone who cares to study them; or, as it became plain she feels, to anyone with the intelligence to interpret them.

She has lived for the last twenty years in a small two-roomed flat high over a busy West London street. The flat is shabby and badly heated. The furniture is old, was never anything but ugly, is now frankly rickety and fraying. She has an income of £200 a year from a dead uncle. She lives on this and what she earns from her poetry, and from lecturing on poetry to night classes and extramural university classes.

She does not smoke or drink, and eats very little, from preference, not self-discipline.

She studied poetry and biology at Oxford, with distinction.

She is a Castlewell. That is, she is a member of one of the academic upper-middle-class families, which have been producing for centuries a steady supply of brilliant but sound men and women who are the backbone of the arts and sciences in Britain. She is on cool terms with her family who respect her and leave her alone.

She goes on long walking tours, by herself, in such places as Exmoor or West Scotland.

Every three or four years she publishes a volume of poems.

The walls of her flat are completely lined with books. They are scientific, classical and historical; there is a great deal of poetry and some drama. There is not one novel. When Judith says: "Of course I don't read novels," this does not mean that novels have no place, or a small place, in literature; or that people should not read novels; but that it must be obvious she can't be expected to read novels.

I had been visiting her flat for years before I noticed two long shelves of books, under a window, each shelf filled with the works of a single writer. The two writers are not, to put it at the mildest, the kind one would associate with Judith. They are mild, reminiscent, vague and whimsical. Typical English belles-lettres, in fact, and by definition abhorrent to her. Not one of the books in the two shelves has been read; some of the pages are still uncut. Yet each book is inscribed or dedicated to her: gratefully, admiringly, sentimentally and, more than once, amorously. In short, it is open to anyone who cares to examine these two shelves, and to work out dates, to conclude that Judith from the age of fifteen to twenty-five had been the beloved young companion of one elderly literary gentleman, and from twenty-five to thirty-five the inspiration of another.

During all that time she had produced her own poetry, and the sort of poetry, it is quite safe to deduce, not at all likely to be admired by her two admirers. Her poems are always cool and intellectual; that is their form, which is contradicted or supported by a gravely sensuous texture. They are poems to read often; one has to, to understand them.

I did not ask Judith a direct question about these two eminent but rather fusty lovers. Not because she would not have answered, or because she would have found the question impertinent, but because such questions are clearly unnecessary. Having those two shelves of books where they are, and books she could not conceivably care for, for their own sake, is publicly giving credit where credit is due. I can imagine her thinking the thing over, and deciding it was only fair, or perhaps honest, to place the books there; and this despite the fact that she would not care at all for the same attention to be paid to her. There is something almost contemptuous in it. For she certainly despises people who feel they need attention.

For instance, more than once a new emerging wave of "modern" young poets have discovered her as the only "modern" poet among their despised and well-credited elders. This is because, since she began writing at fifteen, her poems have been full of scientific, mechanical and chemical imagery. This is how she thinks, or feels.

More than once has a young poet hastened to her flat, to claim her as an ally, only to find her totally and by instinct unmoved by words like modern, new, contemporary. He has been outraged and wounded by her principle, so deeply rooted as to be unconscious, and to need no expression but a contemptuous shrug of the shoulders, that publicity seeking or to want critical attention is despicable. It goes without saying that there is perhaps one critic in the world she has any time for. He has sulked off, leaving her on her shelf, which she takes it for granted is her proper place, to be read by an appreciative minority.

Meanwhile she gives her lectures, walks alone through London, writes her poems, and is seen sometimes at a concert or a play with a middle-aged professor of Greek who has a wife and two children.

Betty and I had speculated about this professor, with such remarks as: Surely she must sometimes be lonely? Hasn't she ever wanted to marry? What about that awful moment when one comes in from somewhere at night to an empty flat?

It happened recently that Betty's husband was on a business trip, her children visiting, and she was unable to stand the empty house. She asked Judith for a refuge until her own home filled again.

Afterwards Betty rang me up to report:

"Four of the five nights Professor Adams came in about ten or so."

"Was Judith embarrassed?"

"Would you expect her to be?"

"Well, if not embarrassed, at least conscious there was a situation?"

"No, not at all. But I must say I don't think he's good enough for her. He can't possibly understand her. He calls her Judy."

"Good God."

"Yes. But I was wondering. Suppose the other two called her Judy—'little Judy'—imagine it! Isn't it awful? But it does rather throw a light on Judith."

"It's rather touching."

"I suppose it's touching. But *I* was embarrassed—oh, not because of the situation. Because of how she was, with him. 'Judy, is there another cup of tea in that pot?' And she, rather daughterly and demure, pouring him one."

"Well yes, I can see how you felt."

"Three of the nights he went to her bedroom with her—very casual about it, because she was being. But he was not there in the mornings. So I asked her. You know how it is when you ask her a question. As if you've been having long conversations on that very subject for years and years, and she is merely continuing where you left off last. So when she says something surprising, one feels such a fool to be surprised?"

"Yes. And then?"

"I asked her if she was sorry not to have children. She said yes, but one couldn't have everything."

"One can't have everything, she said?"

"Quite clearly feeling she *has* nearly everything. She said she thought it was a pity, because she would have brought up children very well."

"When you come to think of it, she would, too."

"I asked about marriage, but she said on the whole the role of a mistress suited her better."

"She used the word mistress?"

"You must admit it's the accurate word."

"I suppose so."

"And then she said that while she liked intimacy and sex and everything, she enjoyed waking up in the morning alone and *her own person*."

"Yes, *of course*."

"Of course. But now she's bothered because the professor would like to marry her. Or he feels he ought. At least, he's getting all guilty and obsessive about it. She says she doesn't see the point of divorce, and anyway, surely it would be very hard on his poor old wife after all these years, particularly after bringing up two children so satisfactorily. She talks about his wife as if she's a kind of nice old charwoman, and it wouldn't be *fair* to sack her, you know. Anyway. What with one thing and another, Judith's going off to Italy soon in order to *collect herself*."

"But how's she going to pay for it?"

"Luckily the Third Programme's commissioning her to do some arty programmes. They offered her a choice of The Cid-El Thid, you know—and the Borgias. Well, the Borghese, then. And Judith settled for the Borgias."

"The Borgias," I said, "*Judith*?"

"Yes, quite. I said that too, in that tone of voice. She saw my point. She says the epic is right up her street, whereas the Renaissance has never been on her wave length. Obviously it couldn't be, all the magnificence and cruelty and *dirt*. But of course chivalry and a high moral code and all those idiotically noble goings-on are right on her wave length."

"Is the money the same?"

"Yes. But is it likely Judith would let money decide? No, she said that one should always choose something new, that isn't up one's street. Well, the Renaissance. She didn't say *that*, of course."

"Of course not."

Judith went to Florence; and for some months postcards informed us tersely of her doings. Then Betty decided she must go by herself for a holiday. She had been appalled by the discovery that if her husband was away for a night she couldn't sleep; and when he went to Australia for three weeks, she stopped living until he came back. She had discussed this with him, and he had agreed that, if she really felt the situation to be serious, he would dispatch her by air, to Italy, in order to recover her self-respect. As she put it.

I got this letter from her: "It's no use, I'm coming home. I might have known. Better face it, once you're really married you're not fit for man nor beast. And if you remember what I used to be like! *Well!* I moped around Milan. I sunbathed in Venice, then I thought my tan was surely worth something, so I was on the point of starting an affair with another lonely soul, but I lost heart, and went to Florence to see Judith. She wasn't there. She'd gone to the Italian Riviera. I had nothing better to do, so I followed her. When I saw the place I wanted to laugh, it's so much not Judith, you know, all those palms and umbrellas and gaiety at all costs and ever such an ornamental blue sea. Judith is in an enormous stone room up on the hillside above the sea, with grape vines all over the place. You should see her, she's got beautiful. It seems for the last fifteen years she's been going to Soho every Saturday morning to buy food at an Italian shop. I must have looked surprised, because she explained she liked Soho. I suppose because all that dreary vice and nudes and prostitutes and everything prove how right she is to be as she is? She told the people in the shop she was going to Italy, and the *signora* said, what a coincidence, she was going back to Italy too, and she did hope an old friend like Miss Castlewell would visit her there. Judith said to me: 'I felt lacking, when she used the word friend. Our relations have always been formal. Can you understand it?' she said to me. 'For fifteen years,' I said to her. She said: 'I think I must feel it's a kind of imposition, don't you know, expecting people to feel friendship for one.' *Well*. I said: 'You ought to understand it, because you're like that yourself.' 'Am I?' she said. 'Well, think about it,' I said. But I could see she didn't want to think about it. Anyway, she's here, and I've spent a week with her. The widow Maria Rineiri inherited her mother's house, so she came home, from Soho. On the ground floor is a tatty little rosticcer*ì*a patronized by the neighbours. They are all working people. This isn't tourist country, up on the hill. The widow lives above the shop with her little boy, a nasty little brat of about ten. Say what you like, the English are the only people who know how to bring up children, I don't care if that's insular. Judith's room is at the back, with a balcony. Underneath her room is the barber's shop, and the barber is Luigi Rineiri, the widow's younger brother. Yes, I was keeping him until the last. He is about forty, tall dark handsome, a great *bull*, but rather a sweet fatherly bull. He has cut Judith's hair and made it lighter. Now it looks like a sort of gold helmet. Judith is all brown. The widow Rineiri has made her a white dress and a green dress. They fit, for a change. When Judith walks down the street to the lower town, all the Italian males take one look at the golden girl and melt in their own oil like ice cream. Judith takes all this in her stride. She sort of acknowledges the homage. Then she strolls into the sea and vanishes into the foam. She swims five miles every day. *Naturally*. I haven't asked Judith whether she has collected herself, because you can see she hasn't. The widow Rineiri is matchmaking. When I noticed this I wanted to laugh, but luckily I didn't because Judith asked me, really wanting to know: 'Can you see me married to an Italian barber?' (Not being snobbish, but stating the position, so to speak.) 'Well, yes,' I said, 'you're the only woman I know who I can see married to an Italian barber.' Because it wouldn't matter who she married, she'd always be her own person. 'At any rate, for a time,' I said. At which she said, asperously: 'You can use phrases like for a time in England but not in Italy.' Did you ever see England, at least London, as the home of licence, liberty and free love? No, neither did I, but of course she's right. Married to Luigi it would be the family, the neighbours, the church and the *bambini*. All the same she's thinking about it, believe it or not. Here she's quite different, all relaxed and free. She's melting in the attention she gets. The widow mothers her and makes her coffee all the time, and listens to a lot of good advice about how to bring up that nasty brat of hers. Unluckily she doesn't take it. Luigi is crazy for her. At mealtimes she goes to the trattoria in the upper square and all workmen treat her like a goddess. Well, a film star then. I said to her, you're mad to come home. For one thing her rent is ten bob a week, and you eat *pasta* and drink red wine till you bust for about one and sixpence. No, she said, it would be nothing but self-indulgence to stay. Why? I said. She said, she's got nothing to stay for. (ho ho.) And besides, she's done her research on the Borghese, though so far she can't see her way to an honest presentation of the facts. What made these people tick? She wants to know. And so she's only staying because of the cat. I forgot to mention the cat. This is a town of cats. The Italians here love their cats. I wanted to feed a stray cat at the table, but the waiter said no; and after lunch, all the waiters came with trays crammed with leftover food and stray cats came from everywhere to eat. And at dark when the tourists go in to feed and the beach is empty—you know how empty and forlorn a beach is at dusk?—well, cats appear from everywhere. The beach seems to move, then you see it's cats. They go stalking along the thin inch of grey water at the edge of the sea, shaking their paws crossly at each step, snatching at the dead little fish, and throwing them with their mouths up on to the dry sand. Then they scamper after them. You've never seen such a snarling and fighting. At dawn when the fishing boats come in to the empty beach, the cats are there in dozens. The fishermen throw them bits of fish. The cats snarl and fight over it. Judith gets up early and goes down to watch. Sometimes Luigi goes too, being tolerant. Because what he really likes is to join the evening promenade with Judith on his arm around and around the square of the upper town. Showing her off. Can you *see* Judith? But she does it. Being tolerant. But she smiles and enjoys the attention she gets, there's no doubt of it.

"She has a cat in her room. It's a kitten really, but it's pregnant. Judith says she can't leave until the kittens are born. The cat is too young to have kittens. Imagine Judith. She sits on her bed in that great stone room, with her bare feet on the stone floor and watches the cat, and tries to work out why a healthy uninhibited Italian cat always fed on the best from the roticcerì a should be neurotic. Because it is. When it sees Judith watching it gets nervous and starts licking at the roots of its tail. But Judith goes on watching, and says about Italy that the reason why the English love the Italians is because the Italians make the English feel superior. They have no discipline. And that's despicable reason for one nation to love another. Then she talks about Luigi and says he has no sense of guilt, but a sense of sin; whereas she has no sense of sin but she has guilt. I haven't asked her if this has been an insuperable barrier, because judging from how she looks, it hasn't. She says she would rather have a sense of sin, because sin can be atoned for, and if she understood sin, perhaps she would be more at home with the Renaissance. Luigi is very healthy, she says, and not neurotic. He is a Catholic of course. He doesn't mind that she's an atheist. His mother has explained to him that the English are all pagans, but good people at heart. I suppose he thinks a few smart sessions with the local priest would set Judith on the right path for good and all. Meanwhile the cat walks nervously around the room, stopping to lick, and when it can't stand Judith watching it another second, it rolls over on the floor, with its paws tucked up, and rolls up its eyes, and Judith scratches its lumpy pregnant stomach and tells it to relax. It makes *me* nervous to see her, it's not like her, I don't know why. Then Luigi shouts up from the barber's shop, then he comes up and stands at the door laughing, and Judith laughs, and the widow says, "Children, enjoy yourselves." And off they go, walking down to the town eating ice cream. The cat follows them. It won't let Judith out of its sight, like a dog. When she swims miles out to sea, the cat hides under a beach hut until she comes back. Then she carries it back up the hill, because that nasty little boy chases it. *Well*, I'm coming home tomorrow thank God, to my dear old Billy, I was mad ever to leave him. There is something about Judith and Italy that has upset me, I don't know what. The point is, what on earth can Judith and Luigi *talk* about? Nothing. How can they? And of course it doesn't matter. So I turn out to be a prude as well. See you next week."

It was my turn for a dose of the sun, so I didn't see Betty. On my way back from Rome I stopped off in Judith's resort and walked up through narrow streets to the upper town, where, in the square with the vine-covered *trattoria* at the corner, was a house with ROSTICCRA written in black paint on a cracked wooden board over a low door. There was a door curtain of red beads, and flies settled on the beads. I opened the beads with my hands and looked in to a small dark room with a stone counter. Loops of salami hung from metal hooks. A glass bell covered some plates of cooked meats. There were flies on the salami and on the glass bell. A few tins on the wooden shelves, a couple of pale loaves, some wine casks and an open case of sticky pale green grapes covered with fruit flies seemed to be the only stock. A single wooden table with two chairs stood in a corner, and two workmen sat there, eating lumps of sausage and bread. Through another bead curtain at the back came a short, smoothly fat, slender-limbed woman with greying hair. I asked for Miss Castlewell, and her face changed. She said in an offended, offhand way: "Miss Castlewell left last week." She took a white cloth from under the counter, and flicked at the flies on the glass bell. "I'm a friend of hers," I said, and she said, "*Si*," and put her hands palm down on the counter and looked at me, expressionless. The workmen got up, gulped down the last of their wine, nodded and went. She *ciao'd* them; and looked back at me. Then, since I didn't go, she called, "Luigi!" A shout came from the back room, there was a rattle of beads, and in came first a wiry sharp-faced boy, and then Luigi. He was tall, heavy-shouldered, and his black rough hair was like a cap, pulled low over his brows. He looked good-natured, but at the moment uneasy. His sister said something, and he stood beside her, an ally, and confirmed, "Miss Castlewell went away." I was on the point of giving up, when through the bead curtain that screened off a dazzling light eased a thin tabby cat. It was ugly and it walked uncomfortably, with its back quarters bunched up. The child suddenly let out a "Sssssss" through his teeth, and the cat froze. Luigi said something sharp to the child, and something encouraging to the cat, which sat down, looked straight in front of it, then began frantically licking at its flanks.

Unit 5 *Our Friend Judith*

"Miss Castlewell was offended with us," said Mrs. Rineri suddenly, and with dignity. "She left early one morning. We did not expect her to go." I said: "Perhaps she had to go home and finish some work."

Mrs. Rineiri shrugged, then sighed. Then she exchanged a hard look with her brother. Clearly the subject had been discussed, and closed forever.

"I've known Judith a long time," I said, trying to find the right note. "She's a remarkable woman. She's a poet." But there was no response to this at all. Meanwhile the child, with a fixed bared-teeth grin, was staring at the cat, narrowing his eyes. Suddenly he let out another "Ssssssss" and added a short high yelp. The cat shot backwards, hit the wall, tried desperately to claw its way up the wall, came to its senses and again sat down and began its urgent, undirected licking at its fur. This time Luigi cuffed the child, who yelped in earnest, and then ran out into the street past the cat. Now that the way was clear the cat shot across the floor, up onto the counter, and bounded past Luigi's shoulder and straight through the bead curtain into the barber's shop, where it landed with a thud.

"Judith was sorry when she left us," said Mrs. Rineiri uncertainly. "She was crying."

"I'm sure she was."

"And so," said Mrs. Rineiri, with finality, laying her hands down again, and looking past me at the bead curtain. That was the end. Luigi nodded brusquely at me, and went into the back. I said goodbye to Mrs. Rineiri and walked back to the lower town. In the square I saw the child, sitting on the running board of a lorry parked outside the *trattoria*, drawing in the dust with his bare toes, and directing in front of him a blank, unhappy stare.

I had to go through Florence, so I went to the address Judith had been at. No, Miss Castlewell had not been back. Her papers and books were still there. Would I take them back with me to England? I made a great parcel and brought them back to England.

I telephoned Judith and she had already written for the papers to be sent, but it was kind of me to bring them. There had seemed to be no point, she said, in returning to Florence.

"Shall I bring them over?"

"I would be very grateful, of course."

Judith's flat was chilly, and she wore a bunchy sage-green woollen dress. Her hair was still a soft gold helmet, but she looked pale and rather pinched. She stood with her back to a single bar of electric fire—lit because I demanded it—with her legs apart and her arms folded. She contemplated me.

"I went to the Rineiris' house."

"Oh. Did you?"

"They seemed to miss you."

She said nothing.

"I saw the cat too."

"Oh. Oh, I suppose you and Betty discussed it?" This was with a small unfriendly smile.

"Well, Judith, you must see we were likely to?"

She gave this her consideration and said: "I don't understand why people discuss other people. Oh—I'm not criticising you. But I don't see why you are so interested. I don't understand human behaviour and I'm not particularly interested."

"I think you should write to the Rineiris."

"I wrote and thanked them, of course."

"I don't mean that."

"You and Betty have worked it out?"

"Yes, we talked about it. We thought we should talk to you, so you should write to the Rineiris."

"Why?"

"For one thing, they are both fond of you."

"Fond," she said smiling.

"Judith, I've never in my life felt such an atmosphere of being let down."

Judith considered this. "When something happens that shows one there is really a complete gulf in understanding, what is there to say?"

"It could scarcely have been a complete gulf in understanding. I suppose you are going to say we are being interfering?"

Judith showed distaste. "That is a very stupid word. And it's a stupid idea. No one can interfere with me if I don't let them. No, it's that I don't understand people. I don't understand why you or Betty should care. Or why the Rineiris should, for that matter," she added with the small tight smile.

"Judith!"

"If you've behaved stupidly, there's no point in going on. You put an end to it."

"What happened? Was it the cat?"

"Yes, I suppose so. But it's not important." She looked at me, saw my ironical face, and said: "The cat was too young to have kittens. That is all there was to it."

"Have it your way. But that is obviously not all there is to it."

"What upsets me is that I don't understand at all why I was so upset then."

"What happened? Or don't you want to talk about it?"

"I don't give a damn whether I talk about it or not. You really do say the most extraordinary things, you and Betty. If you want to know, I'll tell you. What does it matter?"

"I would like to know of course."

"*Of course!*" she said. "In your place I wouldn't care. Well, I think the essence of the thing was that I must have had the wrong attitude to that cat. Cats are supposed to be independent. They are supposed to go off by themselves to have their kittens. This one didn't. It was climbing up onto my bed all one night and crying for attention. I don't like cats on my bed. In the morning I saw she was in pain. I stayed with her all that day. Then Luigi—he's the brother, you know."

"Yes."

"Did Betty mention him? Luigi came up to say it was time I went for a swim. He said the cat should look after itself. I blame myself very much. That's what happens when you submerge yourself in somebody else."

Her look at me was now defiant; and her body showed both defensiveness and aggression. "Yes. It's true. I've always been afraid of it. And in the last few weeks I've behaved badly. It's because I let it happen."

"Well, go on."

"I left the cat and swam. It was late, so it was only for a few minutes. When I came out of the sea the cat had followed me and had had a kitten on the beach. The little beast Michele—the son, you know?—well, he always teased the poor thing, and now he had frightened her off the kitten. It was dead, though. He held it up by the tail and waved it at me as I came out of the sea. I told him to bury it. He scooped two inches of sand away and pushed the kitten in—on the beach, where people are all day. So I buried it properly. He had run off. He was chasing the poor cat. She was terrified and running up the town. I ran too. I caught Michele and I was so angry I hit him. I don't believe in hitting children. I've been feeling beastly about it ever since."

"You were angry."

"It's no excuse. I would never have believed myself capable of hitting a child. I hit him very hard. He went off, crying. The poor cat had got under a big lorry parked in the square. Then she screamed. And then a most remarkable thing happened. She screamed just once, and all at once cats just materialised. One minute there was just one cat, lying under a lorry, all quite still, and watching my poor cat."

"Rather moving," I said.

"Why?"

"There is no evidence one way or the other." I said in inverted commas, "that the cats were there out of concern for a friend in trouble."

"No," she said energetically. "There isn't. It might have been curiosity. Or anything. How do we know? However, I crawled under the lorry. There were two paws sticking out of the cat's back end. The kitten was the wrong way round. It was stuck. I held the cat down with one hand and I pulled the kitten out with the other." She held out her long white hands. They were still covered with fading scars and scratches. "She bit and yelled, but the kitten was alive. She left the kitten and crawled across the square into the house. Then all the cats got up and walked away. It was the most extraordinary thing I've ever seen. They vanished again. One minute they were all there, and then they had vanished. I went after the cat, with the kitten. Poor little thing, it was covered with dust—being wet, don't you know. The cat was on my bed. There was another kitten coming, but it got stuck too. So when she screamed and screamed I just pulled it out. The kittens began to suck. One kitten was very big. It was a nice fat black kitten. It must have hurt her. But she suddenly bit out—snapped, don't you know, like a reflex action, at the back of the kitten's head. It died, just like that. Extraordinary, isn't it?" she said, blinking hard, her lips quivering. "She was its mother, but she killed it. The she ran off the bed and went downstairs into the shop under the counter. I called to Luigi. You know, he's Mrs. Rineiri's brother."

"Yes, I know."

"He said she was too young, and she was badly frightened and very hurt. He took the alive kitten to her but she got up and walked away. She didn't want it. Then Luigi told me not to look. But I followed him. He held the kitten by the tail and he banged it against the wall twice. Then he dropped it into the rubbish heap. He moved aside some rubbish with his toe, and put the kitten there and pushed rubbish over it. Then Luigi said the cat should be destroyed. He said she was badly hurt and it would always hurt her to have kittens."

"He hasn't destroyed her. She's still alive. But it looks to me as if he were right."

"Yes, I expect he was."

"What upset you—that he killed the kitten?"

"Oh, no, I expect the cat would if he hadn't. But that isn't the point, is it?"

"What is the point?"

"I don't think I really know." She had been speaking breathlessly, and fast. Now she said slowly: "It's not a question of right or wrong, is it? Why should it be? It's a question of what one is. That night Luigi wanted to go promenading with me. For him, that was *that*. Something had to be done, and he'd done it. But I felt ill. He was very nice to me. He's a very good person," she said, defiantly.

"Yes, he looks it."

"That night I couldn't sleep. I was blaming myself. I should never have left the cat to go swimming. Well, and then I decided to leave the next day. And I did. And that's all. The whole thing was a mistake, from start to finish."

"Going to Italy at all?"

"Oh, to go for a holiday would have been all right."

"You've done all that work for nothing? You mean you aren't going to make use of all that research?"

"No. It was a mistake."

"Why don't you leave it a few weeks and see how things are then?"

"Why?"

"You might feel differently about it."

"What an extraordinary thing to say. Why should I? Oh, you mean, time passing, healing wounds—that sort of thing? What an extraordinary idea. It's always seemed to me an extraordinary idea. No, right from the beginning I've felt ill at ease with the whole business, not myself at all."

"Rather irrationally, I should have said."

Judith considered this, very seriously. She frowned while she thought it over. Then she said: "But if one cannot rely on what one feels, what can one rely on?"

"On what one thinks, I should have expected you to say."

"Should you? Why? Really, you people are all very strange. I don't understand you." She turned off the electric fire, and her face closed up. She smiled, friendly and distant, and said: "I don't really see any point at all in discussing it."

Topics for Discussion

1) In the story, who are the friends of Judith?
2) What are the three incidents about Judith?
3) What kinds of life philosophy are reflected in the three incidents about Judith?
4) What is the family background of Judith?
5) What is Judith's relationship with the middle-aged professor?
6) Why doesn't Judith accept the professor's proposal to marry her?
7) What does the cat mean to Judith?
8) Why is Judith determined to take care of the kitten?
9) How many love affairs does Judith ever have?
10) What is the theme of "Our Friend Judith"?

Interdisciplinary Concepts for Further Thinking

1. Stereotype

"Stereotype" is a concept used in psychology, neurology, anthropology, sociology, and cultural studies.

A stereotype can refer to a preconceived idea or set of ideas that individuals apply to groups of people, places, or situations, and it is a fixed, oversimplified, and often biased belief. Stereotypes often lead to prejudice, because they lead people to making generalized assumptions about people without having access to very much information. We commonly say that we "should not label" others but we cannot help but do so. We categorize people according to their citizenship, gender, and university affiliation, among other qualities. People are often biased against others outside of their social group, showing prejudice (emotional bias), stereotypes (cognitive bias), and discrimination (behavioral bias).

There are a variety of different ways that stereotypes can develop. Most of the time, stereotypes come from either personal experiences or from things people are taught as they grow up. Very often, stereotypes are formed as a result of social learning, which is information that people learn from their parents and peers. Another element of socialization that can lead to the formation of stereotypes is personality theory, which suggests that someone's personal experiences can lead them to form generalized beliefs. Another theory for how stereotypes form is called motivational theory. This theory argues that people will develop stereotypes about their competitors to increase their own confidence levels. Just as things that someone is told while growing up can influence the creation of stereotypes, so can one's environment. According to social identity theory, people typically believe that their own in-group (which may be racial, religious, national, cultural, familial, and more) is heterogenous, while the out-group is homogenous, with similarities between members of the group amplified and differences ignored.

Often, stereotypes can be negative or even harmful. The most common stereotypes that tend to be negative include: cultural stereotypes, social stereotypes, racial stereotypes, gender stereotypes, and religious stereotypes.

1) How is the image of the spinster stereotype depicted in "Our Friend Judith"?
2) Does Doris Lessing portray Judith under the spinster stereotype?

2. Masking

Masking, a term in psychology and sociology, refers to the process in which an individual can "mask" or camouflage their natural personality or behavior to conform to social pressures, social norms, conventionally expected behaviors, or even abuse and harassment.

Masking can be strongly influenced by environmental factors such as authoritarian parents, rejection, and emotional, physical, or sexual abuse. Masking is often a behavior individuals adopt subconsciously as a coping mechanism or trauma response.

As a term, masking was first used to describe the act of concealing disgust by Ekman (1972) and Friesen (1969). During our everyday social life, the face we present to others is rarely our genuine face. Only in exceptional cases does one display one's real feelings. "Day after day we cover up this bare human being. We hold ourselves in careful control lest our bodies cry out messages our minds are too careless to hide" (Pease, 1993).

Masking is behaving in certain ways that would help one hide or repress emotions that are not approved by those around them. There are types of masks people wear to hide emotions, such as the anger mask, adopted to keep people away rather than to genuinely express emotions, or the people-pleasing mask put on to make other people around them happy. There are various reasons people mask their emotions, for example, to gain social acceptance, to be liked, to hide happiness, vulnerability, fear, anger, sadness, depression, pain, etc.

1) The word "mask" is mentioned twice in "Our Friend Judith". In what sense does Judith have a "mask"?

2) What are the means to figure out the true nature of Judith?

Thinking in Numbers

In "Our Friend Judith", three incidents about Judith and four men related to her are mentioned. What life attitudes or life philosophy are shown through the three incidents, and what roles do these men play in her life? Figure out who these men are, what they mean to Judith and how they affect her life attitude and philosophy.

Visual Thinking with Mind Mapping

In "Our Friend Judith", Judith is labeled as a spinster. Just as Simone de Beauvoir says, "One is not born, but rather becomes a woman" in *The Second Sex*. Similarly, Judith is not born but becomes a spinster. She has a very good family and educational background; however, she has lived in a small, badly-heated two-roomed flat for 20 years. What has happened to her? How does she become a spinster? Create a mind map to analyze it.

Critical Thinking for Reality

Judith is quite different from the traditional concept of a woman. She is beautiful and independent but chooses to keep a low profile and remain single. On the surface, she seems to be lofty and indifferent to others; this makes it hard to know her. From the title of the story, it can be concluded that Judith has two friends Betty and "I". Do you think Betty and "I" are true friends of Judith, or are they regarded as a friend in Judith's eyes? Why?

Unit 6
The White Cat

Joyce Carol Oates

THE WHITE CAT

Introduction to the Author

The American writer Joyce Carol Oates (1938—) has published 58 novels, a number of plays and novellas, and many volumes of short stories, poetry, and nonfiction since the publication of her debut work *By the North Gate* in 1963. She has won many awards for her writing, including the National Book Award for her novel *Them* (1969), two O. Henry Awards, and the National Humanities Medal. Her novels *Black Water* (1992), *What I Lived For* (1994), *Blonde* (2000), and short story collections *The Wheel of Love and Other Stories* (1970) and *Lovely, Dark, Deep: Stories* (2014) were each nominated for the Pulitzer Prize. Particularly effective are her depictions of violence and evil in modern society. Oates's novels encompass a variety of historical settings and literary genres. She typically portrays American individuals whose intensely experienced and obsessive lives end in bloodshed and self-destruction owing to larger forces beyond their control. Her books blend a realistic treatment of everyday life with horrific and even sensational depictions of violence.

Introduction to the Work

In the macabre short tale "The White Cat", Julius and Alissa have an unsatisfactory relationship and it is a story about unharmonious family relationship which results in tragedy. The narration's narrator, Julius Muir, struggles internally with self-discipline and control over his immortal white cat, Miranda. Julius's effort to murder Miranda is also, in a way, a projection of his power over his wife Alissa. In this story, Oates suggests that treating each other as autonomous individuals with free choice is the only way to end loneliness and create a happy family because an unequal connection between men and women can only result in tragedy.

Text

The White Cat

There was a gentleman of independent means who, at about the age of fifty-six, conceived of a passionate hatred for his much-younger wife's white Persian cat.

His hatred for the cat was all the more ironic, and puzzling, in that he himself had given the cat to his wife as a kitten, years ago, when they were first married. And he himself had named her—Miranda—after his favorite Shakespearean heroine.

It was ironic, too, in that he was hardly a man given to irrational sweeps of emotion. Except for his wife (whom he'd married late—his first marriage, her second) he did not love anyone very much, and would have thought it beneath his dignity to hate anyone. For whom should he take that seriously? Being a gentleman of independent means allowed him that independence of spirit unknown to the majority of men.

Julius Muir was of slender build, with deep-set somber eyes of no distinctive color; thinning, graying, baby-fine hair; and a narrow, lined face to which the adjective *lapidary* had once been applied, with no vulgar intention of mere flattery. Being of old American stock he was susceptible to none of the fashionable tugs and sways of "identity": He knew who he was, who his ancestors were, and thought the subject of no great interest. His studies both in America and abroad had been undertaken with a dilettante's rather than a scholar's pleasure, but he would not have wished to make too much of them. Life, after all, is a man's primary study.

Fluent in several languages, Mr. Muir had a habit of phrasing his words within ordinate care, as if he were translating them into a common vernacular. He carried himself with an air of discreet self-consciousness that had nothing in it of vanity, or pride, yet did not bespeak a pointless humility. He was a collector (primarily of rare books and coins), but he was certainly not an obsessive collector; he looked upon the fanaticism of certain of his fellows with a bemused disdain. So his quickly blossoming hatred for his wife's beautiful white cat surprised him, and for a time amused him. Or did it frighten him? Certainly he didn't know what to make of it!

The animosity began as an innocent sort of domestic irritation, a half-conscious sense that being so respected in public—so recognized as the person of quality and importance he assuredly was—he should warrant that sort of treatment at home. Not that he was naively ignorant of the fact that cats have a way of making their preferences known that lacks the subtlety and tact devised by human beings. But as the cat grew older and more spoiled and ever more choosy it became evident that she did not, for affection, choose *him*. Alissa was her favorite, of course; then one or another of the help; but it was not uncommon for a stranger, visiting the Muirs for the first time, to win or to appear to win Miranda's capricious heart. "Miranda! Come here!" Mr. Muir might call—gently enough, yet forcibly, treating the animal in fact with a silly sort of deference—but at such times Miranda was likely to regard him with indifferent, unblinking eyes and make no move in his direction. What a fool, she seemed to be saying, to court someone who cares so little for you!

If he tried to lift her in his arms—if he tried, with a show of playfulness, to subdue her—in true cat fashion she struggled to get down with as much violence as if a stranger had seized her. Once as she squirmed out of his grasp, she accidentally raked the back of his hand and drew blood that left a faint stain on the sleeve of his dinner jacket. "Julius, dear, are you hurt?" Alissa asked. "Not at all," Mr. Muir said, dabbing at the scratches with a handkerchief. "I think Miranda is excited because of the company," Alissa said. "You know how sensitive she is." "Indeed I do," Mr. Muir said mildly, winking at their guests. But a pulse beat hard in his head and he was thinking he would like to strangle the cat with his bare hands—were he the kind of man who was capable of such an act.

More annoying still was the routine nature of the cat's aversion to him. When he and Alissa sat together in the evening, reading, each at an end of their sofa, Miranda would frequently leap unbidden into Alissa's lap—but shrink fastidiously from Mr. Muir's very touch. He professed to be hurt. He professed to be amused. "I'm afraid Miranda doesn't like me any longer," he said sadly. (Though in truth he could no longer remember if there'd been a time the creature *had* liked him when she'd been a kitten, perhaps, and utterly indiscriminate in her affections?) Alissa laughed and said apologetically, "Of course she likes you, Julius," as the cat purred loudly and sensuously in her lap. "But—you know how cats are."

"Indeed, I am learning," Mr. Muir said with a stiff little smile.

And he felt he *was* learning—something to which he could give no name.

WHAT FIRST GAVE him the idea—the fancy, really—of killing Miranda, he could not have afterward said. One day, watching her rubbing about the ankles of a director-friend of his wife's, observing how wantonly she presented herself to an admiring little circle of guests (even people with a general aversion to cats could not resist exclaiming over Miranda—petting her, scratching her behind the ears, cooing over her like idiots), Mr. Muir found himself thinking that, as he had brought the cat into his household of his own volition and had paid a fair amount of money for her, she was his to dispose of as he wished. It was true that the full-blooded Persian was one of the prize possessions of the household—a household in which possessions were not acquired casually or cheaply—and it was true that Alissa adored her. But ultimately she belonged to Mr. Muir. And he alone had the power of life or death over her, did he not?

"What a beautiful animal! Is it a male or a female?"

Mr. Muir was being addressed by one of his guests (in truth, one of Alissa's guests; since returning to her theatrical career she had a new, wide, rather promiscuous circle of acquaintances) and for a moment he could not think how to answer. The question lodged deep in him as if it were a riddle: *Is it a male or a female?*

"Female, of course," Mr. Muir said pleasantly. "Its name after all is Miranda."

HE WONDERED: SHOULD he wait until Alissa began rehearsals for her new play—or should he act quickly, before his resolution faded? (Alissa, a minor but well-regarded actress, was to be an understudy for the female lead in a Broadway play opening in September.) And how should he do it? He could not strangle the cat—could not bring himself to act with such direct and unmitigated brutality—nor was it likely that he could run over her, as if accidentally, with the car. (Though *that* would have been fortuitous, indeed.) One midsummer evening when sly, silky Miranda insinuated herself onto the lap of Alissa's new friend Alban (actor, writer, director; his talents were evidently lavish) the conversation turned to notorious murder cases—to poisons—and Mr. Muir thought simply, *Of course. Poison.*

Next morning he poked about in the gardener's shed and found the remains of a ten-pound sack of grainy white "rodent" poison. The previous autumn they'd had a serious problem with mice, and their gardener had set out poison traps in the attic and basement of the house. (With excellent results, Mr. Muir surmised. At any rate, the mice had certainly disappeared.) What was ingenious about the poison was that it induced extreme thirst—so that after having devoured the bait the poisoned creature was driven to seek water, leaving the house and dying outside. Whether the poison was "merciful" or not, Mr. Muir did not know.

He was able to take advantage of the servants' Sunday night off—for as it turned out, though rehearsals for her play had not yet begun, Alissa was spending several days in the city. So Mr. Muir himself fed Miranda in a corner of the kitchen where she customarily ate—having mashed a generous teaspoon of the poison in with her usual food. (How spoiled the creature was! From the very first, when she was a seven-weeks' kitten, Miranda had been fed a special high-protein, high-vitamin cat food, supplemented by raw chopped liver, chicken giblets, and God knows what all else, though as he ruefully had to admit, Mr. Muir had had a hand in spoiling her, too.)

Miranda ate the food with her usual finicky greed, not at all conscious of, or grateful for, her master's presence. He might have been one of the servants; he might have been no one at all. If she sensed something out of the ordinary—the fact that her water dish was taken away and not returned, for instance—like a true aristocrat she gave no sign. Had there ever been any creature of his acquaintance, human or otherwise, so supremely complacent as this white Persian cat?

Mr. Muir watched Miranda methodically poison herself with an air not of elation as he'd anticipated, not even with a sense of satisfaction in a wrong being righted, in justice being (however ambiguously) exacted—but with an air of profound regret. That the spoiled creature deserved to die he did not doubt; for after all, what incalculable cruelties, over a lifetime, must a cat inflict on birds, mice, rabbits! But it struck him as a melancholy thing, that *he*, Julius Muir—who had paid so much for her, and who in fact had shared in the pride of her—should find himself out of necessity in the role of executioner. But it was something that had to be done, and though he had perhaps forgotten why it had to be done, he knew that he and he alone was destined to do it.

The other evening a number of guests had come to dinner, and as they were seated on the terrace Miranda leapt whitely up out of nowhere to make her way along the garden wall—plumelike tail erect, silky ruff floating about her high-held head, golden eyes gleaming—quite as if on cue, as Alissa said. "This is Miranda, come to say hello to you! Isn't she beautiful?" Alissa happily exclaimed. (For she seemed never to tire of remarking upon her cat's beauty—an innocent sort of narcissism Mr. Muir supposed.) The usual praise, or flattery, was aired; the cat preened herself—fully conscious of being the center of attention-then leapt away with a violent sort of grace and disappeared down the steep stone steps to the river embankment. Mr. Muir thought then that he understood why Miranda was so uncannily *interesting* as a phenomenon: She represented a beauty that was both purposeless and necessary; a beauty that was (considering her pedigree) completely an artifice, and yet (considering she *was* a thing of flesh and blood) completely natural: Nature.

Though was Nature always and invariably—*natural*?

Now, as the white cat finished her meal (leaving a good quarter of it in the dish, as usual), Mr. Muir said aloud, in a tone in which infinite regret and satisfaction were commingled, "But beauty won't save you."

The cat paused to look up at him with her flat, unblinking gaze. He felt an instant's terror: Did she know? Did she know—already? It seemed to him that she had never looked more splendid: fur so purely, silkily white; ruff full as if recently brushed; the petulant pug face; wide, stiff whiskers; finely shaped ears so intelligently erect. And, of course, the eyes . . .

He'd always been fascinated by Miranda's eyes, which were a tawny golden hue, for they had the mysterious capacity to flare up, as if at will, seen at night, of

Unit 6　*The White Cat*

course—by way of the moon's reflection, or the headlights of the Muirs' own homebound car—they were lustrous as small beams of light. "Is that Miranda, do you think?" Alissa would ask, seeing the twin flashes of light in the tall grass bordering the road. "Possibly," Mr. Muir would say. "Ah, she's waiting for us! Isn't that sweet! She's waiting for us to come home!" Alissa would exclaim with childlike excitement. Mr. Muir—who doubted that the cat had even been aware of their absence, let alone eagerly awaited their return—said nothing. Another thing about the cat's eyes that had always seemed to Mr. Muir somehow perverse was the fact that, while the human eyeball is uniformly white and the iris colored, a cat eyeball is colored and the iris purely black. Green, yellow, gray, even blue—the entire eyeball! And the iris so magically responsive to gradations of light or excitation, contracting to razor-thin slits, dilating blackly to fill almost the entire eye ... As she stared up at him now her eyes were so dilated their color was nearly eclipsed.

"No, beauty can't save you. It isn't enough," Mr. Muir said quietly. With trembling fingers he opened the screen door to let the cat out into the night. As she passed him—perverse creature, indeed!—she rubbed lightly against his leg as she had not done for many months. Or had it been years?

ALISSA WAS TWENTY years Mr. Muir's junior but looked even younger: a petite woman with very large, very pretty brown eyes; shoulder-length blond hair; the upbeat if sometimes rather frenetic manner of a well-practiced ingenue. She was a minor actress with a minor ambition—as she freely acknowledged—for after all, serious professional acting is brutally hard work, even if one somehow manages to survive the competition.

"And then, of course, Julius takes such good care of me," she would say, linking her arm through his or resting her head for a moment against his shoulder. "I have everything I want, really, right here ... " By which she meant the country place Mr. Muir had bought for her when they were married. (Of course they also kept an apartment in Manhattan, two hours to the south. But Mr. Muir had grown to dislike the city—it abraded his nerves like a cat's claws raking against a screen—and rarely made the journey in any longer.) Under her maiden name, Howth, Alissa had been employed intermittently for eight years before marrying Mr. Muir; her first marriage—contracted at the age of nineteen to a well-known (and notorious) Hollywood actor, since deceased—had been a disaster of which she cared not to speak in any detail. (Nor did Mr. Muir care to question her about those years. It was as if, for him, they had not existed.)

At the time of their meeting Alissa was in temporary retreat, as she called it, from her career. She'd had a small success on Broadway but the success had not taken hold. And was it worth it, really, to keep going, to keep trying? Season after season, the grinding round of auditions, the competition with new faces, "promising" new talents... Her first marriage had ended badly and she'd had a number of love affairs of varying degrees of worth (precisely how many Mr. Muir was never to learn), and now perhaps it was time to ease into private life. And there was Julius Muir: not young, not particularly charming, but well-to-do, and well-bred, and besotted with love for her, and—*there*.

Of course Mr. Muir was dazzled by her; and he had the time and the resources to court her more assiduously than any man had ever courted her. He seemed to see in her qualities no one else saw; his imagination, for so reticent and subdued a man, was rich, lively to the point of fever, immensely flattering. And he did not mind, he extravagantly insisted, that he loved her more than she loved him—even as Alissa protested she *did* love him—would she consent to marry him otherwise?

For a few years they spoke vaguely of "starting a family," but nothing came of it. Alissa was too busy, or wasn't in ideal health; or they were traveling; or Mr. Muir worried about the unknown effect a child would have upon their marriage. (Alissa would have less time for him, surely?) As time passed he vexed himself with the thought that he'd have no heir when he died—that is, no child of his own—but there was nothing to be done.

They had a rich social life; they were wonderfully *busy* people. And they had, after all, their gorgeous white Persian cat. "Miranda would be traumatized if there was a baby in the household," Alissa said. "We really couldn't do that to her."

"Indeed we couldn't," Mr. Muir agreed.

And then, abruptly, Alissa decided to return to acting. To her "career" as she gravely called it—as if it were a phenomenon apart from her, a force not to be resisted. And Mr. Muir was happy for her—very happy for her. He took pride in his wife's professionalism, and he wasn't at all jealous of her ever-widening circle of friends, acquaintances, associates. He wasn't jealous of her fellow actors and actresses—Rikka, Mario, Robin, Sibyl, Emile, each in turn—and now Alban of the damp dark shiny eyes and quick sweet smile; nor was he jealous of the time she spent away from home; nor, if home, of the time she spent sequestered away in the room they called her studio, deeply absorbed in her work. In her maturity Alissa Howth had acquired a robust sort of good-heartedness that gave her more stage presence even as it relegated her to certain sorts of roles—the roles inevitable, in any case, for older actresses, regardless of their physical beauty. And she'd become a far better, far more subtle actress—as everyone said.

Indeed, Mr. Muir *was* proud of her, and happy for her. And if he felt, now and then, a faint resentment—or, if not quite resentment, a tinge of regret at the way their life had diverged into lives—he was too much a gentleman to show it.

Unit 6   The White Cat

"WHERE IS MIRANDA? Have you seen Miranda today?"

It was noon, it was four o'clock, it was nearly dusk, and Miranda had not returned. For much of the day Alissa had been preoccupied with telephone calls—the phone seemed always to be ringing—and only gradually had she become aware of the cat's prolonged absence. She went outside to call her; she sent the servants out to look for her. And Mr. Muir, of course, gave his assistance, wandering about the grounds and for some distance into the woods, his hands cupped to his mouth and his voice high-pitched and tremulous: "Kitty-kitty-kitty-kitty-kitty! Kitty-kitty-kitty" How pathetic, how foolish-how futile! Yet it had to be performed since it was what, in innocent circumstances, *would* be performed. Julius Muir, that most solicitous of husbands, tramping through the underbrush looking for his wife's Persian cat … Poor Alissa! He thought. She'll be heartbroken for days—or would it be weeks?

And he, too, would miss Miranda—as a household presence at the very least. They would have had her, after all, for ten years this autumn.

Dinner that night was subdued, rather leaden. Not simply because Miranda was missing (and Alissa did seem inordinately and genuinely worried), but because Mr. Muir and his wife were dining alone; the table, set for two, seemed almost aesthetically wrong. And how unnatural the quiet! Mr. Muir tried to make conversation but his voice soon trailed off into a guilty silence. Midmeal Alissa rose to accept a telephone call (from Manhattan, of course—her agent, or her director, or Alban, or a female friend—an urgent call, for otherwise Mrs. Muir did not accept calls at this intimate hour) and Mr. Muir—crestfallen, hurt—finished his solitary meal in a kind of trance, tasting nothing. He recalled the night before—the pungent smelling cat food, the grainy white poison, the way the shrewd animal had looked up at him; and the way she'd brushed against his leg in a belated gesture of … was it affection? Reproach? Mockery? He felt a renewed stab of guilt, and an even more powerful stab of visceral satisfaction. Then, glancing up, he chanced to see something white making its careful way along the top of the garden wall …

Of course it was Miranda come home.

He stared, appalled. He stared, speechless—waiting for the apparition to vanish. Slowly, in a daze, he rose to his feet. In a voice meant to be jubilant he called out the news to Alissa in the adjoining room: "Miranda's come home!"

He called out: "Alissa! Darling! Miranda's come home!"

And there Miranda was, indeed; indeed it *was* Miranda, peering into the dining room from the terrace, her eyes glowing tawny gold. Mr. Muir was trembling, but his brain worked swiftly to absorb the fact, and to construe logic to accommodate it. She'd vomited up the poison, no doubt. Ah, no doubt! Or, after a cold, damp winter in the gardener's shed, the poison had lost its efficacy.

He had yet to bestir himself, to hurry to unlatch the sliding door and let the white cat in, but his voice fairly quavered with excitement: "Alissa! Good news! Miranda's come home!"

Alissa's joy was so extreme and his own initial relief so genuine that Mr. Muir—stroking Miranda's plume of a tail as Alissa hugged the cat ecstatically in her arms—thought he'd acted cruelly, selfishly—certainly he'd acted out of character—and decided that Miranda, having escaped death at her master's hands, should be granted life. He would *not* try another time.

BEFORE HIS MARRIAGE at the age of forty-six Julius Muir, like most never-married men and women of a certain temperament—introverted, self-conscious; observers of life rather than participants—had believed that the marital state was unconditionally *marital*; he'd thought that husband and wife were one flesh in more than merely the metaphorical sense of that term. Yet it happened that his own marriage was a marriage of a decidedly diminished sort. Marital relations had all but ceased, and there seemed little likelihood of their being resumed. He would shortly be fifty-seven years old, after all. (Though sometimes he wondered: Was that truly *old*?)

During the first two or three years of their marriage (when Alissa's theatrical career was, as she called it, in eclipse), they had shared a double bed like any married couple—or so Mr. Muir assumed. (For his own marriage had not enlightened him to what "marriage" in a generic sense meant.) With the passage of time, however, Alissa began to complain gently of being unable to sleep because of Mr. Muir's nocturnal "agitation"—twitching, kicking, thrashing about, exclaiming aloud, sometimes even shouting in terror. Wakened by her he would scarcely know, for a moment or two, where he was; he would then apologize profusely and shamefully, and creep away into another bedroom to sleep, if he could, for the rest of the night. Though unhappy with the situation, Mr. Muir was fully sympathetic with Alissa; he even had reason to believe that the poor woman (whose nerves were unusually sensitive) had suffered many a sleepless night on his account without telling him. It was like her to be so considerate; so loath to hurt another's feelings.

As a consequence they developed a cozy routine in which Mr. Muir spent a half-hour or so with Alissa when they first tired for the night; then, taking care not to disturb her, he would tiptoe quietly away into another room, where he might sleep undisturbed. (If, indeed, his occasional nightmares allowed him undisturbed sleep, he rather thought the worst ones, however, were the ones that failed to wake him.)

Yet a further consequence had developed in recent years: Alissa had acquired the habit of staying awake late—reading in bed, or watching television, or even, from time to time, chatting on the telephone—so it was most practical for Mr. Muir simply to kiss her good-night without getting in bed beside her, and then to go off to his own bedroom. Sometimes in his sleep he imagined Alissa was calling him back—awakened, he would hurry out into the darkened corridor to stand by her door for a minute or two, eager and hopeful. At such times he dared not raise his voice above a whisper: "Alissa? Alissa, dearest? Did you call me?"

Just as unpredictable and capricious as Mr. Muir's bad dreams were the nighttime habits of Miranda, who at times would cozily curl up at the foot of Alissa's bed and sleep peacefully through to dawn, but at other times would insist upon being let outside, no matter that Alissa loved her to sleep on the bed. There was comfort of a kind—childish, Alissa granted—in knowing the white Persian was there through the night, and feeling at her feet the cat's warm, solid weight atop the satin coverlet.

But of course, as Alissa acknowledged, a cat can't be forced to do anything against her will. "It seems almost to be a law of nature," she said solemnly.

A FEW DAYS after the abortive poisoning Mr. Muir was driving home in the early dusk when, perhaps a mile from his estate, he caught sight of the white cat in the road ahead—motionless in the other lane, as if frozen by the car's headlights. Unbidden, the thought came to him: *This is just to frighten her*—and he turned his wheel and headed in her direction. The golden eyes flared up in a blaze of blank surprise—or perhaps it was terror, or recognition—*This is just to redress the balance*, Mr. Muir thought as he pressed down harder on the accelerator and drove directly at the white Persian—and struck her, just as she started to bolt toward the ditch, with the front left wheel of his car. There was a thud and a cat's yowling, incredulous scream—and it was done.

My God! It *was* done!

Dry mouthed, shaking, Mr. Muir saw in his rearview mirror the broken white form in the road; saw a patch of liquid crimson blossoming out around it. He had not meant to kill Miranda, and yet he had actually done it this time—without premeditation, and therefore without guilt.

And now the deed was done forever.

"And no amount of remorse can undo it," he said in a slow, wondering voice. Mr. Muir had driven to the village to pick up a prescription for Alissa at the drugstore—she'd been in the city on theater matters; had returned home late on a crowded commuter train and gone at once to lie down with what threatened to be a migraine headache. Now he felt rather a hypocrite, a brute, presenting headache tablets to his wife with the guilty knowledge that if she knew what he'd done, the severity of her migraine would be tenfold. Yet how could he have explained to her that he had not meant to kill Miranda this time, but the steering wheel of his car had seemed to act of its own volition, wresting itself from his grip? For so Mr. Muir—speeding home, still trembling and excited as though he himself had come close to violent death—remembered the incident.

He remembered too the cat's hideous scream, cut off almost at once by the impact of the collision—but not quite at once.

And was there a dent in the fender of the handsome, English-built car? There was not.

And were there bloodstains on the left front tire? There were not.

Was there in fact any sign of a mishap, even of the mildest, most innocent sort? There was not.

"No proof! No proof!" Mr. Muir told himself happily, taking the stairs to Alissa's room two at a time. It was a matter of some relief as well when he raised his hand to knock at the door to hear that Alissa was evidently feeling better. She was on the telephone, talking animatedly with someone; even laughing in her light, silvery way that reminded him of nothing so much as wind chimes on a mild summer's night. His heart swelled with love and gratitude. "Dear Alissa—we will be so happy from now on!"

THEN IT HAPPENED, incredibly, that at about bedtime the white cat showed up again. *She had not died after all.*

Mr. Muir, who was sharing a late-night brandy with Alissa in her bedroom, was the first to see Miranda: she had climbed up onto the roof—by way, probably, of arose trellis she often climbed for that purpose—and now her pug face appeared a tone of the windows in a hideous repetition of the scene some nights ago. Mr. Muir sat paralyzed with shock, and it was Alissa who jumped out of bed to let the cat in.

"Miranda! What a trick! What *are* you up to?"

Certainly the cat had not been missing for any worrisome period of time, yet Alissa greeted her with as much enthusiasm as if she had. And Mr. Muir—his heart pounding in his chest and his very soul convulsed with loathing—was obliged to go along with the charade. He hoped Alissa would not notice the sick terror that surely shone in his eyes.

The cat he'd struck with his car must have been another cat, not Miranda... Obviously it had not been Miranda. Another white Persian with tawny eyes, and not his own.

Alissa cooed over the creature, and petted her, and encouraged her to settle down on the bed for the night, but after a few minutes Miranda jumped down and scratched to be let out the door: She'd missed her supper; she was hungry; she'd had enough of her mistress's affection. Not so much as a glance had she given her master, who was staring at her with revulsion. He knew now that he *must* kill her—if only to prove he could do it.

FOLLOWING THIS EPISODE the cat shrewdly avoided Mr. Muir—not out of lazy indifference, as in the past, but out of a sharp sense of their altered relations. She could not be conscious, he knew, of the fact that he had tried to kill her—but she must have been able to sense it. Perhaps she had been hiding in the bushes by the road and had seen him aim his car at her unfortunate doppelganger, and run it down.

This was unlikely, Mr. Muir knew. Indeed, it was highly improbable. But how otherwise to account for the creature's behavior in his presence—her demonstration, or simulation, of animal fear? Leaping atop a cabinet when he entered a room, as if to get out of his way; leaping atop a fireplace mantel (and sending it seemed deliberately, one of his carved jade figurines to the hearth, where it shattered into a dozen pieces); skittering gracelessly through a doorway, her sharp toenails clicking against the hardwood floor. When, without intending to, he approached her out of doors, she was likely to scamper noisily up one of the rose trellises, or the grape arbor, or a tree; or run off into the shrubbery like a wild creature. If Alissa happened to be present she was invariably astonished, for the cat's behavior *was* senseless. "Do you think Miranda is ill?" she asked. "Should we take her to the veterinarian?" Mr. Muir said uneasily that he doubted they would be able to catch her for such a purpose—at least, he doubted *he* could.

He had an impulse to confess his crime, or his attempted crime, to Alissa. He had killed the hateful creature—*and she had not died*.

ONE NIGHT AT the very end of August Mr. Muir dreamt of glaring, disembodied eyes. And in their centers those black, black irises like old-fashioned keyholes: slots opening into the Void. He could not move to protect himself. A warm, furry weight settled luxuriantly upon his chest ... upon his very face! The cat's whiskery white muzzle pressed against his mouth in a hellish kiss and in an instant the breath was being sucked from him ...

"Oh, no! Save me! Dear God!"

The damp muzzle against his mouth, sucking his life's breath from him, and he could not move to tear it away—his arms, leaden at his sides; his entire body struck dumb, paralyzed ...

"Save me ... *save me!*"

His shouting, his panicked thrashing about in the bedclothes, woke him. Though he realized at once it had been only a dream, his breath still came in rapid, shallow gasps and his heart hammered so violently he was in terror of dying: Had not his doctor only the other week spoken gravely to him of imminent heart disease, the possibility of heart failure? And how mysterious it was, his blood pressure being so very much higher than ever before in his life ...

Mr. Muir threw himself out of the damp, tangled bedclothes and switched on a lamp with trembling fingers. Thank God he was alone and Alissa had not witnessed this latest display of nerves!

"Miranda?" he whispered. "Are you in here?"

He switched on an overhead light. The bedroom shimmered with shadows and did not seem, for an instant, any room he knew.

"Miranda . . . ?"

The sly, wicked creature! The malevolent beast! To think that cat's muzzle had touched his very lips, the muzzle of an animal that devoured mice, rats—any sort of foul filthy thing out in the woods! Mr. Muir went into his bathroom and rinsed out his mouth even as he told himself calmly that the dream had been only a dream, and the cat only a phantasm, and that of course Miranda was *not* in his room.

Still, she had settled her warm, furry, unmistakable weight on his chest. She had attempted to suck his breath from him, to choke him, suffocate him, stop his poor heart. *It was within her power*. "Only a dream," Mr. Muir said aloud, smiling shakily at his reflection in the mirror. (Oh! To think that pale, haggard apparition was indeed *his* . . .) Mr. Muir raised his voice with scholarly precision. "A foolish dream, a child's dream, a woman's dream."

Back in his room he had the fleeting sense that something—a vague white shape—had just now scampered beneath his bed. But when he got down on his hands and knees to look, of course there was nothing.

He did, however, discover in the deep-pile carpet a number of cat hairs. White rather stiff—quite clearly Miranda's. Ah, quite clearly. "Here's the evidence!" he said excitedly. He found a light scattering of them on the carpet near the door and, nearer his bed, a good deal more—as if the creature had lain there for a while and had even rolled over (as Miranda commonly did out on the terrace in the sun) and stretched her graceful limbs in an attitude of utterly pleasurable abandon. Mr. Muir had often been struck by the cat's remarkable *luxuriance* at such times: a joy of flesh (and fur) he could not begin to imagine. Even before relations between them had deteriorated, he had felt the impulse to hurry to the cat and bring the heel of his shoe down hard on that tender, exposed, pinkish-pale belly . . .

"Miranda? Where are you? Are you still in here?" Mr. Muir said. He was breathless, excited. He'd been squatting on his haunches for some minutes, and when he tried to straighten up his legs ached.

Mr. Muir searched the room, but it was clear that the white cat had gone. He went out onto his balcony, leaned against the railing, blinked into the dimly moonlit darkness, but could see nothing—in his fright he'd forgotten to put on his glasses. For some minutes he breathed in the humid, sluggish night air in an attempt to calm himself, but it soon became apparent that something was wrong. Some vague murmurous undertone of—was it a voice? Voices?

Then he saw it: the ghostly white shape down in the shrubbery. Mr. Muir blinked

Unit 6 *The White Cat*

and stared, but his vision was unreliable. "Miranda?" A scuttling noise rustled above him and he turned to see another white shape on the sharp-slanted roof making its rapid way over the top. He stood absolutely motionless—whether out of terror or cunning, he could not have said. That there was more than one white cat, more than one white Persian—more, in fact, than *merely one Miranda*-was a possibility he had not considered! "Yet perhaps that explains it," he said. He was badly frightened, but his brain functioned as clearly as ever.

It was not so very late, scarcely 1:00 a.m. The undertone Mr. Muir heard was Alissa's voice, punctuated now and then by her light, silvery laughter. One might almost think there was someone in the bedroom with her—but of course she was merely having a late-night telephone conversation, very likely with Alban—they would be chatting companionably, with an innocent sort of malice, about their cofactors and actresses, mutual friends and acquaintances. Alissa's balcony opened out onto the same side of the house that Mr. Muir's did, which accounted for her voice (or *was* it voices? Mr. Muir listened, bemused) carrying so clearly. No light irradiated from her room; she must have been having her telephone conversation in the dark.

Mr. Muir waited another few minutes, but the white shape down in the shrubbery had vanished. And the slate-covered roof overhead was empty, reflecting moonlight in dull, uneven patches. He was alone. He decided to go back to bed but before doing so he checked carefully to see that he *was* alone. He locked all the windows, and the door, and slept with the lights on-but so deeply and with such grateful abandon that in the morning, it was Alissa's rapping on the door that woke him. "Julius? Julius? Is something wrong, dear?" she cried. He saw with astonishment that it was *nearly noon*: he'd slept four hours past his usual rising time!

Alissa said good-bye to him hurriedly. A limousine was coming to carry her to the city; she was to be away for several nights in succession; she was concerned about him, about his health, and hoped there was nothing wrong ... "Of course there is nothing wrong," Mr. Muir said irritably. Having slept so late in the day left him feeling sluggish and confused; it had not at all refreshed him. When Alissa kissed him good-bye he seemed rather to suffer the kiss than to participate in it, and after she had gone he had to resist an impulse to wipe his mouth with the back of his hand. "God help us!" he whispered.

BY DEGREES, AS a consequence of his troubled mind, Mr. Muir had lost interest in collecting. When an antiquarian bookdealer offered him a rare octavo edition of the *Directorium Inquisitorum* he felt only the mildest tinge of excitement, and allowed the treasure to be snatched up by a rival collector. Only a few days afterward he responded with even less enthusiasm when offered the chance to bid on a quarto Gothic edition of Machiavelli's *Belfagor*. "Is something wrong, Mr. Muir?" the dealer asked him. (They had been doing business together for a quarter of a century.) Mr. Muir said ironically, "Is something wrong?" and broke off the telephone connection. He was never to speak to the man again.

Yet more decisively, Mr. Muir had lost interest in financial affairs. He would not accept telephone calls from the various Wall Street gentlemen who managed his money; it was quite enough for him to know that the money was there and would always be there. Details regarding it struck him as tiresome and vulgar.

In the third week of September the play in which Alissa was an understudy opened to superlative reviews, which meant a good, long run. Though the female lead was in excellent health and showed little likelihood of ever missing a performance, Alissa felt obliged to remain in the city a good deal, sometimes for a full week at a time. (What she did there, how she busied herself day after day, evening after evening, Mr. Muir did not know and was too proud to ask.) When she invited him to join her for a weekend (why didn't he visit some of his antiquarian dealers, as he used to do with such pleasure?) Mr. Muir said simply, "But why, when I have all I require for happiness here in the country?"

Since the night of the attempted suffocation Mr. Muir and Miranda were yet more keenly aware of each other. No longer did the white cat flee his presence; rather, as if in mockery of him, she held her ground when he entered a room. If he approached her she eluded him only at the last possible instant, often flattening herself close against the floor and scampering, snakelike, away. He cursed her; she bared her teeth and hissed. He laughed loudly to show her how very little he cared; she leapt atop a cabinet, out of his reach, and settled into a cat's blissful sleep. Each evening Alissa called at an appointed hour; each evening she inquired after Miranda, and Mr. Muir would say, "Beautiful and healthy as ever! A pity you can't see her!"

With the passage of time Miranda grew bolder and more reckless—misjudging, perhaps, the quickness of her master's reflexes. She sometimes appeared underfoot, nearly tripping him on the stairs or as he left the house; she dared approach him as he stood with a potential weapon in hand—a carving knife, a poker, a heavy, leatherbound book. Once or twice, as Mr. Muir sat dreaming through one of his solitary meals, she even leapt onto his lap and scampered across the dining room table, upsetting dishes and glasses. "Devil!" he shrieked, swiping in her wake with his fists. "What do you want of me!"

He wondered what tales the servants told of him, whispered backstairs. He wondered if any were being relayed to Alissa in the city.

One night, however, Miranda made a tactical error, and Mr. Muir did catch hold of her. She had slipped into his study—where he sat examining some of his rarest and most valuable coins (Mesopotamian, Etruscan) by lamplight—having calculated, evidently, on making her escape by way of the door. But Mr. Muir, leaping from his chair with extraordinary, almost feline swiftness, managed to kick the door shut. And now what a chase! What a struggle! What a mad frolic! Mr. Muir caught hold of the animal, lost her, caught hold of her again, lost her; she raked him viciously on the backs of both hands and on his face; he managed to catch hold of her again, slamming her against the wall and closing his bleeding fingers around her throat. He squeezed, he squeezed! He had her now and no force on earth could make him release her! As the cat screamed and clawed and kicked and thrashed and seemed to be suffering the convulsions of death, Mr. Muir crouched over her with eyes bulging and mad as her own. The arteries in his forehead visibly throbbed. "Now! Now I have you! Now!" he cried. And at that very moment when, surely, the white Persian was on the verge of extinction, the door to Mr. Muir's study was flung open and one of the servants appeared, white faced and incredulous: "Mr. Muir? What is it? We heard such—", the fool was saying; and of course Miranda slipped from Mr. Muir's loosened grasp and bolted from the room.

After that incident Mr. Muir seemed resigned to the knowledge that he would never have such an opportunity again. The end was swiftly approaching.

IT HAPPENED QUITE suddenly, in the second week of November, which Alissa returned home.

She had quit the play; she had quit the "professional stage"; she did not even intend, as she told her husband vehemently, to visit New York City for a long time.

He saw to his astonishment that she'd been crying. Her eyes were unnaturally bright and seemed smaller than he recalled. And her prettiness looked worn, as if another face—harder, of smaller dimensions—were pushing through. Poor Alissa! She had gone away with such hope! When Mr. Muir moved to embrace her, however, meaning to comfort her, she drew away from him; her very nostrils pinched as if she found the smell of him offensive. "Please," she said, not looking him in the eye. "I don't feel well. What I want most is to be alone, just to be alone."

She retired to her room, to her bed. For several days she remained sequestered there, admitting only one of the female servants and, of course, her beloved Miranda, when Miranda condescended to visit the house. (To his immense relief Mr. Muir observed that the white cat showed no sign of their recent struggle. His lacerated hands and face were slow to heal, but in her own grief and self-absorption, Alissa seemed not to have noticed.)

In her room, behind her locked door, Alissa made a number of telephone calls to New York City. Often she seemed to be weeping over the phone. But so far as Mr. Muir could determine—being forced, under these special circumstances, to eavesdrop on the line—none of her conversations were with Alban.

Which meant ...? He had to confess he had no idea: nor could he ask Alissa, for that would give away the fact that he'd been eavesdropping, and she would be deeply shocked.

Mr. Muir sent small bouquets of autumn flowers to Alissa's sickroom; bought her chocolates and bonbons, slender volumes of poetry, a new diamond bracelet. Several times he presented himself at her door, ever the eager suitor, but she explained that she was not prepared to see him just yet—not just yet. Her voice was shrill and edged with a metallic tone Mr. Muir had not heard before.

"Don't you love me, Alissa?" he cried suddenly.

There was a moment's embarrassed silence. Then: "Of course I do. But please go away and leave me alone."

So worried was Mr. Muir about Alissa that he could no longer sleep for more than an hour or two at a time, and these hours were characterized by tumultuous dreams. The white cat! The hideous smothering weight! Fur in his very mouth! Yet awake he thought only of Alissa and of how, though she had come home to him, it was not in fact to *him*.

He lay alone in his solitary bed, amidst the tangled bedclothes, weeping hoarsely. One morning he stroked his chin and touched bristles: He'd neglected to shave for several days.

From his balcony he chanced to see the white cat preening atop the garden wall, a larger creature than he recalled. She had fully recovered from his attack ... (If, indeed, she had been injured by it, if, indeed, the cat on the garden wall was the selfsame cat that had blundered into his study.) Her white fur very nearly blazed in the sun; her eyes were miniature golden-glowing coals set deep in her skull. Mr. Muir felt a mild shock seeing her: What a beautiful creature!

Though in the next instant, of course, he realized what she was.

ONE RAINY, GUSTY evening in late November Mr. Muir was driving on the narrow blacktop road above the river, Alissa silent at his side—stubbornly silent, he thought. She wore a black cashmere cloak and a hat of soft black felt that fitted her head tightly, covering most of her hair. These were items of clothing Mr. Muir had not seen before, and in their stylish austerity they suggested the growing distance between them. When he had helped her into the car she'd murmured "*thank you*" *in a tone that indicated* "Oh! Must you touch me?" And Mr. Muir had made a mocking little bow, standing bare-headed in the rain.

And I had loved you so much.

Now she did not speak, sat with her lovely profile turned from him. As if she were fascinated by the lashing rain, the river pocked and heaving below, the gusts of wind that rocked the English-built car as Mr. Muir pressed his foot ever harder on the gas pedal. "It will be better this way, my dear wife," Mr. Muir said quietly. "Even if you love no other man, it is painfully clear that you do not love me." At these solemn words Alissa started guiltily, but still

Unit 6 *The White Cat*

would not face him. "*My dear? Do you understand? It will be better this way—do not be frightened.*" As Mr. Muir drove faster, as the car rocked more violently in the wind, Alissa pressed her hands against her mouth as if to stifle any protest; she was staring transfixed—as Mr. Muir stared transfixed—at the rushing pavement.

Only when Mr. Muir bravely turned the car's front wheels in the direction of a guardrail did her resolve break: she emitted a series of breathless little screams, shrinking back against the seat, but made no effort to seize his arm or the wheel. And in an instant all was over, in any case—the car crashed through the railing, seemed to spin in midair, dropped to the rock-strewn hillside and bursting into flame, turned end over end ...

HE WAS SEATED in a chair with wheels—a wheeled chair! It seemed to him a remarkable invention and he wondered whose ingenuity lay behind it.

Though he had not the capacity, being almost totally paralyzed, to propel it of his own volition.

And, being blind, he had no volition in any case! He was quite content to stay where he was, so long as it was out of the draft. (The invisible room in which he now resided was, for the most part, cozily heated—his wife had seen to that—but there yet remained unpredictable currents of cold air that assailed him from time to time. His bodily temperature, he feared, could not maintain its integrity against any sustained onslaught.)

He had forgotten the names for many things and felt no great grief. Indeed, not knowing *names* relaxes one's desire for the *things* that, ghostlike, forever unattainable, dwell behind them. And of course his blindness had much to do with this-for which he was grateful! Quite grateful!

Blind, yet not wholly blind: for he could see (indeed, could not see) washes of white, gradations of white, astonishing subtleties of white like rivulets in a stream perpetually breaking and falling about his head, not distinguished by any form or outline or vulgar suggestion of an object in space ...

He had had, evidently, a number of operations. How many he did not know; nor did he care to know. In recent weeks they had spoken earnestly to him of the possibility of yet another operation on his brain, the (hypothetical) object being, if he understood correctly, the restoration of his ability to move some of the toes on his left foot. Had he the capacity to laugh he would have laughed, but perhaps his dignified silence was preferable.

Alissa's sweet voice joined with the others in a chorus of bleak enthusiasm, but so far as he knew the operation had never taken place. Or if it had, it had not been a conspicuous success. The toes of his left foot were as remote and lost to him as all the other parts of his body.

"HOW LUCKY YOU were, Julius, that another car came along! Why, you might have *died!*"

It seemed that Julius Muir had been driving alone in a violent thunderstorm on the narrow River Road, high above the embankment; uncharacteristically, he'd been driving at a high speed; he'd lost control of his car, crashed through the inadequate guardrail, and over the side . . . "miraculously" thrown clear of the burning wreckage. Two-thirds of the bones in his slender body broken, skull severely fractured, spinal column smashed, a lung pierced . . . So the story of how Julius had come to this place, his final resting place, this place of milk-white peace, emerged, in fragments shattered and haphazard as those of a smashed windshield.

"Julius, dear? Are you awake, or—?" The familiar, resolutely cheerful voice came to him out of the mist, and he tried to attach a name to it, *Alissa?* or, no, *Miranda?*—which?

There was talk (sometimes in his very hearing) that, one day, some degree of his vision might be restored. But Julius Muir scarcely heard, or cared. He lived for those days when, waking from a doze, he would feel a certain furry, warm weight lowered into his lap—"Julius, dear, someone very special has come to visit!"—soft, yet surprisingly heavy; heated, yet not disagreeably so; initially a bit restless (as a cat must circle fussily about, trying to determine the ideal position before she settles herself down), yet within a few minutes quite wonderfully relaxed, kneading her claws gently against his limbs and purring as she drifted into a companionable sleep. He would have liked to see, beyond the shimmering watery whiteness of his vision, her particular whiteness; certainly he would have liked to feel once again the softness, the astonishing silkiness, of that fur. But he could hear the deep-throated melodic purring. He could feel, to a degree, her warmly pulsing weight, the wonder of her mysterious *livingness* against his—for which he was infinitely grateful.

"My love!"

Topics for Discussion

1) Why does Muir develop a passionate hatred for his much-younger wife's white Persian cat?

2) Why is the white cat named "Miranda"?

3) What caused Muir to decide to kill Miranda?

4) What is the background of Julius Muir?

5) What does Muir mean when he says "beauty can't save you"?

6) How many times does Muir attempt to kill Miranda?

7) What are the similarities between Miranda and Alissa?

8) What is the relationship between Alban and Alissa?

9) Why does Muir want to kill Alissa?
10) What is the theme of the short story?

Interdisciplinary Concepts for Further Thinking

1. Gaze

In critical theory, sociology, and psychoanalysis, the gaze is an individual's or a group's awareness and perception of other individuals, other groups, or oneself philosophically and figuratively.

The French social theorist, and philosopher Michel Foucault (1926—1984), in *Discipline and Punish: The Birth of the Prison* (1975) developed the concept of the gaze to illustrate the dynamics of socio-political power relations and the social dynamics of society's mechanisms of discipline. Another French philosopher Jacques Derrida (1930—2004), in *The Animal that Therefore I Am (More to Come)* (1997), adopted the concept of the gaze to elaborate upon the inter-species relations that exist among human beings and other animals. In psychology, to gaze implies more than to look at—it signifies a psychological relationship of power, in which the gazer is superior to the object of the gaze. In *Practices of Looking: An Introduction to Visual Culture* (2009), Marita Sturken and Lisa Cartwright say that "the gaze is [conceptually] integral to systems of power, and [to] ideas about knowledge".

Three concepts about gaze are mainly discussed in academia: the male gaze, the female gaze, and the animal gaze.

The concept of the "male gaze" was first used by the English art critic John Berger in *Ways of Seeing*, a series of films for the BBC aired in January 1972, and later a book, as part of his analysis of the treatment of the nude in European painting. Berger described the difference between how men and women view and are viewed in art and society. He asserts that men are placed into the role of the watcher and women are to be looked at. Laura Mulvey, a British film critic and feminist, similarly critiqued traditional media representations of the female character in cinema. In her 1975 essay "Visual Pleasure and Narrative Cinema", Mulvey discusses the association between activity and passivity to gender. Essentially, Mulvey argues that masculinity is related to the active, whereas femininity is related to the passive.

The term "female gaze" was created as a response to the proposed concept of the male gaze coined by Laura Mulvey. In particular, it is a rebellion against the viewership censored to only masculine lens and feminine desire regardless of the viewer's gender identity or sexual orientation. In Judith Butler's 1990 book *Gender Trouble*, she proposed the idea of the female gaze as a way in which men choose to perform their masculinity by using women as the ones who force men into self-regulation.

The term "animal gaze" was coined and developed by Wendy Woodward in her book *The Animal Gaze: Animal Subjectivities in Southern African Narratives* (2008) to articulate the autonomy and subjectivity of non-human animals. The concept indicates an attempt to challenge the hierarchical power relation between humanity and other animals.

1) Is Alissa under the gaze of Muir in "The White Cat"?

2) Does Alissa show her female gaze?

3) Can an animal have a gaze?

2. Major Depressive Disorder

Major depressive disorder (MDD) in psychology refers to a mood or emotional state that is marked by feelings of low self-worth or guilt and a reduced ability to enjoy life. It is a common and serious mood disorder. Those who suffer from depression experience persistent feelings of sadness, powerlessness, and hopelessness and lose interest in activities they once enjoyed. Aside from the emotional problems caused by depression, individuals can also present with physical symptoms such as chronic pain or digestive issues.

The DSM-5 outlines the following criterion to make a diagnosis of depression. The individual must be experiencing five or more symptoms during the same 2-week period and at least one of the symptoms should be either (1) depressed mood or (2) loss of interest or pleasure.

a. Depressed mood most of the day, nearly every day.

b. Markedly diminished interest or pleasure in all, or almost all, activities most of the day, nearly every day.

c. Significant weight loss when not dieting or weight gain, or decrease or increase in appetite nearly every day.

d. A slowing down of thought and a reduction of physical movement (observable by others, not merely subjective feelings of restlessness or being slowed down).

e. Fatigue or loss of energy nearly every day.

f. Feelings of worthlessness or excessive or inappropriate guilt nearly every day.

g. Diminished ability to think or concentrate, or indecisiveness, nearly every day.

h. Recurrent thoughts of death, recurrent suicidal ideation without a specific plan, or a suicide attempt or a specific plan for committing suicide.

1) In "The White Cat", Julius Muir attempts to commit suicide. Does he suffer from a major depressive disorder? What are the specific symptoms?

2) Do you have any suggestions for Muir to prevent himself from suffering from major depressive disorder?

Unit 6 *The White Cat*

Thinking in Numbers

1) Undoubtedly, Muir and Alissa's marriage is a failure, but it is not a bad one when they are in love and married. Both of them at least claim that they got married for true love. After a ten years' together, their marriage collapses. Generally speaking, their marriage can be divided into three phases. And also Muir attempts to kill Miranda three times. He has three reasons to kill Miranda. Analyze the story by referring to the number three and have a deeper understanding of it.

2) In the story, the word "telephone" is mentioned 9 times, and the phrase "not jealous of" 4 times. Figure out their implications respectively.

Visual Thinking with Mind Mapping

The white cat Miranda plays an important role in the story, and in some sense, it is the "third person" in Muir and Alissa's marriage. Additionally, there is a similar trajectory between the development of the Muir-Miranda relationship and the Alissa-Miranda relationship. Analyze the multiple roles that Miranda plays in the marriage with a mind map.

Critical Thinking for Reality

From "The White Cat", we know Julius Muir is a gentleman who is well-educated, and well-bred, but single at 46 years old. Meeting Alissa can be thought of as a turning point in his life. After a 10-year marriage, Muir is severely paralyzed in a car accident. At this time, it is no exaggeration to say that Muir is a complete tragedy. What's wrong with Muir? How does the tragedy happen? Is it avoidable? What important life lessons can we learn from Muir's experience?

Unit 7

Runaway

Alice Munro

Introduction to the Author

Alice Munro (1931—) is a Canadian short-story writer who gained international recognition with her exquisitely drawn narratives. Munro's work has been described as revolutionizing the architecture of short stories, especially in its tendency to move forward and backward in time. Munro's writing has established her as "one of our greatest contemporary writers of fiction", or, as Cynthia Ozick puts it, "our Chekhov." Munro has received many literary accolades, including the 2013 Nobel Prize in Literature for her work as "master of the contemporary short story", and the 2009 Man Booker International Prize for her lifetime body of work.

Alice Munro has dedicated her literary career almost exclusively to the short story genre. She grew up in a small Canadian town; the kind of environment that often provides the backdrops for her stories. Munro's work was noted for its precise imagery and narrative style, which is at once lyrical, compelling, economical, and intense, revealing the depth and complexities in the emotional lives of everyday people. Portraying the social and cultural landscape of her native southwest Ontario in most of her well-known works, such as *Dance of the Happy Shades* (1968), *The Progress of Love* (1986), and *Runaway* (2004), Munro embraced the mystery, closeness, and tension of everyday lives of men and women, anchored in the unexplored and contradictory environment of what became known as "Munro country."

Unit 7 Runaway

Introduction to the Work

"Runaway", which had its debut in *The New Yorker's* August 11, 2003 edition, is the tale of a young lady who turns down the opportunity to leave her terrible marriage. Additionally, it was included in the same-named Munro collection from 2004.

The novel is filled with runaway characters, creatures, and emotions. Carla, the husband's wife, has fled twice. She ran away from home to marry Clark when she was 18 and headed off to college, defying her parents' wishes, and hasn't spoken to them since. She then flees once more, this time from Clark, and boards a bus to Toronto. Flora, Carla's beloved white goat, also seems to be on the run after mysteriously disappearing just before the story begins. But by the time the story is over, it appears that Clark has been attempting to get rid of the goat all along. In a manner, Carla and the goat share the miserable and oppressed existence.

Text

Runaway

Carla heard the car coming before it topped the little rise in the road that around here they called a hill. It's her, she thought. Mrs. Jamieson—Sylvia—home from her holiday in Greece. From the barn door—but far enough inside that she could not easily be seen—she watched the road where Mrs. Jamieson would have to drive by, her place being half a mile farther along than Clark and Carla's.

If it was somebody coming to see them, the car would be slowing down by now. But still Carla hoped. Let it not be her.

It was. Mrs. Jamieson turned her head once, quickly—she had all she could do to maneuver her car through the ruts and puddles the rain had made in the gravel—but she didn't lift a hand off the wheel to wave, she didn't spot Carla. Carla got a glimpse of a tanned arm bare to the shoulder, hair bleached a lighter color than it had been before, more white now than silver-blond, and an expression that was both exasperated and amused at her own exasperation—just the way Mrs. Jamieson would look negotiating this road. When she turned her head there was something like a bright flash—of inquiry, of hopefulness—that made Carla shrink back.

So maybe Clark didn't know yet. If he was sitting at the computer, he would have his back to the window and the road.

But he would have to know before long. Mrs. Jamieson might have to make another trip—for groceries, perhaps. He might see her then. And after dark the lights of her house would show. But this was July and it didn't get dark till late. She might be so tired that she wouldn't bother with the lights; she might go to bed early.

On the other hand, she might telephone. Anytime now.

This was the summer of rain and more rain. They heard it first thing in the morning, loud on the roof of the mobile home. The trails were deep in mud, the long grass soaking, leaves overhead sending down random showers even in those moments when there was no actual downpour from the sky. Carla wore a wide-brimmed old Australian felt hat every time she went outside, and tucked her long thick braid down her shirt.

Nobody showed up for trail rides—even though Clark and Carla had gone around posting signs at all the campsites, in the cafés, and on the tourist-office bulletin board, and anywhere else they could think of. Only a few pupils were coming for lessons, and those were regulars, not the batches of schoolchildren on vacation or the busloads from summer camps that had kept them going the summer before. And even the regulars took time off for holiday trips, or simply cancelled their lessons because of the weather. If they called too late, Clark charged them anyway. A couple of them had argued, and quit for good.

There was still some income from the three horses that were boarded. Those three, and the four of their own, were out in the field now, poking disconsolately in the grass under the trees. Carla had finished mucking out in the barn. She had taken her time-she liked the rhythm of her regular chores, the high space under the barn roof, the smells. Now she went over to the exercise ring to see how dry the ground was, in case the five-o'clock pupil did show up.

Most of the steady showers had not been particularly heavy, but last week there had come a sudden stirring and then a blast through the treetops and a nearly horizontal blinding rain. The storm had lasted only a quarter of an hour, but branches still lay across the road, hydro lines were down, and a large chunk of the plastic roofing over the ring had been torn loose. There was a puddle like a lake at that end of the track, and Clark had worked until after dark digging a channel to drain it away.

On the Web, right now, he was hunting for a place to buy roofing. Some salvage outlet, with prices that they could afford, or somebody trying to get rid of such material, secondhand. He would not go to Hy and Robert Buckley's Building Supply in town, which he called Highway Robbers Buggery Supply, because he owed them money and had had a fight with them.

Clark often had fights, and not just with the people he owed money to. His friendliness, compelling at first, could suddenly turn sour. There were places in town that he would not go into, because of some row. The drugstore was one such place. An old woman had pushed in front of him—that is, she had gone to get something she'd forgotten and come back and pushed in front, rather than going to the end of the line, and he had complained, and the cashier had said to him, "She has emphysema." Clark had said, "Is that so? I have piles myself," and the manager had been summoned to tell him that that remark was uncalled for. And in the coffee shop out on the highway the advertised breakfast discount had not been allowed, because it was past eleven o'clock in the morning, and Clark had argued and then dropped his takeout cup of coffee on the floor—just missing, so they said, a child in its stroller. He claimed that the child was half a mile away and he'd dropped the cup because no sleeve had been provided. They said that he hadn't asked for a sleeve. He said that he shouldn't have had to ask.

"You flare up," Carla said.

"That's what men do."

She had not dared say anything about his row with Joy Tucker, whom he now referred to as Joy-Fucker. Joy was the librarian from town who boarded her horse with them, a quick-tempered little chestnut mare named Lizzie. Joy Tucker, when she was in a jokey mood, called her Lizzie Borden. Yesterday, she had driven out, not in a jokey mood at all, and complained about the roof's not being fixed and Lizzie looking so miserable, as if she might have caught a chill. There was nothing the matter with Lizzie, actually. Clark had even tried—for him—to be placating. But then it was Joy Tucker who flared up and said that their place was a dump, and Lizzie deserved better, and Clark said, "Suit yourself." Joy had not—or not yet—removed Lizzie, but Clark, who had formerly made the mare his pet, refused to have anything more to do with her.

The worst thing, as far as Carla was concerned, was the absence of Flora, the little white goat who kept the horses company in the barn and in the fields. There had been no sign of her for two days, and Carla was afraid that wild dogs or coyotes had got her, or even a bear.

She had dreamed of Flora last night and the night before. In the first dream, Flora had walked right up to the bed with a red apple in her mouth, but in the second dream—last night—she had run away when she saw Carla coming. Her leg seemed to be hurt, but she ran anyway. She led Carla to a barbed-wire barricade of the kind that might belong on some battlefield, and then she—Flora—slipped through it, hurt leg and all, just slithered through like a white eel and disappeared.

Up until three years ago, Carla had never really looked at mobile homes. She hadn't called them that, either. Like her parents, she would have thought the term "mobile home" pretentious. Some people lived in trailers, and that was all there was to it. One trailer was no different from another. When she moved in here, when she chose this life with Clark, she began to see things in a new way. After that, it was only the mobile homes that she really looked at, to see how people had fixed them up—the kind of curtains they had hung, the way they had painted the trim, the ambitious decks or patios or extra rooms they had built on. She could hardly wait to get to such improvements herself.

Clark had gone along with her ideas for a while. He had built new steps, and spent a lot of time looking for an old wrought-iron railing for them. He hadn't complained about the money spent on paint for the kitchen and bathroom or the material for curtains.

What he did balk at was tearing up the carpet, which was the same in every room and the thing that she had most counted on replacing. It was divided into small brown squares, each with a pattern of darker brown, rust, and tan squiggles and shapes. For a long time, she had thought that the same squiggles and shapes were arranged the same way in each square. Then, when she had had more time, a lot of time, to examine them, she decided that there were four patterns joined together to make identical larger squares. Sometimes she could pick out the arrangement easily and sometimes she had to work to see it.

She did this at times when Clark's mood had weighted down all their indoor space. The best thing then was to invent or remember some job to do in the barn. The horses would not look at her when she was unhappy, but Flora, who was never tied up, would come and rub against her, and look up with an expression that was not quite sympathy; it was more like comradely mockery in her shimmering yellow-green eyes.

Flora had been a half-grown kid when Clark brought her home from a farm where he'd gone to bargain for some horse tackle. He had heard that a goat was able to put horses at ease and he wanted to try it. At first she had been Clark's pet entirely, following him everywhere, dancing for his attention. She was as quick and graceful and provocative as a kitten, and her resemblance to a guileless girl in love had made them both laugh. But as she grew older she seemed to attach herself to Carla, and in this attachment she was suddenly much wiser, less skittish—she seemed capable, instead, of a subdued and ironic sort of humor. Carla's behavior with the horses was tender and strict and rather maternal, but the comradeship with Flora was quite different. Flora allowed her no sense of superiority.

"Still no sign of Flora?" she said as she pulled off her barn boots. Clark had posted a "lost goat" notice on the Web.

"Not so far," he said, in a preoccupied but not unfriendly voice. He suggested, not for the first time, that Flora might have just gone off to find herself a billy.

No word about Mrs. Jamieson.

Carla put the kettle on. Clark was humming to himself as he often did when he sat in front of the computer. Sometimes he talked back to it. "Bullshit," he might say, replying to some challenge. He laughed occasionally, but rarely remembered what the joke was when she asked him afterward.

Carla called, "Do you want tea?" And to her surprise he got up and came into the kitchen.

"So," he said. "So, Carla."

"What?"

"So she phoned."

"Who?"

"Her majesty. Queen Sylvia. She just got back."

"I didn't hear the car."

"I didn't ask you if you did."

"So what did she phone for?"

"She wants you to go and help her straighten up the house. That's what she said. Tomorrow."

"What did you tell her?"

"I told her sure. But you'd better phone up and confirm."

Carla said, "Why do I have to, if you told her?" She poured their mugs of tea. "I cleaned up her house before she left. I don't see what there could be to do so soon."

"Maybe some coons got in and made a mess of it while she was gone. You never know."

"I don't have to phone her right this minute. I want to drink my tea and I want to take a shower."

"The sooner the better."

Carla took her tea into the bathroom.

"We have to go to the laundromat. When the towels dry out, they still smell moldy."

"We're not changing the subject, Carla."

Even after she'd got in the shower, he stood outside the door and called to her.

"I am not going to let you off the hook, Carla."

She thought he might still be standing there when she came out, but he was back at the computer. She dressed as if she were going to town—she hoped that if they could get out of there, go to the laundromat, get a takeout at the cappuccino place, they might be able to talk in a different way, some release might be possible. She went into the living room with a brisk step and put her arms around him from behind. But as soon as she did that a wave of grief swallowed her up—it must have been the heat of the shower, loosening her tears—and she bent over him, crumbling and crying.

He took his hands off the keyboard but sat still.

"Just don't be mad at me," she said.

"I'm not mad. I hate when you're like this, that's all."

"I'm like this because you're mad."

"Don't tell me what I am. You're choking me. Go and get control of yourself. Start supper."

That was what she did. It was obvious by now that the five-o'clock person wasn't coming. She got out the potatoes and started to peel them, but her tears would not stop. She wiped her face with a paper towel and tore off a fresh one to take with her and went out into the rain. She didn't go into the barn because it was too miserable in there without Flora. She walked along the lane back to the woods. The horses were in the other field. They came over to the fence to watch her, but all except Lizzie, who capered and snorted a bit, had the sense to understand that her attention was elsewhere.

. . .

It had started when they read the obituary, Mr. Jamieson's obituary, in the city paper. Until the year before, they had known the Jamiesons only as neighbors who kept to themselves. She taught botany at the college forty miles away, so she had to spend a good deal of her time on the road. He was a poet. But for a poet, and for an old man—perhaps twenty years older than Mrs. Jamieson—he was rugged and active. He improved the drainage system on his place, cleaning out the culvert and lining it with rocks. He dug and planted and fenced a vegetable garden, cut paths through the woods, looked after repairs on the house—not just the sort of repairs that almost any house owner could manage after a while but those that involved plumbing, wiring, roofing, too.

When they read the obituary, Carla and Clark learned for the first time that Leon Jamieson had been the recipient of a large prize five years before his death. A prize for poetry.

Shortly afterward, Clark said, "We could've made him pay."

Carla knew at once what he was talking about, but she took it as a joke.

"Too late now," she said. "You can't pay once you're dead."

"He can't. She could."

"She's gone to Greece."

"She's not going to stay in Greece."

"She didn't know," Carla said more soberly. "She didn't have anything to do with it."

"I didn't say she did."

"She doesn't have a clue about it."

"We could fix that."

Carla said, "No. No."

Clark went on as if she hadn't spoken.

"We could say we're going to sue. People get money for stuff like that all the time."

"How could you do that? You can't sue a dead person."

"Threaten to go to the papers. Big-time poet. The papers would eat it up. All we have to do is threaten and she'd cave in. How much are we going to ask for?"

"You're just fantasizing," Carla said. "You're joking."

"No. Actually, I'm not."

Carla said that she didn't want to talk about it anymore, and he said O.K. But they talked about it the next day, and the next, and the next. He sometimes got notions like this, which were not practicable, which might even be illegal. He talked about them with growing excitement and then—she wasn't sure why—he dropped them. If the rain had stopped, if this had turned into a normal summer, he might have let this idea go the way of the others. But that had not happened, and during the last month he had harped on about the scheme as if it were perfectly feasible. The question was how much money to ask for. Too little and the woman might not take them seriously; she might think they were bluffing. Too much might get her back up and she might become stubborn.

Carla had stopped pretending she thought he was joking. Instead, she told him that it wouldn't work. She said that, for one thing, people expected poets to behave that way. So it wouldn't be worth paying out money to cover it up.

"How do you know?" Clark said.

He said that it would work if it was done right. Carla was to break down and tell Mrs. Jamieson the whole story. Then Clark would move in, as if it had all been a surprise to him, he had just found out. He would be outraged; he would talk about telling the world. He would let Mrs. Jamieson be the one who first mentioned money.

"You were injured. You were molested and humiliated and I was injured and humiliated because you are my wife. It's a question of respect."

Over and over again he talked to her in this way. She tried to deflect him, but he insisted.

"Promise," he said. "Promise."

All this was because of what she had told him—things she could not now retract or deny.

Sometimes he gets interested in me?

The old guy?

Sometimes he calls me into the room when she's not there?

When she has to go out shopping and the nurse isn't there, either?

A lucky inspiration of hers, one that instantly pleased him.

So what do you do then? Do you go in?

She played shy.

Sometimes.

He calls you into his room. So? Carla? So, then?

I go in to see what he wants.

So what does he want?

This was asked and told in whispers, even when there was nobody to hear, even when they were in the neverland of their bed. A bedtime story, in which the details were important and had to be added to each time, with convincing reluctance, shyness, giggles. (Dirty, dirty.) And it was not only he who was eager and grateful. She was, too. Eager to please and excite him, to excite herself. Grateful every time that it still worked.

And in one part of her mind it was true: she saw the randy old man, the bump he made in the sheet, bedridden, almost beyond speech but proficient in sign language, indicating his desire, trying to nudge and finger her into complicity, into obliging stunts and intimacies. (Her refusal a necessity, but also, perhaps, strangely, slightly disappointing to Clark.)

Now and then came an image that she had to hammer down lest it spoil everything. She would think of the real dim and sheeted body, drugged and shrinking every day in its hospital bed, glimpsed only a few times, when Mrs. Jamieson or the visiting nurse had neglected to close the door. She herself never actually coming closer to him than that.

In fact, she had dreaded going to the Jamiesons', but she needed the money, and she felt sorry for Mrs. Jamieson, who seemed so haunted and bewildered, as if she were walking in her sleep. Once or twice, Carla had burst out and done something really silly just to loosen up the atmosphere. The kind of thing she did when clumsy and terrified riders were feeling humiliated. She used to try it, too, when Clark was stuck in his moods. It didn't work with him anymore. But the story about Mr. Jamieson had worked, decisively.

At the house there was nothing for Sylvia to do except open the windows. And think—with an eagerness that dismayed without really surprising her—of how soon she could see Carla.

All the paraphernalia of illness had been removed. The room that had been Sylvia and her husband's bedroom and then his death chamber had been cleaned out and tidied up to look as if nothing had ever happened in it. Carla had helped with all that, during the few frenzied days between the crematorium and the departure for Greece. Every piece of clothing Leon had ever worn and some things he hadn't, some gifts from his sisters that had never been taken out of their packages, had been piled in the back seat of the car and taken to the thrift shop. His pills, his shaving things, unopened cans of the fortified drink that had sustained him as long as anything could, cartons of the sesame-seed snaps that had at one time been his favorite snack, the plastic bottles full of the lotion that had eased his back, the sheepskins on which he had lain—all of that was dumped into plastic bags to be hauled away as garbage, and

Carla didn't question a thing. She never said, "Maybe somebody could use that," or pointed out that whole cartons of cans were unopened. When Sylvia said, "I wish I hadn't taken the clothes to town. I wish I'd burned them all up in the incinerator," Carla showed no surprise.

They cleaned the oven, scrubbed out the cupboards, wiped down the walls and the windows. One day Sylvia sat in the living room going through all the condolence letters she had received. (There was no accumulation of papers and notebooks to be attended to, as you might have expected with a writer, no unfinished work or scribbled drafts. He had told her, months before, that he had pitched everything. And no regrets.) The sloping south wall of the house was mostly big windows. Sylvia looked up, surprised by the watery sunlight that had come out—or possibly by the shadow of Carla on top of a ladder, bare-legged, bare-armed, her resolute face crowned with a frizz of dandelion hair that was too short for her braid. She was vigorously spraying and scrubbing the glass. When she saw Sylvia looking at her, she stopped and flung out her arms as if she were splayed there, making a preposterous gargoyle-like face. They both began to laugh. Sylvia felt this laughter running through her like a sweet stream. She turned back to her letters and soon decided that all these kind, genuine, or perfunctory words, the tributes and the regrets, could go the way of the sheepskins and the crackers.

When she heard Carla taking the ladder down, heard boots on the deck, she was suddenly shy. She sat where she was with her head bowed as Carla came into the room and passed behind her, on her way to the kitchen to put the pail and the paper towels back under the sink. She hardly halted—she was quick as a bird—but she managed to drop a kiss on Sylvia's bent head. Then she went on. She was whistling something to herself, perhaps had been whistling the whole time.

That kiss had been in Sylvia's mind ever since. It meant nothing in particular. It meant Cheer up. Or Almost done. It meant that they were good friends who had got through a lot of depressing work together. Or maybe just that the sun had come out. That Carla was thinking of getting home to her horses. Nevertheless, Sylvia saw it as a bright blossom, its petals spreading inside her with a tumultuous heat, like a menopausal flash.

Every so often there had been a special girl student in one of her classes—one whose cleverness and dedication and awkward egotism, or even genuine passion for the natural world, reminded her of her young self. Such girls hung around her worshipfully, hoped for some sort of intimacy they could not—in most cases—imagine, and soon got on her nerves.

Carla was nothing like them. If she resembled anybody in Sylvia's life, it would have to be certain girls she had known in high school—those who were bright but not too bright, easy athletes but not competitive, buoyant but not rambunctious. Naturally happy.

The day after Sylvia's return, she was speaking to Carla about Greece.

"Where I was, this little tiny village with my two old friends, well, it was the sort of place where the very occasional tourist bus would stop, as if it had got lost, and the tourists would get off and look around and they were absolutely bewildered because they weren't anywhere. There was nothing to buy."

The large-limbed, uncomfortable, dazzling girl was sitting there at last, in the room that had been filled with thoughts of her. She was faintly smiling, belatedly nodding.

"And at first I was bewildered, too. It was so hot. But it's true about the light. It's wonderful. And then I figured out what there was to do. There were just these few simple things, but they could fill the day. You walk half a mile down the road to buy some oil, and half a mile in the other direction to buy your bread or your wine, and that's the morning. Then you eat some lunch under the trees, and after lunch it's too hot to do anything but close the shutters and lie on your bed and maybe read. Later on, you notice that the shadows are longer and you get up and go for a swim. Oh," she interrupted herself. "Oh, I forgot."

She jumped up and went to get the present she had brought, which in fact she had not forgotten about at all. She had not wanted to hand it to Carla right away—she had wanted the moment to come more naturally, and while she was speaking she had thought ahead to the moment when she could mention the sea, going swimming. And then say, as she now said, "Swimming reminded me of this because it's a little replica, you know, it's a little replica of the horse they found under the sea. Cast in bronze. They dredged it up, after all this time. It's supposed to be from the second century B.C."

When Carla had come in and looked around for work to do, Sylvia had said, "Oh, just sit down a minute. I haven't had anybody to talk to since I got back. Please." Carla had sat down on the edge of a chair, legs apart, hands between her knees, looking somehow desolate. As if reaching for some distant politeness, she had said, "How was Greece?"

Now she was standing, with the tissue paper crumpled around the horse, which she had not fully unwrapped.

"It's said to represent a racehorse," Sylvia said. "Making that final spurt, the last effort in a race. The rider, too—the boy—you can see that he's urging the horse on to the limit of its strength."

She did not mention that the boy had made her think of Carla, and she could not now have said why. He was only ten or eleven years old. Maybe the strength and grace of the arm that must have held the reins, or the wrinkles in his childish forehead, the absorption and the pure effort there. It was, in some way, like Carla cleaning the windows last spring. Her strong legs in her shorts, her broad shoulders, her big dedicated swipes at the glass, and then the way she had splayed herself out as a joke, inviting or even commanding Sylvia to laugh.

"You can see that," Carla said, conscientiously now examining the little bronzy-green statue. "Thank you very much."

"You are welcome. Let's have coffee, shall we? I've just made some. The coffee in Greece was strong, a little stronger than I liked, but the bread was heavenly. Sit down another moment, please do. You should stop me going on and on this way. What about here? How has life been here?"

"It's been raining most of the time."

"I can see that. I can see it has," Sylvia called from the kitchen end of the big room. Pouring the coffee, she decided that she would keep quiet about the other gift she had brought. It hadn't cost her anything (the horse had cost more than the girl could probably guess); it was only a beautiful small pinkish-white stone that she had picked up on the road.

"This is for Carla," she had said to her friend Maggie, who was walking beside her. "I know it's silly. I just want her to have a tiny piece of this land."

She had already mentioned Carla to Maggie, and to Soraya, her other friend there, telling them how the girl's presence had come to mean more and more to her, how an indescribable bond had seemed to grow up between them, and had consoled her in the awful months of last spring.

"It was just to see somebody—somebody so fresh and full of healh coming into the hourse."

Maggie and Soraya had laughed in a kindly but annoying way.

"There's always a girl," Soraya said, with an indolent stretch of her heavy brown arms, and Maggie said, "We all come to it sometime. A crush on a girl."

Sylvia was obscurely angered by that dated word-crush.

"Maybe it's because Leon and I never had children," she said. "It's stupid. Displaced maternal love."

Her friends spoke at the same time, saying in slightly different ways something to the effect that it might be stupid but it was, after all, love.

But the girl was not, today, anything like the Carla Sylvia had been remembering, not at all the calm bright spirit, the carefree and generous young creature who had kept her company in Greece.

She had been hardly interested in her gift. Almost sullen as she reached out for her mug of coffee.

"There was one thing I thought you would have liked a lot," said Sylvia energetically. "The goats. They were quite small even when they were full-grown. Some spotty and some white, and they were leaping around up on the rocks just like—like the spirits of the place." She laughed in an artificial way, she couldn't stop herself. "I wouldn't be surprised if they'd had wreaths on their horns. How is your little goat? I forget her name."

Carla said, "Flora."

"Flora."

"She's gone."

"Gone? Did you sell her?"

"She disappeared. We don't know where."

"Oh, I'm sorry. I'm sorry. But isn't there a chance she'll turn up again?"

No answer. Sylvia looked directly at the girl, something that up to now she had not quite been able to do, and saw that her eyes were full of tears, her face bloated with distress.

She didn't do anything to avoid Sylvia's look. She drew her lips tight over her teeth and shut her eyes and rocked back and forth as if in a soundless howl, and then, shockingly, she did howl. She howled and wept and gulped for air and tears ran down her cheeks and snot out of her nostrils and she began to look around wildly for something to wipe with. Sylvia ran and got handfuls of Kleenex.

"Don't worry, here you are, here, you're all right," she said, thinking that maybe the thing to do would be to take the girl in her arms. But she had not the least wish to do that, and it might make things worse. The girl might feel how little Sylvia wanted to do such a thing, how appalled she was in fact by this noisy fit.

Carla said something, said the same thing again.

"Awful," she said. "Awful."

"No it's not. We all have to cry sometimes. It's all right, don't worry."

"It's awful."

And Sylvia could not help feeling how, with every moment of this show of misery, the girl made herself more ordinary, more like one of those soggy students in her—Sylvia's—office. Some of them cried about their marks, but that was often tactical, a brief unconvincing bit of whimpering. The more infrequent, real waterworks would turn out to have something to do with a love affair, or their parents, or a pregnancy.

"It's not the goat. What is it?"

Carla said, "I can't stand it anymore."

What could she not stand?

It turned out to be the husband.

He was mad at her all the time. He acted as if he hated her. There was nothing she could do right, there was nothing she could say. Living with him was driving her crazy.

Sometimes she thought she already was crazy. Sometimes she thought he was.

"Has he hurt you, Carla?"

No. He hadn't hurt her physically. But he hated her. He despised her. He could not stand it when she cried and she could not help crying because he was so mad. She did not know what to do.

"Perhaps you do know what to do," said Sylvia.

"Get away? I would if I could." Carla began to wail again. "I'd give anything to get away. I can't. I haven't any money. I haven't anywhere in this world to go."

"Well. Think. Is that altogether true?" said Sylvia in her best counseling manner. "Don't you have parents? Didn't you tell me you grew up in Kinston? Don't you have a family there?"

Her parents had moved to British Columbia. They hated Clark. They didn't care if she lived or died.

Brothers or sisters?

One brother nine years older. He was married and in Toronto. He didn't care either. He didn't like Clark. His wife was a snob.

"Have you ever thought of the Women's Shelter?"

"They don't want you there unless you've been beaten up. And everybody would find out and it would be bad for our business."

Sylvia smiled gently. "Is this a time to think about that?"

Then Carla actually laughed. "I know," she said. "I'm insane."

"Listen," Sylvia said. "Listen to me. If you had the money to go, where would you go? What would you do?"

"I would go to Toronto," Carla said, readily enough. "But I wouldn't go near my brother. I'd stay in a motel or something and I'd get a job at a riding stable."

"You think you could do that?"

"I was working at a riding stable the summer I met Clark. I'm more experienced now than I was then. A lot more."

"And all that's stopping you is lack of money?"

Carla took a deep breath. "All that's stopping me," she said.

"All right," Sylvia said. "Now, listen to what I propose. I don't think you should go to a motel. I think you should take the bus to Toronto and go to stay with a friend of mine. Her name is Ruth Stiles. She has a big house and she lives alone and she won't mind having somebody to stay. You can stay there till you find a job. I'll help you with some money. There must be lots of riding stables around Toronto."

"There are."

"So what do you think? Do you want me to phone and find out what time the bus goes?"

Carla said yes. She was shivering. She ran her hands up and down her thighs and shook her head roughly from side to side.

"I can't believe it," she said. "I'll pay you back. I mean, thank you. I'll pay you back. I don't know what to say."

Sylvia was already at the phone, dialling the bus depot.

"Sh-h-h, I'm getting the times," she said. She listened and hung up. "I know you will. You agree about Ruth's? I'll let her know. There's one problem, though." She looked critically at Carla's shorts and T-shirt. "You can't very well go in those clothes."

"I can't go home to get anything," Carla said in a panic. "I'll be all right."

"The bus will be air-conditioned. You'll freeze. There must be something of mine you could wear. Aren't we about the same height?"

"You're ten times skinnier," Carla said.

"I didn't use to be."

In the end, they decided on a brown linen jacket, hardly worn—Sylvia had considered it to be a mistake for herself, the style too brusque-and a pair of tailored tan pants and a cream-colored silk shirt. Carla's sneakers would have to do, because her feet were two sizes larger then Sylvia's.

Carla went to take a shower—something she had not bothered with, in her state of mind that morning—and Sylvia phoned Ruth. Ruth was going to be out at a meeting that evening, but she would leave the key with her upstairs tenants and all Carla would have to do was ring their bell.

"She'll have to take a cab from the bus depot, though. I assume she's O.K. to manage that?" Ruth said.

Sylvia laughed. "She's not a lame duck, don't worry. She is just a person in a bad situation, the way it happens."

"Well, good. I mean, good she's getting out."

"Not a lame duck at all," Sylvia said, thinking of Carla trying on the tailored pants and linen jacket. How quickly the young recover from a fit of despair and how handsome the girl had looked in the fresh clothes.

The bus would stop in town at twenty past two. Sylvia decided to make omelettes for lunch, to set the table with the dark-blue cloth, and to get down the crystal glasses and open a bottle of wine.

"I hope you can eat something," she said, when Carla came out clean and shining in her borrowed clothes. Her softly freckled skin was flushed from the shower and her hair was damp and darkened, out of its braid, the sweet frizz now flat against her head. She said that she was hungry, but when she tried to get a forkful of the omelette to her mouth her trembling hands made it impossible.

"I don't know why I'm shaking like this," she said. "I must be excited. I never knew it would be this easy."

"It's very sudden," Sylvia said judiciously. "Probably it doesn't seem quite real."

"It does, though. Everything now seems really real. It's like the time before—that's when I was in a daze."

"Maybe when you make up your mind to something, when you really make up your mind, that's how it is. Or that's how it should be. Easy."

"If you've got a friend," Carla said with a self-conscious smile and a flush spreading over her forehead. "If you've got a true friend. I mean, like you." She laid down the knife and fork and raised her wineglass with both hands. "Drinking to a true friend," she said, uncomfortably. "I probably shouldn't even take a sip, but I will."

"Me, too," Sylvia said with a pretense of gaiety, but she spoiled the moment by saying, "Are you going to phone him? Or what? He'll have to know. At least he'll have to know where you are by the time he'd be expecting you home."

"Not the phone," Carla said, alarmed. "I can't do it. Maybe if you—"

"No," Sylvia said. "No."

"No, that's stupid of me. I shouldn't have said that. It's just hard to think straight. What I maybe should do is put a note in the mailbox. But I don't want him to get it too soon. I don't want us to even drive past there when we're going into town. I want to go the back way. So if I write it—if I write it, could you, could you maybe slip it in the box when you come back?"

Sylvia agreed to this, seeing no good alternative. She brought pen and paper and poured a little more wine. Carla sat thinking, then wrote a few words.

I have gone away. I will be all write.

These were the words that Sylvia read when she unfolded the paper on her way back from the bus station. She was sure that Carla knew "right" from "write." It was just that she had been talking about writing a note and she was in a state of exalted confusion. More confusion perhaps than Sylvia had realized. The wine had brought out a stream of talk, but it had not seemed to be accompanied by any particular grief or upset. She had talked about the horse barn where she had worked when she was eighteen and just out of high school—that was where she'd met Clark. Her parents had wanted her to go to college, and she had agreed, as long as she could choose to be a veterinarian. She had been one of those dorky girls in high school, one of those girls they made rotten jokes about, but she didn't care. All she really wanted, and had wanted all her life, was to work with animals and live in the country.

Clark was the best riding teacher they had—and good-looking, too. Scads of women were after him—they would take up riding just to get him as their teacher. She had teased him about this, and at first he seemed to like it, but then he got annoyed. She tried to make up for it by getting him talking about his dream—his plan, really—to have a riding school, a horse stable, someplace out in the country. One day, she came in to work and saw him hanging up his saddle and realized that she had fallen in love with him.

Maybe it was just sex. It was probably just sex.

When fall came and she was supposed to leave for college, she refused to go. She said she needed a year off.

Clark was very smart, but he hadn't waited even to finish high school, and he had altogether lost touch with his family. He thought families were like a poison in your blood. He had been an attendant in a mental hospital, a disk jockey on a radio station in Lethbridge, Alberta, a member of a road crew near Thunder Bay, an apprentice barber, a salesman in an Army-surplus store. And those were only the jobs he had told her about.

She had nicknamed him Gypsy Rover, because of the song, an old song her mother used to sing. And she took to singing it around the house all the time, till her mother knew something was up.

Last night she slept on a goose-feather bed
With silken sheets for cover.
Tonight she'll sleep on the cold cold ground—
Beside her gypsy lo-ov-ver.

Her mother had said, "He'll break your heart, that's a sure thing." Her stepfather, who was an engineer, did not even grant Clark that much power. "A loser," he called him. "A drifter." He said this as if Clark were a bug he could just whisk off his clothes.

Carla said, "Does a drifter save up enough money to buy a farm, which, by the way, he has done?" He said, "I'm not about to argue with you." She was not his daughter, anyway, he added, as if that were the clincher.

So, naturally, Carla had had to run away with him. The way her parents behaved, they were practically guaranteeing it.

"Will you get in touch with your parents after you're settled?" Sylvia asked. "In Toronto?"

Carla raised her eyebrows, pulled in her cheeks, and made a saucy O of her mouth. She said, "Nope."

Definitely a little bit drunk.

Back home, having left the note in the mailbox, Sylvia cleaned up the dishes that were still on the table, washed and polished the omelette pan, threw the blue napkins and tablecloth in the laundry basket, and opened the windows. She did this with a confusing sense of regret and irritation. She had put out a fresh cake of apple-scented soap for the girl's shower and the smell of it lingered in the house, as it had in the air of the car.

Sometime in the last hour or so the rain had stopped. She could not stay still, so she went for a walk along the path that Leon had cleared. The gravel he had dumped in the boggy places had mostly washed away. They used to go walking every spring to hunt for wild orchids. She taught him the name of every wildflower—all of which, except for trillium, he forgot. He called her his Dorothy Wordsworth.

Last spring, she had gone out once, and picked him a bunch of dogtooth violets, but he had looked at them—as he sometimes looked at her—with mere exhaustion, disavowal.

She kept seeing Carla, Carla stepping onto the bus. Her thanks had been sincere but already almost casual, her wave jaunty. She had got used to her salvation.

Around six o'clock, Sylvia put in a call to Toronto, to Ruth, knowing that Carla probably wouldn't have arrived yet. She got the answering machine.

"Ruth," Sylvia said. "Sylvia. It's about this girl I sent you. I hope she doesn't turn out to be a bother to you. I hope it'll be all right. You may find her a little full of herself. Maybe it's just youth. Let me know. O.K.? O.K. Bye-bye."

She phoned again before she went to bed but got the machine, so she said, "Sylvia again. Just checking," and hung up. It was between nine and ten o'clock, not even really dark. Ruth would still be out, and the girl would not want to pick up the phone in a strange house. She tried to think of the name of Ruth's upstairs tenants. They surely wouldn't have gone to bed yet. But she could not remember it. And just as well. Phoning them would have been going too far.

She got into bed, but it was impossible, so she took a light quilt and went out to the living room and lay down on the sofa, where she had slept for the last three months of Leon's life. She did not think it likely that she would get to sleep there, either—there were no curtains on the huge south windows and she could tell by the sky that the moon had risen, though she could not see it.

The next thing she knew she was on a bus somewhere—in Greece?—with a lot of people she did not know, and the engine of the bus was making an alarming knocking sound. She woke to find that the knocking was at her front door.

Carla?

Carla had kept her head down until the bus was clear of town. The windows were tinted, nobody could see in, but she had to guard herself against seeing out. Lest Clark appear. Coming out of a store or waiting to cross the street, ignorant of her abandonment, thinking this an ordinary afternoon. No: thinking it the afternoon when their scheme—his scheme—had been put in motion, eager to know how far she had got with it.

Once they were out in the country, she looked up, breathed deeply, took account of the violet-tinted fields. Mrs. Jamieson's presence had surrounded her with a kind of remarkable safety and sanity, had made her escape seem the most rational thing you could imagine—in fact, the only self-respecting thing that a person in Carla's shoes could do. Carla had felt herself capable of an unaccustomed confidence, even a mature sense of humor. She had revealed her life to Mrs. Jamieson in a way that seemed bound to gain sympathy and yet to be ironic and truthful. And adapted to live up to what, as far as she could see, were Mrs. Jamieson's—Sylvia's—expectations.

The sun was shining, as it had been for some time. At lunch, it had made the wineglasses sparkle. And there was enough of a wind blowing to lift the roadside grass, the flowering weeds, out of their drenched clumps. Summer clouds, not rain clouds, were scudding across the sky. The whole countryside was changing, shaking itself loose, into the true brightness of a July day. And as they sped along she didn't see much trace of the recent past—no big puddles in the fields, showing where the seed had washed out, no miserable spindly cornstalks or lodged grain.

It occurred to her that she should tell Clark about this—that perhaps they had chosen what was, for some freakish reason, a very wet and dreary corner of the country, and there were other places where they could have been successful.

Or could be yet?

Then it came to her, of course, that she would not be telling Clark anything. Never again. She would not be concerned about what happened to him, or to the horses. If, by any chance, Flora came back she would not hear about it.

This was her second time, leaving everything behind. The first time had been just like the old Beatles song: she had put a note on the table and slipped out of the house at five o'clock in the morning to meet Clark in the church parking lot down the street. She was even humming that song as they rattled away. She's leaving home, bye-bye. She recalled now how the sun had come up behind them, how she had looked at Clark's hands on the wheel, at the dark hairs on his competent forearms, and breathed in the smell of the truck, a smell of oil and metal tools and horse barns. The cold air of the fall morning had blown in through the rusted seams of the sort of vehicle that nobody in her family ever rode in, that scarcely ever appeared on the streets where she lived. Clark's preoccupation with the traffic, his curt answers, his narrowed eyes, everything about him that ignored her, even his slight irritation at her giddy delight— all of that had thrilled her. As did the disorder of his past life, his avowed loneliness, the unexpectedly tender way he could have with a horse, and with her. She saw him as the sturdy architect of the life ahead of them, herself as a captive, her submission both proper and exquisite.

"You don't know what you're leaving behind," her mother wrote to her, in the one letter she received and never answered. But in those shivering moments of early-morning flight she certainly had known what she was leaving behind, even if she had rather a hazy idea of what she was going to. She despised their house, their back yard, their photo albums, their vacations, their Cuisinart, their powder room, their walk-in closets, their underground lawn-sprinkling system. In the brief note she left, she had used the word "authentic."

I have always felt the need of a more authentic kind of life. I know I cannot expect you to understand this.

The bus had stopped now at a gas station in the first town on the way. It was the very station that she and Clark used to drive to, in their early days, to buy cheap gas. In those days, their world had included several towns in the surrounding countryside, and they had sometimes behaved like tourists, sampling the specialties in grimy hotel bars. Pigs' feet, sauerkraut, potato pancakes, beer. They would sing all the way home like crazy hillbillies.

But after a while all outings came to be seen as a waste of time and money. They were what people did before they understood the realities of their lives.

She was crying now—her eyes had filled up without her realizing it. She tried to think about Toronto, the first steps ahead. The taxi, the house she had never seen, the strange bed she would sleep in alone. Looking in the phone book tomorrow for the addresses of riding stables, then getting to wherever they were, asking for a job.

She could not picture it. Herself riding on the subway or a streetcar, caring for new horses, talking to new people, living among hordes of people every day who were not Clark. A life, a place, chosen for that specific reason: that it would not contain Clark.

The strange and terrible thing about that world of the future, as she now pictured it, was that she would not exist in it. She would only walk around, and open her mouth and speak, and do this and do that. She would not really be there. And what was strange about it was that she was doing all this, she was riding on this bus, in the hope of recovering herself. As Mrs. Jamieson might say—and as she herself might have said with satisfaction—taking charge of her own life. With nobody glowering over her, nobody's mood infecting her with misery, no implacable mysterious silence surrounding her.

But what would she care about? How would she know that she was alive?

While she was running away from him—now—Clark still kept his place in her life. But when she was finished running away, when she just went on, what would she put in his place? What else—who else—could ever be so vivid a challenge?

She managed to stop crying but she had started to shake. She was in a bad way and would have to take hold, get a grip on herself. "Get a grip on yourself," Clark had sometimes told her, passing through a room where she was scrunched up, trying not to weep, and that indeed was what she must do now.

They had stopped in another town. This was the third town away from the one where she had got on the bus, which meant that they had passed through the second town without her even noticing. The bus must have stopped, the driver must have called out the name, and she had not heard or seen anything, in her fog of fright. Soon enough, they would reach the highway, they would be tearing along toward Toronto.

And she would be lost.

She would be lost. What would be the point of getting into a taxi and giving the new address, of getting up in the morning and brushing her teeth and going into the world?

Her feet seemed now to be at some enormous distance from her body. Her knees in the unfamiliar crisp pants were weighted with irons. She was sinking to the ground like a stricken horse.

Already the bus had loaded on the few passengers and parcels that had been waiting in this town. A woman and a baby in its stroller were waving goodbye to somebody. The building behind them, the café that served as a bus stop, was also in motion; a liquefying wave passed through the bricks and windows as if they were about to dissolve. In peril, Carla pulled her huge body, her iron limbs, forward. She stumbled. She cried out, "Let me off."

The driver braked. He called back irritably, "I thought you were going to Toronto." People gave her casually curious looks. No one seemed to understand that she was in anguish.

"I have to get off here."

"There's a washroom in the back."

"No. No. I have to get off."

"I'm not waiting. You understand that? You got luggage underneath?"

"No. Yes. No."

"No luggage?"

A voice in the bus said, "Claustrophobia. That's what's the matter with her."

"You sick?" the driver said.

"No. No. I just want off."

"O.K. O.K. Fine by me."

Come and get me. Please. Come and get me.
I will.

Sylvia had forgotten to lock her door. She realized that she should be locking it now, not opening it, but it was too late, she had it open.

And nobody there.

Yet she was sure, sure, the knocking had been real.

She closed the door and this time she locked it.

There was a playful sound, a tinkling tapping sound, coming from the wall of windows. She switched the light on, but saw nothing there, and switched it off again. Some animal—maybe a squirrel? The French doors that opened between windows, leading to the patio, had not been locked either. Not even really closed, having been left open an inch or so from her airing of the house. She started to close them and somebody laughed, nearby, near enough to be in the room with her.

"It's me," a man said. "Did I scare you?"

He was pressed against the glass of the door; he was right beside her.

"It's Clark," he said. "Clark from down the road."

She was not going to ask him in, but she was afraid to shut the door in his face. He might grab it before she could get it closed. She didn't want to turn on the light, either. She slept in a T-shirt. She should have pulled the quilt from the sofa and wrapped it around herself, but it was too late now.

"Did you want to get dressed?" he said. "What I got in here could be the very things you need."

He had a shopping bag in his hand. He thrust it at her, but did not try to move forward with it.

"What?" she said in a choppy voice.

"Look and see. It's not a bomb. There, take it."

She felt inside the bag, not looking. Something soft. And then she recognized the buttons of the jacket, the silk of the shirt, the belt on the pants.

"Just thought you'd better have them back," he said. "They're yours, aren't they?"

She tightened her jaw so that her teeth wouldn't chatter. A fearful dryness had attacked her mouth and throat.

"I understood they were yours," he said.

Her tongue moved like a wad of wool. She forced herself to say, "Where's Carla?"

"You mean my wife Carla?"

Now she could see his face more clearly. She could see how he was enjoying himself.

"My wife Carla is at home in bed. Where she belongs."

He was both handsome and silly-looking. Tall, lean, well-built, but with a slouch that seemed artificial. A contrived, self-conscious air of menace. A lock of dark hair falling over his forehead, a vain little mustache, eyes that appeared both hopeful and mocking, a boyish smile perpetually on the verge of a sulk.

She had always disliked the sight of him—she had mentioned her dislike to Leon, who said that the man was just unsure of himself, just a bit too friendly. The fact that he was unsure of himself would not make her any safer.

"Pretty worn out," he said. "After her little adventure. You should have seen your face—you should have seen the look on you when you recognized those clothes. What did you think? Did you think I'd murdered her?"

"I was surprised," Sylvia said.

"I bet you were. After you were such a big help to her running away."

"I helped her—" Sylvia said with considerable effort. "I helped her because she seemed to be in distress."

"Distress," he said, as if examining the word. "I guess she was. She was in very big distress when she jumped off that bus and got on the phone to me to come and get her. She was crying so hard I could hardly make out what it was she was saying."

"She wanted to come back?"

"Oh, yeah. You bet she wanted to come back. She was in real hysterics to come back. She is a girl who is very up and down in her emotions. But I guess you don't know her as well as I do."

"She seemed quite happy to be going."

"Did she really? Well, I have to take your word for it. I didn't come here to argue with you."

Sylvia said nothing.

"Actually, I came here not just to return those clothes. I came here to tell you that I don't appreciate you interfering in my life with my wife."

"She is a human being," Sylvia said, though she knew that it would be better if she could keep quiet. "Besides being your wife."

"My goodness, is that so? My wife is a human being? Really? Thank you for the information. But don't try getting smart with me. Sylvia."

"I wasn't trying to get smart."

"Good. I'm glad you weren't. I don't want to get mad. I just have a couple of important things to say to you. One thing—that I don't want you sticking your nose in anywhere, anytime, in my life. Another—that I'm not going to want her coming around here anymore. Not that she is going to want to come, I'm pretty sure of that. She doesn't have too good an opinion of you at the moment. And it's time you learned how to clean your own house. Now—" he said. "Now. Has that sunk in?"

"Quite sufficiently."

"Oh, I really hope it has. I hope so."

Sylvia said, "Yes."

"And you know what else I think?"

"What?"

"I think you owe me something."

"What?"

"I think you owe me—you owe me an apology."

Sylvia said, "All right. If you think so. I'm sorry."

He shifted, perhaps just to put out his hand, and with the movement of his body she shrieked.

He laughed. He put his hand on the doorframe to make sure she didn't close it.

"What's that?"

"What's what?" he said, as if she were trying out a trick and it would not work. But then he caught sight of something reflected in the window, and he snapped around to look.

Not far from the house was a wide shallow patch of land that often filled up with night fog at this time of year. The fog was there tonight, had been there all this while. But now the fog had changed. It had thickened, taken on a separate shape, transformed itself into something spiky and radiant. First, a live dandelion ball, tumbling forward, then it condensed itself into an unearthly sort of animal, pure white, hellbent, something like a giant unicorn rushing at them.

"Jesus Christ," Clark said softly. He grabbed hold of Sylvia's shoulder. This touch did not alarm her at all—she accepted it with the knowledge that he did it either to protect her or to reassure himself.

Then the vision exploded. Out of the fog, and out of the magnifying light—now revealed to be that of a car travelling along this back road, probably in search of a place to park—out of this appeared a white goat. A little dancing white goat, hardly bigger than a sheepdog.

Clark let go. He said, "Where the Christ did you come from?"

"It's your goat," Sylvia said. "Isn't it your goat?"

"Flora," he said. "Flora."

The goat had stopped a yard or so away from them, had turned shy, and hung her head.

"Flora," Clark said. "Where the hell did you come from? You scared the shit out of us."

Us.

Flora came closer but still did not look up. She butted against Clark's legs.

"Goddam stupid animal," he said shakily.

"She was lost," Sylvia said.

"Yeah. She was. Never thought we'd see her again, actually."

Flora looked up. The moonlight caught a glitter in her eyes.

"Scared the shit out of us," Clark said to her. "We thought you were a ghost."

"It was the effect of the fog," Sylvia said. She stepped out of the door now, onto the patio. Quite safe.

"Yeah."

"Then the lights of that car."

"Like an apparition," he said, recovering. And pleased that he had thought of this description.

"Yes."

"The goat from outer space. That's what you are. You are a goddam goat from outer space," he said, patting Flora. But when Sylvia put out her hand to do the same Flora immediately lowered her head as if preparing to butt.

"Goats are unpredictable," Clark said. "They can seem tame but they're not really. Not after they grow up."

"Is she grown up? She looks so small."

"She's as big as she's ever going to get."

They stood looking down at the goat, as if hoping that she would provide them with more conversation. But she apparently was not going to. From this moment, they could go neither forward nor back. Sylvia believed that she might have seen a shadow of regret in his eyes that this was so.

But he acknowledged it. He said, "It's late."

"I guess it is," Sylvia said, just as if this had been an ordinary visit.

"O.K., Flora. Time for us to go home."

"I'll make other arrangements for help if I need it," she said. "I probably won't need it now, anyway." She added lightly, "I'll stay out of your hair."

"Sure," he said. "You'd better get inside. You'll get cold."

"Good night," she said. "Good night, Flora."

The phone rang then.

"Excuse me."

"Good night."

It was Ruth.

"Ah," Sylvia said. "A change in plans."

She did not sleep, thinking of the little goat, whose appearance out of the fog seemed to her more and more magical. She even wondered if, possibly, Leon could have had something to do with it. If she were a poet, she would write a poem about something like this. But in her experience the subjects that she thought a poet would write about had not appealed to Leon, who was—who had been—the real thing.

Carla had not heard Clark go out, but she woke when he came in.

He told her that he had just been checking around the barn.

"A car went along the road a while ago, and I wondered what it was doing here. I couldn't get back to sleep till I went out and checked whether everything was O.K."

"So, was it?"

"Far as I could see. And then while I was up," he said, "I thought I might as well pay a visit up the road. I took the clothes back."

Carla sat up in bed.

"You didn't wake her up?"

"She woke up. It was O.K. We had a little talk."

"Oh."

"It was O.K."

"You didn't mention any of that stuff, did you?"

"I didn't mention it."

"It really was all made up. It really was. You have to believe me. It was all a lie."

"O.K."

"You have to believe me."

"Then I believe you."

"I made it all up."

"O.K."

He got into bed.

"Did you get your feet wet?" she said.

"Heavy dew."

He turned to her.

"Come here," he said. "When I read your note, it was just like I went hollow inside. It's true. I felt like I didn't have anything left in me."

The bright weather had continued. On the streets, in the stores, in the post office, people greeted each other by saying that summer had finally arrived. The pasture grass and even the poor beaten crops lifted up their heads. The puddles dried up, the mud turned to dust. A light warm wind blew and everybody felt like doing things again. The phone rang. Inquiries about trail rides, about riding lessons. Summer camps cancelled their trips to museums, and minivans drew up, loaded with restless children. The horses pranced along the fences, freed from their blankets.

Clark had managed to get hold of a piece of roofing at a good price. He had spent the whole first day after Runaway Day (that was how they referred to Carla's bus trip) fixing the roof of the exercise ring.

For a couple of days, as they went about their chores, he and Carla would wave at each other. If she happened to pass close to him and there was nobody else around, Carla might kiss his shoulder through the light material of his summer shirt.

"If you ever try to run away on me again I'll tan your hide," he said to her, and she said, "Who are you now—Clint Eastwood?"

Then she said, "Would you?"

"What?"

"Tan my hide?"

"Damn right."

Birds were everywhere. Red-winged blackbirds, robins, a pair of doves that sang at daybreak. Lots of crows, and gulls on reconnoitering missions from the lake, and big turkey buzzards that sat in the branches of a dead oak about half a mile away, at the edge of the woods. At first they just sat there, drying out their voluminous wings, lifting themselves occasionally for a trial flight, flapping around a bit, then composing themselves, to let the sun and the warm air do their work. In a day or so, they were restored, flying high, circling and dropping to earth, disappearing over the woods, coming back to rest in the familiar bare tree.

Lizzie Borden's owner—Joy Tucker—showed up again, tanned and friendly. She had got sick of the rain, and gone off on her holidays to hike in the Rocky Mountains. Now she was back. Perfect timing.

She and Clark treated each other warily at first, but they were soon joking as if nothing had happened.

"Lizzie looks to be in good shape," she said. "But where's her little friend?"

"Gone," Clark said. "Maybe she took off to the Rocky Mountains."

"Lots of wild goats out there. With fantastic horns."

"So I hear."

For three or four days they had been too busy to go down and look in the mailbox. When Carla opened it, she found the phone bill, a promise that if they subscribed to a certain magazine they could win a million dollars, and Mrs. Jamieson's letter.

> *My Dear Carla,*
> *I have been thinking about the (rather dramatic) events of the last few days and I find myself talking to myself, but really to you, so often that I thought I must speak to you, even if—the best way I can do now—only in a letter. And don't worry—you do not have to answer me.*

Mrs. Jamieson went on to say that she was afraid she had involved herself too closely in Carla's life and had made the mistake of thinking somehow that Carla's freedom and happiness were the same thing. All she cared for was Carla's happiness, and she saw now that she—Carla—had found that in her marriage. All she could hope was that perhaps Carla's flight and turbulent emotions had brought her true feelings to the surface, and perhaps a recognition in her husband of his true feelings as well.

She said that she would perfectly understand if Carla wished to avoid her in the future and that she would always be grateful for Carla's presence in her life during such a difficult time.

The strangest and most wonderful thing in this whole string of events seems to me the reappearance of Flora. In fact, it seems rather like a miracle. Where had she been all that time and why did she choose just that moment to reappear? I am sure your husband has described it to you. We were talking at the patio door, and I—facing out—was the first to see this white something, descending on us out of the night. Of course it was the effect of the ground fog. But truly terrifying. I think I shrieked out loud. I had never in my life felt such bewitchment, in the true sense. I suppose I should be honest and say fear. There we were, two adults, frozen, and then out of the fog comes little lost Flora.

There has to be something special about this. I know, of course, that Flora is an ordinary little animal and that she probably spent her time away getting herself pregnant. In a sense, her return has no connection at all with our human lives. Yet her appearance at that moment did have a profound effect on your husband and me. When two human beings divided by hostility are both, at the same time, mystified by the same apparition, there is a bond that springs up between them, and they find themselves united in the most unexpected way. United in their humanity—that is the only way I can describe it. We parted almost as friends. So Flora has her place as a good angel in my life and perhaps also in your husband's life and yours.

With all my good wishes,
Sylvia Jamieson

As soon as Carla had read this letter she crumpled it up. Then she burned it in the sink. The flames leaped up alarmingly and she turned on the tap, then scooped up the soft disgusting black stuff and put it down the toilet, as she should have done in the first place.

She was busy for the rest of that day, and the next, and the next. During that time, she had to take two parties out on the trails, she had to give lessons to children, individually and in groups. At night when Clark put his arms around her—he was generally in good spirits now—she did not find it hard to be cooperative. She dreamed of things that were of no importance, that made no sense.

It was as if she had a murderous needle somewhere in her lungs, and by breathing carefully she could avoid feeling it. But every once in a while she had to take a deep breath, and it was still there.

Sylvia Jamieson had taken an apartment in the college town where she taught. The house was not up for sale—or at least there wasn't a sign out in front of it. Leon Jamieson had got some kind of posthumous award—news of this was in the papers. There was no mention of any money.

As the dry golden days of fall came on—an encouraging and profitable season— Carla found that she had got used to the sharp thought that had lodged inside her. It wasn't so sharp anymore; in fact, it no longer surprised her. She was inhabited now by an almost seductive notion, a constant low-lying temptation.

She had only to raise her eyes, she had only to look in one direction, to know where she might go. An evening walk, once her chores for the day were finished. To the edge of the woods, and the bare tree where she had seen the buzzards.

Where she might find the little dirty bones in the grass. The skull, with shreds of bloodied skin still clinging to it, that she could settle in one hand. Knowledge in one hand.

Or perhaps not.

Suppose something else had happened. Suppose he had chased Flora away, or tied her in the back of the truck and driven some distance and let her loose. Taken her back to the place they'd got her from. Not to have her around, reminding them of this bad time.

The days passed and she didn't go. She held out against the temptation.

Topics for Discussion

1) What do you think of the relationship between Carla and Clark?
2) When does the story happen?
3) What is Clark's temper like?
4) How does the relationship between Clark and Flora change?
5) What's Sylvia's attitude when Carla runs away?
6) Why does Carla return from running away?
7) What does Clark imply when he says "[g]oats are unpredictable"?
8) What role does the description of the weather play in narration?
9) Why does Clark kill Flora?
10) What does "runaway" indicate in the story?

Interdisciplinary Concepts for Further Thinking

Scapegoating

A scapegoat referred literally to an "escaped goat" in the wilderness. It was necessary because the people of Israel could not enter into any kind of relationship with God unless that which separated them from Him—sins and transgressions—were "sent away".

Emile Durkheim put forth a theory of scapegoating that connects perspectives in sociology, anthropology, psychology, law, and religion. Durkheim believed that, when any misfortune that causes feelings of disquiet and fear occurs, both the individual and society are threatened with disintegration, and they resort to a specific set of rituals to regain the stability and sense of integration that they had lost. These rites involve the processes of blame, sacrifice, and scapegoating. Fauconnet (1920) elaborated on Durkheim's insight by saying that, historically, animals and inanimate objects as well as people and groups have been blamed, condemned, and punished as a way to atone for death. For example, animals and insects have been killed and driven out of European countries as scapegoats for the plague and other misfortunes. This happens not because these things or groups of people are objectively responsible, but because responsibility must fall on someone or something.

Sociologists generally recognize four ways in which scapegoating takes place and through which scapegoats are created: one-on-one form, one-on-group form, group-on-one form and group-on-group form. As for one-on-one phenomenon, one person blames another for something they did. In a one-on-group manner, one person blames a group for a problem they did not cause, which involves war, deaths, financial losses, or other personal struggles. This form of scapegoating can be put on racial, ethnic, religious, or class groups. Scapegoating can also take on a group-on-one form, meaning that a group of people singles out and blames one person for a problem. Finally, scapegoating can have a group-on-group form. This is of particular interest to sociologists, and can happen when one group blames another for problems that the group collectively experiences.

 1) Who is a scapegoat in "Runaway"?
 2) Why is the scapegoat needed in human society?

Thinking in Numbers

In the story, Carla runs away multiple times either physically or spiritually. She elopes with Clark to avoid going back to her parents, but returns after a short time, leaving Clark. What are three reasons she decided to return?

Visual Thinking with Mind Mapping

In the short story, "Runaway" is the central topic. In reality, every one has some occasions, harsh or dark moments, when he or she wants to flee. Carla elopes with Clark from her parents because of love, and she runs away from Clark because of dullness and frustration in family life. Does she lose her love for Clark? And then why does she choose to come back? Is her behavior reasonable? Create a mind map to analyze Carla's actions.

Critical Thinking for Reality

In our life, every one of us might have some moments to have the impulse to run away from our parents, friends, the school, or the environment. On these occasions, how will you control your emotions, and will you compromise with an unsatisfactory life? Why?

Section Three

Body-Mind Harmony: Self-Relationship

In modern society, people are becoming more and more anxious in an increasingly competitive environment, particularly young people who have only begun to face all kinds of fierce challenges in their studies and work. Relevant studies show that the percentage of young people experiencing mental health disorders has risen significantly over the past decade. More adolescents and young adults have experienced serious psychological distress, major depression, or even suicidal thoughts. Young people are the future of the nation and world. Therefore, body and mind harmony, that is, balancing one's physical and mental health, is becoming an important social issue.

As the world's second-largest economy since 2010, China has now achieved, on schedule, its first centenary goal of building a moderately prosperous society in all respects. It also has begun a new journey toward the second centenary goal of building a modern socialist country in all respects, which depends on the efforts of our nation's youth. Their career development and contributions to China are essential to the whole society. They are endowed with a lot of expectations, and there is still a lot of work to be done to make sure they are healthy and happy. Harmony between the mind and body is, without doubt, the foundation for young people's well-being. In this case, young people must become more aware of the issue and learn to balance their bodies and minds throughout daily life.

In English literature, numerous works disclose the tragedy of main characters regarding the imbalance of mind and body during different time periods. Manifestations of the human psyche and the natural consequences of an unbalanced state of mind and body are depicted in these works. Despite being fictional, these works provide readers across time and space a chance to delve into the human psyche and consider psychological issues they might or might not encounter in real life. Therefore, understanding important psychological theories and key concepts, such as

trauma, major depression, psychological disorder, etc., is critical, not only to better appreciate and analyze these literary works but also to guide and assist young people in attaching enough importance to their well-being and improving their health. In this way, they can gradually learn to build a harmonious self-relationship to better face the pressure, difficulties, and opportunities of the present and the future.

Unit 8
A Rose for Emily

William Faulkner

Introduction to the Author

William Faulkner (1897—1962) was an American novelist and short-story writer, often cited as one of the most celebrated writers in the history of American literature and the greatest writer of Southern literature. During his lifetime, he wrote 19 novels and nearly 100 short stories, most of which took place in a county called Yoknapatawpha, a fictional Mississippi county. Faulkner was best known for his pioneering use of "stream of consciousness" technique and in-depth characterization. He was awarded the 1949 Nobel Prize for Literature "for his powerful and artistically unique contribution to the modern American novel." And he won the Pulitzer Prize for Fiction in 1955 and 1963 respectively. His most famous works include novels such as *The Sound and the Fury* (1929), *As I Lay Dying* (1930) and *Absalom, Absalom!* (1936).

Introduction to the Work

First published on April 30, 1930, "A Rose for Emily" is a short story by William Faulkner. This story takes place in Jefferson, a fictional city in the fictional Yoknapatawpha County. The story is told in a non-linear way from the townspeople's point of view. Emily Grierson, an aristocratic woman, is the subject of the story. The first person plural narrator "we" speculates Emily's abnormal relationships with her father and her lover, the Yankee road worker Homer Barron, as well as the strange circumstances of her life. Many residents of the town believe she plans to kill herself with the arsenic she bought earlier. Homer Barron is presumed to have returned north after he is not heard from again. Despite the fact that Emily does not kill herself, Jefferson's residents continue to spread rumors about her aloofness and the history of her family. She becomes more and more self-reclusive and is heard from less and less. After Emily dies, Homer's corpse was found in her upstairs bedroom, which explains the smell of decay emanating from her house 40 years ago.

Suspense and disorderly narration make this story intriguing enough for readers. The juxtaposition of external and internal conflicts helps clarify the message of the story. The external conflict between the tradition and progress is drawn by Faulkner. At the same time, Emily's internal conflict revolves around the shifts in society and her outmoded mentalities, which appear to be destructive. She is unable to adapt her actions and thoughts to the new reality anymore.

Text

A Rose For Emily

I

When Miss Emily Grierson died, our whole town went to her funeral: the men through a sort of respectful affection for a fallen monument, the women mostly out of curiosity to see the inside of her house, which no one save an old manservant—a combined gardener and cook—had seen in at least ten years.

It was a big, squarish frame house that had once been white, decorated with cupolas and spires and scrolled balconies in the heavily lightsome style of the seventies, set on what had once been our most select street. But garages and cotton gins had encroached and obliterated even the august names of that neighborhood; only Miss Emily's house was left, lifting its stubborn and coquettish decay above the cotton wagons and the gasoline pumps—an eyesore among eyesores. And now Miss Emily had gone to join the representatives of those august names where they lay in the cedar-bemused cemetery among the ranked and anonymous graves of Union and Confederate soldiers who fell at the battle of Jefferson.

Alive, Miss Emily had been a tradition, a duty, and a care; a sort of hereditary obligation upon the town, dating from that day in 1894 when Colonel Sartoris, the mayor—he who fathered the edict that no Negro woman should appear on the streets without an apron—remitted her taxes, the dispensation dating from the death of her father on into perpetuity. Not that Miss Emily would have accepted charity. Colonel Sartoris invented an involved tale to the effect that Miss Emily's father had loaned money to the town, which the town, as a matter of business, preferred this way of repaying. Only a man of Colonel Sartoris' generation and thought could have invented it, and only a woman could have believed it.

When the next generation, with its more modern ideas, became mayors and aldermen, this arrangement created some little dissatisfaction. On the first of the year they mailed her a tax notice. February came, and there was no reply. They wrote her a formal letter, asking her to call at the sheriff's office at her convenience. A week later the mayor wrote her himself, offering to call or to send his car for her, and received in reply a note on paper of an archaic shape, in a thin, flowing calligraphy in faded ink, to the effect that she no longer went out at all. The tax notice was also enclosed, without comment.

They called a special meeting of the Board of Aldermen. A deputation waited upon her, knocked at the door through which no visitor had passed since she ceased giving china-painting lessons eight or ten years earlier. They were admitted by the old Negro into a dim hall from which a stairway mounted into still more shadow. It smelled of dust and disuse—a close, dank smell. The Negro led them into the parlor. It was furnished in heavy, leather-covered furniture. When the Negro opened the blinds of one window, they could see that the leather was cracked; and when they sat down, a faint dust rose sluggishly about their thighs, spinning with slow motes in the single sun-ray. On a tarnished gilt easel before the fireplace stood a crayon portrait of Miss Emily's father.

They rose when she entered—a small, fat woman in black, with a thin gold chain descending to her waist and vanishing into her belt, leaning on an ebony cane with a tarnished gold head. Her skeleton was small and spare; perhaps that was why what would have been merely plumpness in another was obesity in her. She looked bloated, like a body long submerged in motionless water, and of that pallid hue. Her eyes, lost in the fatty ridges of her face, looked like two small pieces of coal pressed into a lump of dough as they moved from one face to another while the visitors stated their errand.

She did not ask them to sit. She just stood in the door and listened quietly until the spokesman came to a stumbling halt. Then they could hear the invisible watch ticking at the end of the gold chain.

Her voice was dry and cold. "I have no taxes in Jefferson. Colonel Sartoris explained it to me. Perhaps one of you can gain access to the city records and satisfy yourselves."

"But we have. We are the city authorities, Miss Emily. Didn't you get a notice from the sheriff, signed by him?"

"I received a paper, yes," Miss Emily said. "Perhaps he considers himself the sheriff... I have no taxes in Jefferson."

"But there is nothing on the books to show that, you see We must go by the—"

"See Colonel Sartoris. I have no taxes in Jefferson."

"But, Miss Emily—"

"See Colonel Sartoris." (Colonel Sartoris had been dead almost ten years.) "I have no taxes in Jefferson. Tobe!" The Negro appeared. "Show these gentlemen out."

II

So she vanquished them, horse and foot, just as she had vanquished their fathers thirty years before about the smell.

That was two years after her father's death and a short time after her sweetheart—the one we believed would marry her—had deserted her. After her father's death she went out very little; after her sweetheart went away, people hardly saw her at all. A few of the ladies had the temerity to call, but were not received, and the only sign of life about the place was the Negro man—a young man then—going in and out with a market basket.

"Just as if a man—any man—could keep a kitchen properly, "the ladies said; so they were not surprised when the smell developed. It was another link between the gross, teeming world and the high and mighty Griersons.

A neighbor, a woman, complained to the mayor, Judge Stevens, eighty years old.

"But what will you have me do about it, madam?" he said.

"Why, send her word to stop it," the woman said. "Isn't there a law?"

"I'm sure that won't be necessary," Judge Stevens said. "It's probably just a snake or a rat that nigger of hers killed in the yard. I'll speak to him about it."

The next day he received two more complaints, one from a man who came in diffident deprecation. "We really must do something about it, Judge. I'd be the last one in the world to bother Miss Emily, but we've got to do something." That night the Board of Aldermen met—three graybeards and one younger man, a member of the rising generation.

"It's simple enough," he said. "Send her word to have her place cleaned up. Give her a certain time to do it in, and if she don't..."

"Dammit, sir," Judge Stevens said, "will you accuse a lady to her face of smelling bad?"

So the next night, after midnight, four men crossed Miss Emily's lawn and slunk about the house like burglars, sniffing along the base of the brickwork and at the cellar openings while one of them performed a regular sowing motion with his hand out of a sack slung from his shoulder. They broke open the cellar door and sprinkled lime there, and in all the outbuildings. As they recrossed the lawn, a window that had been dark was lighted and Miss Emily sat in it, the light behind her, and her upright torso motionless as that of an idol. They crept quietly across the lawn and into the shadow of the locusts that lined the street. After a week or two the smell went away.

That was when people had begun to feel really sorry for her. People in our town, remembering how old lady Wyatt, her great-aunt, had gone completely crazy at last, believed that the Griersons held themselves a little too high for what they really were. None of the young men were quite good enough for Miss Emily and such. We had long thought of them as a tableau, Miss Emily a slender figure in white in the background, her father a spraddled silhouette in the foreground, his back to her and clutching a horsewhip, the two of them framed by the back-flung front door. So when she got to be thirty and was still single, we were not pleased exactly, but vindicated; even with insanity in the family she wouldn't have turned down all of her chances if they had really materialized.

When her father died, it got about that the house was all that was left to her; and in a way, people were glad. At last they could pity Miss Emily. Being left alone, and a pauper, she had become humanized. Now she too would know the old thrill and the old despair of a penny more or less.

The day after his death all the ladies prepared to call at the house and offer condolence and aid, as is our custom Miss Emily met them at the door, dressed as usual and with no trace of grief on her face. She told them that her father was not dead. She did that for three days, with the ministers calling on her, and the doctors, trying to persuade her to let them dispose of the body. Just as they were about to resort to law and force, she broke down, and they buried her father quickly.

We did not say she was crazy then. We believed she had to do that. We remembered all the young men her father had driven away, and we knew that with nothing left, she would have to cling to that which had robbed her, as people will.

III

She was sick for a long time. When we saw her again, her hair was cut short, making her look like a girl, with a vague resemblance to those angels in colored church windows—sort of tragic and serene.

The town had just let the contracts for paving the sidewalks, and in the summer after her father's death they began the work. The construction company came with riggers and mules and machinery, and a foreman named Homer Barron, a Yankee—a big, dark, ready man, with a big voice and eyes lighter than his face. The little boys would follow in groups to hear him cuss the riggers, and the riggers singing in time to the rise and fall of picks. Pretty soon he knew everybody in town. Whenever you heard a lot of laughing anywhere about the square, Homer Barron would be in the center of the group. Presently we began to see him and Miss Emily on Sunday afternoons driving in the yellow-wheeled buggy and the matched team of bays from the livery stable.

At first we were glad that Miss Emily would have an interest, because the ladies all said, "Of course a Grierson would not think seriously of a Northerner, a day laborer." But there were still others, older people, who said that even grief could not cause a real lady to forget noblesse oblige—without calling it noblesse oblige. They just said, "Poor Emily. Her kinsfolk should come to her." She had some kin in Alabama; but years ago her father had fallen out with them over the estate of old lady Wyatt, the crazy woman, and there was no communication between the two families. They had not even been represented at the funeral.

And as soon as the old people said, "Poor Emily," the whispering began. "Do you suppose it's really so?" they said to one another. "Of course it is. What else could . . ." This behind their hands; rustling of craned silk and satin behind jalousies closed upon the sun of Sunday afternoon as the thin, swift clop-clop-clop of the matched team passed: "Poor Emily."

She carried her head high enough—even when we believed that she was fallen. It was as if she demanded more than ever the recognition of her dignity as the last Grierson; as if it had wanted that touch of earthiness to reaffirm her imperviousness. Like when she bought the rat poison, the arsenic. That was over a year after they had begun to say "Poor Emily," and while the two female cousins were visiting her.

"I want some poison," she said to the druggist. She was over thirty then, still a slight woman, though thinner than usual, with cold, haughty black eyes in a face the flesh of which was strained across the temples and about the eyesockets as you imagine a lighthouse-keeper's face ought to look. "I want some poison," she said.

"Yes, Miss Emily. What kind? For rats and such? I'd recom—"

"I want the best you have. I don't care what kind."

The druggist named several. "They'll kill anything up to an elephant. But what you want is—"

"Arsenic," Miss Emily said. "Is that a good one?"

"Is . . . arsenic? Yes, ma'am. But what you want—"

"I want arsenic."

The druggist looked down at her. She looked back at him, erect, her face like a strained flag. "Why, of course," the druggist said. "If that's what you want. But the law requires you to tell what you are going to use it for."

Miss Emily just stared at him, her head tilted back in order to look him eye for eye, until he looked away and went and got the arsenic and wrapped it up. The Negro delivery boy brought her the package; the druggist didn't come back. When she opened the package at home there was written on the box, under the skull and bones: "For rats."

IV

So the next day we all said, "She will kill herself"; and we said it would be the best thing. When she had first begun to be seen with Homer Barron, we had said, "She will marry him." Then we said, "She will persuade him yet," because Homer himself had remarked—he liked men, and it was known that he drank with the younger men in the Elks' Club—that he was not a marrying man. Later we said, "Poor Emily" behind the jalousies as they passed on Sunday afternoon in the glittering buggy, Miss Emily with her head high and Homer Barron with his hat cocked and a cigar in his teeth, reins and whip in a yellow glove.

Then some of the ladies began to say that it was a disgrace to the town and a bad example to the young people. The men did not want to interfere, but at last the ladies forced the Baptist minister—Miss Emily's people were Episcopal—to call upon her. He would never divulge what happened during that interview, but he refused to go back again. The next Sunday they again drove about the streets, and the following day the minister's wife wrote to Miss Emily's relations in Alabama.

So she had blood-kin under her roof again and we sat back to watch developments. At first nothing happened. Then we were sure that they were to be married. We learned that Miss Emily had been to the jeweler's and ordered a man's toilet set in silver, with the letters H. B. on each piece. Two days later we learned that she had bought a complete outfit of men's clothing, including a nightshirt, and we said, "They are married." We were really glad. We were glad because the two female cousins were even more Grierson than Miss Emily had ever been.

So we were not surprised when Homer Barron—the streets had been finished some time since—was gone. We were a little disappointed that there was not a public blowing-off, but we believed that he had gone on to prepare for Miss Emily's coming, or to give her a chance to get rid of the cousins. (By that time it was a cabal, and we were all Miss Emily's allies to help circumvent the cousins. Sure enough, after another week they departed. And, as we had expected all along, within three days Homer Barron was back in town. A neighbor saw the Negro man admit him at the kitchen door at dusk one eventing.

And that was the last we saw of Homer Barron. And of Miss Emily for some time. The Negro man went in and out with the market basket, but the front door remained closed. Now and then we would see her at a window for a moment, as the men did that night when they sprinkled the lime, but for almost six months she did not appear on the streets. Then we knew that this was to be expected too; as if that quality of her father which had thwarted her woman's life so many times had been too virulent and too furious to die.

When we next saw Miss Emily, she had grown fat and her hair was turning gray. During the next few years it grew grayer and grayer until it attained an even pepper-

and-salt iron-gray, when it ceased turning. Up to the day of her death at seventy-four it was still that vigorous iron-gray, like the hair of an active man.

From that time on her front door remained closed, save for a period of six or seven years, when she was about forty, during which she gave lessons in china-painting. She fitted up a studio in one of the downstairs rooms, where the daughters and granddaughters of Colonel Sartoris' contemporaries were sent to her with the same regularity and in the same spirit that they were sent to church on Sundays with a twenty-five-cent piece for the collection plate. Meanwhile her taxes had been remitted.

Then the newer generation became the backbone and the spirit of the town, and the painting pupils grew up and fell away and did not send their children to her with boxes of color and tedious brushes and pictures cut from the ladies' magazines. The front door closed upon the last one and remained closed for good. When the town got free postal delivery, Miss Emily alone refused to let them fasten the metal numbers above her door and attach a mailbox to it. She would not listen to them.

Daily, monthly, yearly we watched the Negro grow grayer and more stooped, going in and out with the market basket. Each December we sent her a tax notice, which would be returned by the postoffice a week later, unclaimed. Now and then we would see her in one of the downstairs windows—she had evidently shut up the top floor of the house—like the carven torso of an idol in a niche, looking or not looking at us, we could never tell which. Thus she passed from generation to generation—dear, inescapable, impervious, tranquil, and perverse.

And so she died. Fell ill in the house filled with dust and shadows, with only a doddering Negro man to wait on her. We did not even know she was sick; we had long since given up trying to get any information from the Negro.

He talked to no one, probably not even to her, for his voice had grown harsh and rusty, as if from disuse.

She died in one of the downstairs rooms, in a heavy walnut bed with a curtain, her gray head propped on a pillow yellow and moldy with age and lack of sunlight.

V

The negro met the first of the ladies at the front door and let them in, with their hushed, sibilant voices and their quick, curious glances, and then he disappeared. He walked right through the house and out the back and was not seen again.

The two female cousins came at once. They held the funeral on the second day, with the town coming to look at Miss Emily beneath a mass of bought flowers, with the crayon face of her father musing profoundly above the bier and the ladies sibilant and macabre; and the very old men—some in their brushed Confederate uniforms—on the porch and the lawn, talking of Miss Emily as if she had been a contemporary of theirs, believing that they had danced with her and courted her perhaps, confusing time with its mathematical progression, as the old do, to whom all the past is not a diminishing road but, instead, a huge meadow which no winter ever quite touches, divided from them now by the narrow bottle neck of the most recent decade of years.

Already we knew that there was one room in that region above stairs which no one had seen in forty years, and which would have to be forced. They waited until Miss Emily was decently in the ground before they opened it.

The violence of breaking down the door seemed to fill this room with pervading dust. A thin, acrid pall as of the tomb seemed to lie everywhere upon this room decked and furnished as for a bridal: upon the valance curtains of faded rose color, upon the rose-shaded lights, upon the dressing table, upon the delicate array of crystal and the man's toilet things backed with tarnished silver, silver so tarnished that the monogram was obscured. Among them lay a collar and tie, as if they had just been removed, which, lifted, left upon the surface a pale crescent in the dust. Upon a chair hung the suit, carefully folded; beneath it the two mute shoes and the discarded socks.

The man himself lay in the bed.

For a long while we just stood there, looking down at the profound and fleshless grin. The body had apparently once lain in the attitude of an embrace, but now the long sleep that outlasts love, that conquers even the grimace of love, had cuckolded him. What was left of him, rotted beneath what was left of the nightshirt, had become inextricable from the bed in which he lay; and upon him and upon the pillow beside him lay that even coating of the patient and biding dust.

Then we noticed that in the second pillow was the indentation of a head. One of us lifted something from it, and leaning forward, that faint and invisible dust dry and acrid in the nostrils, we saw a long strand of iron-gray hair.

Topics for Discussion

1) What are the main incidents of the story?
2) What are the multiple identities of Emily?
3) When and where does the story happen?
4) How much do you know about Emily from her birth to her death?
5) How many people die in the story and how does it happen?
6) What is the historical background of the story?
7) When do townspeople begin to say "Poor Emily" and why?
8) What is the timeline of the story?

9) What are the possible reasons for Homer Barren to say that he loves men?

10) Why does Emily refuse to pay the tax and what does it imply?

Interdisciplinary Concepts for Further Thinking

Hierarchy of Needs

"Hierarchy of Needs" is a concept in psychology.

Abraham Maslow first introduced the concept of hierarchy of needs in his 1943 paper, titled "A Theory of Human Motivation," and again in his subsequent book, *Motivation and Personality*. This hierarchy suggests that people are motivated to fulfill basic needs before moving on to other more advanced needs.

Maslow's hierarchy of needs theory is a motivational theory that states that humans are motivated by a distinct set of needs placed on an upward trajectory. Maslow placed these needs into five distinct tiers, namely: physiological needs, safety and security needs, love and belonging needs, esteem needs, and self-actualization needs.

The two bottom levels—physiological needs and safety and security needs—are within the "basic needs" category. The next two tiers—love and belonging needs and esteem needs—are within the "psychological needs" category. And finally, the top tier—self-actualization—is in the "self-fulfillment needs" category. Within the basic needs and psychological needs categories there are "deficiency needs," which are needs you are deprived of and must gain in order to move up Maslow's pyramid of needs. Within the self-fulfillment needs category there are "growth needs", which, as the name suggests, are needs that allow you to grow as a human being. This is to say, these needs are hierarchical in nature.

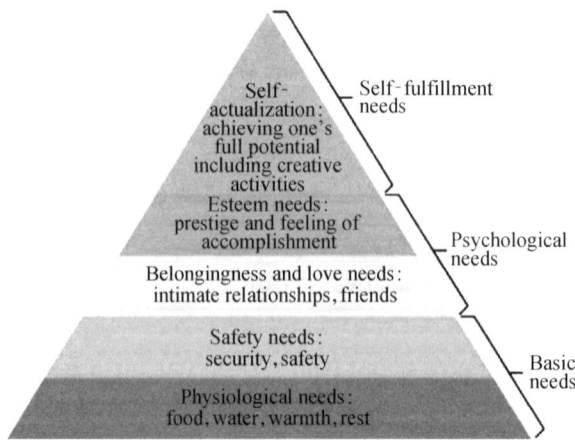

Choice theory contends that every part of our behavior—thoughts, feelings, physiology and doings—is a choice.

Choice Theory understands that humans have five basic needs—freedom, power, fun, love and belonging and security. Our needs may vary but they remain the same throughout our lives, although our behavior—our attempts to meet the needs—may change. Glasser's term "Quality World" refers to all the significant things or people and relationships that are important to us. All of those things in the Quality World are meeting one of our "five basic needs" and can usually be replaced, apart from our parents, who are irreplaceable.

1) Adopt the theory of hierarchy of needs to analyze all of eccentric behaviours of Emily.

2) What do you think the quality of Emily's world is?

Thinking in Numbers

1) The number "three" can be effective in thinking and analyzing "A Rose for Emily". Three important characters die in the narration; three men who play important roles in Emily's life; Emily's life can be divided into three periods; Emily's relationship with Homer Barron can be thought of as three phases and Emily's hair is mentioned three times. Please analyze these "threes" and their inner connections in the story.

2) The word "dust" appears 4 times and "smell" 7 times in the story. What do they indicate respectively? How are these words employed to demonstrate Emily's choices and life condition?

Visual Thinking with Mind Mapping

One of the biggest features of "A Rose for Emily" is its chaotic time sequence. The story covers the whole life of Emily Grierson, but it is not narrated chronologically. Create a mind map to reorganize and demonstrate Emily's life experience, highlighting the important events and turning points of her life.

Critical Thinking for Reality

In "A Rose for Emily", Emily is a noblewoman in the American South. What is hard to understand is that she chooses to condescend to be together with Homer Barron, a Yankee. The townspeople feel their relationship is a disgrace to the whole town. What are the possible considerations of Emily? What are the pros and cons of it? Do you think Emily makes a wise choice? Why?

Unit 9
From *An American Tragedy*

Theodore Dreiser

Introduction to the Author

Theodore Dreiser (1871—1945) was an American novelist, journalist and one of the representative practitioners of the school of naturalism. His novels mostly investigated the emerging social issues in a rapidly industrializing American society which was replete with abundant material possessions and spiritual dilemma. Theodore Dreiser's works were successful because they dealt with the subject matter realistically and drew out the tragic aspects of the American pursuit of success in the 20th century in a powerful and intense way. Dreiser was up against the censorship forces due to his authentic portrayals of characters whose lives were thought to be amoral in reality at that time, like infidelity and prostitution. *Sister Carrie* (1900) and *The American Tragedy* (1925) are the most well-known works of Theodore Dreiser.

Introduction to the Work

The American Tragedy is a novel by Theodore Dreiser, published in 1925. It recounts the life and death of a young antihero named Clyde Griffiths. It begins with Clyde's troubled upbringing, his rise to success, and ends with his capture, trial, and execution for murder. Like what the title suggests, the story was a tragedy. Clyde's demise is caused by his inherent weaknesses: moral and physical cowardice, a lack of self-control and scruples, a muddled mind, and a vague goal. The perplexing speculations that Dreiser makes regarding the extent of Clyde's guilt do not lessen his fiery critique of materialism and the American dream of success in the 20th century.

By adding details and constantly varying his "emotional distance" from Clyde and other characters, from in-depth examinations of their inner thoughts and motivations to objective description, Dreiser manages to hold reader's attention throughout the whole novel. *The American Tragedy* was considered Theodore Dreiser's first commercial success, which has been adapted into other artistic forms for several times.

Text

The American Tragedy
(Excerpt)

Chapter 42

TWO letters, which arrived at this time and simultaneously, but accentuated the difficulty of all this.

Pine Point Landing, June 10th

CLYDE MYDIE:

How is my pheet phing? All whytie? It's just glorious up here. Lots of people already here and more coming every day. The Casino and golf course over at Pine Point are open and lots of people about. I can hear Stuart and Grant with their launches going up toward Gray's Inlet now. You must hurry and come up, dear. It's too nice for words. Green roads to gallop through, and swimming and dancing at the Casino every afternoon at four. Just back from a wonderful gallop on Dickey and going again after luncheon to mail these letters. Bertine says she'll write you a letter to-day or tomorrow good for any week-end or any old time, so when Sonda says come, you come, you hear, else Sonda whip hard. You baddie, good boy.

Is he working hard in the baddie old factory? Sonda wisses he was here wiss her instead. We'd ride and drive and swim and dance. Don't forget your tennis racquet and golf clubs. There's a dandy course on the Casino grounds.

This morning when I was riding a bird flew right up under Dickey's heels. It scared him so that he bolted, and Sonda got all switched and scwatched. Isn't Clydie sorry for his Sonda?

She is writing lots of notes to-day. After lunch and the ride to catch the down mail, Sonda and Bertine and Nina going to the Casino. Don't you wish you were going to be there? We could dance to "Taudy." Sonda just loves that song. But she has to dress now. More to-morrow, baddie boy. And when Bertine writes, answer right away. See all 'ose dots? Kisses. Big and little ones. All for baddie boy. And wite Sonda every day and she'll write 'oo.

More kisses.

To which Clyde responded eagerly and in kind in the same hour. But almost the same mail, at least the same day, brought the following letter from Roberta.

Biltz, June 10th.

DEAR CLYDE:

I am nearly ready for bed, but I will write you a few lines. I had such a tiresome journey coming up that I was nearly sick. In the first place I didn't want to come much (alone) as you know. I feel too upset and uncertain about everything, although I try not to feel so now that we have our plan and you are going to come for me as you said.

(At this point, while nearly sickened by the thought of the wretched country world in which she lived, still, because of Roberta's unfortunate and unavoidable relation to it, he now experienced one of his old time twinges of remorse and pity in regard to her. For after all, this was not her fault. She had so little to look forward to—nothing but her work or a commonplace marriage. For the first time in many days, really, and in the absence of both, he was able to think clearly—and to sympathize deeply, if gloomily. For the remainder of the letter read:)

But it's very nice here now. The trees are so beautifully green and the flowers in bloom. I can hear the bees in the orchard whenever I go near the south windows. On the way up instead of coming straight home I decided to stop at Homer to see my sister and brother-in-law, since I am not so sure now when I shall see them again, if ever, for I am resolved that they shall see me respectable, or never at all any more. You mustn't think I mean anything hard or mean by this. I am just sad. They have such a cute little home there, Clyde—pretty furniture, a victrola and all, and Agnes is so very happy with Fred. I hope she always will be. I couldn't help thinking of what a dear place we might have had, if only my dreams had come true. And nearly all the time I was there Fred kept teasing me as to why I don't get married, until I said, "Oh, well, Fred, you mustn't be too sure that I won't one of these days. All good things come to him who waits, you know." "Yes, unless you just turn out to be a waiter," was the way he hit me back.

But I was truly glad to see mother again, Clyde. She's so loving and patient and helpful. The sweetest, dearest mother that ever, ever was. And I just hate to hurt her in any way. And Tom and Emily, too. They have had friends here every evening since I've been here—and they want me to join in, but I hardly feel well enough now to do all the things they want me to do—play cards and games—dance.

(At this point Clyde could not help emphasizing in his own mind the shabby home world of which she was a part and which so recently he had seen—that rickety house! those toppling chimneys! Her uncouth father. And that in contrast to such a letter as this other from Sondra.)

Father and mother and Tom and Emily just seem to hang around and try to do things for me. And I feel remorseful when I think how they would feel if they knew, for, of course, I have to pretend that it is work that makes me feel so tired and depressed as I am sometimes. Mother keeps saying that I must stay a long time or quit entirely and rest and get well again, but she just don't know of course—poor dear. If she did! I can't tell you how that makes me feel sometimes, Clyde. Oh, dear!

But there, I mustn't put my sad feelings over on you either. I don't want to, as I told you, if you will only come and get me as we've agreed. And I won't be like that either, Clyde. I'm not that way all the time now. I've started to get ready and do all the things it'll take to do in three weeks and that's enough to keep my mind off everything but work. But you will come for me, won't you, dear? You won't disappoint me any more and make me suffer this time like you have so far, for, oh, how long it has been now—ever since I was here before at Christmas time, really. But you were truly nice to me. I promise not to be a burden on you, for I know you don't really care for me any more and so I don't care much what happens now, so long as I get out of this. But I truly promise not to be a burden on you.

Oh, dear, don't mind this blot. I just don't seem to be able to control myself these days like I once could.

But as for what I came for, the family think they are clothes for a party down in Lycurgus and that I must be having a wonderful time. Well, it's better that way than the other. I may have to come as far as Fonda to get some things, if I don't send Mrs. Anse, the dressmaker, and if so, and if you wanted to see me again before you come, although I don't suppose you do, you could. I'd like to see you and talk to you again if you care to, before we start. It all seems so funny to me, Clyde, having these clothes made and wishing to see you so much and yet knowing that you would rather not do this. And yet I hope you are satisfied now that you have succeeded in making me leave Lycurgus and come up here and are having what you call a good time. Are they so very much better than the ones we used to have last summer when we went about to the lakes and everywhere? But whatever they are, Clyde, surely you can afford to do this for me without feeling too bad. I know it seems hard to you now, but you don't want to forget either that if I was like some that I know, I might and would ask more. But as I told you I'm not like that and never could be. If you don't really want me after you have helped me out like I said, you can go.

Please write me, Clyde, a long, cheery letter, even though you don't want to, and tell me all about how you have not thought of me once since I've been away or missed me at all—you used to, you know, and how you don't want me to come back and you can't possibly come up before two weeks from Saturday if then.

Oh, dear, I don't mean the horrid things I write, but I'm so blue and tired and lonely that I can't help it at times. I need someone to talk to—not just any one here, because they don't understand, and I can't tell anybody.

But there, I said I wouldn't be blue or gloomy or cross and yet I haven't done so very well this time, have I? But I promise to do better next time—tomorrow or next day, because it relieves me to write to you, Clyde. And won't you please write me just a few words to cheer me up while I'm waiting, whether you mean it or not, I need it so. And you will come, of course. I'll be so happy and grateful and try not to bother you too much in any way.

Your lonely
BERT

And it was the contrast presented by these two scenes which finally determined for him the fact that he would never marry Roberta—never—nor even go to her at Biltz, or let her come back to him here, if he could avoid that. For would not his going, or her return, put a period to all the joys that so recently in connection with Sondra had come to him here—make it impossible for him to be with Sondra at Twelfth Lake this summer—make it impossible for him to run away with and marry her? In God's name was there no way? No outlet from this horrible difficulty which now confronted him?

And in a fit of despair, having found the letters in his room on his return from work one warm evening in June, he now threw himself upon his bed and fairly groaned. The misery of this! The horror of his almost insoluble problem! Was there no way by which she could be persuaded to go away—and stay—remain at home, maybe for a while longer, while he sent her ten dollars a week, or twelve, even—a full half of all his salary? Or could she go to some neighboring town—Fonda, Gloversville, Schenectady—she was not so far gone but what she could take care of herself well enough as yet, and rent a room and remain there quietly until the fatal time, when she could go to some doctor or nurse? He might help her to find some one like that when the time came, if only she would be willing not to mention his name.

But this business of making him come to Biltz, or meeting her somewhere, and that within two weeks or less. He would not, he would not. He would do something desperate if she tried to make him do that—run away—or—maybe go up to Twelfth Lake before it should be time for him to go to Biltz, or before she would think it was time, and then persuade Sondra if he could-but oh, what a wild, wild chance was that—to run away with and marry him, even if she wasn't quite eighteen—and then—and then—being married, and her family not being able to divorce them, and Roberta not being able to find him, either, but only to complain—well, couldn't he deny it—say that it was not so—that he had never had any relationship, other than that which any department head might have with any girl working for him. He had not been introduced to the Gilpins, nor had he gone with Roberta to see that Dr. Glenn near Gloversville, and she had told him at the time, she had not mentioned his name.

But the nerve of trying to deny it!

The courage it would take.

The courage to try to face Roberta when, as he knew, her steady, accusing, horrified, innocent, blue eyes would be about as difficult to face as anything in all the world. And could he do that? Had he the courage? And would it all work out satisfactorily if he did? Would Sondra believe him—once she heard?

But just the same in pursuance of this idea, whether finally he executed it or not, even though he went to Twelfth Lake, he must write Sondra a letter saying that he was coming. And this he did at once, writing her passionately and yearningly. At the same time he decided not to write Roberta at all. Maybe call her on long distance, since she had recently told him that there was a neighbor near-by who had a telephone, and if for any reason he needed to reach her, he could use that. For writing her in regard to all this, even in the most guarded way, would place in her hands, and at this time, exactly the type of evidence in regard to this relationship which she would most need, and especially when he was so determined not to marry her. The trickery of all this! It was low and shabby, no doubt. Yet if only Roberta had agreed to be a little reasonable with him, he would never have dreamed of indulging in any such low and tricky plan as this. But, oh, Sondra! Sondra! And the great estate that she had described, lying along the west shore of Twelfth Lake. How beautiful that must be! He could not help it! He must act and plan as he was doing! He must!

And forthwith he arose and went to mail the letter to Sondra. And then while out, having purchased an evening paper and hoping via the local news of all whom he knew, to divert his mind for the time being, there, upon the first page of the *Times-Union* of Albany, was an item which read:

ACCIDENTAL DOUBLE TRAGEDY AT PASS LAKE—UPTURNED CANOE AND FLOATING HATS REVEAL PROBABLE LOSS OF TWO LIVES AT RESORT NEAR PITTSFIELD—UNIDENTIFIED BODY OF GIRL RECOVERED—THAT OF COMPANION STILL MISSING

Because of his own great interest in canoeing, and indeed in any form of water life, as well as his own particular skill when it came to rowing, swimming, diving, he now read with interest:

Pancoast, Mass., June 7th ... What proved to be a fatal boat ride for two, apparently, was taken here day before yesterday by an unidentified man and girl who came presumably from Pittsfield to spend the day at Pass Lake, which is fourteen miles north of this place.

Tuesday morning a man and a girl, who said to Thomas Lucas, who conducts the Casino Lunch and Boat House there, that they were from Pittsfield, rented a small row-boat about ten o'clock in the morning and with a basket, presumably containing lunch, departed for the northern end of the lake. At seven o'clock last evening, when they did not return, Mr. Lucas, in company with his son Jeffrey, made a tour of the lake in his motor boat and discovered the row-boat upside down in the shallows near the north shore, but no trace of the occupants. Thinking at the time that it might be another instance of renters having decamped in order to avoid payment, he returned the boat to his own dock.

But this morning, doubtful as to whether or not an accident had occurred, he and his assistant, Fred Walsh, together with his son, made a second tour of the north shore and finally came upon the hats of both the girl and the man floating among some rushes near the shore. At once a dredging party was organized, and by three o'clock to-day the body of the girl, concerning whom nothing is known here, other than that she came here with her companion, was brought up and turned over to the authorities. That of the man has not yet been found. The water in the immediate vicinity of the accident in some places being over thirty feet deep, it is not certain whether the trolling and dredging will yield the other body or not. In the case of a similar accident which took place here some fifteen years ago, neither body was ever recovered.

To the lining of the small jacket which the girl wore was sewed the tag of a Pittsfield dealer. Also in her shoe lining was stamped the name of Jacobs of this same city. But other than these there was no evidence as to her identity. It is assumed by the authorities here that if she carried a bag of any kind it lies at the bottom of the lake.

The man is recalled as being tall, dark, about thirty-five years of age, and wore a light green suit and straw hat with a white and blue band. The girl appears to be not more than twenty-five, five feet five inches tall, and weighs 130 pounds. She wore her hair, which was long and dark brown, in braids about her forehead. On her left middle finger is a small gold ring with an amethyst setting. The police of Pittsfield and other cities in this vicinity have been notified, but as yet no word as to her identity has been received.

This item, commonplace enough in the usual grist of summer accidents, interested Clyde only slightly. It seemed odd, of course, that a girl and a man should arrive at a small lake anywhere, and setting forth in a small boat in broad daylight thus lose their lives. Also it was odd that afterwards no one should be able to identify either of them. And yet here it was. The man had disappeared for good. He threw the paper down, little concerned at first, and turned to other things—the problem that was confronting him really—how he was to do. But later—and because of that, and as he was putting out the light before getting into bed, and still thinking of the complicated problem which his own life here presented, he was struck by the thought (what devil's whisper?—what evil hint of an evil spirit?)—supposing that he and Roberta—no, say he and Sondra—(no, Sondra could swim so well, and so could he)—he and Roberta were in a small boat somewhere and it should capsize at the very time, say, of this dreadful complication which was so harassing him? What an escape? What a relief from a gigantic and by now really destroying problem! On the other hand—hold—not so fast!—for could a man even think of such a solution in connection with so difficult a problem as his without committing a crime in his heart, really—a horrible, terrible crime? He must not even think of such a thing. It was wrong—wrong—terribly wrong. And yet, supposing—by accident, of course—such a thing as this did occur? That would be the end, then, wouldn't it, of all his troubles in connection with Roberta? No more terror as to her—no more fear and heartache even as to Sondra. A noiseless, pathless, quarrelless solution of all his present difficulties, and only joy before him forever. Just an accidental, unpremeditated drowning—and then the glorious future which would be his!

But the mere thinking of such a thing in connection with Roberta at this time—(why was it that his mind persisted in identifying her with it?) was terrible, and he must not, he must not, allow such a thought to enter his mind. Never, never, never! He must not. It was horrible! Terrible! A thought of murder, no less! Murder?!!! Yet so wrought up had he been, and still was, by the letter which Roberta had written him, as contrasted with the one from Sondra—so delightful and enticing was the picture of her life and his as she now described it, that he could not for the life of him quite expel that other and seemingly easy and so natural a solution of all his problem—if only such an accident could occur to him and Roberta. For after all he was not planning any crime, was he? Was he not merely thinking of an accident that, had it occurred or could it but occur in his case … Ah—but that "could it but occur." There was the dark and evil thought about which he must not, he must not think. He MUST NOT. And yet—and yet, … He was an excellent swimmer and could swim ashore, no doubt—whatever the distance. Whereas Roberta, as he knew from swimming with her at one beach and another the previous summer, could not swim. And then—and then—well and then, unless he chose to help her, of course …

As he thought, and for the time, sitting in the lamplight of his own room between nine-thirty and ten at night, a strange and disturbing creepiness as to flesh and hair and finger-tips assailed him. The wonder and the horror of such a thought! And presented to him by this paper in this way. Wasn't that strange? Besides, up in that lake country to which he was now going to Sondra, were many, many lakes about everywhere—were there not? Scores up there where Sondra was. Or so she had said. And Roberta loved the out-of-doors and the water so—although she could not swim—could not swim—could not swim. And they or at least he was going where lakes were, or they might, might they not—and if not, why not? since both had talked of some Fourth of July resort in their planning, their final departure—he and Roberta.

But, no! no! The mere thought of an accident such as that in connection with her, however much he might wish to be rid of her—was sinful, dark and terrible! He must not let his mind run on any such things for even a moment. It was too wrong—too vile—too terrible! Oh, dreadful thought! To think it should have come to him! And at this time of all times—when she was demanding that he go away with her!

Death!

Murder!

The murder of Roberta!

But to escape her of course—this unreasonable, unshakable, unchangeable demand of hers! Already he was quite cold, quite damp—with the mere thought of it. And now—when—when—! But he must not think of that! The death of that unborn child, too!!

But how could any one even think of doing any such thing with calculation—deliberately? And yet—many people were drowned like that—boys and girls—men and women—here and there—everywhere the world over in the summer time. To be sure, he would not want anything like that to happen to Roberta. And especially at this time. He was not that kind of a person, whatever else he was. He was not. He was not. He was not. The mere thought now caused a damp perspiration to form on his hands and face. He was not that kind of a person. Decent, sane people did not think of such things. And so he would not either—from this hour on.

In a tremulous state of dissatisfaction with himself—that any such grisly thought should have dared to obtrude itself upon him in this way—he got up and lit the lamp—re-read this disconcerting item in as cold and reprobative way as he could achieve, feeling that in so doing he was putting anything at which it hinted far from him once and for all. Then, having done so, he dressed and went out of the house for a walk—up Wykeagy Avenue, along Central Avenue, out Oak, and then back on Spruce and to Central again—feeling that he was walking away from the insinuating thought or suggestion that had so troubled him up to now. And after a time, feeling better, freer, more natural, more human, as he so much wished to feel—he returned to his room, once more to sleep, with the feeling that he had actually succeeded in eliminating completely a most insidious and horrible visitation. He must never think of it again! He must never think of it again. He must never, never, never think of it—never.

And then falling into a nervous, feverish doze soon thereafter, he found himself dreaming of a savage black dog that was trying to bite him. Having escaped from the fangs of the creature by waking in terror, he once more fell asleep. But now he was in some very strange and gloomy place, a wood or a cave or narrow canyon between deep hills, from which a path, fairly promising at first, seemed to lead. But soon the path, as he progressed along it, became narrower and narrower and darker, and finally disappeared entirely. And then, turning to see if he could not get back as he had come, there directly behind him were arrayed an entangled mass of snakes that at first looked more like a pile of brush. But above it waved the menacing heads of at least a score of reptiles, forked tongues and agate eyes. And in front now, as he turned swiftly, a horned and savage animal—huge, it was—its heavy tread crushing the brush—blocked the path in that direction. And then, horrified and crying out in hopeless desperation,

Unit 9　From *An American Tragedy*

once more he awoke—not to sleep again that night.

Topics for Discussion

1) Who are the main characters in *The American Tragedy*?
2) What do you know about Sondra from her letter to Clyde?
3) What do you know about Roberta from her letter to Clyde?
4) What are the differences between the letters from Sondra and Roberta to Clyde in terms of wording and emotion?
5) What effects do Sondra's and Roberta's letters have upon Clyde?
6) Why does Clyde feel anxious?
7) Is Clyde the master of his own life?
8) What figures of speech are adopted in the excerpt?
9) What is Clyde's dream about?
10) Why is the work titled "The American Tragedy"?

Interdisciplinary Concepts for Further Thinking

1. Id, Ego, and Superego

The id, the ego, and the superego are three concepts by Sigmund Freud (1856—1939) who is regarded as the "father of psychoanalysis".

In 1930, Sigmund Freud published one of the most influential books of the time about human psychology: *The Introduction to Psychoanalysis*. The book describes his ideas about the human mind, which changed the way psychiatrists treated their patients. Freud's revolutionary new theory argued that human beings are completely controlled by their unconscious mind. According to Freud, humans are not in control of the everyday decisions they make, but they are completely controlled by three sections of the unconscious mind: the id, the ego, and the superego, which are also the components of the human personality.

According to Freud, the id is the most primitive part of the human mind. It is the source of our bodily needs, wants, desires, and impulses and acts according to the "pleasure principle". The id is the most selfish part of our mind and is only concerned with the immediate satisfaction of whatever want or need the body is experiencing at the moment. The ego is the rational part of our mind and acts according to the reality principle. It seeks to please the id's drive in realistic ways that will be of long-term benefit. Freud considered it a mediator "between id and reality". The superego plays a critical and moralizing role in our mind. It reflects the internalization of cultural rules that are mainly taught by parents applying their guidance and influence. The superego is not inborn and is developed through the rules and expectations of our caregivers.

According to Freud, most people should be able to balance the three parts of their unconscious mind in a way that keeps them happy and healthy. When the three components of the mind become out of balance a person can suffer physical or emotional repercussions.

1) What kind of mental state does Clyde exhibit in the excerpt?
2) Analyze Clyde's state of mind in reference to Freud's personality theory.

2. *The Interpretation of Dreams*

Sigmund Freud's *The Interpretation of Dreams* was one of the most important books of the 20th century. First published in 1900, it provides a groundbreaking theory of dreams and an innovative method for interpreting them that captivates readers to this day.

For Freud, dreaming is a mental activity that has its own logic. By identifying its mechanisms, Freud also shed new light on the workings of the unconscious and its powerful role in human life. For Freud, "The interpretation of dreams is the royal road to a knowledge of the unconscious activities of the mind." Our dreams are nothing more than wishes that we are looking to fulfill in our waking lives. Some of these wishes are relatively innocent, and in these cases, our dreams depict the wish just as it is. However, other wishes are so unacceptable to us (such as sexual or aggressive impulses that we can't admit to or act out) that our dreams censor them. Such unacceptable wishes are typically suppressed by the conscious waking mind but turn up in the dream in an unrecognizable and often bizarre way. But with the help of a psychoanalyst and methods like free association, Freud argued, the wish behind the dream could be discovered.

1) What is Clyde's dream mainly about in the excerpt?
2) Interpret Clyde's dream in reference to Freud's argument of dreams.

Thinking in Numbers

1) Sometimes a choice can completely change one's life. The choice before Clyde seems to be such a challenging one. In this situation, choosing the best strategy might include having "second thoughts" before making the decision. Think about Clyde's relationship with Sondra and Roberta and figure out three reasons for him to choose either Sondra or Roberta.

2) The word "terrible" appears 5 times in the excerpt. Figure out why the author uses the word so many times and what kind of state of mind is reflected through the repetition.

Visual Thinking with Mind Mapping

The triangle is the strongest and most stable shape used in construction but is the most vulnerable and troublesome in love affairs. Create a mind map to analyze the vulnerability and collapse of the love triangle between Sondra, Clyde, and Roberta.

Critical Thinking for Reality

If you are in a similar situation as Clyde, what would you do? Would you choose Sondra or Roberta, dream or responsibility?

Unit 10
The Fly

Katherine Mansfield

Introduction to the Author

Katherine Mansfield (1888—1923) was a New Zealand-born novelist, often regarded as one of the most influential writers during modernist period. As a master of short stories, Katherine Mansfield explored anxiety, sexuality and existentialism as well as a developing New Zealand identity. Her emphasis on psychological conflicts, oblique narration and subtle observation unveiled the influence of Anton Chekhov. She herself also had a significant impact on the development of the short story as a literary form. By examining women's living condition in her writing, Katherine Mansfield also provided a literary solution to the social problem of women's liberation. Therefore, she has been widely regarded by later generations as one of the pioneers of New Zealand feminism.

Mansfield left New Zealand when she was 19 and moved to England, where she became friends with D. H. Lawrence, Virginia Woolf, Lady Ottoline Morrell, and other Bloomsbury Group members in England. In 1917, Mansfield was diagnosed with pulmonary tuberculosis, and she passed away at the age of 34 in France. Her most notable works include *At the Bay* (1922), *Bliss and Other Stories* (1920) and *The Garden Party* (1922), etc. Mansfield's writing was deeply influenced by World War

Ⅰ, which changed the fate of a whole generation. Mansfield was part of that generation and lost her brother in the conflict. Mansfield ever wrote to her husband John Middleton Murry: "I feel in the profoundest sense that nothing can ever be the same—that, as artists, we are traitors if we feel otherwise: we have to take it into account and find new expressions, new moulds for our thoughts and feelings." The critic Vincent O'Sullivan stated that, "[f]rom any perspective, the most important public event in Mansfield's lifetime was the First World War."

Introduction to the Work

First written in February 1922, "The Fly" was published the following month in *The Nation and Athenaeum*. In 1923, after Mansfield's death, "The Fly" was published in *The Doves' Nest and Other Stories*. The story takes place in the life of a boss who is still grieving the loss of his son when a friend named Mr. Woodifield brings up his son at a meetup. His daughters have visited Belgium to visit both the grave of their brother, Woodifield's son and the boss's son's grave. Woodifield leaves after stating that the grave is well-kept. The boss wants to weep alone but he cannot easily. He sees a fly in the ink pot, pulls it out, places it on a blotter, and then tortures it by applying one drop of ink to it at a time until the fly appears to have escaped and gained hope. The boss continues to spray ink on the fly. Consequently, in the agony, he kills the fly.

Mansfield describes the mental breakdown of a person who lacks self-knowledge in the story. Beneath the surface storyline of killing a fly is an allegory of political and moral implications. Mansfield focuses on a man's internal struggle with himself, others, nature, and society. Written shortly after World War Ⅰ, key issues like postwar trauma and existential crisis are portrayed in the narrative. Many people consider "The Fly" to be one of Katherine Mansfield's finest short stories.

Text

The Fly

"Y'are very snug in here," piped old Mr. Woodifield, and he peered out of the great, green-leather armchair by his friend the boss's desk as a baby peers out of its pram. His talk was over; it was time for him to be off. But he did not want to go. Since he had retired, since his ... stroke, the wife and the girls kept him boxed up in the house every day of the week except Tuesday. On Tuesday he was dressed and brushed and allowed to cut back to the City for the day. Though what he did there the wife and girls couldn't imagine. Made a nuisance of himself to his friends, they supposed ... Well, perhaps so. All the same, we cling to our last pleasures as the tree clings to its last leaves. So there sat old Woodifield, smoking a cigar and staring almost greedily at the boss, who rolled in his office chair, stout, rosy, five years older than he, and still going strong, still at the helm. It did one good to see him. Wistfully, admiringly, the old voice added, "It's snug in here, upon my word!"

"Yes, it's comfortable enough," agreed the boss, and he flipped the *Financial Times* with a paper-knife. As a matter of fact he was proud of his room; he liked to have it admired, especially by old Woodifield. It gave him a feeling of deep, solid satisfaction to be planted there in the midst of it in full view of that frail old figure in the muffler.

"I've had it done up lately," he explained, as he had explained for the past—how many!—weeks. "New carpet," and he pointed to the bright red carpet with a pattern of large white rings. "New furniture," and he nodded towards the massive bookcase and the table with legs like twisted treacle. "Electric heating!" He waved almost exultantly towards the five transparent, pearly sausages glowing so softly in the tilted copper pan.

But he did not draw old Woodifield's attention to the photograph over the table of a grave-looking boy in uniform standing in one of those spectral photographers' parks with photographers' storm-clouds behind him. It was not new. It had been there for over six years.

"There was something I wanted to tell you," said old Woodifield, and his eyes grew dim remembering. "Now what was it? I had it in my mind when I started out this morning." His hands began to tremble, and patches of red showed above his beard.

Poor old chap, he's on his last pins, thought the boss. And, feeling kindly, he winked at the old man, and said jokingly, "I tell you what. I've got a little drop of something here that'll do you good before you go out into the cold again. It's beautiful stuff. It wouldn't hurt a child." He took a key off his watch-chain, unlocked a cupboard below his desk, and drew forth a dark, squat bottle. "That's the medicine," said he. "And the man from whom I got it told me on the strict Q.T. it came from the cellars at Windsor Castle."

Old Woodifield's mouth fell open at the sight. He couldn't have looked more surprised if the boss had produced a rabbit.

"It's whisky, ain't it?" he piped, feebly.

The boss turned the bottle and lovingly showed him the label. Whisky it was.

"D'you know," said he, peering up at the boss wonderingly, "they won't let me touch it at home." And he looked as though he was going to cry.

"Ah, that's where we know a bit more than the ladies," cried the boss, swooping across for two tumblers that stood on the table with the water-bottle, and pouring a generous finger into each. "Drink it down. It'll do you good. And don't put any water with it. It's sacrilege to tamper with stuff like this. Ah!" He tossed off his, pulled out his handkerchief, hastily wiped his moustaches, and cocked an eye at old Woodifield, who was rolling his in his chaps.

The old man swallowed, was silent a moment, and then said faintly, "It's nutty!"

But it warmed him; it crept into his chill old brain—he remembered.

"That was it," he said, heaving himself out of his chair. "I thought you'd like to know. The girls were in Belgium last week having a look at poor Reggie's grave, and they happened to come across your boy's. They're quite near each other, it seems."

Old Woodifield paused, but the boss made no reply. Only a quiver in his eyelids showed that he heard.

"The girls were delighted with the way the place is kept," piped the old voice. "Beautifully looked after. Couldn't be better if they were at home. You've not been across, have yer?"

"No, no!" For various reasons the boss had not been across.

"There's miles of it," quavered old Woodifield, "and it's all as neat as a garden. Flowers growing on all the graves. Nice broad paths." It was plain from his voice how much he liked a nice broad path.

The pause came again. Then the old man brightened wonderfully.

"D'you know what the hotel made the girls pay for a pot of jam?" he piped. "Ten francs! Robbery, I call it. It was a little pot, so Gertrude says, no bigger than a half-crown. And she hadn't taken more than a spoonful when they charged her ten francs. Gertrude brought the pot away with her to teach 'em a lesson. Quite right, too; it's trading on our feelings. They think because we're over there having a look round we're ready to pay anything. That's what it is." And he turned towards the door.

"Quite right, quite right!" cried the boss, though what was quite right he hadn't the least idea. He came round by his desk, followed the shuffling footsteps to the door, and saw the old fellow out. Woodifield was gone.

For a long moment the boss stayed, staring at nothing, while the grey-haired office messenger, watching him, dodged in and out of his cubby hole like a dog that expects to be taken for a run. Then: "I'll see nobody for half an hour, Macey," said the boss. "Understand? Nobody at all."

"Very good, sir."

The door shut, the firm heavy steps recrossed the bright carpet, the fat body plumped down in the spring chair, and leaning forward, the boss covered his face with his hands. He wanted, he intended, he had arranged to weep ...

It had been a terrible shock to him when old Woodifield sprang that remark upon him about the boy's grave. It was exactly as though the earth had opened and he had seen the boy lying there with Woodifield's girls staring down at him. For it was strange. Although over six years had passed away, the boss never thought of the boy except as lying unchanged, unblemished in his uniform, asleep for ever. "My son!" groaned the boss. But no tears came yet. In the past, in the first months and even years after the boy's death, he had only to say those words to be overcome by such grief that nothing short of a violent fit of weeping could relieve him. Time, he had declared then, he had told everybody, could make no difference. Other men perhaps might recover, might live their loss down, but not he. How was it possible? His boy was an only son. Ever since his birth the boss had worked at building up this business for him; it had no other meaning if it was not for the boy. Life itself had come to have no other meaning. How on earth could he have slaved, denied himself, kept going all those years without the promise for ever before him of the boy's stepping into his shoes and carrying on where he left off?

And that promise had been so near being fulfilled. The boy had been in the office learning the ropes for a year before the war. Every morning they had started off together; they had come back by the same train. And what congratulations he had received as the boy's father! No wonder; he had taken to it marvellously. As to his popularity with the staff, every man jack of them down to old Macey couldn't make enough of the boy. And he wasn't in the least spoilt. No, he was just his bright, natural self, with the right word for everybody, with that boyish look and his habit of saying, "Simply splendid!"

But all that was over and done with as though it never had been. The day had come when Macey had handed him the telegram that brought the whole place crashing about his head. "Deeply regret to inform you . . ." And he had left the office a broken man, with his life in ruins.

Six years ago, six years ... How quickly time passed! It might have happened yesterday. The boss took his hands from his face; he was puzzled. Something seemed to be wrong with him. He wasn't feeling as he wanted to feel. He decided to get up and have a look at the boy's photograph. But it wasn't a favourite photograph of his; the expression was unnatural. It was cold, even stern-looking. The boy had never looked like that.

At that moment the boss noticed that a fly had fallen into his broad inkpot, and was trying feebly but desperately to clamber out again. Help! help! said those struggling legs. But the sides of the inkpot were wet and slippery; it fell back again and began to swim. The boss took up a pen, picked the fly out of the ink, and shook it on to a piece of blotting-paper. For a fraction of a second it lay still on the dark patch that oozed round it. Then the front legs waved, took hold, and, pulling its small, sodden body up it began the immense task of cleaning the ink from its wings. Over and under, over and under, went a leg along a wing, as the stone goes over and under the scythe. Then there was a pause, while the fly, seeming to stand on the tips of its toes, tried to expand first one wing and then the other. It succeeded at last, and, sitting down, it began, like a minute cat, to clean its face. Now one could imagine that the little front legs rubbed against each other lightly, joyfully. The horrible danger was over; it had escaped; it was ready for life again.

But just then the boss had an idea. He plunged his pen back into the ink, leaned his thick wrist on the blotting paper, and as the fly tried its wings down came a great heavy blot. What would it make of that? What indeed! The little beggar seemed absolutely cowed, stunned, and afraid to move because of what would happen next. But then, as if painfully, it dragged itself forward. The front legs waved, caught hold, and, more slowly this time, the task began from the beginning.

He's a plucky little devil, thought the boss, and he felt a real admiration for the fly's courage. That was the way to tackle things; that was the right spirit. Never say die; it was only a question of ... But the fly had again finished its laborious task, and the boss had just time to refill his pen, to shake fair and square on the new-cleaned body yet another dark drop. What about it this time? A painful moment of suspense followed. But behold, the front legs were again waving; the boss felt a rush of relief. He leaned over the fly and said to it tenderly, "You artful little b..." And he actually had the brilliant notion of breathing on it to help the drying process. All the same, there was something timid and weak about its efforts now, and the boss decided that this time should be the last, as he dipped the pen deep into the inkpot.

It was. The last blot fell on the soaked blotting-paper, and the draggled fly lay in it and did not stir. The back legs were stuck to the body; the front legs were not to be seen.

"Come on," said the boss. "Look sharp!" And he stirred it with his pen—in vain. Nothing happened or was likely to happen. The fly was dead.

The boss lifted the corpse on the end of the paper-knife and flung it into the waste-paper basket. But such a grinding feeling of wretchedness seized him that he felt positively frightened. He started forward and pressed the bell for Macey.

"Bring me some fresh blotting-paper," he said sternly, "and look sharp about it." And while the old dog padded away he fell to wondering what it was he had been thinking about before. What was it? It was ... He took out his handkerchief and passed it inside his collar. For the life of him he could not remember.

Topics for Discussion

1) Where and when does the story happen?
2) Why does old Woodifield pay a visit to the boss?
3) What is the turning point of the story?
4) Why does the boss feel "a real admiration for the fly's courage"?
5) Has the boss visited his son's cemetery?
6) Why doesn't the boss "draw old Woodifield's attention to the photograph" when he shows off his new office?
7) Why does the boss "[make] no reply" when Mr. Woodifield mentions his son's grave?

8) Why does the boss drop the ink on the fly?
9) Why does the boss "[take] out his handkerchief and [pass] it inside his collar"?
10) What does the fly symbolize in the story?

Interdisciplinary Concepts for Further Thinking

1. Trauma

Trauma is the Greek word for "wound". Although the Greeks used the term only for physical injuries, nowadays trauma is just as likely to refer to emotional wounds. Trauma is a person's emotional response to a distressing experience. Few people go through life without encountering some kind of trauma. Unlike ordinary hardships, traumatic events tend to be sudden and unpredictable, involve a serious threat to life—like bodily injury or death—and feel beyond a person's control.

According to the *Comprehension Textbook of Psychiatry*, the psychological trauma is a feeling of intense fear, helplessness, loss of control, and the threat of annihilation. According to Cathy Caruth, trauma is "an overwhelming experience of sudden or catastrophic events in which the response to the events occur in the often delayed, uncontrolled repetitive appearance of hallucination and other intrusive phenomenon", and to be "traumatized" means "precisely to be possessed by an image or event".

1) What is the essence of trauma?
2) What kind of trauma does the boss suffer from?

2. PTSD

Post-traumatic stress disorder (PTSD) is a psychiatric disorder that may occur in people who have experienced or witnessed a traumatic event such as a natural disaster, a serious accident, a terrorist act, war/combat, or rape when someone has been threatened with death, sexual violence or serious injury. PTSD can occur in all people, of any ethnicity, nationality, or culture, and at any age.

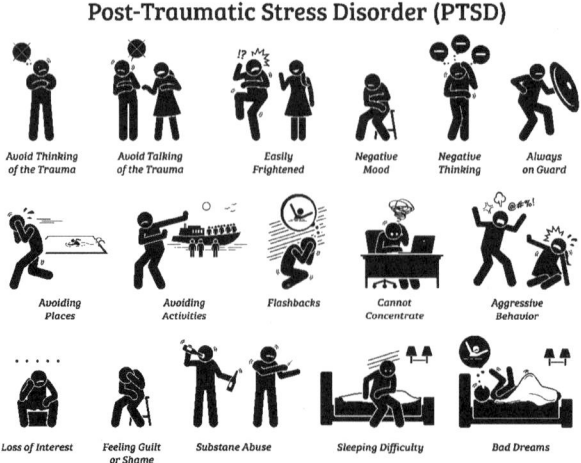

The formal diagnostic criteria for PTSD are outlined in the Diagnostic and Statistical Manual of Mental Disorders-Text Revision (DSM-TR). In 2013, the American Psychiatric Association revised the PTSD diagnostic criteria in the fifth edition of its Diagnostic and Statistical Manual of Mental Disorders (DSM-5). There are five criteria to evaluate the demonstration of PTSD.

The third PTSD criterion captures typical symptoms of avoidance and hyperarousal: Persistent avoidance of stimuli associated with the trauma and numbing of general responsiveness, as indicated by three of the following: a. efforts to avoid thoughts, feelings, or conversations associated with the trauma; b. efforts to avoid activities, places, or people that arouse recollections of the trauma; c. inability to recall an important aspect of the event; d. markedly diminished interest or participation in significant activities; e. feeling of detachment or estrangement from others.

Stages of Recovery and Healing from Trauma
Judith Herman

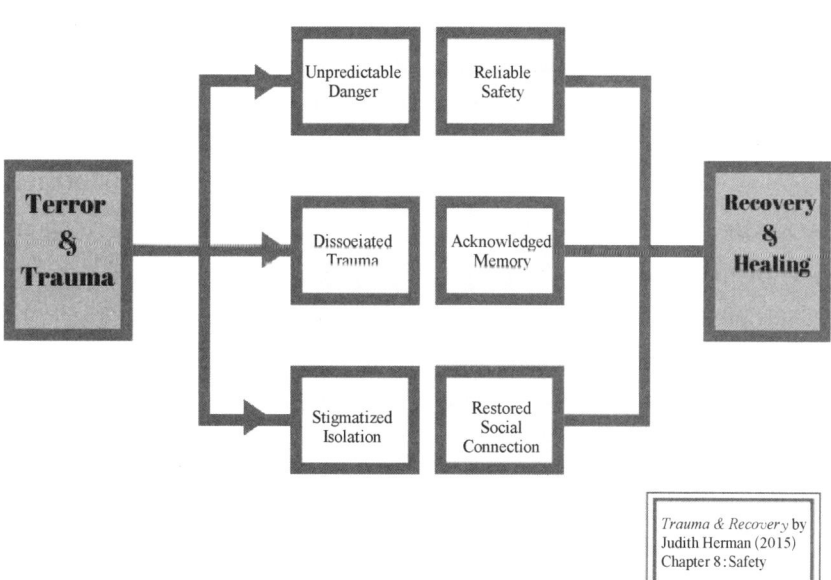

Trauma & Recovery by Judith Herman (2015)
Chapter 8: Safety

3MMM | TRAUMA HEALING AND RECOVERY

In *Trauma and Recovery: The Aftermath of Violence* (1992), Judith L. Herman argues that the core experiences of psychological trauma are "disempowerment" and "disconnection" from others. Recovery, therefore, is based upon the empowerment of the survivor and the creation of new connections. Recovery can take place only within the context of relationships; it cannot occur in isolation. In her renewed connections with other people, the sufferer re-creates the psychological faculties that are damaged or deformed by traumatic experiences. Recovery unfolds in three stages. The central task of the first stage is the establishment of safety. The central task of the second stage is remembrance and mourning. The central task of the third stage is reconnection with ordinary life.

1) Does the boss have PTSD and what are the symptoms?

2) There are mainly 3 steps that allow a person to recover from a traumatic event. Is it possible for the boss to recover from his trauma? Explain it by referring to the three steps of recovery.

Thinking in Numbers

1) The number 6 is important in the story. In the story, "six years" is mentioned 4 times in three places. It can be said that the "six years" has been the longest time that the boss has ever experienced in his life; it is also the shortest time since he can go back to that moment at any time, of which he is not even conscious. Have a further consideration of the function of time in the story.

2) In the story, the boss drops 3 "heavy blot[s]" on the fly. What do the 4 times symbolize or indicate about the boss? Can we see through the boss's life as well as fate?

Visual Thinking with Mind Mapping

Undoubtedly, the fly is the core image in "The Fly". The boss's strange behavior in dealing with the fly is even beyond his comprehension, which is concluded in the last paragraph of the story. Create a mind map to analyze the abnormality of the boss in dealing with the fly and show the connection between his inner mind and his treatment of the fly.

Critical Thinking for Reality

Everyone will witness some traumatic events such as the loss of parents, a good friend, or something disastrous in his or her life. At that moment, he or she might feel that the world collapses or life itself does not make any sense. People might rethink the meaning of life in their darkest moments. What do you think the meaning of life is and how will you get through the dark moments?

Unit 11

From *The Goat, or Who is Sylvia?*

Edward Albee

Introduction to the Author

Edward Albee (1958—2016) was one of America's greatest modern playwrights, known for his sharp insight and his grasp of the Theatre of the Absurd. His works were often considered to be a candid inspection of modern condition and existential conflicts. As Albee himself commented on his body of work in a 1991 interview: "All of my plays are about people missing the boat, closing down too young, coming to the end of their lives with regret at things not done, as opposed to things done." One-act plays, represented by *The Zoo Story* (1959), made Edward Albee known as an astute critic of American values. His first play, *Who's Afraid of Virginia Woolf?* (1962) was his best-known work, which won a Tony Award and was adapted into a movie. *A Delicate Balance* (1966), *Seascape* (1972), and *Three Tall Women* (1994) all won him the Pulitzer Prize for Drama. Delving into American morality, Albee continued to be experimental in his later works, such as *The Goat, or Who Is Sylvia?* (2002).

Introduction to the Work

The Goat, or Who Is Sylvia? is a full-length written by Edward Albee in 2000 and premiered on Broadway in 2002. It was also a finalist for the 2003 Pulitzer Prize for Drama and won the Tony Award for Best Play in 2002. The play is about Martin, a hugely successful architect who has just turned fifty, who leads an ostensibly ideal life with his loving wife Stevie and gay teenage son Billy. But when he confides to his best friend that he is in love with a goat (named Sylvia), their marriage falls apart. The play is Albee's most provocative, daring, and controversial play since *Who's Afraid of Virginia Woolf*. The Subtitle "Notes Toward a Definition of Tragedy" was added when Albee first published this play. The ancient Greek word for tragedy has the literal meaning of "goat song", which was ingeniously employed by Albee in a modern circumstance.

The Goat, or Who Is Sylvia? is ostensibly an absurd tale of bestiality that raises deeper concerns and engages audience regarding social taboos, hypocrisy, and ethics, focusing on the boundaries of a seemingly liberal society. As Albee himself commented this play in *Stretching My Mind*, "The play is about love, and loss, the limits of our tolerance and who, indeed, we really are." Featuring linguistic disputes and language games amid the domestic conflicts, the play plumbs the issue of self-relationship, concerning the way in which people understand, support and value themselves in the context of a modern society.

Text

The Goat, or Who is Sylvia?
(Excerpt)

Scene One

(*The living room*)

(STEVIE *onstage, arranging flowers*)

STEVIE

(*Calling offstage*) What time are they coming? (*No response*) Martin? What time are they coming?

MARTIN

(*Offstage*) What? (*Entering*) What?

STEVIE

(*A little smile; a slowish statement*) What … time … are … they … coming.

MARTIN

Who? (*Recalling*) Oh! Oh. (*Looks at watch*) Soon; very soon. Why can't I remember anything?

STEVIE

(*Finishing flowers*) Why can't you remember?

MARTIN

Anything; nothing; can't remember a thing. This morning—so far!—I couldn't

Unit 11　From *The Goat, or Who is Sylvia?*

remember where I'd put the new head for the razor; I couldn't recall Ross's son's name—still can't; two cards in my jacket make no sense to me whatever, and I'm not sure I know why I came in here.

STEVIE

Todd.

MARTIN

What?

STEVIE

Ross's son is called Todd.

MARTIN

(*Slaps his forehead*) Right! Why the flowers?

STEVIE

To brighten up the corner …

MARTIN

… where you *are*? Where *I* am?

STEVIE

… where you'll probably be sitting, to make the cameras happy.

MARTIN

(*Smelling the flowers*) What are they?

STEVIE

Cameras?

MARTIN

No; these.

STEVIE

Ranunculus. I (*Then*) I: ranunculi.

MARTIN

Pretty. Why don't they smell?

STEVIE

They're secretive; probably too subtle for your forgetful nose.

MARTIN

(*Shakes his head, mock concern*) Every sense going! Taste next! Touch; hearing. Hah! Hearing!

STEVIE

What?

MARTIN

What?

STEVIE

And to think you're only fifty. Did you find it?

MARTIN

What?

STEVIE

The new head for the razor.

MARTIN

Right! A new head! I'll need that next—the whole thing.

STEVIE

Why did you want to remember Todd's name?

MARTIN

Well, to begin with, I shouldn't be forgetting it, and when Ross shows up and he asks about Billy I can't say "He's fine; how's ... you know ... *your* son ..."

STEVIE

Todd.

MARTIN

Todd. "How's old Todd?"

STEVIE

Young Todd.

MARTIN

Yes. It's the little slips.

STEVIE

I wouldn't worry about it. Are you going to offer them stuff? Coffee? Beer?

MARTIN

(*Preoccupied*) Probably. Do you think it means anything?

STEVIE

I don't know what "it" is.

MARTIN

That I can't remember anything.

STEVIE

Probably not: you have too much to remember, that's all. You could go in for a checkup ... if you can remember our doctor's name.

MARTIN

(*Nailing it*) Percy!

STEVIE

Right!

MARTIN

(*To himself*) Who could forget that? Nobody has a doctor named Percy. (*To STEVIE*) What's the matter with me?

STEVIE

You're fifty.

MARTIN

Unit 11　From *The Goat, or Who is Sylvia?*

No; more than that.

STEVIE

The old foreboding? The sense that everything going right is a sure sign that everything's going wrong, of all the awful to come? All that?

MARTIN

(*Rueful*) Probably. Why did I come in here?

STEVIE

I heard you in the hall; I called you.

MARTIN

Aha.

STEVIE

What's my *name*?

MARTIN

Pardon?

STEVIE

Who *am* I? Who am *I*?

MARTIN

(*Acted*) You're the love of my life, the mother of my handsome and worrisome son, my playmate, my cook, my bottlewasher. Do you?

STEVIE

What?

MARTIN

Wash my bottles?

STEVIE

(*Puzzles it*) Not as a habit. I may have—washed one of your bottles. Do you have bottles?

MARTIN

Everyone has bottles.

STEVIE

Right. But what's my *name*?

MARTIN

(*Pretending confusion*) Uh ... Stevie?

STEVIE

Good. Will this be a long one?

MARTIN

A long what?

STEVIE

Interview.

MARTIN

The usual, I guess. Ross said it wasn't going to be a feature—sort of a catch-up.

STEVIE

On your fiftieth.

MARTIN

(*Nods*) On my fiftieth. I wonder if I should tell him that my mind's going? If I can remember.

STEVIE

(*Laughs; hugs him from behind*) Your mind's not going.

MARTIN

My what?

STEVIE

Your mind, darling; it's not going ... anywhere.

MARTIN

(*Serious*) Am I too young for Alzheimer's?

STEVIE

Probably. Isn't it nice to be too young for something?

MARTIN

(*Mind elsewhere*) Um-hum.

STEVIE

The joke is, if you can remember what it's called you don't have it.

MARTIN

Have what?

STEVIE

Alz ... (*they both laugh; he kisses her forehead*) Oh, you know how to turn a girl on! Forehead kisses! (*Sniffs him*) Where have you been?

MARTIN

(*Releases her; preoccupied*) What time are they coming?

STEVIE

Soon, you said; very soon.

MARTIN

I did? Good.

STEVIE

Did you find it?

MARTIN

What?

STEVIE

The head for your razor.

MARTIN

No; it's around somewhere. (*Fishes in a pocket, brings out cards*) But these! Now these! What the hell are these!? "Basic Services, Limited." Basic Services, Limited?? Limited to what!? (*The other card*) "Clarissa Atherton." (*Shrugs*) Clarissa Atherton? No number, no ... internet thing? Clarissa Atherton?

STEVIE

Basic services? Clarissa Atherton, basic services?

MARTIN

Hm? Every time someone gives me one of these, I know I'm supposed to give them one back, and I don't have them. It's embarrassing.

STEVIE

I've told you to have them made ... cards.

MARTIN

I don't want to.

STEVIE

Then don't. Who is she?

MARTIN

Who?

STEVIE

Clarissa Atherton, basic services. Does she smell funny?

MARTIN

I don't know. (*Afterthought*) I don't know who she is, as far as I know. Where were we this week?

STEVIE

(*Overly casual; stretches*) Oh, it doesn't matter sweetie. If you're seeing this Atherton woman, this ... dominatrix ... who smells funny ...

MARTIN

How could I be seeing her—whoever she is? There's nothing on the card. Dominatrix!?

STEVIE

Why not?

MARTIN

Maybe you know things I don't.

STEVIE

Maybe.

MARTIN

And I probably know one or two things you *don't*.

STEVIE

It evens out.

MARTIN

Yes. Do I look OK?

STEVIE

For the TV? Yes.

MARTIN

Yes. (*Turning*) Really?

STEVIE

I said: yes; fine. (*Indicates*) The old prep school tie?

MARTIN

(*Genuine, as he looks*) Is it? Oh, yeah; so it is.

STEVIE

(*Not letting him have it*) *No* one puts on their prep school tie by accident. *No* one.

MARTIN

(*Considers*) What if you can't remember that's what it is?

STEVIE

No one!! If you do get Alzheimer's, and you get to the stage you don't know who *I* am, who *Billy* is, who *you* are, for that matter …

MARTIN

Billy?

STEVIE

(*Laughs*) Stop it! When you get to the point you can't remember anything, someone will hand you *that* (*indicates his tie*) and you'll look at it and you'll say (*terrible imitation of aged man*)

"Ahhhhh! My prep school tie! My prep school tie!"

(*They chuckle; the doorbell rings/chimes*)

MARTIN

Ah! Doom time!

STEVIE

(*Quite matter of fact*) If you *are* seeing that woman, I think we'd better talk about it.

MARTIN

(*Stops. Long pause; matter of fact*) If I were … we *would*.

STEVIE

(*As offhand as possible*) If not the dominatrix, then some blonde half your age, some … chippie, as they used to call them …

MARTIN

… or, worst of all, someone just like you? As bright; as resourceful; as intrepid; … merely … new?

STEVIE

(*Warm smile; shake of head*) You win 'em all, don't you.

Unit 11 From *The Goat, or Who is Sylvia?*

MARTIN

(*Same smile*) Enough. (*Door again. The next several speeches are done in a greatly exaggerated Noel Coward manner: English accents, flamboyant gestures*)

STEVIE

Something's going on, isn't it!?

MARTIN

Yes! I've fallen in love!

STEVIE

I knew it!

MARTIN

Hopelessly!

STEVIE

I knew it!

MARTIN

I fought against it!

STEVIE

Oh, you poor darling!

MARTIN

Fought hard!

STEVIE

I suppose you'd better tell me!

MARTIN

I can't! I can't!

STEVIE

Tell me! Tell me!

MARTIN

Her name is Sylvia!

STEVIE

Sylvia? Who is Sylvia?

MARTIN

She's a goat; Sylvia is a goat! (*Acting manner dropped; normal tone now; serious, flat*) She's a goat.

STEVIE

(*Long pause; she stares, finally smiles. She giggles, chortles, moves toward the hall; normal tone*)

You're too much! (*Exits*)

MARTIN

I am? (*Shrugs; to himself*) You try to *tell* them; you try to be *honest*. What do they do? They laugh at you. (*Imitation*) "You're too much!" (*Thinks about it*) I suppose I am.

ROSS

Hey honey.

STEVIE

Hi Ross. (ROSS *enters with* STEVIE)

ROSS

Hello there, old man!

MARTIN

I'm fifty!

ROSS

It's a term of endearment. Nice flowers.

MARTIN

It is?

ROSS

What? What is?

MARTIN

"Hello there, old man." Ranunculi.

ROSS

Pardon?

STEVIE

The proper plural of ranunculus-the flowers, according to old Martin here.

MARTIN

Some say ranunculuses, but that sounds wrong, even though it's probably perfectly acceptable.

ROSS

(*Not interested*) Aha! Let's move that chair over to the ... whatever they are ... the flowers. (*To* MARTIN) Are you happy in that chair?

MARTIN

Am I happy in it? I don't even know if I've ever sat in it. (*To* STEVIE) Have I? Have I ever sat in it?

STEVIE

You just did, and you sat in it the last time Ross did the program with you.

ROSS

That's *right*!

MARTIN

Yes ... but was I happy? Did I sit there and did contentment bathe me in its warm light?

ROSS

You got me, fella.

Unit 11 From *The Goat, or Who is Sylvia?*

STEVIE

Yes; contentment fell; you sat there and I watched it bathe you in its warm light. I've got to go.

MARTIN

Where are you going?

STEVIE

(*No information*) Out.

MARTIN

Are we in tonight?

STEVIE

Yes. I think Billy's going out.

MARTIN

Naturally!

STEVIE

We're in. (*Glee*) TV time! I'm getting my hair done, and then I thought I'd stop by the feed store.

(*Exits, giggling*)

ROSS

By *what*? She's going to stop by *what*?

MARTIN

(*Staring after her*) Nothing; nowhere. (*To* ROSS) No crew?

ROSS

Just me this time—the old hand-held. (*Indicates camera*) You ready for the chair?

MARTIN

(*Sing-song*) Ha, ha. (*Suddenly remembering*) How's old *Todd*!?

ROSS

"Old Todd?"

MARTIN

You know: old *Todd*!

ROSS

You mean my baby son who just last week it seems I dandled on my knee? *That* old Todd?

MARTIN

Lovely word—dandled. Yes: *that* old Todd.

ROSS

Who I cannot accept having become eighteen?

MARTIN

Whom.

ROSS

Maybe.

MARTIN

Yes; that one. Can any of us? Ever?

ROSS

Pushing me further into middle age?

MARTIN

Yes; that one.

ROSS

(*Offhand*) He's OK. (*Laughs*) He asked me last week—first time since he was four, or something—why he didn't have a brother, or a sister, or whatever—why April and I never had another kid.

MARTIN

April, May, June—the pastel months. You name girl babies after them.

ROSS

(*Doesn't care*) Right. (*Does care*) I told him if you do it right the first time, why take a chance on another.

MARTIN

Did he like that one?

ROSS

Seemed to. Of course, I could have told him the whole graduating class got together and vowed that we would all have only one kid each—keep the population down. Speaking of which, how's Billy? How's *yours*—*your* one and only?

MARTIN

(*Attempted throw-away tone*) Ohhhh, seventeen last week—didn't Todd come to the party? No, I guess he didn't. Real cute kid, Billy, bright as you'd ever want, gay as the nineties.

ROSS

Passing phase. Have you had the old serious talk?

MARTIN

The "You'll get over it once you meet the right girl" lecture? Nah, I'm too smart for that, so's he, so's Billy. I told him to be sure. Says he's sure; loves it, he says.

ROSS

Well, of course he loves it; he's getting laid, for God's sake! Don't worry about him.

…

Scene Three

(*An hour or so later.* MARTIN *is sitting in the ruins. Maybe he is examining a*

Unit 11 From *The Goat, or Who is Sylvia?*

broken piece of something. The room is as it was at the end of Scene Two. The front door slams; BILLY enters; MARTIN rises and stands in the middle of the room.)

BILLY

(*Looking around*) Wow!

MARTIN

(*Realizing* BILLY *is there*) Yes; wow.

BILLY

(*Seemingly casual*) You guys really had it out, hunh.

MARTIN

(*Subdued; almost laughing*) Oh, yes.

BILLY

Where is she?

MARTIN

Hm? Who?

BILLY

(*Not friendly; overly articulated*) My mother. Where is my mother?

MARTIN

(*Mocking*) Where is "my mother"? Not "Mother—where's Mother?" Not that, but ... "Where is my mother?"

BILLY

(*Anger rising*) Whatever! Where *is* she? Where is *my mother*?

MARTIN

(*Arms out; helplessly*) I ... I ...

BILLY

(*Angrier*) Where *is* she?! What did you do ... kill her?

MARTIN

(*Softly*) Yes; I think so.

BILLY

(*Dropping something he has picked up*) What!!?

MARTIN

(*Quietly, with a restraining hand*) Stop. No. No, I did not kill her—of *course* not—but I think I might as well have. I think we've killed each other.

BILLY

(*Driving*) Where *is* she!?

MARTIN

(*Simply*) I don't know.

BILLY

What do you mean you don't ...

MARTIN

(*Loud*) She left!

BILLY

What do you mean she left? Where ...

MARTIN (*Snappish*)

Stop asking me what I mean! (*Quieter*) She said what she wanted to say; she finished ... and she left. She slammed the front door and left. I assume she drove somewhere.

BILLY

Yeah, the wagon's gone. (*Harder*) Where *is* she!?

MARTIN

(*Loud*) She *left!* I don't know where she *is*! It's English! "She left." It's English. No, I did not kill her, yes, I think I did, I think we killed each other. That's English, too: one of your courses!

BILLY

(*Is his rage close to tears? Probably*) I know who you *are*. I know you're my father. I know who you are, and I know who you're supposed to be, but ...

MARTIN

You, too?

BILLY

Hunh?

MARTIN

You don't know who I *am* anymore.

BILLY

(*Flat*) No.

MARTIN

Well ... neither does your mother.

BILLY

(*Trying to explain, but, still, rage underneath*) Parents fight; I know that; all kids know that. There are good times and rotten ones, and sometimes the blanket is pulled out from under you, and ...

MARTIN

(*Can't help saying it*) You're mixing your metaphors.

BILLY

(*Furious*) What!?

MARTIN

Never mind; probably not the best time to bring it up. You were saying ... "There are good times and rotten ones"?

BILLY

Yes. (*Quick sarcasm*) Thanks.

MARTIN

(*Noncommittal*) Welcome.

BILLY

But sometimes the whatever is pulled out from under you.

MARTIN

Rug, I think.

BILLY

Right! Now shut the fuck up! (MARTIN *opens his mouth, closes it. Spits out*) Semanticist!

MARTIN

Very good! Where did you learn that?

BILLY

I go to a good school. Remember?

MARTIN

Yes, but still ...

BILLY

I said, shut the fuck up!

MARTIN

(*Subsiding*) Right.

BILLY

There are good times, and there are rotten ones. There are times we are so ... deep in content, in happiness, that we think we'll probably drown in it but we won't mind. There are *some* of those—not too many. There are times we don't know what the fuck's going on—*to* us, *with* us, *about* us—and that's most of the time. I'm talking about us so-called adolescents.

MARTIN

I know.

BILLY

And then there are the times we wish we were old enough to ... just walk out the door and start all over again, somewhere else—blank it all out.

MARTIN

(*Quietly*) And this?

BILLY

(*Hard*) One guess, you *fuck*!! (*Huge*) What have you done with my *mother*!!??

MARTIN

(*Calm*) We finished our conversation (*gestures at ruined room*)—you see how we talk?—we finished our conversation, and she said a final ... *thing*, and she left. She walked out, out the front door, slam.

BILLY

How long ago?

MARTIN

(*Shrugs*) An hour; maybe more; maybe two. I'm not very good at time and stuff right now.

BILLY

Two hours? And you haven't . . .

MARTIN

(*A little angry himself*) What!? called the police? (*Awful imitation of distress*) "Oh, Officer, help me! My wife just found out I've been doing it with livestock, and she's run off, and can you help me find her?" What!? Take off after her!? She's a grown woman; she could be having her hair done, for all I know.

BILLY

(*Dogged*) What did she *say* to you?

MARTIN

(*Rueful chuckle*) Oh . . . quite a few things.

BILLY

(*Bigger*) When she left! What did she say when she left!?

MARTIN

Something about . . . bringing me down—or whatever.

BILLY

Be specific.

MARTIN

Well, it's hard to be specific. We *were* busy after all, and . . .

BILLY

(*Big*) Exactly what she said, and *now*!

MARTIN

(*Clears his throat*) "You have brought me down, and . . . I will bring you down with me."

BILLY

(*Puzzled; trying to get it*) What does that *mean*?

MARTIN

(*Almost sweet*) No one's ever brought you down? No, I suppose not—not yet. It means . . . (*fails*) it means what it says: that you have done to me what cannot be undone and . . . and you won't get away with it.

(BILLY *stands for a moment and then spontaneously cries for a little, stops*)

BILLY

(*Wiping his eyes*) I see.

Unit 11 From *The Goat, or Who is Sylvia?*

MARTIN

(*Further explanation*) You destroy me—I destroy you.

BILLY

Yes; I see. (*Indicates wreckage*) Then there's no point in setting all this right.

MARTIN

(*Sad chuckle*) It does look pretty awful, *doesn't* it.

BILLY

Let's do it anyway.

MARTIN

Set the stage for the next round? (*Some self-pity and irony*) Hunh! *What* next round!? It's all behind me, isn't it?—everything? All hope … all … "salvation"? (*Fast litany*) Dead-end-rock-bottom-out-with-the-garbage flushed-down-the-toilet-ground-up-spit-out-over-the-edge with heavy weights, down-down-sunk … whatever? All hope, everything? Gone? Right?

BILLY

(*Shrugs*) Whatever. (BILLY *begins to right a few things, not much; then quits*) What is it going to be then? Divorce?

MARTIN

(*Simply*) I don't know, Billy; I don't know that there are any rules for where we are.

BILLY

Beyond all the rules, eh?

MARTIN

(*Some rue*) I think so.

BILLY

I wouldn't know. I guess I've never been in love. Yet, I mean. Oh, lots of crushes, and all.

MARTIN

Only twice for me—your mother and … Sylvia.

BILLY

You're really holding onto this, *aren't* you.

MARTIN

To …?

BILLY

(*Sneering*) This goat! This big love affair!

MARTIN

(*Shrugs*) It's true.

BILLY

Grow up!

MARTIN

Ah! Is *that* it! (BILLY *laughs, in spite of himself*. MARTIN *tries to right a chair*) Help me with this. (BILLY *helps him*) Thanks!

BILLY

(*Shrugs*) Any time. (*Pause*) They asked us at school—when? Last week, last month?—they asked each of us in this class to talk about how normal our lives were, how ... how conventional it all was and how did we feel about it.

MARTIN

What kind of school *is* this!?

BILLY

(*Shrugs*) You chose it; you two chose it. And a lot of the guys got up and talked about—you know—our home lives, how our parents get on, and all; and it wasn't very special except the guys whose parents are divorced or one has died or gone crazy, or whatever.

MARTIN

Really? Crazy?

BILLY

Sure. Good private school. All guys, too; thanks. I mean, it was all about what you'd expect. Maybe everybody left all the juicy stuff out, or they didn't know it. (*Picks up a shard*) Where does this go?

MARTIN

Trash, I suspect.

BILLY

(*Looks at it*) Too bad. (*Drops it*) So, it was all pretty dull, pretty much what you'd expect.

MARTIN

I take it you haven't gotten up and spoken yet.

BILLY

(*Noncommittal*) Nope. Haven't. (*Waits a little*) You know what I'm going to tell them—when I get up there on my hind legs?

MARTIN

(*Winces*) Do I *want* to know?

BILLY

Sure; you're a big guy.

MARTIN

I am diminished.

BILLY

Yeah? Well ... whatever. I think what I'll tell them is this: that I've been living with two people about as splendid as you can get; that if I'd been born to other people, it couldn't have been any better. (MARTIN *sighs heavily, puts a protesting hand up*) No; really; I mean it. You two guys are about as good as they come. You're smart, and fair, and you have a sense of humor—both of you—and ... and you're Democrats. You *are* Democrats, aren't you?

MARTIN

More than *they* are, sometimes.

BILLY

That's what I thought, and you've figured out that raising a kid does *not* include making him into a carbon copy of *you*, that you're letting me think you're putting up with me being gay far better than you probably really are.

MARTIN

Oh, now ...

BILLY

Thank you, by the way.

MARTIN

It's the least.

BILLY

(*Nodding*) Right.

MARTIN

(*Feigned surprise*) You're *gay*!?

BILLY

(*Smiles*) Shut up. Anyway, you've let me have it better than a lot of kids, better than a lot of "Moms and Dads" have, a lot closer to what being grown up will look like—as far as I can tell. Good guidance; it's great to see how two people can love each other ...

MARTIN

Don't!

BILLY

At least that's what I thought—until yesterday, until the shit hit the fan!

MARTIN

Billy, please don't.

BILLY

(*Big crying underneath*) ... until the shit hit the fan, and the talk I was going to do at school became history. (*Exaggerated*) What will I say *now*!? Goodness me! The Good Ship Lollipop has gone and sunk. (*More normal tone*) What will I say!? Well, let's see: I came home yesterday and everything had been great—absolutely normal, therefore great. Great parents, great house, great trees, great cars—you know: the old "great." (*Bigger now, more exaggerated*) But then today I come home, and what do I *find*? I find my great Mom and my great Dad talking about a letter from great good friend Ross . . .

MARTIN

(*Deep anger*) Fuck Ross!!

BILLY

Yes? A letter from great good friend Ross written to great good Mom about how great good Dad has been out in the barnyard fucking *animals*!!

MARTIN

Don't . . . *do* this.

BILLY

Animals! Well, one in particular. A goat! A fucking goat! You see, guys, your stories are swell or whatever, but I've got one'll knock your socks off, as they used to say, wipe the tattoos right off your butts. Ya see, while great old Mom and great old Dad have been doing the great old parent thing, one of them has been underneath the house, down in the cellar, digging a pit so deep!, so wide!, so . . . HUGE! . . . we'll all fall in and (*crying now*) and never . . . be . . . able . . . to . . . climb . . . out . . . again—no matter how much we want to, how hard we try. And you see, kids, fellow students, you see, I love these people. I love the man who's been down there digging—when he's not giving it to a goat! I love this man! I love him! (*Drops whatever he's holding, moves to* MARTIN, *arms out*) I love him! (*Wraps his arms around* MARTIN, *who doesn't know what to do. Starts kissing* MARTIN *on the hands, then on the neck, crying the while. Then it turns—or does it?—and he kisses* MARTIN *full on the mouth—a deep, sobbing, sexual kiss.* ROSS *has entered, stands watching.* MARTIN *tries to disengage from* BILLY, *but* BILLY *moans, holds on. Finally* MARTIN *shoves him away.* BILLY *stands there, still sobbing, arms around nothing. They have not seen* ROSS.)

MARTIN

Don't *do* that!!

BILLY

I *love* you!

MARTIN

Sure you do, you . . . you . . .

BILLY

Faggot? You faggot?

MARTIN

(*Enraged*) That's not what I was going to say!!

BILLY

(*So sad; so sincere*) Dad! I *love* you! Hold me! Please!

MARTIN

(*Holds him; strokes him*) Shhhhhh; shhh; shhhhh now.

BILLY

(*Disengaging finally*) I'm sorry; I didn't mean to ...

MARTIN

No; it's all right. (*Arms out*) Here; let me hold you.

(BILLY *moves to him again; a momentary silent embrace*)

ROSS

Excuse me. (*They are startled, split. Maybe* BILLY *stumbles over something.*) I'm sorry; I didn't mean to interrupt your little ...

MARTIN

(*Cold fury*) What!? See a man and his son kissing? That would go nicely in one of your fucking letters. Judas! Get out of here!

BILLY

(*To* ROSS) It wasn't what you think!

MARTIN

(*At* BILLY) Yes! Yes, it was! Don't apologize. (*To* ROSS) Too bad you couldn't have brought your fucking TV crew over! Don't you and *your* son ever kiss? Don't you and—what's his name?—*Todd* love one another?

ROSS

(*Hard; contemptuous*) Not *that* way!

MARTIN

(*Angry and reckless*) *That* way!? *What* way!? (*Points vigorously at* BILLY) This boy is hurt! I've hurt him, and he still loves me! You fucker! He loves his father, and if it ... clicks over and becomes—what?—sexual for ... just a moment ... so what!? So fucking what!? He's hurt and he's lonely and mind your own fucking business!

ROSS

(*A sneer*) You're sicker than I thought.

MARTIN

No! I'm hysterical!

BILLY

(*Rueful wonder*) It *did*. It clicked over, and you were just another ...

MARTIN

It's all right.

BILLY

... another man. I get confused ... sex and love; loving and ... (*To* ROSS) I probably *do* want to sleep with him. (*Rueful laugh*) I want to sleep with everyone.

MARTIN

(*To quiet him*) It's all right.

BILLY

(*Still to* ROSS) Except you, probably.

ROSS

Jesus! Sick! What is it . . . contagious?

BILLY

(*Confused*) What? Is what?

MARTIN

(*Moves over to comfort* BILLY) There was a man told me once—a friend; we went to the same gym—he told me he had his kid on his lap one day—not even old enough to be a boy or a girl: a baby—and he had . . . *it* on his lap, and it was gurgling at him and making giggling sounds, and he had it with his arms around it, (*demonstrates*) in his lap, shifting it a little from side to side to make it happier, to make it giggle more . . . and all at once he realized he was getting hard.

ROSS

Jesus!

BILLY

Oh my God . . .

MARTIN

. . . that the baby in his lap was making him hard—not arousing him; it wasn't sexual, but it was happening.

ROSS

Jesus!

MARTIN

. . . his dick was rising to the baby in his lap—his baby; his lap. And when he realized what was happening, he thought he would die; his pulse was going a mile a minute; his ears were ringing-loud! Very *loud*! And he was going to faint; he *knew* it, and then the moment passed, and he knew it had all been an accident, that it meant . . . nothing—that nothing was connected to anything else. His wife came in; she smiled; he smiled and handed her the baby. And that was it; it was over. (*Shrugs*) Things happen. Besides—I'm hysterical. Remember?

ROSS

What are you doing? *Defending* yourself?! Jesus. You're sick.

MARTIN

(*Contempt*) Do you have any other words? Sick and Jesus? Is that all you have?

BILLY

(*Shy*) Was it me? Was it me, Dad? Was the baby me?

MARTIN

(*To* BILLY; *after a pause; gently*) Hush.

BILLY

(*Almost frightened*) Was it?

MARTIN

(*Turning to* ROSS) So, what do you want here now, motherfucker!? Judas!?

ROSS

Stevie called—what? An hour ago? More? She said you needed me; she said to come over.

MARTIN

I don't! Get out! (*Surprise*) She *called* you?

ROSS

Yes. (*Shakes his head*) Getting hard with a baby! Is there anything you people don't get off on!?

BILLY

(*Once more*) Was it, Dad?

MARTIN

(*So clearly a lie; gently*) Of course not, Billy. (*To* ROSS; *hard, eyes narrowing*) Is there anything "we people" don't get off on? Is there anything anyone doesn't get off on, whether we admit it or not—whether we *know* it or not? Remember Saint Sebastian with all the arrows shot into him? He probably came! God knows the faithful did! Shall I go on!? You want to hear about the cross!?

BILLY

(*Quietly; smiling*) No, of course it wasn't ... wasn't me.

ROSS

(*Shaking his head; sad, but with a lip curled*) Sick; sick; sick.

MARTIN

(*At* ROSS; *growing rage*) I'll tell you what's sick! Writing that fucking letter to Stevie—why doesn't matter!!—that's what's sick! I *tell* you about it; I share it with you, the ... the ... whole ... awful ... thing, because I think I've lost it, maybe; I *tell* you; I *share* it with you because you're ... what!? ... you're my best friend in the whole world? Because I needed to tell *somebody*, somebody with his head on straight enough to hear it? I *tell* you, and you fucking turn around and ...

ROSS

I *had* to!!

MARTIN

No! You *didn't*! You didn't *have* to!

ROSS

(*Dogmatic*) I couldn't let you *continue*!

MARTIN

(*Near tears*) I could have worked it out. I could have stopped, and no one would have known. Except you, motherfucker. Mister one strike and you're out. I could have ...

ROSS

No! You couldn't!

MARTIN

I could have worked it out! And now nothing can *ever* be put back together! *Ever*!

BILLY

(*Trying to help*) Dad . . .

MARTIN

(*Savage*) You shut up! (BILLY *winces*. MARTIN *reacts*) Oh, God! I'm sorry. (*To* ROSS) Yes; all right, it *was* sick, and yes, it *was* compulsive, and . . .

ROSS

IS! Not *was*! IS!

MARTIN

(*Stopped in his tracks*) I . . . I . . .

ROSS

IS!

MARTIN

(*Gathering himself*) *Is*. All right. *Is*. *Is* sick; *is* compulsive.

ROSS

(*Pushing*) And it was *wrong*!

MARTIN

It was . . . it was . . . what?

ROSS

Wrong! Deeply, destructively *wrong*!

MARTIN

Whatever you want. (*Rage growing*) But I could have handled it! You didn't have to bring it all down! You didn't have to destroy both of us; you didn't have to destroy Stevie, too! ROSS Me!? *Me* bring you down!? This isn't . . . embezzlement, honey; this isn't stealing from helpless widows; this isn't going to whores and coming down with the clap, or whatever, you know. This isn't the stuff that stops a career in its tracks for a little while—humiliation, public remorse, and then back up again. This is *beyond* that—*way* beyond it! You go on and you'll slip up one day. Somebody'll see you. Somebody'll surprise you one day, in whatever barn you put her in, no matter where you put her. Somebody'll see you, on your knees behind the damn animal; your pants around your ankles. Somebody will catch you at it.

BILLY

Let him alone. For God's sake, Ross . . .

ROSS

(*Waving* BILLY *off*; *to* MARTIN) Do you know there are prison terms for this?

Some states they kill you for it? Do you know what they'd *do* to you. The press? Everybody? Down it all comes—your career; your life ... everything. (*So cold; so rational*) For fucking a goat. (*Shakes his head sadly*; BILLY *is weeping quietly*)

MARTIN

(*Long pause*) Is *that* what it is, then? That people will *know*!? That people will find *out*!? That I can do whatever I want, and that's what matters!? That people will find *out*!? Fuck the ... thing it *self*!? Fuck what it *means*!? That people will find *out*!?

ROSS

Your soul is your own business. The rest I can *help* you with.

MARTIN

Of course it's my business, and clearly you don't have one.

ROSS

(*Mild interest*) Oh?

MARTIN

So that's what it comes down to, eh? ... what we can get away with?

ROSS

Sure.

MARTIN

(*Heavy irony*) Oh, thank God! It's so simple! I thought it was ... I thought it had to do with love and loss, and it's only about ... getting *by*. Well, Stevie and I have been wrestling with the wrong angel! When she comes back—*if* she comes back—I'll have to set her straight about what matters. (*Intense; not looking at* ROSS *or* BILLY; *pounding his hands on his knees perhaps*) Does nobody understand what happened!?

ROSS

Oh, for Christ's sake, Martin!

BILLY

Dad ...

MARTIN

(*Crying a little*) Why can't anyone understand this ... that I am *alone* ... all ... *alone*!

(*A silence. Then we hear a sound at the door.*)

BILLY

Mom? (BILLY *going into the hall. Gone.*)

MARTIN

(*Pause; to* ROSS, *begging*) You *do* understand; *don't* you.

ROSS

(*Long pause; shakes his head*) No.

(STEVIE *is dragging a dead goat. The goat's throat is cut; the blood is down*

STEVIE's *dress, on her arms. She stops*)

ROSS

Oh, my God.

MARTIN

What have you done!?

STEVIE

Here.

BILLY

(*Generally; to no one; helpless; a quiet plea*) Help. Help.

ROSS

Oh, my God.

(MARTIN *moves toward* STEVIE)

MARTIN

What have you done!? Oh, my God, what have you *done*!?

(BILLY *is crying*. STEVIE *regards* MARTIN *for a moment*; ROSS *is immobile*.)

STEVIE

(*Turns to face him; evenly, without emotion*) I went where Ross told me I would find ... your friend. I found her. I killed her. I brought her here to you. (*Odd little question*) No?

MARTIN

(*A profound cry*) ANNNNNNH!

STEVIE

Why are you surprised? What did you expect me to do.

MARTIN

(*Crying*) What did she *do*!? What did she ever *do*!? (*To* STEVIE) I ask you: what did she ever *do*!?

STEVIE

(*Pause; quietly*) She loved you ... you say. As much as *I* do.

MARTIN

(*To* STEVIE; *empty*) I'm sorry. (*To* BILLY; *empty*) I'm sorry. (*Then* ...) I'm sorry.

BILLY

(*To one, then the other; no reaction from them*) Dad? Mom?

(*Tableau*)

End

Topics for Discussion

1) What is the excerpt mainly about?

2) Why does Martin fall in love with a goat?
3) How is the goat described in the play?
4) What impact does Martin's abnormal behavior have?
5) What is Martin's wife's reaction after learning of his love for Sylvia?
6) What is Billy's reaction when he learns of his father's love for Sylvia?
7) What role does Sylvia play?
8) Why does Martin's wife kill Sylvia?
9) What is the theme of the play?
10) What would you do if you were Martin's wife?

Interdisciplinary Concepts for Further Thinking

Ethical Literary Criticism

Ethical literary criticism is a theory of interpreting and analyzing literature from an ethical perspective. It examines literature as a unique expression of ethics and morality within a certain historical period, and argues that literature is not just an art of language, but also an art of text. Ethical literary criticism is aimed at interpreting literary texts and claims that almost all literary texts are the records of human beings' moral experiences and contain ethical structures or ethical lines. Ethical lines form the main ethical structure.

1) What moral problem arises when Martin falls in love with Sylvia?
2) Analyze the moral problem in the play.

Thinking in Numbers

In this excerpt, the image of the goat appears for many times. Figure out how many and explain their implications in the different scenes.

Visual Thinking with Mind Mapping

The human-animal boundary has long been a topic that philosophers and anthropologists think about. In the modern world, human beings are often considered the measure of all things which reflects a typical anthropocentric way of thinking. However, in *The Goat, or Who is Sylvia?* the situation is quite different. Martin regards himself as the equal of Sylvia, a goat. Create a mind map to demonstrate the aspects that subvert the idea of anthropocentrism.

Critical Thinking for Reality

In the contemporary world, more and more people love raising pets and even consider their pets to be family members. It is not uncommon for some to develop an attachment to their pets. Can you accept that a person falls in love with his or her pet, or any other non-human being? Why?

Section Four

Diversity and Respect: Ethnic/Racial Relationship

There exist diverse civilizations and cultures in the world, just like there are diverse species in the nature. The world today is home to over 200 countries and regions, more than 2,500 ethnic groups and 6,000-plus languages. As different musical notes make a beautiful melody, people of different ethnicities, colors and historical and cultural backgrounds have jointly made our world a splendid and colorful place.

Since different ethnicities and races have developed their own cultures, it is safe to say that no single criterion can evaluate good or bad in an easy way. There is no one word that can be adopted to describe the culture in the world. In modern world, globalization has made the whole world one village. There has never been so much communication among different ethnicities and races. However, what should not be neglected is the fact that Western colonialism and imperialism brought devastating consequences to the diversity of ethnicities and races.

In the 21st century, people all over the world are unprecedentedly connected. The Chinese nation has always emphasized harmony through difference, concerted effort, and mutual cooperation. The community with a shared future for mankind is that the future and destiny of each nation and country are closely connected. Everyone should pull together for a common cause, share weal and woe, and strive to build our planet into a harmonious big family, thus turning the wish for a better life for people all over the world into reality. Although different countries and ethnicities have different histories and cultures, they should live in harmony and treat each other as equals. They should respect and learn from each other, and abandon all arrogance and prejudice. It is the responsibility of the whole world to deepen exchanges and mutual learning among civilizations.

Civilizations can be different, but no civilization is superior to others. Each civilization embodies the common vision and common aspirations of mankind shaped in the course of development and progress. There are a lot of works that reflect and explore into the colonial oppression, and the power relationship between different ethnicities and races, and the integration and clashes of different civilizations in English literature. Reading and having some discussion about these works will shed light on the western colonial history as well as the evolution of civilization, which is inspiring for us to have a better understanding of the significance of building a community of shared future for mankind.

Unit 12
My People

Langston Hughes

Introduction to the Author

Langston Hughes (1901—1967) was one of the most important writers and thinkers of the Harlem Renaissance and one of the earliest innovators of the then new literary art form called "jazz poetry". As simple as it is, his poetry stands for the height of literature in the New Negro Movement, after which he pursued his literary career and, in time, established himself as a columnist, dramatist, essayist, and novelist. Hughes's creative genius was influenced by his life in New York City's Harlem, a primarily African American neighborhood. His writing tapped into the common experience of Black life in America.

Distinct from the stereotypes of miserable downtrodden Negroes or "polished" middle class blacks, the blacks depicted in Hughes's book were the working-class who are "full of struggle, joy, laughter and music". He had a strong sense of racial pride. Through his poetry, novels, plays, essays, and children's books, he promoted equality, condemned racism and injustice, and celebrated African American culture, humor, and spirituality. His poems and novels, brimming over with his pride in his African ancestry, focus on "a racial consciousness and cultural nationalism devoid of self-hate", as he wrote "if people suffered, they suffered in beautiful language, not in monosyllables."

Introduction to the Work

Throughout the short lines of this poem, Hughes uses very few words to create effective images. His passion for the people he cares for is clear from the first lines. Beauty is the motif of this simple, rhythmic poem. Images of the night, stars and the sun are used in each of the three stanzas, representing the beauty of nature while the faces, eyes and souls pair with each image, highlighting the beauty and kindness of the black people inside out. To some extent, the darkness shading through dim into bright resonates with the wakening and struggle of the blacks, as well as the author's optimism for a bright future.

Text

My People

The night is beautiful,
So the faces of my people.
The stars are beautiful,
So the eyes of my people.
Beautiful, also, is the sun.
Beautiful, also, are the souls of my people.

Topics for Discussion

1) What does the poet convey throughout the poem?
2) What the important images are employed in the poem?
3) Can you find other words to replace "beautiful" in the poem?
4) What figures of speech are used in the poem?
5) Do you think the poem is powerful?

Interdisciplinary Concepts for Further Thinking

1. Internalized Oppression

In social justice theory, internalized oppression is a concept in which an oppressed group uses the methods of the oppressing group against itself.

Oppression occurs when one group has more access to power and privilege than another group, and when that power and privilege are used to maintain the status quo (i.e., domination of one group over another). Thus, oppression is both a state and a process, with the state of oppression being unequal group access to power and privilege, and the process of oppression being how inequality between groups is maintained. Oppression, therefore, results in the differentiation of people into groups (e. g., dominant/dominated, powerful/powerless, superior/inferior, oppressor/oppressed), and group membership determines the degree to which an individual has power or the opportunity and ability to access resources. Differentiating people into groups can be done in many ways (e. g., race, sex, sexual orientation, abilities) and, thus, oppression based on group membership also comes in various forms (e.g., racism, sexism, and ableism).

The persons who are the target of the hatred often believe the lie that they are inferior, that they are the problem, and that they are less worthy. The persons who are discriminated against over time will often shift from a healthy self-image into a self-image that exemplifies the lies of inferiority and inadequacy. When oppressed persons believe the lies that the oppressors tell them about their status as inferior—they have internalized the oppression.

1) What is the main idea of internalized oppression?

2) How is internalized oppression implied in "My People"?

2. Community

German sociologist Ferdinand Tönnies's book *Gemeinschaft und Gesellschaft* (*Community and Society*) published in 1887 is one of the most influential works in sociology and the politics that have been produced in the name of community. Community means genuine, enduring life together, whereas society is a transient and superficial thing. Thus, Gemeinschaft must be understood as a living organism in its own right, while Gesellschaft is a mechanical aggregate and artifact. Tönnies explains the evolution of community into a wider social area: "Community by blood, indicating primal unity of existence, develops more specifically into community of place, which is expressed first of all as living in close proximity to one another. This in turn becomes community of the spirit, working together for the same end and purpose." With this, he characterized the three forms of community: community by blood, community by place and community by spirit. An imagined community is a concept developed by Benedict Anderson in his 1983 book *Imagined Communities* to analyze nationalism. Anderson depicts a nation as a socially-constructed community, imagined by people who perceive themselves.

1) What kind of community is advocated in "My People" and what are its limits?

2) How is the sense of an imagined community enhanced?

Thinking in Numbers

In the poem, the poet uses the word "beautiful" 4 times. What do you think of the repetition? Will it be a better wording if we find another three words to replace "beautiful"? Why?

Visual Thinking with Mind Mapping

1) Create a mind map to demonstrate the influential figures throughout the Harlem Renaissance.

2) Analyze the Movements where black people pursue their rights with a mind map.

Critical Thinking for Reality

Building up confidence whether it concerns your skin, body, or just yourself in general is a personal journey that can take a lot of time, work, and self-love. There are a few starting points that are popular ways of beginning a confidence journey, from slow beauty rituals to daily affirmations. Is there anything that you do not feel confident about? How will you boost your confidence? Also, as a member of a nation, how will you enhance your sense of nationality?

Unit 13
Flying Home

Ralph Ellison

Introduction to the Author

Ralph Waldo Ellison (1913—1994) was a famous American writer, whose literary accomplishments span essays, criticisms, novels, and short stories. Ellison's early years as an outsider at Tuskegee Institute, a "prestigious all-black university" but "no less class-conscious than white institutions were", inspired his creation of *Invisible Man*, which won him the US National Book Award for Fiction in 1953 and secured him a place in the American Academy of Arts and Letters in 1975. The African American protagonist narrating his search for an identity and place in the society in the 1930s remained unnamed throughout. Fiction had been his major literary career. Some of his novels published posthumously include *Flying Home and Other Stories* in 1996, *Juneteenth* in 1999, and *Three Days Before the Shooting* in 2010. He was also a prolific writer of critical essays, which nourished his novels.

Introduction to the Work

"Flying Home", a short story published in 1943, is set in WWII, when the FDR administration decided to enlist African Americans into the Army Air Corps. Since childhood, the hero, Todd, had a deep-rooted self-hate and hostility toward his fellow blacks because his dream of having a toy plane like the white kids never came true. Eventually, his childhood dream translated into flying a real plane as a pilot, whereby he could be identified as a member of the white community. It turned out that the Army was just as segregated, where no amount of effort and talent on Todd's part could earn him the respect and equal treatment he had been craving. His status in the Army never rose above that of the maintenance crew, medics, or other support units. Even though he refused to come to terms with his black identity, he was an outsider either in the company of his black brothers or in the mainstream society dominated by the whites.

Text

Flying Home

When Todd came to, he saw two faces suspended above him in a sun so hot and blinding that he could not tell if they were black or white. He stirred, feeling a pain that burned as though his whole body had been laid open to the sun which glared into his eyes. For a moment an old fear of being touched by white hands seized him. Then the very sharpness of the pain began slowly to clear his head. Sounds came to him dimly. *He done come to.* Who are they? he thought. *Naw he ain't, I coulda sworn he was white.* Then he heard clearly,

"You hurt bad?"

Something within him uncoiled. It was a Negro sound.

"He's still out," he heard.

"Give 'im time ... Say, son, you hurt bad?"

Was he? There was that awful pain. He lay rigid, hearing their breathing and trying to weave a meaning between them and his being stretched painfully upon the ground. He watched them warily, his mind traveling back over a painful distance. Jagged scenes, swiftly unfolding as in a movie trailer, reeled through his mind, and he saw himself piloting a tailspinning plane and landing and falling from the cockpit and trying to stand. Then, as in a great silence, he remembered the sound of crunching bone and, now, looking up into the anxious faces of an old Negro man and a boy from where he lay in the same field, the memory sickened him and he wanted to remember no more.

"How you feel, son?"

Todd hesitated, as though to answer would be to admit an inacceptable weakness. Then, "It's my ankle," he said.

"Which one?"

"The left."

With a sense of remoteness he watched the old man bend and remove his boot, feeling the pressure ease.

"That any better?"

"A lot. Thank you."

He had the sensation of discussing someone else, that his concern was with some far more important thing, which for some reason escaped him.

"You done broke it bad," the old man said. "We have to get you to a doctor."

He felt that he had been thrown into a tailspin. He looked at his watch; how long had he been here? He knew there was but one important thing in the world, to get the plane back to the field before his officers were displeased.

"Help me up," he said. "Into the ship."

"But it's broke too bad ..."

"Give me your arm!"

"But, son ..."

Clutching the old man's arm he pulled himself up, keeping his left leg clear, thinking, "I'd never make him understand," as the leather-smooth face came parallel with his own.

"Now, let's see."

He pushed the old man back, hearing a bird's insistent shrill. He swayed, giddily. Blackness washed over him, like infinity.

"You best sit down."

"No, I'm O.K."

"But, son. You jus' gonna make it worse ..."

It was a fact that everything in him cried out to deny, even against the flaming pain in his ankle. He would have to try again.

"You mess with that ankle they have to cut your foot off," he heard.

Holding his breath, he started up again. It pained so badly that he had to bite his lips to keep from crying out and he allowed them to help him down with a pang of despair.

"It's best you take it easy. We gon' git you a doctor."

Of all the luck, he thought. Of all the rotten luck, now I have done it. The fumes of high-octane gasoline clung in the heat, taunting him.

"We kin ride him into town on old Ned," the boy said.

Ned? He turned, seeing the boy point toward an ox team, browsing where the buried blade of a plow marked the end of a furrow. Thoughts of himself riding an ox through the town, past streets full of white faces, down the concrete runways of the airfield made swift images of humiliation in his mind. With a pang he remembered his girl's last letter. "Todd," she had written, "I don't need the papers to tell me you had the intelligence to fly. And I have always known you to be as brave as anyone else. The papers annoy me. Don't you be contented to prove over and over again that you're brave or skillful just because you're black, Todd. I think they keep beating that dead horse because they don't want to say why you boys are not yet fighting. I'm really disappointed, Todd. Anyone with brains can learn to fly, but then what. What about using it, and who will you use it for? I wish, dear, you'd write about this. I sometimes think they're playing a trick on us. It's very humiliating ..." He whipped cold sweat from his face, thinking, What does she know of humiliation? She's never been down South. *Now* the humiliation would come. When you must have them judge you, knowing that they never accept your mistakes as your own, but hold it against your whole race—that was humiliation. Yes, and humiliation was when you could never be simply yourself; when you were always a part of this old black ignorant man. Sure, he's all right. Nice and kind and helpful. But he's not you. Well, there's one humiliation I can spare myself.

"No," he said, "I have orders not to leave the ship ..."

"Aw," the old man said. Then turning to the boy, "Teddy, then you better hustle down to Mister Graves and get him to come ..."

"No, wait!" he protested before he was fully aware. Graves might be white. "Just have him get word to the field, please. They'll take care of the rest."

He saw the boy leave, running.

"How far does he have to go?"

"Might' nigh a mile."

He rested back, looking at the dusty face of his watch. But now they know something has happened, he thought. In the ship there was a perfectly good radio, but it was useless. The old fellow would never operate it. That buzzard knocked me back a hundred years, he thought. Irony danced within him like the gnats circling the old man's head. With all I've learned I'm dependent upon this "peasant's" sense of time and space. His leg throbbed. In the plane, instead of time being measured by the rhythms of pain and a kid's legs, the instruments would have told him at a glance. Twisting upon his elbows he saw where dust had powdered the plane's fuselage, feeling the lump form in his throat that was always there when he thought of flight. It's crouched there, he thought, like the abandoned shell of a locust. I'm naked without it. Not a machine, a suit of clothes you wear. And with a sudden embarrassment and wonder he whispered, "It's the only dignity I have ..."

He saw the old man watching, his torn overalls clinging limply to him in the heat. He felt a sharp need to tell the old man what he felt. But that would be meaningless. If I tried to explain why I need to fly back, he'd think I was simply afraid of white officers. But it's more than fear ... a sense of anguish clung to him like the veil of sweat that hugged his face. He watched the old man, hearing him humming snatches of a tune as he admired the plane. He felt a furtive sense of resentment. Such old men often came to the field to watch the pilots with childish eyes. At first it had made him proud; they had been a meaningful part of a new experience. But soon he realized they did not understand his accomplishments and they came to shame and embarrass him, like the distasteful praise of an idiot. A part of the meaning of flying had gone, then, and he had not been able to regain it. If I were a prize-fighter I would be more human, he thought. Not a monkey doing tricks, but a man. They were pleased simply that he was a Negro who could fly, and that was not enough. He felt cut off from them by age, by understanding, by sensibility, by technology and by his need to measure himself against the mirror of other men's appreciation. Somehow he felt betrayed, as he had when as a child he grew to discover that his father was dead. Now, for him, any real appreciation lay with his white officers; and with them he could never be sure. Between ignorant black men and condescending whites, his course of flight seemed mapped by the nature of things away from all needed and natural landmarks. Under some sealed orders, couched in ever more technical and mysterious terms, his path curved swiftly away from both the shame the old man symbolized and the cloudy terrain of white man's regard. Flying blind, he knew but one point of landing and there he would receive his wings. After that the enemy would appreciate his skill and he would assume his deepest meaning, he thought sadly, neither from those who condescended nor from those who praised without understanding, but from the enemy who would recognize his manhood and skill in terms of hate ...

He sighed, seeing the oxen making queer, prehistoric shadows against the dry brown earth.

"You just take it easy, son," the old man soothed. "That boy won't take long. Crazy as he is about airplanes."

"I can wait," he said.

"What kinda airplane you call this here'n?"

"An Advanced Trainer," he said, seeing the old man smile. His fingers were like gnarled dark wood against the metal as he touched the low-slung wing.

"'Bout how fast can she fly?"

"Over two hundred an hour."

"Lawd! That's so fast I bet it don't seem like you moving!"

Holding himself rigid, Todd opened his flying suit. The shade had gone and he lay in a ball of fire.

"You mind if I take a look inside? I was always curious to see ..."

"Help yourself. Just don't touch anything."

He heard him climb upon the metal wing, grunting. Now the questions would start. Well, so you don't have to think to answer ...

He saw the old man looking over into the cockpit, his eyes bright as a child's.

"You must have to know a lot to work all these here things."

He was silent, seeing him step down and kneel beside him.

"Son, how come you want to fly way up there in the air?"

Because it's the most meaningful act in the world . . . because it makes me less like you, he thought.

But he said: "Because I like it, I guess. It's as good a way to fight and die as I know."

"Yeah? I guess you right," the old man said. "But how long you think before they gonna let you all fight?"

He tensed. This was the question all Negroes asked, put with the same timid hopefulness and longing that always opened a greater void within him than that he had felt beneath the plane the first time he had flown. He felt lightheaded. It came to him suddenly that there was something sinister about the conversation, that he was flying unwillingly into unsafe and uncharted regions. If he could only be insulting and tell this old man who was trying to help him to shut up!

"I bet you one thing . . ."

"Yes?"

"That you was plenty scared coming down."

He did not answer. Like a dog on a trail the old man seemed to smell out his fears and he felt anger bubble within him.

"You sho' scared *me*. When I seen you coming down in that thing with it a-rollin' and a-jumpin' like a pitchin' hoss, I thought sho' you was a goner. I almost had me a stroke!"

He saw the old man grinning, "Ever'thin's been happening round here this morning, come to think of it."

"Like what?" he asked.

"Well, first thing I know, here come two white fellers, looking for Mister Rudolph, that's Mister Graves' cousin. That got me worked up right away . . ."

"Why?"

"Why? 'Cause he done broke outta the crazy house, that's why. He liable to kill somebody," he said. "They oughta have him by now though. Then here *you* come. First I think it's one of them white boys. Then dog-gone if you don't fall outta there. Lawd, I'd done heard about you boys but I haven't never *seen* one o' you-all. Cain't tell you how it felt to see somebody what look like me in a airplane!"

The old man talked on, the sound streaming around Todd's thoughts like air flowing over the fuselage of a flying plane. You were a fool, he thought, remembering how before the spin the sun had blazed, bright against the billboard signs beyond the town, and how a boy's blue kite had bloomed beneath him, tugging gently in the wind like a strange, odd-shaped flower. He had once flown such kites himself and tried to find the boy at the end of the invisible cord. But he had been flying too high and too fast. He had climbed steeply away in exultation. Too steeply, he thought. And one of

Unit 13　*Flying Home*

the first rules you learn is that if the angle of thrust is too steep the plane goes into a spin. And then, instead of pulling out of it and going into a dive you let a buzzard panic you. A lousy buzzard!

"Son, what made all that blood on the glass?"

"A buzzard," he said, remembering how the blood and feathers had sprayed back against the hatch. It had been as though he had flown into a storm of blood and blackness.

"Well, I declare! They's lots of 'em around here. They after dead things. Don't eat nothing what's alive."

"A little bit more and he would have made a meal out of me," Todd said grimly.

"They bad luck all right. Teddy's got a name for 'em, calls 'em 'jim-crows,'" the old man laughed.

"It's a damned good name."

"They the damnedest birds. Once I seen a hoss all stretched out like he was sick, you know. So I hollers, 'Gid up from there, suh!' Just to make sho! An, doggone, son, if I don't see two ole jimcrows come flying right up outa that hoss's insides! Yessuh! The sun was shinin' on 'em and they couldn't a been no greasier if they'd been eating barbecue!"

Todd thought he would vomit, his stomach quivered.

"You made that up," he said.

"Nawsuh! Saw him just like I see you."

"Well, I'm glad it was you."

"You see lots a funny things down here, son."

"No, I'll let you see them," he said.

"By the way, the white folks round here don't like to see you boys up there in the sky. They ever bother you?"

"No."

"Well, they'd like to."

"Someone always wants to bother someone else," Todd said. "How do you know?"

"I just know."

"Well," he said defensively, "no one has bothered us."

Blood pounded in his ears as he looked away into space. He tensed, seeing a black spot in the sky and strained to confirm what he could not clearly see.

"What does that look like to you?" he asked excitedly.

"Just another bad luck, son."

Then he saw the movement of wings with disappointment. It was gliding smoothly down, wings outspread, tail feathers gripping the air, down swiftly—gone behind the green screen of trees. It was like a bird he had imagined there, only the sloping branches of the pines remained, sharp against the pale stretch of sky. He lay barely breathing and stared at the point where it had disappeared, caught in a spell of loathing and admiration. Why did they make them so disgusting and yet teach them to fly so well? *It's like when I was up in heaven* he heard, starting.

The old man was chuckling, rubbing his stubbed chin.

"What did you say?"

"Sho', I died and went to heaven ... maybe by time I tell you about it they be done come after you."

"I hope so," he said wearily.

"You boys ever sit around and swap lies?"

"Not often. Is this going to be one?"

"Well, I ain't so sho', on account of it took place when I was dead."

The old man paused, "That wasn't no lie 'bout the buzzards, though."

"All right," he said.

"Sho' you want to hear 'bout heaven?"

"Please," he answered, resting his head upon his arm.

"Well, I went to heaven and right away started to sproutin' me some wings. Six foot ones, they was. Just like them the white angels had. I couldn't hardly believe it. I was so glad that I went off on some clouds by myself and tried 'em out. You know, 'cause I didn't want to make a fool outta myself the first thing . . . ."

It's an old tale, Todd thought. Told me years ago. Had forgotten. But at least it will keep him from talking about buzzards.

He closed his eyes, listening.

" . . . First thing I done was to git up on a low cloud and jump of. And doggone, boy, if them wings didn't work! First I tried the right; then I tried the left; then I tried 'em both together. Then, Lawd, I started to move on out among the folks. I let 'em see me . . ."

He saw the old man gesturing flight with his arms, his face full of mock pride as he indicated an imaginary crowd, thinking, *I'll be in the newspapers*, as he heard, " . . . so I went and found me some colored angels—somehow I didn't believe I was an angel 'til I seen a real black one, ha, yes! Then I was sho'—but they tole me I better come down 'cause us colored folks had to wear a special kin'a harness when we flew. That was how come *they* wasn't flyin'. Oh yes, an' you had to be extra strong for a black man even, to fly with one of them harnesses . . ."

This is a new turn, Todd thought, what's he driving at?

"So I said to myself, I ain't gonna be bothered with no harness! Oh naw! 'Cause if God let you sprout wings you oughta have sense enough not to let nobody make you wear something what gits in the way of flyin'. So I starts to flyin', Hecks, son," he chuckled, his eyes twinkling, "you know I had to let eve'ybody know that old Jefferson could fly good as anybody else. And I could too, fly smooth as a bird! I could even loop-the-loop—only I had to make sho' to keep my long white robe down roun' my ankles ... "

Todd felt uneasy. He wanted to laugh at the joke, but his body refused, as of an independent will. He felt as he had as a child when after he had chewed a sugar-coated pill which his mother had given him, she had laughed at his efforts to remove the terrible taste.

" ... Well," he heard. "I was doing all right 'til I got to speeding. Found out I could fan up a right strong breeze, I could fly so fast. I could do all kin'sa stunts too. I started flying up to the stars and divin' down and zooming roun' the moon. Man, I like to scare the devil outa some ole white angels. I was raisin' hell. Not that I meant any harm, son. But I was just feeling good. It was so good to know I was free at last. I accidently knocked the tips offa some stars and they tell me I caused a storm and a coupla lynchings down here in Macon County—though I swear I believe them boys what said that was making up lies on me ... "

He's mocking me, Todd thought angrily. He thinks it's a joke. Grinning down at me ... His throat was dry. He looked at his watch; why the hell didn't they come? Since they had to, why? *One day I was flying down one of them heavenly streets.* You got yourself into it, Todd thought. Like Jonah in the whale.

"Justa throwin' feathers in everybody's face. An' ole Saint Peter called me in. Said, 'Jefferson, tell me two things, what you doin' flyin' without a harness; an' how come you flyin' so fast?' So I tole him I was flyin' without a harness 'cause it got in my way, but I couldn'ta been flyin' so fast, 'cause I wasn't usin' but one wing. Saint Peter said, 'You wasn't flyin' with but *one* wing?' 'Yessuh,' I says, scared-like. So he says, 'Well, since you got sucha extra fine pair of wings you can leave off yo' harness awhile. But from now on none of that there one-wing flyin', 'cause you gittin' up too damn much speed!'"

And with one mouth full of bad teeth you're making too damned much talk, thought Todd. Why don't I send him after the boy? His body ached from the hard ground and seeking to shift his position he twisted his ankle and hated himself for crying out.

"It gittin' worse?"

"I ... I twisted it," he groaned.

"Try not to think about it, son. That's what I do."

He bit his lip, fighting pain with counter pain as the voice resumed its rhythmical droning. Jefferson seemed caught in his own creation.

" ... After all that trouble I just floated roun' heaven in slow motion. But I forgot like colored folks will do and got to flyin' with one wing agin. This time I was restin' my ole broken arm and got to flyin' fast enough to shame the devil. I was comin' so fast, Lawd, I got myself called befo' ole Saint Peter agin. He said, 'Jeff, didn't I warn you 'bout that speedin'?' 'Yessuh,' I says, 'but it was an accident.' He looked at me sad-like and shook his head and I knowed I was gone. He said, 'Jeff, you and that speedin' is a danger to the heavenly community. If I was to let you keep on flyin', heaven wouldn't be nothin' but uproar. Jeff, you got to go!' Son, I argued and pleaded with that old white man, but it didn't do a bit of good. They rushed me straight to them pearly gates and gimme a parachute and a map of the state of Alabam ..."

Todd heard him laughing so that he could hardly speak, making a screen between them upon which his humiliation glowed like fire.

"Maybe you'd better stop a while," he said, his voice unreal.

"Ain't much more," Jefferson laughed. "When they gimme the parachute ole Saint Peter ask me if l wanted to say a few words before I went. I felt so bad I couldn't hardly look at him, specially with all them white angels standin' around. Then somebody laughed and made me mad. So I tole him, 'Well, you done took my wings. And you puttin' me out. You got charge of things so's I can't do nothin' about it. But you got to admit just this: While I was up here I was the flyinest son of a bitch what ever hit heaven!"

At the burst of laughter Todd felt such an intense humiliation that only great violence would wash it away. The laughter which shook the old man like a boiling purge set up vibrations of guilt within him which not even the intricate machinery of the plane would have been adequate to transform and he heard himself screaming, "Why do you laugh at me this way?"

He hated himself at that moment, but he had lost control. He saw Jefferson's mouth fall open, "What—?"

"Answer me!"

His blood pounded as though it would surely burst his temples and he tried to reach the old man and fell, screaming, "Can I help it because they won't let us actually fly? Maybe we are a bunch of buzzards feeding on a dead horse, but we can hope to be eagles, can't we? *Can't we?*"

He fell back, exhausted, his ankle pounding. The saliva was like straw in his mouth. If he had the strength he would strangle this old man. This grinning, grey-headed clown who made him feel as he felt when watched by the white officers at the field. And yet this old man had neither power, prestige, rank nor technique. Nothing that could rid him of this terrible feeling. He watched him, seeing his face struggle to express a turmoil of feeling.

"What you mean, son? What you talking 'bout ...?"

"Go away. Go tell your tales to the white folks."

"But I didn't mean nothing like that ... I ... I wasn't tryin' to hurt your feelings ..."

"Please. Get the hell away from me!"

"But I didn't, son. I didn't mean all them things a-tall."

Todd shook as with a chill, searching Jefferson's face for a trace of the mockery he had seen there. But now the face was somber and tired and old. He was confused. He could not be sure that there had ever been laughter there, that Jefferson had ever really laughed in his whole life. He saw Jefferson reach out to touch him and shrank away, wondering if anything except the pain, now causing his vision to waver, was real. Perhaps he had imagined it all.

"Don't let it get you down, son," the voice said pensively.

He heard Jefferson sigh wearily, as though he felt more than he could say. His anger ebbed, leaving only the pain.

"I'm sorry," he mumbled.

"You just wore out with pain, was all ..."

He saw him through a blur, smiling. And for a second he felt the embarrassed silence of understanding flutter between them.

"What you was doin' flyin' over this section, son? Wasn't you scared they might shoot you for a crow?"

Todd tensed. Was he being laughed at again? But before he could decide the pain shook him and a part of him was lying calmly behind the screen of pain that had fallen between them, recalling the first time he had ever seen a plane. It was as though an endless series of hangars had been shaken ajar in the air base of his memory and from each, like a young wasp emerging from its cell, arose the memory of a plane.

> *The first time I ever saw a plane I was very small and planes were new in the world. I was four-and-a-half and the only plane that I had ever seen was a model suspended from the ceiling of the automobile exhibit at the State Fair. But I did not know that it was only a model. I did not know how large a real plane was, nor how expensive. To me it was a fascinating toy, complete in itself, which my mother said could only be owned by rich little white boys. I stood rigid with admiration, my head straining backwards as I watched the grey little plane describing arcs above the gleaming tops of the automobiles. And I vowed that, rich or poor, some day I would own such a toy. My mother had to drag me out of the exhibit, and not even the merry-go-round, the Ferris wheel, or the racing horses could hold my attention for the rest of the Fair. I was too busy imitating the tiny drone of the plane with my lips, and imitating with my hands the motion, swift and circling, that it made in flight.*
>
> *After that I no longer used the pieces of lumber that lay about our back yard to construct wagons and autos ... now it was used for airplanes. I built bi-planes, using pieces of board for wings, a small box for the fuselage, another piece of wood for the rudder. The trip to the Fair had brought something new into my small world. I asked my mother repeatedly when the Fair would come back again. I'd lie in the grass and watch the sky and each fighting bird became a soaring plane. I would have been good a year just to have seen a plane again. I became a nuisance to everyone with my questions about airplanes. But planes were new to the old folks,*

too, and there was little that they could tell me. Only my uncle knew some of the answers. And better still, he could carve propellers from pieces of wood that would whirl rapidly in the wind, wobbling noisily upon oiled nails.

I wanted a plane more than I'd wanted anything; more than I wanted the red wagon with rubber tires, more than the train that ran on a track with its train of cars. I asked my mother over and over again:

"Mamma?"

"What do you want, boy?" she'd say.

"Mamma, will you get mad if I ask you?" I'd say.

"What do you want now, I ain't got time to be answering a lot of fool questions. What you want?"

"Mamma, when you gonna get me one . . . ?" I'd ask.

"Get you one what?" she'd say.

"You know, Mamma; what I been asking you . . ."

"Boy," she'd say, "if you don't want a spanking you better come on 'n tell me what you talking about so I can get on with my work."

"Aw, Mamma, you know . . ."

"What I just tell you?" she'd say.

"I mean when you gonna buy me a airplane."

"AIRPLANE! Boy, is you crazy? How many times I have to tell you to stop that foolishness. I done told you them things cost too much, I bet I'm gon' wham the living daylight out of you if you don't quit worrying me 'bout them things!"

But this did not stop me, and a few days later I'd try all over again.

Then one day a strange thing happened. It was spring and for some reason I had been hot and irritable all morning. It was a beautiful spring. I could feel it as I played barefoot in the backyard. Blossoms hung from the thorny black locust trees like clusters of fragrant white grapes. Butterflies flickered in the sunlight above the short new dew-wet grass. I had gone in the house for bread and butter and coming out I heard a steady unfamiliar drone. It was unlike anything I had ever heard before. I tried to place the sound. It was no use. It was a sensation like that I had when searching for my father's watch, heard ticking unseen in a room. It made me feel as though I had forgotten to perform some task that my mother had ordered . . . then I located it, overhead. In the sky, flying quite low and about a hundred yards off was a plane! It came so slowly that it seemed barely to move. My mouth hung wide; my bread and butter fell into the dirt. I wanted to jump up and down and cheer. And when the idea struck I trembled with excitement: "Some little white boy's plane's done flew away and all I got to do is stretch out my hands and it'll be mine!" It was a little plane like that at the Fair, flying no higher than the eaves of our roof. Seeing it come steadily forward I felt the world grow warm with promise. I opened the screen and climbed over it and clung there, waiting. I would catch the plane as it came over and swing down fast and run into the house before anyone could see me. Then no one could come to claim the plane. It droned nearer. Then when it hung like a silver cross in the blue directly above me I stretched out my hand and grabbed. It was like sticking my finger through a soap bubble. The plane flew on, as though I had simply blown my breath after it. I grabbed again, frantically, trying to catch the tail. My fingers clutched the air and disappointment surged tight and hard in my throat. Giving one last desperate grasp, I strained forward. My fingers ripped from the screen. I was falling. The ground burst hard against me. I drummed the earth with my heels and when my breath returned, I lay there bawling.

My mother rushed through the door.

"What's the matter, chile! What on earth is wrong with you?"

"It's gone! It's gone!"

"What gone?"

"The airplane ..."

"Airplane?"

"Yessum, jus' like the one at the Fair ... I ... I tried to stop it an' it kep' right on going ..."

"When, boy?"

"Just now," I cried through my tears,

"Where it go, boy, what way?"

"Yonder, there ..."

She scanned the sky, her arms akimbo and her checkered apron flapping in the wind as I pointed to the fading plane. Finally she looked down at me, slowly shaking her head.

"It's gone! It's gone!" I cried.

"Boy, is you a fool?" she said, "Don't you see that there's a real airplane 'stead of one of them toy ones?"

"Real ...?" I forgot to cry. "Real?"

"Yass, real. Don't you know that thing you reaching for is bigger'n a auto? You here trying to reach for it and I bet it's flying 'bout two hundred miles higher'n this roof." She was disgusted with me. "You come on in this house before somebody else sees what a fool you done turned out to be. You must think these here li'l ole arms of your'n is mighty long ..."

I was carried into the house and undressed for bed and the doctor was called. I cried bitterly; as much from the disappointment of finding the plane so far beyond my reach as from the pain.

When the doctor came I heard my mother telling him about the plane and asking if anything was wrong with my mind. He explained that I had had a fever for several hours. But I was kept in bed for a week and I constantly saw the plane in my sleep, flying just beyond my finger tips, sailing so slowly that it seemed barely to move. And each time I'd reach out to grab it I'd miss and through each dream I'd hear my grandma warning:

"Young man, young man
Yo' arm's too short
To box with God ..."

"Hey, son!"

At first he did not know where he was and looked at the old man pointing, with blurred eyes.

"Ain't that one of you-all's airplanes coming after you?"

As his vision cleared he saw a small black shape above a distant field, soaring through waves of heat. But he could not be sure and with the pain he feared that somehow a horrible recurring fantasy of being split in twain by the whirling blades of a propeller had come true.

"You think he sees us?" he heard.

"See? I hope so."

"He's coming like a bat outa hell!"

Straining, he heard the faint sound of a motor and hoped it would soon be over.

"How you feeling?"

"Like a nightmare," he said.

"Hey, he's done curved back the other way!"

"Maybe he saw us," he said. "Maybe he's gone to send out the ambulance and ground crew." And, he thought with despair, maybe he didn't even see us.

"Where did you send the boy?"

"Down to Mister Graves," Jefferson said. "Man what owns this land."

"Do you think he phoned?"

Jefferson looked at him quickly.

"Aw sho'. Dabney Graves is got a bad name on accounta them killings but he'll call though . . ."

"What killings?"

"Them five fellers . . . ain't you heard?" he asked with surprise.

"No."

"Everybody knows 'bout Dabney Graves, especially the colored. He done killed enough of us."

Todd had the sensation of being caught in a white neighborhood after dark.

"What did they do?" he asked.

"Thought they was men," Jefferson said. "An' some he owed money, like he do me . . ."

"But why do you stay here?"

"You black, son."

"I know, but . . ."

"You have to come by the white folks, too."

He turned away from Jefferson's eyes, at once consoled and accused. And I'll have to come by them soon, he thought with despair. Closing his eyes, he heard Jefferson's voice as the sun burned blood red upon his lids.

"I got nowhere to go," Jefferson said, "an' they'd come after me if I did. But

Dabney Graves is a funny fellow. He's all the time making jokes. He can be mean as hell, then he's liable to turn right around and back the colored against the white folks. I seen him do it. But me, I hates him for that more'n anything else. 'Cause just as soon as he gits tired helping a man he don't care what happens to him. He just leaves him stone cold. And then the other white folks is double hard on anybody he done helped. For him it's just a joke. He don't give a hilla beans for nobody—but himself . . ."

Todd listened to the thread of detachment in the old man's voice. It was as though he held his words at arm's length before him to avoid their destructive meaning.

"He'd just as soon do you a favor and then turn right around and have you strung up. Me, I stays outa his way 'cause down here that's what you gotta do."

If my ankle would only ease for a while, he thought. The closer I spin toward the earth the blacker I became, flashed through his mind. Sweat ran into his eyes and he was sure that he would never see the plane if his head continued whirling. He tried to see Jefferson, what it was that Jefferson held in his hand? It was a little black man, another Jefferson! A little black Jefferson that shook with fits of belly-laughter while the other Jefferson looked on with detachment. Then Jefferson looked up from the thing in his hand and turned to speak but Todd was far away, searching the sky for a plane in a hot dry land on a day and age he had long forgotten. He was going mysteriously with his mother through empty streets where black faces peered from behind drawn shades and someone was rapping at a window and he was looking back to see a hand and a frightened face frantically beckoning from a cracked door and his mother was looking down the empty perspective of the street and shaking her head and hurrying him along and at first it was only a flash he saw and a motor was droning as through the sun-glare he saw it gleaming silver as it circled and he was seeing a burst like a puff of white smoke and hearing his mother yell, Come along, boy, I got no time for them fool airplanes, I got no time, and he saw it a second time, the plane flying high, and the burst appeared suddenly and fell slowly, billowing out and sparkling like fireworks and he was watching and being hurried along as the air filled with a flurry of white pin-wheeling cards that caught in the wind and scattered over the roof-tops and into the gutters and a woman was running and snatching a card and reading it and screaming and he darted into the shower, grabbing as in winter he grabbed for snowflakes and bounding away at his mother's, Come on here, boy! Come on, I say! and he was watching as she took the card away seeing her face grow puzzled and turning taut as her voice quavered, "Niggers Stay From The Polls," and died to a moan of terror as he saw the eyeless sockets of a white hood staring at him from the card and above he saw the plane spiraling gracefully, agleam in the sun like a fiery sword. And seeing it soar he was caught, transfixed between a terrible horror and a horrible fascination.

The sun was not so high now, and Jefferson was calling and gradually he saw three figures moving across the curving roll of the field.

"Look like some doctors, all dressed in white," said Jefferson.

They're coming at last, Todd thought. And he felt such a release of tension within him that he thought he would faint. But no sooner did he close his eyes than he was seized and he was struggling with three white men who were forcing his arms into some kind of coat. It was too much for him, his arms were pinned to his sides and as the pain blazed in his eyes, he realized that it was a straight-jacket. What filthy joke was this?

"That oughta hold him, Mister Graves," he heard.

His total energies seemed focused in his eyes as he searched their faces. That was Graves, the other two wore hospital uniforms. He was poised between two poles of fear and hate as he heard the one called Graves saying,

"He looks kinda purty in that there suit, boys. I'm glad you dropped by."

"This boy ain't crazy, Mister Graves," one of the others said. "He needs a doctor, not us. Don't see how you led us way out here anyway. It might be a joke to you, but your cousin Rudolph liable to kill somebody. White folks or niggers don't make no difference . . ."

Todd saw the man turn red with anger. Graves looked down upon him, chuckling.

"This nigguh belongs in a straight-jacket, too, boys. I knowed that the minit Jeff's kid said something 'bout a nigguh flyer. You all know you cain't let the nigguh git up that high without his going crazy. The nigguh brain ain't built right for high altitudes . . ."

Todd watched the drawling red face, feeling that all the unnamed horror and obscenities that he had ever imagined stood materialized before him.

"Let's git outta here," one of the attendants said.

Todd saw the other reach toward him, realizing for the first time that he lay upon a stretcher as he yelled,

"Don't put your hands on me!"

They drew back, surprised.

"What's that you say, nigguh?" asked Graves.

He did not answer and thought that Graves' foot was aimed at his head. It landed in his chest and he could hardly breathe. He coughed helplessly, seeing Graves' lips stretch taut over his yellow teeth and tried to shift his head. It was as though a half-dead fly was dragging slowly across his face and a bomb seemed to burst within him. Blasts of hot, hysterical laughter tore from his chest, causing his eyes to pop and he felt that the veins in his neck would surely burst. And then a part of him stood behind it all, watching the surprise in Graves' red face and his own hysteria. He thought he would never stop, he would laugh himself to death. It rang in his ears like Jefferson's laughter and he looked for him, centering his eyes desperately upon his face, as though somehow he had become his sole salvation in an insane world of outrage and humiliation. It brought a certain relief. He was suddenly aware that although his body was still contorted it was an echo that no longer rang in his ears. He heard Jefferson's voice with gratitude.

"Mister Graves, the Army done tole him not to leave his airplane."

"Nigguh, Army or no, you gittin' off my land! That airplane can stay 'cause it was paid for by taxpayers' money. But you gittin' off. An' dead or alive, it don't make no difference to me."

Todd was beyond it now, lost in a world of anguish.

"Jeff," Graves said, "you and Teddy come and grab holt. I want you to take this here black eagle over to that nigguh airfield and leave him."

Jefferson and the boy approached him silently. He looked away, realizing and doubting at once that only they could release him from his overpowering sense of isolation.

They bent for the stretcher. One of the attendants moved toward Teddy.

"Think you can manage it, boy?"

"I think I can, suh," Teddy said.

"Well, you better go behind then, and let yo' pa go ahead so's to keep that leg elevated."

He saw the white men walking ahead as Jefferson and the boy carried him along in silence. Then they were pausing and he felt a hand wiping his face, then he was moving again. And it was as though he had been lifted out of his isolation, back into the world of men. A new current of communication flowed between the man and boy and himself. They moved him gently. Far away he heard a mocking-bird liquidly calling. He raised his eyes, seeing a buzzard poised unmoving in space. For a moment the whole afternoon seemed suspended and he waited for the horror to seize him again. Then like a song within his head he heard the boy's soft humming and saw the dark bird glide into the sun and glow like a bird of flaming gold.

Topics for Discussion

1) What is Todd's racial identity?
2) What is the central event in the story?
3) How does the airplane crash happen in the story?
4) What are the consequences of the airplane crash?
5) What is Todd's first response after he regains consciousness?
6) Why does Todd want to become a pilot so much?
7) What does the phrase "the eyeless sockets of a white hood" indicate in the story?
8) What kind of racial relationship is shown in the story?
9) What is the feature of language used by Jefferson in the story?

10) What does the title "Flying Home" mean and imply?

Interdisciplinary Concepts for Further Thinking

1. Collective Trauma

Whereas the term "trauma" typically refers to the impact that a traumatic incident has on an individual or a few people, collective trauma refers to the impact of a traumatic experience that affects and involves entire groups of people, communities, or societies. Collective trauma is extraordinary in that it can not only bring distress and negative consequences to individuals but can also change the entire fabric of a community (Erikson, 1976). Situations that may elicit a collective trauma response may include, but are not limited to: wars, natural disasters, mass shootings, terrorism, pandemics, systematic and historical oppression, recessions, and famine or severe poverty.

1) Is there any collective trauma described in "Flying Home"?
2) Can Todd recover from collective trauma? Why?

2. Violence Triangle

Violence triangle is a term used in peace and conflict studies.

In his 1969 paper "Violence, Peace and Peace Research", Johan Galtung presents his theory of the Violence Triangle, a framework used in the study of peace and conflict. The theory is based on the principle that any state of peace is characterized by the absence of violence. As for him, violence falls into three categories: direct violence, structural violence, and cultural violence.

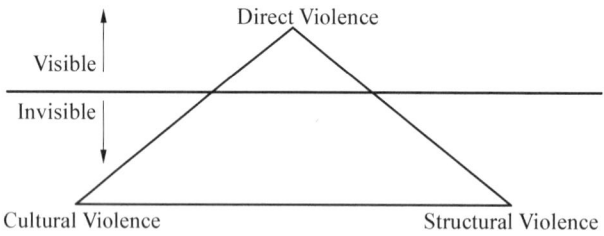

Direct violence takes many forms. In its typical form, it involves the use of physical force, like killing or torture, rape and sexual assault, and beatings. Further, verbal violence, like humiliation, is also recognized as violence.

Structural violence exists when groups, classes, genders, and nationalities have more access to goods, resources, and opportunities than others. This unequal advantage is built into the very social, political, and economic systems that govern societies, states, and the world. These tendencies may be overt such as apartheid, or more subtle traditions or tendencies that award some groups privileges over another.

Cultural violence is the prevailing attitudes and beliefs that we have been taught since childhood that surround us in daily life about the power and necessity of violence. Almost all cultures recognize that killing a person is murder, but killing tens, hundreds, or thousands during a declared conflict is called "war". Cultural violence makes direct and structural violence look, even feel right—at least not wrong.

Racial and Sexual Violence Pyramid

According to Galtung's violence triangle, direct violence is the worst form of violence; structural violence makes violence invisible and cultural violence makes violence justifiable. Direct violence reinforces structural and cultural violence, and cultural and structural violence causes direct violence.

1) How are the three different forms of violence shown in "Flying Home"?

2) What is the connection between violence and collective trauma in "Flying Home"?

Thinking in Numbers

1) In "Flying Home", there are three important scenes with the plane which represent Todd's dreams, hopes and regrets. Figure out the three scenes and further analyze them by referring to the theme of the story.

2) The words "pain" and "humiliation" appear in "Flying Home" many times. Figure out how many times they are used respectively and analyze what the writer is intending to tell us.

3) For the young Todd, there are 3 different groups of people in the world. The first group is those who are condescending to him, the second is those who "praised without understanding" him, and the third is the enemy. Does he have any sense of

belonging? Why or not?

4) There are 3 different phases of Todd's attitude toward the buzzard. What are they and what do they represent respectively?

Visual Thinking with Mind Mapping

1) In general, all different forms of trauma are due to violence. Trauma occurs from the loss of safety or controllability. Create a mind map to show the connection between violence and trauma that Todd suffers from.

2) Essentially, the short story "Flying Home" focuses on the process of Todd's attempt to flee his own community, his failure to do so, and his return to his racial community. Create a mind map to show these three phases and Todd's psychological changes.

Critical Thinking for Reality

"Home" is a sweet place and it is a keyword in "Flying Home". It is worth noting that the word is not mentioned at all except in the title of the story. How do you understand the implication of "home" in the story? What's your understanding of the word?

Unit 14
Still I Rise

Maya Angelou

Introduction to the Author

Maya Angelou (1928—2014) was an American poet, author, actress, dancer, playwright, film director, television producer, and civil rights activist. She was best known for the first of her seven subsequent autobiographies, *I Know Why the Caged Bird Sings*, which was published in 1969. This book brought her international recognition and won her nomination for the National Book Award. It also made literary history as the first nonfiction bestseller by an African American woman. She stood out as the first memoirist who presented herself as the central character and wrote about "blackness from the inside, without apology or defense". She also innovated the notion of autobiography as truth by employing fictional aspects.

Angelou was also a successful poet. American president Clinton invited Angelou to recite her poem "On the Pulse of Morning" at his inauguration in 1993. And she was nominated for a Pulitzer Prize for her poetry, *Just Give Me a Cool Drink of Water 'fore I Diiie*. In 2011, President Barack Obama awarded Angelou the Presidential Medal of Freedom, the country's highest civilian honor. It was a fitting recognition for Angelou's remarkable and inspiring career in the arts. She was known for "theatrical" performances of her poems, that is, "using skills she learned as an actor and speaker". Her poems are characterized by "the African-American oral tradition of speakers such as Frederick Douglass, Martin Luther King Jr. and Malcolm X".

Introduction to the Work

"Still I Rise" is one of Maya Angelou's popular poems, published in 1978. It is about the power of the human spirit to overcome discrimination and hardship, with Angelou specifically reflecting her attitudes as a black American woman. The refrain of "I'll rise" divides the poem into four stanzas. The first stanza starts with the hardship and suffering of the black people in history while the last stanza displays the image of a black woman fighting unrelentingly and hopefully for a life without discrimination. The two middle stanzas serve as a bridge between the two poles of living. They stand for the awakening of black women, who are not afraid to display their feminine attributes.

Text

Still I Rise

You may write me down in history
With your bitter, twisted lies,
You may trod me in the very dirt
But still, like dust, I'll rise.

Does my sassiness upset you?
Why are you beset with gloom?
'Cause I walk like I've got oil wells
Pumping in my living room.

Just like moons and like suns,
With the certainty of tides,
Just like hopes springing high,
Still I'll rise.

Did you want to see me broken?
Bowed head and lowered eyes?
Shoulders falling down like teardrops,
Weakened by my soulful cries?

Does my haughtiness offend you?
Don't you take it awful hard
'Cause I laugh like I've got gold mines

Diggin' in my own backyard.

You may shoot me with your words,
You may cut me with your eyes,
You may kill me with your hatefulness,
But still, like air, I'll rise.

Does my sexiness upset you?
Does it come as a surprise
That I dance like I've got diamonds
At the meeting of my thighs?

Out of the huts of history's shame
I rise
Up from a past that's rooted in pain
I rise
I'm a black ocean, leaping and wide,
Welling and swelling I bear in the tide.

Leaving behind nights of terror and fear
I rise
Into a daybreak that's wondrously clear
I rise
Bringing the gifts that my ancestors gave,
I am the dream and the hope of the slave.
I rise
I rise
I rise.

Topics for Discussion

1) What is the poem mainly about?
2) What is the racial identity of the "narrator" in the poem?
3) What are the important images used in the poem?
4) How many times is the verb "rise" used in the poem?
5) What figures of speech are used in the poem?

Interdisciplinary Concepts for Further Thinking

Social Identity Theory

Social identity theory is a theory in psychology. Social identity is a person's sense of who they are based on their group membership(s). Henri Tajfel proposed that the groups (e.g. social class, family, football team, etc.) that people belong to are an important source of pride and self-esteem. Groups give us a sense of social identity: a sense of belonging to the social world.

The central hypothesis of social identity theory is that group members of an in-group will seek to find negative aspects of an out-group, thus enhancing their self-image. Prejudiced views between cultures may result in racism; in its extreme forms, racism may result in genocide, such as occurred in Germany with the Jews, and in Rwanda between the Hutus and Tutsis.

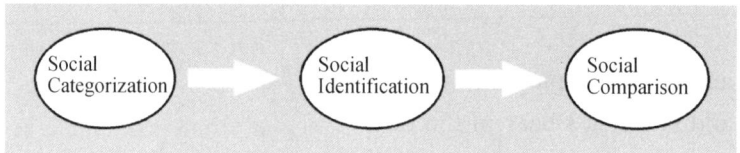

Tajfel and Turner (1979) proposed that there are three mental processes involved in evaluating others as "us" or "them" (i.e. "in-group" and "out-group"). These take place in a particular order. The first is categorization. We categorize objects in order to understand them and identify them. In a very similar way we categorize people (including ourselves) in order to understand the social environment. We use social categories like black, white, Australian, Christian, Muslim, student, and bus driver because they are useful.

In the second stage, social identification, we adopt the identity of the group we have categorized ourselves as belonging to. If you have categorized yourself as a student, the chances are you will adopt the identity of a student and begin to act in the ways you believe students act (and conform to the norms of the group).

The final stage is social comparison. Once we have categorized ourselves as part of a group and have identified with that group we then tend to compare that group with other groups. If our self-esteem is to be maintained, our group needs to compare favorably with other groups. This is critical to understanding prejudice, because once two groups identify themselves as rivals, they are forced to compete in order for the members to maintain their self-esteem. Competition and hostility between groups are thus not only a matter of competing for resources like jobs but also the result of competing identities.

Thinking in Numbers

How many times does the sentence "I'll rise" appear in the poem? What kind of effect is achieved through repetition?

Visual Thinking with Mind Mapping

1) Create a mind map to demonstrate the means to "rise" for Blacks.
2) Analyze the important images that reflect the miseries of Blacks with a mind map.

Critical Thinking for Reality

Have you ever had the sensation of being belittled or looked down upon by others? Have you ever felt that someone is consciously marginalizing you in a group? Does this poem give you power?

Unit 15

From *Waiting for the Barbarians*

J. M. Coetzee

Introduction to the Author

John Maxwell Coetzee (1940—) is a South African-born novelist, essayist, linguist, and translator. He gained Australian citizenship in 2006 and currently lives in Adelaide. He is one of the most critically acclaimed and decorated authors in the English language. The major awards that he won include two Booker Prizes in 1983 and in 1999 and, eventually, the Nobel Prize for Literature in 2003. Coetzee has published 14 novels and most of his fame and awards come from them. As noted by the Swedish Academy, his writing in "innumerable guises portrays the surprising involvement of the outsider", and his novels are characterized by well-crafted composition, pregnant dialogue and analytical brilliance. The major concerns of Coetzee's literary career are the limitations of art in South African society, "whose structure had resulted in deformed and stunted relationship between human beings and a deformed and stunted inner life".

Introduction to the Work

Waiting for the Barbarians was published in 1980. The story is set in a settlement on the territorial frontier of "Empire". The Third Bureau, the special forces of the Empire, starts a rumor that the indigenous people, the so-called barbarians, might

Unit 15 From *Waiting for the Barbarians*

attack the town. Under the cover of self-defense, a series of brutal slaughters of indigenous people and animals are carried out by them to secure their exploitation of lands and resources.

Though fictional, *Waiting for the Barbarians* is full of allusions to the western imperialism and colonialism in Africa. In the novel, ecological themes and postcolonial themes are interwoven. The protagonist is an unnamed magistrate, who is persecuted by the bureau because of his sympathy for the indigenous people. His experiences are a clue to Coetzee's ethics of fighting hegemony, respecting life, and upholding the harmony between man and nature.

Text

Waiting for the Barbarians
(Excerpt)

First there is the sound of muskets far away, as diminutive as popguns. Then from nearer by, from the ramparts themselves, come volleys of answering shots. There is a stampede of footsteps across the barracks yard. "The barbarians!" someone shouts; but I think he is wrong. Above all the clamour the great bell begins to peal.

Kneeling with an ear to the crack of the door I try to make out what is going on.

The noise from the square mounts from a hubbub to a steady roar in which no single voice can be distinguished. The whole town must be pouring out in welcome, thousands of ecstatic souls. Volleys of musket-shots keep cracking. Then the tenor of the roar changes, rises in pitch and excitement. Faintly above it come the brassy tones of bugles.

The temptation is too great. What have I to lose? I unlock the door. In glare so blinding that I must squint and shade my eyes, I cross the yard, pass through the gate, and join the rear of the crowd. The volleys and the roar of applause continue. The old woman in black beside me takes my arm to steady herself and stands on her toes. "Can you see?" she says. "Yes, I can see men on horseback," I reply; but she is not listening.

I can see a long file of horsemen who, amid flying banners, pass through the gateway and make their way to the centre of the square where they dismount. There is a cloud of dust over the whole square, but I see that they are smiling and laughing: one of them rides with his hands raised high in triumph, another waves a garland of flowers. They progress slowly, for the crowd presses around them, trying to touch them, throwing flowers, clapping their hands above their heads in joy, spinning round and round in private ecstasies. Children dive past me, scrambling through the legs of the grownups to be nearer to their heroes. Fusillade after fusillade comes from the ramparts, which are lined with cheering people.

One part of the cavalcade does not dismount. Headed by a stern-faced young corporal bearing the green and gold banner of the battalion, it passes through the press of bodies to the far end of the square and then begins a circuit of the perimeter, the crowd surging slowly in its wake. The word runs like fire from neighbour to neighbour: "*Barbarians*!"

The standard-bearer's horse is led by a man who brandishes a heavy stick to clear his way. Behind him comes another trooper trailing a rope; and at the end of the rope, tied neck to neck, comes a file of men, barbarians, stark naked, holding their hands up to their faces in an odd way as though one and all are suffering from toothache. For a moment I am puzzled by the posture, by the tiptoeing eagerness with which they follow their leader, till I catch a glint of metal and at once comprehend. A simple loop of wire runs through the flesh of each man's hands and through holes pierced in his cheeks. "It makes them meek as lambs," I remember being told by a soldier who had once seen the trick: "they think of nothing but how to keep very still." My heart grows sick. I know now that I should not have left my cell.

I have to turn my back smartly to avoid being seen by the two who, with their mounted escort, bring up the rear of the procession: the bareheaded young captain whose first triumph this is, and at his shoulder, leaner and darker after his months of campaigning, Colonel of Police Joll.

The circuit is made, everyone has a chance to see the twelve miserable captives, to prove to his children that the barbarians are real. Now the crowd, myself reluctantly in its wake, flows towards the great gate, where a half-moon of soldiers blocks its way until, compressed at front and rear, it cannot budge.

"What is going on?" I ask my neighbour.

"I don't know," he says, "but help me to lift him." I help him to lift the child he carries on his arm on to his shoulders. "Can you see?" he asks the child.

"Yes."

"What are they doing?"

"They are making those barbarians kneel. What are they going to do to them?"

"I don't know. Let's wait and see."

Slowly, titanically, with all my might, I turn and begin to squeeze my body out. "Excuse me. Excuse me . . ." I say: "the heat—I'm going to be sick." For the first time I see heads turn, fingers point.

I ought to go back to my cell. As a gesture it will have no effect, it will not even be noticed. Nevertheless, for my own sake, as a gesture to myself alone, I ought to return to the cool dark and lock the door and bend the key and stop my ears to the noise of patriotic bloodlust and close my lips and never speak again. Who knows, perhaps I do my fellow-townsmen an injustice, perhaps at this very minute the shoemaker is at home tapping on his last, humming to himself to drown the shouting, perhaps there are housewives shelling peas in their kitchens, telling stories to occupy their restless children, perhaps there are farmers still going calmly about the repair of the ditches. If comrades like these exist, what a pity I do not know them! For me, at this moment, striding away from the crowd, what has become important above all is that I should neither be contaminated by the atrocity that is about to be committed nor poison myself with impotent hatred of its perpetrators. I cannot save the prisoners, therefore let me save myself. Let it at the very least be said, if it ever comes to be said, if there is ever anyone in some remote future interested to know the way we lived, that in this farthest outpost of the Empire of light there existed one man who in his heart was not a barbarian.

I pass through the barracks gate into my prison yard. At the trough in the middle of the yard I pick up an empty bucket and fill it. With the bucket held up before me, slopping water over its sides, I approach the rear of the crowd again. "Excuse me," I say, and push. People curse me, give way, the bucket tilts and splashes, I forge forward till in a minute I am suddenly clear in the frontmost rank of the crowd behind the backs of the soldiers who, holding staves between them, keep an arena clear for the exemplary spectacle.

Four of the prisoners kneel on the ground. The other eight, still roped together, squat in the shade of the wall watching, their hands to their cheeks.

The kneeling prisoners bend side by side over a long heavy pole. A cord runs from the loop of wire through the first man's mouth, under the pole, up to the second man's loop, back under the pole, up to the third loop, under the pole, through the fourth loop. As I watch a soldier slowly pulls the cord tighter and the prisoners bend further till finally they are kneeling with their faces touching the pole. One of them writhes his shoulders in pain and moans. The others are silent, their thoughts wholly concentrated on moving smoothly with the cord, not giving the wire a chance to tear their flesh.

Directing the soldier with little gestures of the hand is Colonel Joll. Though I am only one in a crowd of thousands, though his eyes are shaded as ever, I stare at him so hard with a face so luminous with query that I know at once he sees me.

Behind me I distinctly hear the word magistrate. Do I imagine it or are my neighbours inching away from me?

The Colonel steps forward. Stooping over each prisoner in turn he rubs a handful of dust into his naked back and writes a word with a stick of charcoal. I read the words upside down: *ENEMY ... ENEMY ... ENEMY ... ENEMY*. He steps back and folds his hands. At a distance of no more than twenty paces he and I contemplate each other.

Then the beating begins. The soldiers use the stout green cane staves, bringing them down with the heavy slapping sounds of washing-paddles, raising red welts on the prisoners' backs and buttocks. With slow care the prisoners extend their legs until they lie flat on their bellies, all except the one who had been moaning and who now gasps with each blow.

The black charcoal and ochre dust begin to run with sweat and blood. The game, I see, is to beat them till their backs are washed clean.

I watch the face of a little girl who stands in the front rank of the crowd gripping her mother's clothes. Her eyes are round, her thumb is in her mouth: silent, terrified, curious, she drinks in the sight of these big naked men being beaten. On every face around me, even those that are smiling, I see the same expression: not hatred, not bloodlust, but a curiosity so intense that their bodies are drained by it and only their eyes live, organs of a new and ravening appetite.

The soldiers doing the beating grow tired. One stands with his hands on his hips panting, smiling, gesturing to the crowd. There is a word from the Colonel: all four of them cease their labour and come forward offering their canes to the spectators.

A girl, giggling and hiding her face, is pushed forward by her friends. "Go on, don't be afraid!" they urge her. A soldier puts a cane in her hand and leads her to the place. She stands confused, embarrassed, one hand still over her face. Shouts, jokes, obscene advice are hurled at her. She lifts the cane, brings it down smartly on the prisoner's buttocks, drops it, and scuttles to safety to a roar of applause.

There is a scramble for the canes, the soldiers can barely keep order, I lose sight of the prisoners on the ground as people press forward to take a turn or simply watch the beating from nearer. I stand forgotten with my bucket between my feet.

Then the flogging is over, the soldiers reassert themselves, the crowd scrambles back, the arena is reconstituted, though narrower than before.

Over his head, exhibiting it to the crowd, Colonel Joll holds a hammer, an ordinary four-pound hammer used for knocking in tent-pegs. Again his gaze meets mine. The babble subsides.

"*No!*" I hear the first word from my throat, rusty, not loud enough. Then again: "*No!*" This time the word rings like a bell from my chest. The soldier who blocks my way stumbles aside. I am in the arena holding up my hands to still the crowd: "*No! No! No!*"

When I turn to Colonel Joll he is standing not five paces from me, his arms folded. I point a finger at him. "*You!*" I shout. Let it all be said. Let him be the one on whom the anger breaks. "You are depraving these people!"

He does not flinch, he does not reply.

"You!" My arm points at him like a gun. My voice fills the square. There is utter silence; or perhaps I am too intoxicated to hear.

Something crashes into me from behind. I sprawl in the dust, gasp, feel the sear of old pain in my back. A stick thuds down on me. Reaching out to ward it off, I take a withering blow on my hand.

It becomes important to stand up, however difficult the pain makes it. I come to my feet and see who it is that is hitting me. It is the stocky man with the sergeant's

Unit 15　From *Waiting for the Barbarians*

stripes who helped with the beatings. Crouched at the knees, his nostrils flaring, he stands with his stick raised for the next blow. "Wait!" I gasp, holding out my limp hand. "I think you have broken it!" He strikes, and I take the blow on the forearm. I hide my arm, lower my head, and try to grope towards him and grapple. Blows fall on my head and shoulders. Never mind: all I want is a few moments to finish what I am saying now that I have begun. I grip his tunic and hug him to me. Though he wrestles, he cannot use his stick; over his shoulder I shout again.

"Not with that!" I shout. The hammer lies cradled in the Colonel's folded arms. "You would not use a hammer on a beast, not on a beast!" In a terrible surge of rage I turn on the sergeant and hurl him from me. Godlike strength is mine. In a minute it will pass: let me use it well while it lasts! "Look!" I shout. I point to the four prisoners who lie docilely on the earth, their lips to the pole, their hands clasped to their faces like monkeys' paws, oblivious of the hammer, ignorant of what is going on behind them, relieved that the offending mark has been beaten from their backs, hoping that the punishment is at an end. I raise my broken hand to the sky. "Look!" I shout. "We are the great miracle of creation! But from some blows this miraculous body cannot repair itself! How—!" Words fail me. "Look at these men!" I recommence. "*Men!*" Those in the crowd who can crane to look at the prisoners, even at the flies that begin to settle on their bleeding welts.

I hear the blow coming and turn to meet it. It catches me full across the face. "I am blind!" I think, staggering back into the blackness that instantly falls. I swallow blood; something blooms across my face, starting as a rosy warmth, turning to fiery agony. I hide my face in my hands and stamp around in a circle trying not to shout, trying not to fall.

What I wanted to say next I cannot remember. A miracle of creation—I pursue the thought but it eludes me like a wisp of smoke. It occurs to me that we crush insects beneath our feet, miracles of creation too, beetles, worms, cockroaches, ants, in their various ways.

I take my fingers from my eyes and a grey world re-emerges swimming in tears. I am so profoundly grateful that I cease to feel pain. As I am hustled, a man at each elbow, back through the murmuring crowd to my cell, I even find myself smiling.

That smile, that flush of joy, leave behind a disturbing residue. I know that they commit an error in treating me so summarily. For I am no orator. What would I have said if they had let me go on? That it is worse to beat a man's feet to pulp than to kill him in combat? That it brings shame on everyone when a girl is permitted to flog a man? That spectacles of cruelty corrupt the hearts of the innocent? The words they stopped me from uttering may have been very paltry indeed, hardly words to rouse the rabble. What, after all, do I stand for besides an archaic code of gentlemanly behaviour towards captured foes, and what do I stand against except the new science of degradation that kills people on their knees, confused and disgraced in their own eyes? Would I have dared to face the crowd to demand justice for these ridiculous barbarian prisoners with their backsides in the air? *Justice*: once that word is uttered, where will it all end? Easier to shout *No*! Easier to be beaten and made a martyr. Easier to lay my head on a block than to defend the cause of justice for the barbarians: for where can that argument lead but to laying down our arms and opening the gates of the town to the people whose land we have raped? The old magistrate, defender of the rule of law, enemy in his own way of the State, assaulted and imprisoned, impregnably virtuous, is not without his own twinges of doubt.

My nose is broken, I know, and perhaps also the cheekbone where the flesh was laid open by the blow of the stick. My left eye is swelling shut.

As the numbness wears off the pain begins to come in spasms a minute or two apart so intense that I can no longer lie still. At the height of the spasm I trot around the room holding my face, whining like a dog; in the blessed valleys between the peaks I breathe deeply, trying to keep control of myself, trying not to make too disgraceful an outcry. I seem to hear surges and lulls in the noise from the mob on the square but cannot be sure that the roar is not simply in my eardrums.

They bring me my evening meal as usual but I cannot eat. I cannot keep still, I have to walk back and forth or rock on my haunches to keep myself from screaming, tearing my clothes, clawing my flesh, doing whatever people do when the limit of their endurance is reached. I weep, and feel the tears stinging the open flesh. I hum the old song about the rider and the juniper bush over and over again, clinging to the remembered words even after they have ceased to make any sense. One, two, three, four ... I count. It will be a famous victory, I tell myself, if you can last the night.

In the early hours of the morning, when I am so giddy with exhaustion that I reel on my feet, I finally give way and sob from the heart like a child: I sit in a corner against the wall and weep, the tears running from my eyes without stop. I weep and weep while the throbbing comes and goes according to its own cycles. In this position sleep bursts upon me like a thunderbolt. I am amazed to come to myself in the thin grey light of day, slumped in a corner, with not the faintest sense that time has passed. Though the throbbing is still there I find I can endure it if I remain still. Indeed, it has lost its strangeness. Soon, perhaps, it will be as much part of me as breathing.

So I lie quietly against the wall, folding my sore hand under my armpit for comfort, and fall into a second sleep, into a confusion of images among which I search out one in particular, brushing aside the others that fly at me like leaves. It is of the girl. She is kneeling with her back to me before the snowcastle or sandcastle she has built. She wears a dark blue robe. As I approach I see that she is digging away in the bowels of the castle.

She becomes aware of me and turns. I am mistaken, it is not a castle she has built but a clay oven. Smoke curls up from the vent at the back. She holds out her hands to me offering me something, a shapeless lump which I peer at unwillingly through a mist. Though I shake my head my vision will not clear.

She is wearing a round cap embroidered in gold. Her hair is braided in a heavy plait which lies over her shoulder: there is gold thread worked into the braid. "Why are you dressed in your best?" I want to say: "I have never seen you looking so lovely." She smiles at me: what beautiful teeth she has, what clear jet-black eyes! Also now I can see that what she is holding out to me is a loaf of bread, still hot, with a coarse steaming broken crust. A surge of gratitude sweeps through me. "Where did a child like you learn to bake so well in the desert?" I want to say. I open my arms to embrace her, and come to myself with tears stinging the wound on my cheek. Though I scrabble back at once into the burrow of sleep I cannot re-enter the dream or taste the bread that has made my saliva run.

...

5

I have barbarians come out at night. Before darkness falls the last goat must be brought in, the gates barred, a watch set in every lookout to call the hours. All night, it is said, the barbarians prowl about bent on murder and rapine. Children in their dreams see the shutters part and fierce barbarian faces leer through. "The barbarians are here!" the children scream, and cannot be comforted. Clothing disappears from washing-lines, food from larders, however tightly locked. The barbarians have dug a tunnel under the walls, people say; they come and go as they please, take what they like; no one is safe any longer. The farmers still till the fields, but they go out in bands, never singly. They work without heart: the barbarians are only waiting for the crops to be established, they say, before they flood the fields again.

Why doesn't the army stop the barbarians? People complain. Life on the frontier has become too hard. They talk of returning to the Old Country, but then remember that the roads are no longer safe because of the barbarians. Tea and sugar can no longer be bought over the counter as the shopkeepers hoard their stocks. Those who eat well eat behind closed doors, fearful of awaking their neighbour's envy.

Three weeks ago a little girl was raped. Her friends, playing in the irrigation ditches, did not miss her till she came back to them bleeding, speechless. For days she lay in her parents' home staring at the ceiling. Nothing would induce her to tell her story. When the lamp was put out she would begin to whimper. Her friends claim a barbarian did it. They saw him running away into the reeds. They recognized him as a barbarian by his ugliness. Now all children are forbidden to play outside the gates, and the farmers carry clubs and spears when they go to the fields.

The higher feeling runs against the barbarians, the tighter I huddle in my corner, hoping I will not be remembered.

It is a long time since the second expeditionary force rode out so bravely with its flags and trumpets and shining armour and prancing steeds to sweep the barbarians from the valley and teach them a lesson they and their children and grandchildren would never forget. Since then there have been no dispatches, no communiqués. The exhilaration of the times when there used to be daily military parades on the square, displays of horsemanship, exhibitions of musketry, has long since dissipated. Instead the air is full of anxious rumours. Some say that the entire thousand-mile frontier has erupted into conflict, that the northern barbarians have joined forces with the western barbarians, that the army of the Empire is too thinly stretched, that one of these days it will be forced to give up the defence of remote outposts like this one to concentrate its resources on the protection of the heartland. Others say that we receive no news of the war only because our soldiers have thrust deep into the enemy's territory and are too busy dealing out heavy blows to send dispatches. Soon, they say, when we least expect it, our men will come marching back weary but victorious, and we shall have peace in our time.

Among the small garrison that has been left behind there is more drunkenness than I have ever known before, more arrogance towards the townspeople. There have been incidents in which soldiers have gone into shops, taken what they wanted, and left without paying. Of what use is it for the shopkeeper to raise the alarm when the criminals and the civil guard are the same people? The shopkeepers complain to Mandel, who is in charge under the emergency powers while Joll is away with the army. Mandel makes promises but does not act. Why should he? All that matters to him is that he should remain popular with his men. Despite the parade of vigilance on the ramparts and the weekly sweep along the lakeshore (for lurking barbarians, though none has ever been caught), discipline is lax.

Meanwhile I, the old clown who lost his last vestige of authority the day he spent hanging from a tree in a woman's underclothes shouting for help, the filthy creature who for a week licked his food off the flagstones like a dog because he had lost the use of his hands, am no longer locked up. I sleep in a corner of the barracks yard; I creep around in my filthy smock; when a fist is raised against me I cower. I live like a starved beast at the back door, kept alive perhaps only as evidence of the animal that skulks within every barbarian-lover. I know I am not safe. Sometimes I can feel the weight of a resentful gaze resting upon me; I do not look up; I know that for some the attraction must be strong to clear the yard by putting a bullet through my skull from an upstairs window.

There has been a drift of refugees to the town, fisherfolk from the tiny settlements dotted along the river and the northern lakeshore, speaking a language no one understands, carrying their households on their backs, with their gaunt dogs and rickety children trailing behind them. People crowded around them when they first came. "Was it the barbarians who chased you out?" they asked, making fierce faces, stretching imaginary bows. No one asked about the imperial soldiery or the brush-fires they set.

There was sympathy for these savages at first, and people brought them food and old clothing, until they began to put up their thatched shelters against the wall on the side of the square near the walnut trees, and their children grew bold enough to sneak into kitchens and steal, and one night a pack of their dogs broke into the sheepfold and tore out the throats of a dozen ewes. Feelings then turned against them. The soldiers took action, shooting their dogs on sight and, one morning when the men were still down at the lake, tearing down the entire row of shelters. For days the fisherfolk hid out in the reeds. Then one by one their little thatched huts began to reappear, this time outside the town under the north wall. Their huts were allowed to stand, but the sentries at the gate received orders to deny them entry. Now that rule has been relaxed, and they can be seen hawking strings of fish from door to door in the mornings. They have no experience of money, they are cheated outrageously, they will part with anything for a thimbleful of rum.

They are a bony, pigeon-chested people. Their women seem always to be pregnant; their children are stunted; in a few of the young girls there are traces of a fragile, liquid-eyed beauty; for the rest I see only ignorance, cunning, slovenliness. Yet what do they see in me, if they ever see me? A beast that stares out from behind a gate: the filthy underside of this beautiful oasis where they have found a precarious safety.

One day a shadow falls across me where I doze in the yard, a foot prods me, and I look up into Mandel's blue eyes.

"Are we feeding you well?" he says. "Are you growing fat again?"

I nod, sitting at his feet.

"Because we can't go on feeding you forever."

There is a long pause while we examine each other.

"When are you going to begin working for your keep?"

"I am a prisoner awaiting trial. Prisoners awaiting trial are not required to work for their keep. That is the law. They are maintained out of the public coffer."

"But you are not a prisoner. You are free to go as you please." He waits for me to take the ponderously offered bait. I say nothing. He goes on: "How can you be a prisoner when we have no record of you? Do you think we don't keep records? We have no record of you. So you must be a free man."

I rise and follow him across the yard to the gate. The guard hands him the key and he unlocks it. "You see? The gate is open."

I hesitate before I pass through. There is something I would like to know. I look into Mandel's face, at the clear eyes, windows of his soul, at the mouth from which his spirit utters itself. "Have you a minute to spare?" I say. We stand in the gateway, with the guard in the background pretending not to hear. I say: "I am not a young man any more, and whatever future I had in this place is in ruins." I gesture around the square, at the dust that scuds before the hot late summer wind, bringer of blights and plagues. "Also I have already died one death, on that tree, only you decided to save me. So there is something I would like to know before I go. If it is not too late, with the barbarian at the gate." I feel the tiniest smile of mockery brush my lips, I cannot help it. I glance up at the empty sky. "Forgive me if the question seems impudent, but I would like to ask: How do you find it possible to eat afterwards, after you have been ... working with people? That is a question I have always asked myself about executioners and other such people. Wait! Listen to me a moment longer, I am sincere, it has cost me a great deal to come out with this, since I am terrified of you, I need not tell you that, I am sure you are aware of it. Do you find it easy to take food afterwards? I have imagined that one would want to wash one's hands. But no ordinary washing would be enough, one would require priestly intervention, a ceremonial of cleansing, don't you think? Some kind of purging of one's soul too—that is how I have imagined it. Otherwise how would it be possible to return to everyday life—to sit down at table, for instance, and break bread with one's family or one's comrades?"

He turns away, but with a slow claw-like hand I manage to catch his arm. "No, listen!" I say. "Do not misunderstand me, I am not blaming you or accusing you, I am long past that. Remember, I too have devoted a life to the law, I know its processes, I know that the workings of justice are often obscure. I am only trying to understand. I am trying to understand the zone in which you live. I am trying to imagine how you breathe and eat and live from day to day. But I cannot! That is what troubles me! If I were he, I say to myself, my hands would feel so dirty that it would choke me—"

He wrenches himself free and hits me so hard in the chest that I gasp and stumble backwards. "You bastard!" he shouts. "You fucking old lunatic! Get out! Go and die somewhere!"

"When are you going to put me on trial?" I shout at his retreating back. He pays no heed.

* * *

There is nowhere to hide. And why should I? From dawn to dusk I am on view on the square, roaming around the stalls or sitting in the shade of the trees. And gradually, as word gets around that the old Magistrate has taken his knocks and come through, people cease to fall silent or turn their backs when I come near. I discover that I am not without friends, particularly among women, who can barely conceal their eagerness to hear my side of the story. Roaming the streets, I pass the quartermaster's plump wife hanging out the washing. We greet. "And how are you, sir?" she says. "We heard that you had such a hard time." Her eyes glitter, avid though cautious. "Won't you come in and have a cup of tea?" So we sit together at the kitchen table, and she sends the children to play outside, and while I drink tea and munch steadily at a plate of the delicious oatmeal biscuits she bakes, she plays out the first moves in this roundabout game of question and answer: "You were gone so long, we wondered if you would ever be coming back ... And then all the trouble you had! How things have changed! There was none of this commotion when you were in charge. All these strangers from the capital, upsetting things!" I take my cue, sigh: "Yes, they don't understand how we go about things in the provinces, do they. All this trouble over a girl ... " I gobble another biscuit. A fool in love is laughed at but in the end always forgiven. "To me it was simply a matter of common sense to take her back to her family, but how could one make them understand that?" I ramble on; she listens to these half-truths, nodding, watching me like a hawk; we pretend that the voice she hears is not the voice of the man who swung from the tree shouting for mercy loud enough to waken the dead. " ... Anyhow, let us hope it is all over. I still have pains"—I touch my shoulder—"one's body heals so slowly as one gets older ... "

So I sing for my keep. And if I am still hungry in the evening, if I wait at the barracks gate for the whistle that calls the dogs and slip in quietly enough, I can usually wheedle out of the maids the leftovers from the soldiers' supper, a bowl of cold beans or the rich scrapings of the soup-pot or half a loaf of bread.

Or in the mornings I can saunter over to the inn and, leaning over the flap of the kitchen door, breathe in all the good smells, marjoram and yeast and crisp chopped onions and smoky mutton-fat. Mai the cook greases the baking-pans: I watch her deft fingers dip into the pot of lard and coat the pan in three swift circles. I think of her pastries, the renowned ham and spinach and cheese pie she makes, and feel the saliva spurt in my mouth.

"So many people have left," she says, turning to the great ball of dough, "I can't even begin to tell you. A sizable party left only a few days ago. One of the girls from here—he little one with the long straight hair, you may remember her—she was one of them, she left with her fellow." Her voice is flat as she imparts the information to me, and I am grateful for her considerateness. "Of course it makes sense," she continues, "if you want to leave you must leave now, it's a long road, dangerous too, and the nights are getting colder." She talks about the weather, about the past summer and signs of approaching winter, as though where I had been, in my cell not three hundred paces from where we stand, I had been sealed off from hot and cold, dry and wet. To her, I realize, I disappeared and then reappeared, and in between was not part of the world.

I have been listening and nodding and dreaming while she talks. Now I speak. "You know," I say, "when I was in prison—in the barracks, not in the new prison, in a little room they locked me into—I was so hungry that I did not give a thought to women, only to food. I lived from one mealtime to the next. There was never enough for me. I bolted my food like a dog and wanted more. Also there was a great deal of pain, at different times: my hand, my arms, as well as this"—I touch the thickened nose, the ugly scar under my eye by which, I am beginning to learn, people are surreptitiously fascinated. "When I dreamed of a woman I dreamed of someone who would come in the night and take the pain away. A child's dream. What I did not know was how longing could store itself away in the hollows of one's bones and then one day without warning flood out. What you said a moment ago, for instance—the girl you mentioned—I was very fond of her, I think you know that, though delicacy prevented you . . . When you said she was gone, I confess, it was as if something had struck me here, in the breast. A blow."

Her hands move deftly, pressing circles out of the sheet of dough with the rim of a bowl, catching up the scraps, rolling them together. She avoids my eyes.

"I went upstairs to her room last night, but the door was locked. I shrugged it off. She has a lot of friends, I never thought I was the only one . . . But what did I want? Somewhere to sleep, certainly; but more too. Why pretend? We all know, what old men seek is to recover their youth in the arms of young women." She pounds the dough, kneads it, rolls it out: a young woman herself with children of her own, living with an exacting mother: what appeal am I making to her as I ramble on about pain, loneliness? Bemused I listen to the discourse that emerges from me. "Let everything be said!" I told myself when I first faced up to my tormentors. "Why clamp your lips stupidly together? You have no secrets. Let them know they are working on flesh and blood! Declare your terror, scream when the pain comes! They thrive on stubborn silence: it confirms to them that every soul is a lock they must patiently pick. Bare yourself! Open your heart!" So I shouted and screamed and said whatever came into my head. Insidious rationale! For now what I hear when I loosen my tongue and let it sail free is the subtle whining of a beggar. "Do you know where I slept last night?" I hear myself saying. "Do you know that little lean-to at the back of the granary? . . ."

. . .

I wander down the wide road down to the lakeside. The horizon ahead is already grey, merging into the grey water of the lake. Behind me the sun is setting in streaks of gold and crimson. From the ditches comes the first cricketsong. This is a world I know and love and do not want to leave. I have walked this road by night since my youth and come to no harm. How can I believe that the night is full of the flitting shadows of barbarians? If there were strangers here I would feel it in my bones. The barbarians have withdrawn with their flocks into the deepest mountain valleys, waiting for the soldiers to grow tired and go away. When that happens the barbarians will come out again. They will graze their sheep and leave us alone, we will plant our fields and leave them alone, and in a few years the frontier will be restored to peace.

I pass the ruined fields, cleared by now and ploughed afresh, cross the irrigation ditches and the shore-wall. The ground beneath my soles grows soft; soon I am walking on soggy marshgrass, pushing my way through reedbrakes, striding ankle-deep in water in the last violet light of dusk. Frogs plop into the water before me; nearby I hear a faint rustle of feathers as a marshbird crouches ready to fly.

I wade deeper, parting the reeds with my hands, feeling the cool slime between my toes; the water, holding the warmth of the sun longer than the air, resists, then gives way, before each stride. In the early hours of the morning the fishermen pole their flat-bottomed boats out across this calm surface and cast their nets. What a peaceful way to make a living! Perhaps I should leave off my beggar's trade and join them in their camp outside the wall, build myself a hut of mud and reeds, marry one of their pretty daughters, feast when the catch is plentiful, tighten my belt when it is not.

Calf-deep in the soothing water I indulge myself in this wistful vision. I am not unaware of what such daydreams signify, dreams of becoming an unthinking savage, of taking the cold road back to the capital, of groping my way out to the ruins in the desert, of returning to the confinement of my cell, of seeking out the barbarians and offering myself to them to use as they wish. Without exception they are dreams of ends: dreams not of how to live but of how to die. And everyone, I know, in that walled town sinking now into darkness (I hear the two thin trumpet calls that announce the closing of the gates) is similarly preoccupied. Everyone but the children! The children never doubt that the great old trees in whose shade they play will stand forever, that one day they will grow to be strong like their fathers, fertile like their mothers, that they will live and prosper and raise their own children and grow old in the place where they were born. What has made it impossible for us to live in time like fish in water, like birds in air, like children? It is the fault of Empire! Empire has created the time of history. Empire has located its existence not in the smooth recurrent spinning time of the cycle of the seasons but in the jagged time of rise and fall, of beginning and end, of catastrophe. Empire dooms itself to live in history and plot against history. One thought alone preoccupies the submerged mind of Empire: how not to end, how not to die, how to prolong its era. By day it pursues its enemies. It is cunning and ruthless, it sends its bloodhounds everywhere. By night it feeds on images of disaster: the sack of cities, the rape of populations, pyramids of bones, acres of desolation. A mad vision yet a virulent one: I, wading in the ooze, am no less infected with it than the faithful Colonel Joll as he tracks the enemies of Empire through the boundless desert, sword unsheathed to cut down barbarian after barbarian until at last he finds and slays the one whose destiny it should be (or if not he then his son's or unborn grandson's) to climb the bronze gateway to the Summer Palace and topple the globe surmounted by the tiger rampant that symbolizes eternal dominion, while his comrades below cheer and fire their muskets in the air.

There is no moon. In darkness I grope my way back to dry land and on a bed of grass, wrapped in my cloak, fall asleep. I wake up stiff and cold from a flurry of confused dreams. The red star has barely moved in the sky.

As I pass along the road to the fishermen's camp a dog starts to bark; in a moment it is joined by another, and the night bursts out in a clamour of barking, shouts of alarm, screams. Dismayed, I shout out at the top of my voice, "It is nothing!" but I am not heard. I stand helpless in the middle of the road. Someone runs past me down towards the lake; then another body cannons into me, a woman, I know at once, who gasps in terror in my arms before she breaks free and is gone. There are dogs, too, snarling about me: I whirl and cry out as one snaps at my legs, tears my skin, retreats. The frenzied yapping is all round me. From behind the walls the dogs of the town bay their response. I crouch and circle, tensed for the next attack. The brassy wail of trumpets cuts through the air. The dogs bark louder than ever. Slowly I shuffle towards the camp, till one of the huts suddenly looms against the sky. I push aside the mat that hangs over the doorway and pass into the sweaty warmth where until a few minutes ago people slept.

The clamour outside dies down, but no one returns. The air is stale, drowsy. I would like to sleep, yet I am disturbed by the resonance of that soft impact on me in the road. Like a bruise my flesh retains the imprint of the body that for a few seconds rested against me. I fear what I am capable of: of coming back tomorrow in daylight still aching with the memory and asking questions until I discover who it was who ran into me in the dark, so as to build upon her, child or woman, an even more ridiculous erotic adventure. There is no limit to the foolishness of men of my age. Our only excuse is that we leave no mark of our own on the girls who pass through our hands: our convoluted desires, our ritualized lovemaking, our elephantine ecstasies are soon forgotten, they shrug off our clumsy dance as they drive straight as arrows into the arms of the men whose children they will bear, the young and vigorous and direct. Our loving leaves no mark. Whom will that other girl with the blind face remember: me with my silk robe and my dim lights and my perfumes and oils and my unhappy pleasures, or that other cold man with the mask over his eyes who gave the orders and pondered the sounds of her intimate pain? Whose was the last face she saw plainly on this earth but the face behind the glowing iron? Though I cringe with shame, even here and now, I must ask myself whether, when I lay head to foot with her, fondling and kissing those broken ankles, I was not in my heart of hearts regretting that I could not engrave myself on her as deeply. However kindly she may be treated by her own people, she will never be courted and married in the normal way: she is marked for life as the property of a stranger, and no one will approach her save in the spirit of lugubrious sensual pity that she detected and rejected in me. No wonder she fell asleep so often, no wonder she was happier peeling vegetables than in my bed! From the moment my steps paused and I stood before her at the barracks gate she must have felt a miasma of deceit closing about her: envy, pity, cruelty all masquerading as desire. And in my lovemaking not impulse but the laborious denial of impulse! I remember her sober smile. From the very first she knew me for a false seducer. She listened to me, then she listened to her heart, and rightly she acted in accord with her heart. If only she had found the words to tell me! "That is not how you do it," she should have said, stopping me in the act. "If you want to learn how to do it, ask your friend with the black eyes." Then she should have continued, so as not to leave me without hope: "But if you want to love me you will have to turn your back on him and learn your lesson elsewhere." If she had told me then, if I had understood her, if I had been in a position to understand her, if I had believed her, if I had been in a position to believe her, I might have saved myself from a year of confused and futile gestures of expiation.

For I was not, as I liked to think, the indulgent pleasure-loving opposite of the cold rigid Colonel. I was the lie that Empire tells itself when times are easy, he the truth that Empire tells when harsh winds blow. Two sides of imperial rule, no more, no less. But I temporized, I looked around this obscure frontier, this little backwater with its dusty summers and its cartloads of apricots and its long siestas and its shiftless garrison and the waterbirds flying in and flying out year after year to and from the dazzling waveless sheet of the lake, and I said to myself, "Be patient, one of these days he will go away, one of these days quiet will return: then our siestas will grow longer and our swords rustier, the watchman will sneak down from his tower to spend the night with his wife, the mortar will crumble till lizards nest between the bricks and owls fly out of the belfry, and the line that marks the frontier on the maps of Empire will grow hazy and obscure till we are blessedly forgotten." Thus I seduced myself, taking one of the many wrong turnings I have taken on a road that looks true but has delivered me into the heart of a labyrinth.

. . .

I wrap myself tighter in my cloak and walk up the road past the main gate, which is still closed, as far as the north-west watchtower, which does not appear to be manned; then back down the road and, cutting across the fields, over the earthwall towards the lakeside.

A hare starts at my feet and dashes away in a zigzag. I keep track of it until it has circled back and is lost behind the ripe wheat in the far fields.

A little boy stands in the middle of the path fifty yards from me, peeing. He watches the arc of his urine, watching me too out of the corner of his eye, curving his back to make the last spurt go further. Then with his golden trail still hanging in the air he is suddenly gone, snatched away by a dark arm from the reeds.

I stand on the spot where he stood. There is nothing to be seen but tossing reed-crests through which flickers the dazzling half-globe of the sun.

"You can come out," I say, barely raising my voice. "There is nothing to be afraid of." The finches, I notice, are avoiding this patch of reeds. I have no doubt that thirty pairs of ears hear me.

I turn back to the town.

The gates are open. Soldiers, heavily armed, poke around among the huts of the fisherfolk. The dog that awoke me trots with them from hut to hut, tail high, tongue lolling, ears alert.

One of the soldiers heaves at the rack where the gutted and salted fish hang to dry. It comes creaking down.

"Don't do that!" I call, hurrying my steps. Some of these men I recognize from the long days of torment in the barracks yard. "Don't do it, it wasn't their fault!"

With deliberate nonchalance the same soldier now strolls over to the largest of the huts, braces himself against two of the projecting roof-struts, and tries to lift the thatched roof off. Though he strains he cannot do it. I have watched these fragile-seeming huts being built. They are built to withstand the tugging of winds in which no bird can fly. The roof frame is lashed to the uprights with thongs that pass through wedge-shaped notches. One cannot lift it without cutting the thongs.

I plead with the man. "Let me tell you what happened last night. I was walking past in the dark and the dogs began to bark. The people here were frightened, they lost their heads, you know how they are. They probably thought the barbarians had come. They ran away down to the lake. They are hiding in the reeds—I saw them a short while ago. You can't punish them for such a ridiculous incident."

He ignores me. A comrade helps him to clamber on to the roof. Balancing on two struts, he begins to stamp holes in the roof with the heel of his boot. I hear the thuds inside as the grass and clay plastering falls.

"Stop it!" I shout. The blood pounds in my temples. "What have they done to harm you?" I grab at his ankle but he is too far away. I could tear out his throat in this mood.

Someone thrusts himself before me: the friend who helped him up. "Why don't you fuck off," he murmurs. "Why don't you just fuck off. Why don't you go and die somewhere."

Under the thatch and clay I hear the roof-strut snap cleanly. The man on the roof throws out his hands and plunges through. One moment he is there, his eyes wide with surprise, the next moment there is only a puff of dust hanging in the air.

The mat over the doorway is pushed aside and he staggers out clutching his hands together, covered from head to toe in ochre dust. "Shit!" he says. "Shit, shit, shit,

shit, shit!" His friends howl with laughter. "It's not funny!" he shouts. "I've hurt my fucking thumb!" He squeezes his hand between his knees. "It's fucking sore!" He swings a kick at the wall of the hut and again I hear plaster fall inside. "Fucking savages!" he says. "We should have lined them up against a wall and shot them long ago—with their friends!"

Looking past me, looking through me, declining in every way to see me, he swaggers off. As he passes the last hut he rips off the mat over the doorway. The strings of beads with which it is decorated, red and black berries, dried melon-seeds, break and cascade everywhere. I stand in the road waiting for the quivering of rage in me to subside. I think of a young peasant who was once brought before me in the days when I had jurisdiction over the garrison. He had been committed to the army for three years by a magistrate in a far-off town for stealing chickens. After a month here he tried to desert. He was caught and brought before me. He wanted to see his mother and his sisters again, he said. "We cannot just do as we wish," I lectured him. "We are all subject to the law, which is greater than any of us. The magistrate who sent you here, I myself, you—we are all subject to the law." He looked at me with dull eyes, waiting to hear the punishment, his two stolid escorts behind him, his hands manacled behind his back. "You feel that it is unjust, I know, that you should be punished for having the feelings of a good son. You think you know what is just and what is not. I understand. We all think we know." I had no doubt, myself, then, that at each moment each one of us, man, woman, child, perhaps even the poor old horse turning the mill-wheel, knew what was just: all creatures come into the world bringing with them the memory of justice. "But we live in a world of laws," I said to my poor prisoner, "a world of the second-best. There is nothing we can do about that. We are fallen creatures. All we can do is to uphold the laws, all of us, without allowing the memory of justice to fade." After lecturing him I sentenced him. He accepted the sentence without murmur and his escort marched him away. I remember the uneasy shame I felt on days like that. I would leave the courtroom and return to my apartment and sit in the rocking-chair in the dark all evening, without appetite, until it was time to go to bed. "When some men suffer unjustly," I said to myself, "it is the fate of those who witness their suffering to suffer the shame of it." But the specious consolation of this thought could not comfort me. I toyed more than once with the idea of resigning my post, retiring from public life, buying a small market garden. But then, I thought, someone else will be appointed to bear the shame of office, and nothing will have changed. So I continued in my duties until one day events overtook me.

Topics for Discussion

1) Who is referred to as the barbarian in the novel?

2) How are the "barbarians" treated?

3) What is the identity of the narrator?

4) Why is the narrator maltreated?

5) How are barbarians characterized in the story?

6) What does the Magistrate mean when he says "We are the great miracle of creation!"?

7) What is the distinction between the Magistrate and Colonel Joll?

8) What are the rumors about barbarians?

9) How does the Magistrate reflect on imperialism?

10) According to your understanding, who are the real barbarians in the story?

Interdisciplinary Concepts for Further Thinking

Orientalism

In art history, literature, and cultural studies, the concept of "Orientalism" is the imitation or depiction of the Eastern world. These depictions are usually created by writers, designers, and artists from the Western world. In its original medieval usage, the "Orient" refers to the "East".

In his groundbreaking *Orientalism*, published in 1978, the cultural critic and theorist Edward Said argues that a dominant European political ideology created the notion of the Orient to subjugate and control it. Orientalism is a Western way of seeing that imagines, emphasizes, exaggerates, and distorts the differences between non-European peoples and cultures. It claims they are exotic, inferior, primitive, backward, and uncivilized and in need of civilized leadership because being civilized is "good" and being uncivilized is "bad". Said explained that the concept embodied distinctions between "East" (the Orient) and "West" (the Occident) so that the "West" could control and authorize views of the "East". For Said, this nexus of power and knowledge enabled the "West" to generalize and misrepresent North Africa, the Middle East, and Asia.

1) How is the idea of Orientalism demonstrated in the excerpt of *Waiting for the Barbarians*?

2) How is the power of Orientalism challenged in the novel?

Thinking in Numbers

"Barbarian" is a keyword in *Waiting for the Barbarians* and it can be understood in different ways since people's understanding is influenced and determined by their position. Figure out how many times the word appears in the excerpt and expound three meanings of the word to have a better understanding of the novel.

Visual Thinking with Mind Mapping

In *Waiting for the Barbarians*, both the Magistrate and Colonel Joll are servants of the Empire. The Magistrate makes his contribution to the Empire. However, the conflicts between him and Colonel Joll seem to be inevitable after the arrival of the latter. Create a mind map to show and analyze the root of the conflict between the Magistrate and Colonel Joll.

Critical Thinking for Reality

In *Waiting for the Barbarians*, the Magistrate criticizes the Empire bluntly, which reminds readers of the criticism of George Orwell in his short story "Shooting an Elephant". The description of the Empire seems to indicate its inevitable collapse. World civilization is and should be diverse, and different races and cultures should respect each other. What's your reflection on the collapse of the Western Empire?

Appendix

Chinese Translation of Some Selected Texts

附 录

部分文本译文

附：

飞蛾茫茫——自然与欢愉（节选）

迈克尔·麦卡锡

对于自然界而言，21世纪简直就是一场灾难。而我在孩提时，就与大自然结下了不解之缘。

我是婴儿潮的一员，我们这代人在"二战"后富裕的西方降生，在20世纪60年代爆发的新自由主义思潮中成年，年轻气盛地认为自己就是宇宙的主宰。也许事实的确如此。正是我们这代人年轻时的主宰观念形塑了我们，并且持续至今。正如两次世界大战对我们父辈和祖辈的影响一样，摇滚是我们的标签。但是，当我们这一代人行将谢幕之时，新的标签正开始显现：正是我们这一代人，在漫漫人生路上，目睹了阴影笼罩地球。

我们来理理头绪。我们的世界正面临着前所未有的威胁，这种威胁来自一种"弊病"，完全超出先辈的想象：人口数量呈现出一种指数式的迅猛增长，令人瞠目结舌。谁能想到这种增长没发生在漫长的人类故事里，没发生在数千年的史前历史长河里，而是发生在最近短短的近40年。这几乎是一个人的一生就得以见证的事，实际上恰恰是我自己的一生：从少年到中年，从1960年到2000年，世界人口翻了一番，从30亿增加到60亿。（随后的10年里又增加了10亿，并将在未来的40年里将再增加30亿。）近40年来，不仅人口数量迅速增加，这在贫困国家尤其明显，而且在较为富裕的国家，人们日益富有，消费大爆炸时代随之来临，婴儿潮一代——有史以来最幸运的一代，对此欣然接受。在人口翻番的同时，同期世界经济增长了6倍多。现在看来，这似乎是20世纪后半叶最为重要的历史事件，甚至比核武器的研发和扩散、帝国的撤退陨落、阿以冲突，或社会主义建设的失败都更具重要性。

人类，智人属的生物，是什么时候开始对世界产生显著的影响？几乎可以肯定的是，从解剖学和行为学角度来看的现代人，也就是智人，在大约6万年前的某个时候走出非洲，开始向东传播到世界各地，到亚洲，然后到大洋洲，然后回到西北向欧洲，最后通过白令海峡大陆桥从西伯利亚进入美洲。他们通过掌握语言而取得了惊人的进步，他们——我们——几乎肯定地消灭了并取代了比他们早很久走出非洲的更早期的人类物种，亚洲的直立人和欧洲的尼安德特人（他们可能还没有完全拥有发达的语言能力）；在此过程中，他们拥有了类似的命运，这些巨大的动物，在数百万年的时间里，从各个方面到处进化成哺乳动物和有袋动物的顶层，在今天我们仍拥有此地位。我们对这些消失的庞然大物并没有太多的想象。但我们应该保持想象。这是一场惨绝人寰的大屠杀。到了更新世末期，冰河时代的漫长时期，整个大陆的巨型动物群已经被人类和采集狩猎者灭绝，例如澳大利亚巨型动物群中重达两吨的袋熊和双原齿兽，还有属于南美洲巨型动物群的大地獭，其化石为达尔文所发现。此外，包括爱尔兰麋鹿在内的欧亚大陆巨型动物群也消失了踪迹。这种麋鹿的宽和高都足有10英尺。当你在杜伦大学生物科学系的中庭见到它们时，你会瞠目结舌。

当然，没有人知道真正的原因。一些古生物学家认为气候变化可能是罪魁祸首，但最有说服力的观点更倾向于远古巨兽的灭绝是人类所为，我们才是始作俑者。两万、三万甚至四万年前，人类就已经在改变周遭世界，尽管人口稀少，却进行大肆破坏。从手斧到电锯，从原始工具鹿肩骨到推土机，从鱼钩到一英里长的漂网，从投掷矛到自动步枪，人类科技不断取得激动人心的进展，改造地球的手段也在进步。那么，随之而来的巨幅激增的人口又会对世界产生怎样的影响呢？

我们正像肆意破坏房屋的窃贼一样糟蹋地球，这不合常理。史上离奇而可怕的一幕发生了。我们明明完全依赖于这个薄薄的、环绕地球的生命圈，却在其中弃掷废料，疯狂地通过攫取、撕裂、乱扔、硬扯、火烧、劈砍、排泄等一系列手段蹂躏大气层、海洋和中心土壤及其供养的一切。过半的热带雨林已不复存在，杀虫剂的使用杀死了大量野花和分布于农田与河流的昆虫种群；海床严重退化，大部分鱼类群落濒危，海洋酸度持续升高，珊瑚礁遭受多重破坏；每年有 400 亿吨造成气候变化的碳充斥着大气；目前五分之一的脊椎动物，包括哺乳动物、鸟类、鱼类、爬行动物和两栖动物正濒临灭绝，且这一比例仍在上升。……处处千疮百孔，生灵涂炭。21 世纪自然界的特征不再是美丽、丰饶、富足，也不再是生机勃勃，而是"脆弱"。

再三强调：这些恶果不是由海啸或火山爆发这样的自然灾害酿成的，而是人类，是我们自己干的"好事"。并且随着人口的继续增长，我们对自然界的需求持续扩大，造成的破坏也会进一步加剧。其直接原因众所周知——破坏、污染栖息地、过度开发或过度捕猎、物种入侵成灾，以及逐渐凸显的气候变化问题；但究其根本，导致如此大规模毁灭性灾难的依然是人类——我们仅仅是地球上林林总总数百万生命形式之一，繁衍至今却已使我们的栖地不堪重负，现在更是要毁掉它才罢休。

在人口爆炸时代开始之际，一个不寻常的历史巧合为我们开辟了崭新的视野，让我们认识到地球受到了何等严重的影响。准确地说，那是在 1968 年的平安夜，记录下这一巧合的美国宇航员威廉·安德斯，作为第一艘离开地球轨道并绕月飞行的载人航天器阿波罗 8 号的机组成员之一，于 12 月 24 日与同事弗兰克·博尔曼及吉姆·洛威尔驾驶飞船出现在月球背面时，他们目睹到令人震撼的景象：一个精致的蓝色球体悬挂在广袤太空的无边黑暗之中。安德斯拍下了这个画面，即那张为人所熟知的《地出》，这无疑是人类文化史上最意义深远的事件之一，因为在那一刻，我们第一次从远处看到了自己，地球在它周围一片漆黑的空旷中，不仅美丽得不可思议，而且脆弱得不可思议。最重要的是，我们可以清楚地看到它的边际，而这在地球表面是看不到的。我们在地球上只能看到陆地或海洋一直延伸到地平线，地平线之外总是还有着别的什么，无论我们跨越多少地平线，总有下一条地平线在等待。然而，当从太空深处瞥见这颗行星时，我们不仅看到了它闪耀澄蓝之美的真正奇观，而且看到了它真正的边际。我们所见到的这个圆形一点也不大——阿波罗 8 号的宇航员只需一个拇指就能盖住它——而且可以肯定的是，它是孤立的，独一无二。在这永无止境的黑暗中，我们无别处可去。感谢《地出》使我们从灵魂深处直观认识到：我们正在毁坏的是自己的家园。

这一不被大多数人承认的问题带来了极其棘手的压力，所以在 20 世纪最后 25 年里，世上最严峻的道德与智力挑战之一摆在了人类面前：我们需要为此做些什么，我们需要寻找办法阻止人类在全球范围所带来的毁灭恶潮。意识到这个问题的人相对较少，通常被界定为环境保护主义者或生态保护主义者。他们分布在各个国家，往往极力发声并带来影响，但在全球范围来看他们仍是少数。大多数普通人对此不以为意，因为其恶果尚未降临到他们身上（尽管恶果终会降临），也因为人们会自然而然地将注意力集中在他们自己那些看似足够无害的点上，没有意识到那些亟待降临的麻烦其实是他们自己的个人选择放大了70亿倍的结果。

再者，人类现行的信仰体系，也就是自由世俗人文主义，使人类无法妥善应对自身行为对人类家园造成的破坏。这一信条自第二次世界大战结束以来一直占据着（人们思想的）主导地位，它期望世界各地的人们免于饥饿、恐惧与疾病，尽可能心情愉悦并过上充实的生活。这样的信条有理有据且公平正直，固然是值得赞赏的，但究其核心却存在着缺陷：未能认识到人类不一定是善良的；它更没能认识到的是：人类物种可能在本质上就存在某些问题，即人类物种可能是地球上的问题儿童。

事实上，许多人会被上述观点所激怒，因为即使不考虑人类作为一个整体在某种程度上存在缺陷，贫穷、饥饿和疾病问题对人们而言已经是足够棘手的了。然而，对于我们文化的奠基者希腊人来说，这一思想是他们道德的核心。人类一直面临着这样的问题：人类自以为是光荣的，几近于神，并在通往神殿的云梯上不断攀登。但是真正的至高无上只有神才能抵达，如果人类爬得太高，像他们过去常常所做的那样，最终会为神所"毁灭"。神代表着人类的极限。当然，我们会想起伊卡洛斯（他因飞得太高太接近太阳而使其蜡翼融化，最终坠海身亡），但是我们还需要吸取一些更加深刻的教训。请记住，在索福克勒斯的戏剧《俄狄浦斯王》中，俄狄浦斯的主要过错并不是弑父娶母，这些只是他命运中的偶然。他真正的错误在于自认为通晓一切，他解答了斯芬克斯之谜，遂自认为智慧超常。不过，诸神向他证明他并非如此。

在自由世俗人文主义的影响下，人类的观念具有其局限性应成为当代共识：人类应受规则制约，不能随心所欲、逾矩而为。人类的存在已成为潜在的威胁，哪有物种会毁坏自己的家园？当然，上述的这些宗教思想早已无迹可寻了，提起它们，只会引起人们的反感。随着宗教和自然灵性的消亡，人类成了自身道德的标杆，区分善恶的核心标准在于人类是否在遭受苦难，以及我们如何做才能避免苦难。这一观点在我们心中如此根深蒂固，甚至深深影响了我们所使用的语言：最值得珍视的美德叫作人性，对别人最崇高的赞扬是称之为人道的。他或她是一个具有人道主义的人，无非是在说，他或她是一个活得像人的人。我们的道德完全以人类为中心，我们自然而然地把对自身最有益的界定为客观意义上的善。因此，当人类自身的利益与其他利益冲突时，人类倾向于会漠视其他利益，全然忘却除人类外的所有生物、非生物也是地球正常运转所不可或缺的一部分，而地球是我们的唯一家园……

我们正处在特殊的历史时刻，自然界正遭受着前所未有的威胁，热爱自然的人们热切呼吁保护自然。尽管新的保护措施比以往的保护手段更符合实际，更具有可行性，也必然更有可能取得成功，然而，当我们审视这些新的保护手段时，我们发现其也仍然存在着极为致命的缺陷。

那我们该怎么办呢？

约瑟夫·康拉德曾在一部短篇小说的序言中指出，科学家或知识分子所做的努力会更加直接有效,然而艺术家的作用会更加持久而深入人心。讲道理摆事实,固然具有说服力,但是却不能像艺术形象那么富有感染力……

那些人类从未涉足的荒原,不应仅仅被视为废弃之地。反之,荒原对于人类而言是有价值的,我们应该加以珍惜和保护。从历史的角度来看,这种观点是近年来才出现的。当然,曾经世界上并没有荒原这一说;我们历经50000多代的时间从冰河时代进化而来,成为狩猎者。当时,人类本身便是自然界的有机组成部分,而非凌驾于整个食物链之上。由于当时的人类文明还处于起步阶段,世界各地必然都是荒野。大约12000年前,随着最后一块冰川消失不见,在人类最为伟大的一次变革中,农业应运而生。随着农作物的种植和动物的驯化,定居的概念诞生了。农业促使人类聚居,这些聚居点逐渐形成了村落、乡镇和城市,农业也促进了其他事物的兴起,我们将这一切称之为文明。不过农业的影响绝不仅限于此,农业从根本上改变了人类与自然界的关系,从或深或浅的合作关系——因为即便人类作为狩猎采集者,也需要合作者——转变成了人类正式掌管统治自然界的关系。全新世之后的500代时间中,我们大部分时间都在开垦草皮,砍伐森林,并宣称上帝赋予了我们这样做的权利。上帝赋予我们的权利是有书面记载的——《旧约》直截了当地阐明了农民拥有对自然界的统治权,并指出他们有权利对自然为所欲为。《创世纪》中有这样的几句名句:"上帝对他们说,你们要繁衍后代,生生不息,遍布大地,你们要治理这片土地,也要管理各种飞禽走兽。"因此,我们长期以来对荒原,也就是那些我们尚未成功征服和统治的地方,有着普遍的不满。实际上,我们有时甚至对荒野怀有一种近乎恐怖的厌恶之情。毕竟,我们正在进行的文明化斗争便是针对荒野的,我们砍伐森林以便在那片土地上种植玉米;森林是人类的敌人,它滋养了凶残的野兽,有时还有凶猛的野人,沙漠和山川亦是如此。以文明自居的人类向往都市、崇拜都市,也长久地憎恨、惧怕荒原。荒原之所以为荒原,因其除了荒凉一无所有。

18世纪初,人类的观念发生了转变,随之而来的是人类对待荒野态度的转变。不过这种观念的转变仅仅局限于审美层面,相对而言较为肤浅。但是,这种转变仍然是有效的。这一观念的转变始于英国绅士的欧洲大旅行,旅行过程中,他们历经千难万险才翻越了阿尔卑斯山,但与此同时又享受着那种惊险刺激的感觉。于是,颇具影响力的"崇高"概念就此诞生,即欣赏大自然令人敬畏的一面,这与美不尽相同,但又和美一样具有强大的力量,能够激发人们的敬佩之情。这一概念成为一种颇具影响力的文化风尚和艺术风尚,并于18世纪下半叶与另一种稍显温和的观念相融合,即"如画"的概念,这种新观念主张以积极的艺术眼光看待自然界、荒野和所有事物。这两个观念相互作用,产生了共同影响,到18世纪80年代,尤其是随着公路的修建和公共交通的改善,英国曾遭鄙视的荒野风景,特别是威尔士的怀伊河和英格兰的湖区,吸引了越来越多的游客。而在欧洲大陆,让·雅克·卢梭对阿尔卑斯山大加赞赏,并坚持认为自然界和人类都是天生善良的。直到19世纪初,威廉·华兹华斯声明自己自始至终都对大自然怀有深切的热爱,所有这些思想流派才汇入了浪漫主义这条波澜壮阔的思想长河之中,并且华兹华斯也因此受到了很多人的追随。

因此,大自然终于找到了它的拥护者们;但他们并不是荒野的拥护者,也不是所谓的净土(未被人类踏足的土地)的拥护者。华兹华斯笔下的湖区,大多山脉绵延,令人惊叹,但那已经相继沦为耕地,遍布人类的足迹。那里有迈克尔,有露西,但就是没有真正的荒野之地。50年后,美国开始真正地出现了一批荒野的拥护者。

这是自然而然的事情。在美国这个新世界里,未开垦的土地广袤无际,特别是大陆的中部和西部,荒无人烟。荒野实际上是这个国家的标志性景观。即使荒野无边无际,然而随着19世纪的到来,它还是遭受到了致命的威胁。这个年轻的国家以世界上有史以来最快的速度和最大的规模实施了人类对自然的掌控。短短几十年间,人类在整个大陆范围内破开草皮和砍伐森林,以此作为边疆向西扩张的一部分。美国人将这当作英雄之举,认为是民族性格的象征,是个人主义、自力更生和独立等美德的体现。年复一年,拓荒者们一路向西,建起了一桩桩木屋,犁过一片片原始大草原,砍倒成千上万的古树,赶走祖祖辈辈生活在这片土地上的原住居民(即美洲土著人),野牛、熊、猞猁和狼等野生动物被赶走,取而代之的是家畜们的到来。人们对此举赞叹不绝。

然而,在这一切发生的时候,以拉尔夫·瓦尔多·爱默生和亨利·戴维·梭罗为首的年轻的美国自然作家们开始怀疑:在西部发现的奇异野生景观,比欧洲的任何地方都更新奇壮丽,那么用这种往往带来破坏作用的方式强行驯服这些地方是否明智。作为超验主义者,他们两人将未受破坏的自然世界视为通往精神真理之路。梭罗在这条路上走得更远——也许是第一个这样做的人——他明确支持了野性/荒野的概念。尽管他最出名的作品是《瓦尔登湖》,书中记录了他在森林小木屋里两年的生活经历,但他关于野性的有力观点却发表于《散步》一文。这篇文章经过多次演讲,在1862年他去世后出版,其中有一句著名的话:"世界存乎野性"。梭罗认为人是自然的一部分,荒野不仅对人类的福祉至关重要,更是原始力量的源泉。他说,罗马的创始人罗慕路斯和雷穆斯曾被一只母狼哺乳,这"不是一个无意义的寓言"。

他对"荒野"的支持很快得到了19世纪美国最著名的公众人物之一乔治·帕金斯·马什的响应,尽管他在英国鲜为人知,但其实他在这一方面做出了很大成就。马什是一名律师、政治家、外交家和杰出的语言学家,先后担任过美国驻奥斯曼帝国和意大利的特使。他博学多才,几乎可与维多利亚时代的托马斯·杰斐逊比肩而立,同时也是一位生态学先驱。1864年,他写了一本书,首次总结了《创世纪》鼓励我们做的事情和征服地球的生态后果。美国批评家经常把它和5年前出版的达尔文的《物种起源》联系在一起。马什尽管没有像达尔文那样,推翻之前全部旧有的人类概念,也未能在才智上比肩达尔文,但是毫无疑问,通过挑战另一种关乎世界的传统宏伟设想,他的独创性体现出了无可比拟的价值。

这个设想是:我们对地球的所作所为都不用付出代价。这必然是因为《圣经》中提到,地球上的资源是上帝给予的,意味着资源是无限的。这一点深深地植根于基督徒的思想中。在一个基督教主导的世界里,马什提出的争辩不可撼动。但在《人与自然》一书中,他详细阐述了自己的观点,强调早期的地中海社会之所以分崩离析,正是因为人们乱砍滥伐的行为阻碍了水源供应。鉴于《人与自然》晦涩难懂,他便以自己丰富的旅行经验和博学的知识为佐证,并严肃地指出,在快速开拓边区的过程中,美国正重蹈早期社会的覆辙,自毁其身。

马什是当时第一个阐明这些观点的人,而这些观点现在已是老生常谈。他的眼光比同期的其他人更长远。凭借广博的学识和深入的思考,马什足以概括出人类对整个自然造成的破坏性影响。正如亚当·斯密客观地道出屠夫、酿酒者和面包师为我们提供晚餐的原因,马什的结论悲观而令人难忘:"人类在任何地方都不安生。每到一处,大自然的和谐都将不复存在。"

保持着自然的和谐,与自然世界的平衡和美丽,才是荒野和无人区的真正价值所在。也许一位绅士会对这种更深刻的荒野价值评价感到吃惊,而它已成为热爱荒野人们的精神支柱,且这种热爱开始在美国人对自然世界的思考中获得越来越高的地位。但精心促成这一切的并非马什。

接过马什手中火炬的是苏格兰作家约翰·缪尔。缪尔生于1849年,11岁的他移民美国。他的青少年时期是在父亲的农场度过的,农场位于威斯康星州边境的偏远地区。在一次事故中,他几乎失明。随后他意识到荒野将是他度过余生之地。1868年,他搬到加州,发现了"荒野之最"内华达山脉。在接下来的40多年里,他用抒情的、有时又带有些许神秘的语言,向越来越多的听众讲述了这些山脉的超凡之处及其重要的原因。他说,未被干扰的自然是"一扇通向天堂的窗户,一面映照造物主的镜子"。到19世纪末,尽管其他社会对此几乎不予承认,荒野的价值在美国得到了正式且广泛的认可。荒野一词,过去长期带有贬义,如"荒野中的耶稣",而现在它首次被赋予了褒义色彩。梭罗、马什和缪尔都在荒野中看到了苍茫的原始土地对人类灵魂最有力的呼唤,而且越来越多的人对此深以为然。

缪尔能够闻名大江南北,不仅因其作品,还因其为保护荒野做出的努力。他在1890年促成建立加利福尼亚州约塞米蒂国家公园,创建了美国第一个以荒野保护为主的团体——塞拉俱乐部,并担任主席。到1914年他去世时,对荒野的热爱已经深深地植根于每一位美国人的内心。随着新世纪的到来,这种热爱只增不减,并得到了一些思想家的支持,比如抒情派林学家和哲学家奥尔多·利奥波德,他呼吁建立一种新的"土地伦理"生态责任体系。1964年,林登·约翰逊总统签署《荒野法案》。至此,荒野保护运动迈向了高潮。该法案为美国打造了一个独一无二的国家荒野保护系统,为大片未经开发、未经人类踏足的土地提供了一个巨大的保护伞,这在全世界范围内都是绝无仅有的。

年复一年,当我们提出诸多强有力的思想,致力于拯救人们在全球范围内对自然的无情破坏;当无数专家学者投身经济学和生态学研究,并试图寻找经济发展与生态保护之间的平衡;当我们制定并实施成千上万详尽的政策;当我们投入大量的智力劳动与美好期待,问题却昭然若揭:我们所做的这些能从根本上更好地保护自然,保护这个自然界,保护半个多世纪前某个秋日午后,少年在望见清澈的河水时那瞬间的喜悦吗?

我们认为自身是绝对理性的生物,这在西方基督教思想日渐式微,并为自由世俗的人文主义逐渐取代的背景下,尤为如此。我们沉迷于一种盲目的自豪:在危机面前,我们可以运用绝对的理性,找到绝佳的解决方案,并且我们相信这将永远奏效。理性植根于我们的思维之中。然而,世界并不总是这样运转。在当前这个星球面临致命威胁时,我们除了思考该怎样做,更应当转而思考我们作为人的本质。

我们中的大多数人不加思考就觉得我们知道问题的答案。但是在过去的30多年里,一种对人类本质的鲜为人知的认识诞生了。这种认识基于简单但却是里程碑式的认知:人类作为狩猎—采集者所经历的50000万世代中的演化过程,即使在今天,对人类心理的影响也比从农耕文明出现后人类所经历的500世代更重要……

恐怖的是这个世纪正气势汹汹地向自然界袭来。事实上,在当前自然界遭受如此快速度与大规模的破坏下,新的问题随之出现:我们难以准确描述这种损失的程度,难以真正客观地表达损失背后的含义,难以详细阐明这种损失,也无法笼统地概括一番。你最终只能借冰冷的统计数据来说明这一切,正如我在这里所做的一样。五分之一的脊椎动物面临灭绝的危险……也许值得我们深思的是,随着环境退化的问题日益理论化、抽象化以及学术化,我们有可能会忽略一些至关重要的东西。

这方面的一个重要的例子,就是人们创造出了两个新的隐喻来描述正在发生的事情。其中一个隐喻是"第六次大灭绝"。在地质记录中,研究人员发现从 4.4 亿年前的奥陶纪末期至今,地球上已经发生了 5 次灾难性的生命灭绝事件,每一次事件发生,地球上的大多数物种就会灭绝。其中一些灭绝事件可能是由气候的剧烈变化所引起的;而另一些则是由于小行星或彗星撞击地球导致的,例如在 6500 万年前白垩纪末期,有一颗小行星撞击了如今的墨西哥尤卡坦半岛,恐龙因此灭绝了,这次物种灭绝是前 5 次大灭绝中距离我们最近的一次。但是就现在物种消失的速度看来,许多生物学家都认为我们如今正在经受另一场大灭绝,也就是我们所说的"第六次大灭绝",其规模和前 5 次相当——当然,不同的是这次大灭绝是由我们人类自己造成的。

另一个隐喻是用"人类世"这个新标签来指代我们现在所生活的时代。这个隐喻也是受到了地质记录的启发,具体来说是受到了地质年代表的启发。我们所处时代的官方命名仍是"全新世"。全新世这个词来自希腊语,意为"最近完全",涵盖了最后一次冰河时代结束以来的这段时期,在这段时期内农业得以发展,文明得以涌现。但如今我们人类对地球的影响竟如此之大,首当其冲的就是大气层:人类活动正在迅速地改变大气层的组成部分,埋下灾难的祸根。正因为如此,越来越多的科学家认为,当下时代有其自身鲜明的特征,我们应该以此来重新命名这个时代。所以,欢迎大家来到人类世:一个人类改变地球的时代。

这些宏观的概念非常具有启发性。"人类世"以及"第六次大灭绝"这两个概念影响深远,揭示出地球所面临的真实困境,以及,我们人类恐怕正在按下自毁的启动键。这些概念极具价值,我们每天都在探讨。事实上,这些概念本身就在创造一个学术领域……

粗略估计,世界上大约有 20 万种飞蛾,但其中蝴蝶只有大约 2 万种:蝴蝶只是飞蛾进化树上的一个分支。在进化中途,部分飞蛾开始在白天外出飞行,为方便相互辨识,它们还进化出了鲜艳的颜色。由此,这些飞蛾从进化树上分裂出来,演化成了蝴蝶。这种物种数量上的差异在英国更加明显:规律繁衍的蝴蝶只有 58 种,但是飞蛾总共约有 2500 种,其中约 900 种体型较大,另外约 1600 种体型偏小或极小。因此,就整个世界而言,飞蛾的种类可能是蝴蝶种类的 10 倍,但在英国,飞蛾的种类将近蝴蝶的 50 倍。

当然,这意味着夜间外出活动的飞蛾要比白天的蝴蝶多得多,只是囿于黑暗,我们没有看到它们而已。或者说,至少在汽车发明之前,我们没有发现它们。乡间闷热的夏夜,汽车飞驰而过。前灯就像长焦镜头,光束中飞蛾丛簇,车速越快堆积得越多,如同茫茫雪花一般。这时,它们惊人的真实数量才突然显现出来。飞蛾纷纷附着在前灯和挡风玻璃上,甚至将车子糊得寸步难行,人们不得不停下车来将玻璃表面擦拭干净。英国自然生物种类繁多,其中飞蛾品种尤为繁多,飞蛾雪暴非同寻常,因为它只有在内燃机时代才会被人们察觉。然而经过短短一个世纪,茫茫飞蛾如今已经消失无踪了。

近年来,我经常和人们谈起这件事。让我倍感惊讶的不仅是那些 50 岁以上的(尤其是60岁以上的)老人仍然对此记忆犹新,更是他们开始回忆这段过往时那突然生动鲜活的情态。仿佛这段记忆只是锁在了他们脑海的某个角落里,一经回想,意识到飞蛾雪暴已经消失,他们就能发觉这个现象有多么特殊。而在当时,这事似乎不足为道。

正是在千禧年,即2000年,我开始意识到飞蛾雪暴已经消失了,自此便开始把飞蛾数量减少作为昆虫总体数量减少的一个方面来写。在我看来,这个问题涉及面很广,而且至关重要……

对人类本质的新认识在许多重要方面都有着重要意义,其中最重要的当然是它的产生背景:正是在毁灭自然的时刻,我们开始以新的视角理解它,思考自然对我们的真正意义是什么,自然的价值又在何处。正如《地出》这张太空照片第一次将地球的脆弱和美丽,以及它的独特和孤独展现在我们面前,心理学和进化生物学的观点第一次向我们展示了我们人类是何以与地球紧密相连的。我们的灵魂与地球密不可分,如果我们破坏地球,我们破坏的不仅是自己的家园,这一点已经很可怕了,而且还破坏了自身赖以生存之根本……

自然界可以给我们带来平和,也可以给我们带来快乐;许多人也许可以本能地感觉到这些,但却无法表达。自然绝不是身外物或奢侈品,相反,它是不可或缺的,是我们本质的一部分。

(方璐璐,温　昕　译;秦梓林,李懿澎　校)

夺命灵猫

斯蒂芬·金

哈斯顿心想,这个坐在轮椅上的老头满面病容,神色可怖,看起来命不久矣。他对死亡这种事早已司空见惯,他就是干这一行的。他是个独来独往的杀手,在他的"职业生涯"中,有18个男人和6个女人的性命都葬送在他的手上。他见惯了将死之人的面孔。

这栋房子,准确地说是座豪宅,静谧又阴冷。只能听见宽敞的石质壁炉里木头燃烧的噼啪声,以及窗外11月寒风的呼啸声。

"我要你干掉一个家伙,"老头说道,他颤抖的声音高亢又暴躁,"我知道你就是干这行的。"

"你怎么找到我的?"哈斯顿问。

"一个叫索尔·罗吉亚的人,他说你认识他。"

哈斯顿点点头。如果中间人是罗吉亚,那就没问题。房间里倘若有诈,那么这个叫德罗根的老头说的一切都是圈套。

"你要把谁干掉?"

德罗根按下了安装在轮椅扶手控制台上的一个按钮,轮椅开始嗡嗡地向前移动。凑近了,哈斯顿能闻得到他身上难闻的气味,那气味混合着恐惧的情绪、衰老的无力感,以及黄色尿液的恶臭。

这气味让他感到恶心,但他却不动声色、镇定自若。"那个家伙就在你身后,"德罗根柔声说道。

哈斯顿动如闪电。对于他而言,反应力就是生命,他时刻保持警惕。刹那间,他的身躯跳离沙发,单膝点地,随即转身,一只手伸进特制的短外套里,同时紧握住藏在腋下的0.45口径短管手枪的柄,只需手指轻轻一动,枪套上的装置可以立即把枪弹出。一瞬间,枪已在手上,瞄准的……竟然是一只猫。

那一刻,哈斯顿和那只猫互相盯着对方。哈斯顿没什么想象力,也从不迷信,但是此刻他却觉得很奇怪。就在他跪下瞄准的那一刻,他觉得同这只猫似曾相识,尽管如果他曾见过有如此不寻常特征的猫,他肯定会记得。

这只猫的脸是均分的,一半黑,一半白。黑白的分界线笔直地从它扁平的头顶延伸至鼻子再到嘴巴。它的眼睛在暗处显得尤为巨大,近似圆形的黑瞳宛如棱镜般折射着火光,像一块阴沉的煤在含恨燃烧。

我们彼此认识,这个念头在哈斯顿脑海中转瞬即逝。他收起枪,站了起来:"我真该杀了你,老头,我是不开玩笑的。"

"我也不开玩笑,"德罗根说,"坐下,看看这。"他从盖在腿上的毯子下掏出一个厚厚的信封。

哈斯顿坐下了。那只猫本来一直蜷伏在沙发后面,突然轻轻跳到他的膝盖上。它仰起头用那双又大又黑的眼睛望了哈斯顿一会儿,瞳孔周围环绕着薄薄的金绿环,然后伏下开始呜呜低吟。

哈斯顿疑惑地看着德罗根。

"它很乖,"德罗根说,"一开始是这样。这只温顺的小猫已经杀了家里3个人了。如今就剩下我了。我老了,也病了……但我只想安度晚年。"

"实在难以置信,"哈斯顿说,"你找我只是为了杀一只猫?"

"请你看看这个信封。"

哈斯顿打开信封一看,里面全是面值50、100的旧钞票。

"这是多少钱?"

"6000美元。等你杀死这只猫之后,带着证据来找我,我会再付6000。罗吉亚先生说,你的报价一般是12000?"

哈斯顿点点头,他的手不由自主地抚摸着膝上的猫。它睡得正酣,依然发出呼噜声。他喜欢猫,确切地说,他唯一真正喜欢的动物只有猫。它们特立独行。上帝——如果真的存在的话——把它们变成了完美冷漠的捕杀机器。猫是动物界的杀手,这为哈斯顿所欣赏和敬重。

"我本不需要做任何解释,但是我还是想提醒你,"德罗根说,"常言道,凡事预则立,不预则废。我希望你不要掉以轻心。我似乎需要进行充分的说明,这样你才不会觉得我精神错乱了。"

哈斯顿又点了点头。他已经决定接下这桩特别的生意,也不需要再谈下去。但是如果德罗根想说,他也会听下去。"首先,你知道我是谁吗? 知道你手里的钱都是从哪来的吗?"

"德罗根制药公司。"

"是的,全世界最大的制药公司之一。我们就是主要靠这个赚的钱。"他从长袍口袋里掏出一小瓶没有标记的药丸递给哈斯顿,"三多默尔镇静安眠丸,复方G,专门为患绝症的病人准备的。这种药物兼具止痛、镇定和轻度迷幻的功效,对身患绝症的人缓解痛苦、调节情绪很有帮助。"

"你自己吃吗?"哈斯顿问。

德罗根并未回应,他接着说:"全世界的医生都在开这种药,它是合成药,50年代由我们公司在新泽西州的实验室研制的。我们只用猫做临床试验,因为猫科动物有独特的神经系统。"

"你们谋害了多少只猫?"

德罗根僵住了。"你这么说,有失公允,还带着偏见。"

哈斯顿耸了耸肩。

"通过4年的实验,三多默尔镇静安眠丸获得食品药物管理局的批准,期间大约有15000只……嗯,被终结了。"

哈斯顿戏谑地吹了声口哨。这也就相当于每年屠杀约4000只猫。"所以你现在觉得这只猫是回来索命了,嗯?"

"我一点也不内疚,"德罗根说,但他的声音中又带上了些许颤抖与暴躁,"15000只动物在试验中死亡,换来的是数十万人的……"

"不要跟我提这个。"哈斯顿道。他讨厌别人辩解。

"那只猫7个月前来到这里。我向来不喜欢猫。这些肮脏、携带疾病的动物……总是在野外游荡……在谷仓里爬来爬去……谁知道它们毛上沾了什么病菌……还老是将些内脏都翻出来的玩意儿带到家里给你看……是我姐姐想收留它。猫是她发现的,她也为此付出了代价。"他恶狠狠地盯着睡在哈斯顿腿上的那只猫。

"你说这猫杀了3个人。"

德罗根开始讲述经过。而那只猫,在哈斯顿那职业杀手强壮手指的轻抚下,趴在他的腿上呼呼大睡。

壁炉里的松枝节时不时地爆裂,就像皮肉包裹着的钢簧一样紧绷着。在这间远在康涅狄格州乡村的大石屋周围,寒风哀号着冬天的到来。老人低沉的语声不断传出。

7个月前,这里还住着4个人——72岁的德罗根、比他大两岁的姐姐阿曼达、阿曼达的挚友、患有严重的肺气肿的卡罗琳·布罗德莫尔(据德罗根说"是韦斯特切斯特·布罗德莫尔斯家的"),还有在这家干了20年的雇工——迪克·盖奇。盖奇年过六旬,为主人驾豪华林肯、烹饪、斟夜饮雪利酒。白天还有个女仆来帮忙干活。几个风烛残年的老人凑在一起再加上家仆,他们4个人就这样生活了近两年。他们唯一的乐趣是看电视节目——好莱坞问答游戏,以及比谁活得更长。

接着,猫就来了。

"盖奇先看见的它,它在房子周围徘徊,呜呜叫个不停。他想赶走它,朝它扔树枝和小石头,揍了它好几次,但它就是不肯走。它当然是嗅到了食物的味道。这只猫已经瘦得皮包骨头了。你知道的,人们在夏末时把这些猫丢到路边,让它们自生自灭。真是太可怕、太残忍了。"

"摧残它们的神经比这好一点?"哈斯顿问。

德罗根没理会他的讽刺,继续讲着。他恨猫,一向如此。猫赖着不走,于是他让盖奇准备了有毒的食物,实际上就是大份香喷喷的卡洛牌猫粮拌上三多默尔。猫置之不理。这时阿曼达·德罗根注意到了那只猫,并坚持要收留它。德罗根强烈反对,但阿曼达还是一如既往地遂愿了。

"然而她发现了这只猫的不寻常,"德罗根说,"她把它抱在怀里。它就像现在这样哼着。但它就是不愿靠近我。从来不……至少暂时还没有。她倒了一碟牛奶给它。'哦,看看这可怜的小东西,饿坏了吧,'她低声说道。她和卡罗琳都对这猫柔声细语。令人作呕。当然了,这是她们恶心我的方式。她们都知道自从20年前的三多默尔-G试验项目之后,我就对猫科动物感到憎恶。她们借此戏弄、激怒我,并以此为乐。"他冷冷地看着哈斯顿,"但她们为此付出了代价。"

5月中旬的一天,盖奇起床准备早餐时,发现阿曼达·德罗根躺在主楼梯脚下,身旁一地碎陶片和猫粮。她双眼略凸望向天花板,口鼻大量流血,背部摔伤,双腿跌折,脖子像玻璃一样粉碎。

"猫睡在她的房间里,"德罗根说,"她就像对待婴儿一样对它……'宝宝饿了吗?要出去便便吗?'这些话竟从我那凶悍的姐姐口中说出来,真是倒胃口。我猜它把她喊醒了,喵喵叫着。她就去拿食盆。她过去常说山姆只爱吃用牛奶泡过的猫粮。她打算下楼去,而猫一直在蹭她的腿。她老了,脚踩不太稳。半睡半醒间他们走到楼梯边,猫走到她前面……绊倒了她……"

没错,可能就是这样,哈斯顿想。他的脑海中浮现出当时的情景:老妇人摔了下来,惊得叫不出声。猫粮在她跌落时,抛撒了一地,碗也打碎了。最后她瘫倒在楼梯下,一把老骨头都碎裂了,眼睛瞪得大大的,耳鼻在滴血。猫咕噜咕噜叫着走下楼梯,满足地大嚼着食物……

"法医怎么说?"他问德罗根。

"当然是意外死亡。但我知道是猫搞的鬼。"

"那你为什么不把猫扔了呢?反正阿曼达已经不在了。"

很显然,是因为卡罗琳·布罗德莫尔威胁说,如果他扔了猫,她就出走。她当时已经歇斯底里,有些魔怔了。她是个病态的女人,痴迷于招魂术。哈特福德的一个灵媒告诉她(只收了她20美元),阿曼达的灵魂已经进入了山姆体内。卡罗琳告诫德罗根,山姆与阿曼达是一体的,如果这猫走了,阿曼达也就没了。

哈斯顿算是个老江湖了,他一眼看穿德罗根跟那个布拉莫家的老姑娘早年是一对儿,而德罗根这个老家伙不愿意因为一只猫而从此失去她。

"简直就是自寻死路,"德罗根说道,"她心里头还把自己当成富婆,完全有能力把那只猫收养下来,带去纽约、伦敦甚至蒙特卡洛。实际上她的那个大家族就剩她一个人了,又因为60年代投资屡屡失败,她只能靠着微薄津贴过活。她住在二楼的一间极为逼仄且潮湿的屋子里。哈斯顿先生,这个女人70岁了。她烟瘾很重,死前两年才收敛了点,又得了很严重的肺气肿。我想让她就住在这儿,但是要是这个猫也得留下来……"

哈斯顿点了点头,然后意味深长地瞥了眼他的手表。

"大概在6月末的某天晚上,她死了。医生似乎觉得是正常死亡……就只是过来看了看,开了张死亡证明,就完事了。但是猫当时在房间里。这是盖奇告诉我的。"

"老兄,谁都有走的一天。"哈斯顿说。

"是这样。医生确实是这么说的。但是我心里清楚,我记得,猫喜欢在老人孩子熟睡的时候悄悄钻到他们身边,偷他们的精气。"

"那都是老太婆们胡诌的。"

"但正如大部分所谓的妇人的疯人疯语一样,这是有事实依据的。"德罗根回答道。

"你晓得的,猫都喜欢在软趴趴的东西上踩奶。比如枕头、厚长绒垫子……或者毯子。睡毯或者老人用的毯子。令一个身子本来就虚弱的人身上重上加重……"

德罗根的声音渐渐变弱,哈斯顿脑中的画面则开始成形:卡罗琳·布拉莫睡在她的卧室中,呼吸间,她残破的双肺发出刺耳的刮擦声,这一声音几乎被特制增湿器和空调的微小噪声盖过去了。那只长着奇异的黑白花色的猫悄无声息地跳上那老姑娘的床,用它闪烁的黑绿双眸盯着她沟壑纵横的老脸。它爬上她枯瘦的胸脯,把全身重量压上去,呼呼地睡了……然后女人的呼吸变慢,再变慢……那只猫在呼呼大睡,老妇人却因为它压在胸上的重量慢慢窒息而死。

哈斯顿不是一个想象力丰富的人,但他还是小小打了个寒战。

"德罗根,"他问道,手上还在抚摸那只熟睡的猫。"你为什么不干脆做掉它?只用20美元,兽医就能了结它。"

附录　部分文本译文

德罗根说:"葬礼安排在7月1日,我把卡罗琳埋在我们家的墓园里,紧挨着我姐姐的坟。她本来也是这么希望的。7月3日,我把盖奇叫到这间屋子里,递给他一个柳条筐……类似于那种野餐篮。你知道我是什么意思吧?"

哈斯顿点了点头。

"我让他把猫放进去,带到米尔福德的兽医那里,叫它永远睡过去。他说'好的,先生',然后拿上篮子走了出去。他做事就这样。但我再也见不到活生生的他了。收费公路上出了场车祸。林肯车以每小时60多英里的速度冲上了桥台。迪克·盖奇当场就死了。人们发现他的时候,他的脸上全是抓痕。"

哈斯顿沉默不语,脑海里又浮现出盖奇死时的场景。屋子里一片死寂,只剩下火星轻微的噼啪声和哈斯顿膝上那只猫平稳的呼噜声。他与猫一块儿待在炉火前,完美再现了埃德加·盖斯特一首诗的意境:"膝上蜷猫,炉中焰高……吾生安乐,告之来询。"

迪克·盖奇开着林肯车驶离收费公路,前往米尔福德,每小时的车速比限速时可能要高上5英里左右。身边放着一个类似野餐篮的柳条筐。他正注意着路况,可能正想超过一辆小货车,并没有发现那只阴阳脸的怪猫从朝向驾驶座的篮子一侧探出了头。他还是没有注意到它,因为他正在超过一辆拖斗货车。就在此时,那只猫跳到他的脸上,又咬又挠,爪子掏向盖奇的一只眼睛,刺进去,血流了出来,盖奇什么也看不见了。林肯车强大的马力仍在嗡鸣,以每小时60英里的速度疾驰着。猫的另一只爪子钩住了他的鼻梁,刺入肉中,让他疼痛难忍。车这时开始向右偏转,冲上了货车道,喇叭高鸣,震耳欲聋,但是盖奇听不到,因为那只猫在大声嘶叫,它张开的身体盖在他的脸上,像只硕大的黑毛蜘蛛,它的耳朵向后倒,绿色的眼睛直射出地狱鬼火般的亮光,后腿狂乱地抓进老人盖奇松软的脖颈肉中。车向后猛转,桥台隐约可见。猫这时跳下车,林肯车则像颗乌黑油亮的鱼雷,一头撞到水泥墩上,炸弹似的炸开。

哈斯顿艰难地咽下一口吐沫,听到喉中干涩的倒吸气声。"猫后来回来了?"

德罗根点点头:"一周后,迪克·盖奇下葬的那天,那只猫回来了,就像那首老歌唱的:猫儿回来了。"

"它在时速60英里的车祸中还能活下来?真是不敢相信。"

"人们都说猫有9条命。它回来时……我就开始怀疑它会不会是一只……一只……"

"地狱之猫?"哈斯顿喃喃道。

"说得好听点,或许,恶魔使者……"

"来惩罚你。"

"我不知道,但我太害怕了。我养着它,准确来说是来帮我的那个女佣在喂它,她也不喜欢这只猫,她说这张猫脸简直是上帝的诅咒。当然,这是当地的迷信,"老头想笑却笑不出来,"我想让你杀了它,我已经忍了它4个月了,它隐匿在黑暗中,就那样看着我,似乎是在……等待。每晚我都把房门锁得紧紧的,仍然免不了胡思乱想,想第二天早上醒来时它会不会蜷着身子趴在我胸前……发出呼噜呼噜的喘息声。"

门外的风低声呜咽着,吹的石烟囱也籁籁作响。

"最后我联系上了索尔·罗吉亚,他向我推荐了你。我记得,他说你是个独行侠。"

"独行侠,也就是我自己单干。"

"是的。他说你从未失过手,甚至从未受人怀疑过,总能干净利落地完成任务。"

看着坐在轮椅中的老头,哈斯顿用他那修长的手指与宽大有力的手掌在猫的颈上摩挲着。

"如果你想的话,我现在就了结了它,"他轻声说,"我会瞬间折断它的脖子,它甚至无声无息就死了……"

"不!"德罗根大叫一声,哆嗦着长吸一口气,苍白的脸都憋红了,"别……别在这儿,把它带走。"

哈斯顿冷笑两声,再一次轻柔地抚摸起熟睡的猫儿的头肩背。"好吧,"他说,"成交,你要尸体吗?"

"不。杀了,直接埋了。"德罗根顿了顿,像只老秃鹰一般伏着身子向前滑动着轮椅。

"把它的尾巴交给我,"他说,"我要把它扔进火里,亲眼看着它一点一点被火焰舔舐、吞没、烧成灰烬。"

哈斯顿开着辆1973年产的普利茅斯车,这辆车配有定制的飓风破坏者引擎,车底盘加高并加了盖,引擎盖向下倾斜20度。哈斯顿自己重装了差速器和后盖,用的是潘西牌的换挡装置与赫斯特产的联动装置。整车安在大型波比·安瑟宽纹轮胎上,最高时速可达160多英里。

9点半刚过,他就离开了德罗根家。一轮阴冷的新月穿过11月稀疏的云层高悬头顶。他把车窗全部打开,因为德罗根那因衰老与恐惧散发出来的恶臭似乎已经渗透进他的衣服里了,他对此甚是厌恶。寒气刺骨,直到使人麻木,但这正合他意,可以让寒气将那股恶臭吹走。他在普雷瑟的格兰镇出口下了高速公路,穿过寂静的小镇,那儿的十字路口只有一个交通灯,于是他全程规规矩矩地以35英里的速度前行。出城后,他开始提速,开着普利茅斯车飞驰。引擎发出的呜呜声好像今晚早些时候猫在他腿上发出的呼噜声。想到这个比喻,哈斯顿不由得咧嘴一笑,驾着车以70多英里的速度飞驰在结着白霜、两旁铺满作物秸秆的秋天的田野上。

这只猫被放在一个双层购物袋里,袋子顶部用粗麻绳捆着,袋子搁在客座上。哈斯顿把它放进袋子里的时候,它正发出呼噜呼噜的睡梦声,一路上它一直在呼呼大睡。也许它感觉到哈斯顿喜欢它,就像待在自己家里一样。像哈斯顿一样,这只猫也是独行侠。

真是一个奇怪的任务,哈斯顿想,并且惊讶地发现自己把它当真了。也许最奇怪之处就在于,他真的很喜欢这只猫,一只感到亲近的猫。如果它能摆脱那3个老不死的,它将更为强大……尤其是盖奇,曾带着它去米尔福德一位平头的兽医那儿,兽医可是非常乐意把它捆起来,塞进微波炉大小的陶瓷嵌边的气室中杀死它。纵使对它有亲切感,哈斯顿依然不愿意放弃这单生意。他要干净利落地解决了它。他可以把车停在秋日的荒野中,把它从袋子里拿出来,安抚一会儿,然后扭断它的脖子,再用小刀割下它的尾巴。他想,要体面地安葬了它,免得落入食腐肉动物之口。虽不能避免虫蚁咬蚀,但我可以使它免受蛆虫之扰。

汽车像个暗蓝色幽灵一样穿行在夜色中,他正想到这里,忽然,那只猫出现在他眼前,它端立于仪表盘上,尾巴高傲地翘起,那张阴阳脸蓦地转向他,似乎在对他冷笑。

"嘘——"哈斯顿朝它嘘了一声,他向右边瞥了一眼,看到那个双层购物袋的侧面被咬了个洞,也许是抓的。再抬头一看,只见猫在向他张牙舞爪,一只爪子划过了他的前额。他急忙躲过去,普利茅斯车巨大的轮胎在狭窄的柏油路上左摇右摆,吱吱作响。

附录 部分文本译文

　　哈斯顿对着站在仪表盘上的猫狠狠挥去一拳,猫挡住了他的视线,让他没法开车。它喉咙里发出蔑视的咕噜咕噜声,弓着背但没有动。哈斯顿又一挥拳,可它不但没有退缩,反而向哈斯顿扑来。

　　盖奇,他想,就像是对付盖奇一样……

　　哈斯顿一脚踩住刹车。这只猫已经跳到了他头上,毛茸茸的腹部挡住了他的视线,爪子在他头顶又挠又抓。哈斯顿神色阴冷,紧紧握住方向盘。1次、2次、3次,他伸手去击打那只猫。倏尔,前方的道路不见了,他的普利茅斯车冲进了一条沟里,车子被撞得东倒西歪、砰砰作响。紧接着,一阵猛烈的撞击将系着安全带的他向前甩去,他最后听到的声音是那只猫发出的凄厉嚎叫,那声音像极了妇人痛苦的尖叫抑或是女人性高潮时发出的声音。

　　他握紧拳头向猫挥了过去,却感觉只是落在了几块富有弹性、柔软的肌肉上。

　　接着,第二次猛烈的撞击来临,哈斯顿感到眼前一片漆黑,晕了过去。

　　月亮缓缓下山,离黎明还有一小时。

　　这辆普利茅斯车栽进了一个雾霭弥漫的峡谷中。车的散热器护栅和一条乱成一团的带刺铁丝纠缠在一起,引擎盖弹开了,缕缕蒸汽从裂开的散热器开口中飘出来,与浓雾混作一团。

　　哈斯顿的腿没有了知觉。

　　他向下一看,只见普利茅斯车的防火层已经在撞击中塌陷。庞大的"水星旋风"牌发动机的后部缸体撞到了他,死死地压着他的双腿。

　　汽车外边,远处传来捕食者凄厉的叫声,一只猫头鹰正在扑食一只慌忙逃窜的小型动物。

　　汽车里边,近在咫尺的猫咕噜咕噜地持续低吟着。

　　它似乎在咧着嘴笑,就像《爱丽丝梦游奇境》里的那只柴郡猫一样。

　　哈斯顿看着它,这只猫站起来弓起背然后伸了个懒腰。突然,它敏捷一跃,如同丝绸一阵起伏,跳上了哈斯顿的肩膀。哈斯顿试图抬手把猫赶下去。

　　但是他的胳膊不听使唤,抬不起来。

　　他想了想,应该是脊髓休克。这种瘫痪的状态也许一会儿就能恢复,但更可能永远无法恢复。

　　猫在他耳旁咕噜咕噜地叫着,如同雷鸣一般。

　　"从我身上滚下来。"哈斯顿叫着,他的嗓音又干又涩。猫紧紧绷住身子,过了一会儿在他身上坐了下来。突然,它露出利爪,挠到哈斯顿脸上。一道道带着灼热痛觉的伤痕延伸到他的喉咙。

　　接着,滚热的血一滴一滴淌了出来。

　　疼痛。

　　他感受着疼痛。

　　他吃力地把头转到右边。一下子,他的脸埋进了一团柔顺干燥的毛里。哈斯顿猛地向猫咬去,这让猫吓了一跳,它喉中发出沙哑可怖的声音——喵呜——而后一跃,跳上了车椅。

　　它愤怒地盯着他,耳朵向后竖起。

"我不该接这个活,是吗?"哈斯顿哑着嗓子喃喃道。猫张开嘴巴,对他发出嘶嘶声。面对着这张奇异的、如同精神分裂的脸,他终于明白德罗根怎么会认为这是只来自地狱的猫。它……

一阵隐约的刺痛从他的双手和前臂传来,他的思绪戛然而止。

痛痛麻麻的感觉又回来了。

猫跳回到他的面前,张开利爪,愤怒地发出嘶嘶声。

哈斯顿紧闭双目,张开嘴巴,向猫的腹部咬去,但只咬到一嘴猫毛。而猫的两只前爪紧紧抓住他的双耳,戳了进去。哈斯顿感受到一股剧痛,想要抬起他的双手。

双手在微微颤抖,但是怎么也不能从腿下拔出来。

他把头向前方探去,来回摇摆着,想把猫甩下来,和甩掉眼睛里泡沫的动作如出一辙。猫继续号叫着,发出嘶嘶的声音,前爪紧紧地抓着他的脑袋不放。哈斯顿感受到血液从他的双颊流淌下来。猫的胸部紧紧地压在他的鼻子上,让他难以呼吸。他只能勉强从嘴部吸入一点点空气,这点空气是从猫毛里流进来的。他的耳朵疼得像是浸在了打火机油里,然后被放在火上烤。

他猛地把头往后一仰,痛苦地嚎叫了起来——普利茅斯车跌落山谷时,他肯定扭伤了脖子。猫被他的动作一惊,跳走了。哈斯顿听到它砰的一声落到了后座上。

血液汩汩地淌进了他的眼睛里。他再次尝试移动双手,想要抬起一只手来把血擦掉。

双手在腿下微微颤抖,还是拔不出来。他想到左臂下的手枪皮套里还有一把0.45口径的转轮手枪。

小猫呀,如果我能够拿着我的手枪,你的9条小命要一次付清了。

现在更疼了。他的双脚一阵阵地抽痛,肯定被发动机缸体压碎了。腿部的力量和痛觉在慢慢恢复——像是被枕着睡觉的手臂或腿,在慢慢醒来恢复知觉。那时,哈斯顿已无暇顾及他的脚了。脊柱没断就已经是万幸了,他后半生不会活得像一具会说话的死尸——只有头部能活动,其他地方都是一摊死肉,这就足够了。

也许我也还有好几条命呢。

目前的首要任务是时刻关注那只猫。其次是要从这废车里爬出去——也许会有人经过,那么这两个问题就都能解决了。但在凌晨4:30这个点,在这样一条乡间小路上,这几乎是不可能发生的。而且……

那只猫在后座干什么呢?

他讨厌它紧贴在自己脸上,但也讨厌它脱离自己的视线,埋伏在他身后。他试着看向后视镜,但那只不过是白费力气。从撞歪的后视镜里看到的只有他落入的长满荒草的沟渠。

身后传来一阵声响,低沉如裂帛。

是猫在打呼噜。

去他的地狱灵猫,它这会儿正在后座呼呼大睡呢。

不过即使这只猫没有睡着,即使它真的打算杀了自己,它又能做些什么呢?它不过就是一只瘦弱的小猫罢了,最多也就4磅重。而过不了多久……过不了多久他的手就能动了,就能拿起手枪。他对此深信不疑。

哈斯顿静坐着等待,针刺般的酥麻阵阵流淌在他的四肢百骸,他的身体逐渐恢复了知

附录 部分文本译文

觉。荒谬的是(或许这可能是他与死神擦肩而过时的本能反应),他竟然勃起了一分钟左右。他暗想现在这副样子,动手纾解下可有点困难。

东方的天空逐渐显现出一道曙光,不知何处传来了鸟儿的啼鸣。

哈斯顿试着抬起手,仅仅抬起了几毫米,便又掉了下去。

现在还不是时候,不过很快了。

哈斯顿身旁的后座上传来一声轻柔的扑通声。他扭头往后看,只见一张半黑半白的阴阳脸,两只眼睛闪闪发光,瞳孔大而深邃。

哈斯顿对它说道:

"小猫啊小猫,凡是我接下的生意,就从来没有失手过,你这桩可能是头一次。你可给我等着,我的手就要恢复过来了。再过5分钟,顶多10分钟就能完全恢复。你想听听我的劝告吗?从窗户那儿跳出去吧,窗户都是打开的,夹着你的尾巴滚开吧。"

那只猫死死地盯着他。

哈斯顿再次试着抬起手,两只手剧烈抖动着抬高了半英寸,一英寸,随后又无力地掉了下去,从他的大腿上滑落,砰地摔在普利茅斯车的座位上。两只灰白的手映着暗光,像是两只巨大的热带蜘蛛。

那只猫正咧着嘴对着他笑。

我是失算了吗?他困惑不解。哈斯顿向来直觉敏锐,意识到这次恐怕是失算了,这瞬间让他难以接受,不知所措。随即,那只猫绷紧身体,一跃而起。正是此时,他知道它要动手了,不由得张大嘴巴尖叫起来。

那猫跳到了哈斯顿的胯上,伸出爪子挖挠起来。

此刻,哈斯顿真希望自己已经麻痹了。这种痛苦过于剧烈,叫他生不如死,他从来不知道这世界上还有这种痛苦。猫愤怒极了,嘴里发出咕噜咕噜的叫声,像螺旋弹簧一样,反复用爪子抓他的睾丸。

哈斯顿张大嘴巴,惨叫起来。就在此时,那只猫调转方向,跳到了他的面前,朝着他的嘴巴一跃而下。也正是此刻,哈斯顿知道了这不仅仅是只猫,更是一个恶毒凶残的天生杀手。

哈斯顿最后匆匆瞥了一眼那张阴阳脸。就在那因愤怒而压低的双耳下面,它瞪着大大的双眼,眼中满是疯狂的仇恨。它已经干掉了那3个老家伙,现在就要了结约翰·哈斯顿了。

它像一枚毛茸茸的炮弹一样发射出去,钻进了哈斯顿的嘴里,引得他作呕。猫的前爪轮番撕扯着他的舌头,像撕碎一片肝脏一样。随着胃的收缩蠕动,他开始呕吐。呕吐物涌上来,堵在气管里,哈斯顿开始感到窒息。

绝境之中,求生的本能将他从车祸冲击导致的暂时性麻痹中拽了出来。他慢慢抬起双手,尝试抓住那只猫。我的天呐,他想。

当时,那只猫正强行往他嘴巴里面钻,它放平身体,左右扭动,一点一点往更深处去。哈斯顿能感觉到他的嘴巴被越撑越大,下颌吱嘎作响,才能容得下它。

抬手抓住猫,猛地把它拽出去,然后就能杀了它……然而,哈斯顿的手只握住了猫的尾巴。

不知怎的,那猫已经将整个身子塞进了哈斯顿的嘴里,它那诡异的、半黑半白的脸一定已经堵住了他的喉咙。

哈斯顿的喉咙活活胀开了,像花园里浇水的软管似的肿胀起来。喉咙里发出低沉而可怕的吞咽声。

他的身体抽搐着,双手落回腿面,手指无意识地敲打着大腿。他的眼睛突然一亮,继而发直,没了光彩。透过挡风玻璃,可以看到他两眼空空,直直地望着黎明将至的曙光。

一条两英寸长的尾巴从他张开的嘴巴里伸了出来,毛茸茸的,一半黑,一半白。那尾巴懒洋洋地来回摆动着,随后消失不见了。

不知何处又传来了鸟儿的叫声。曙光,终于在令人窒息的寂静中,笼罩在康涅狄格州郊外冰霜覆盖的田野上。

有一个叫威尔·罗伊斯的农民。

当天上午,他开着农用卡车,去普雷塞尔峡谷检验车辆,更换标贴,在明晃晃的阳光下,看到道路旁边的溪谷里有什么东西在闪闪发亮。他把车停在路边。那是一辆普利茅斯车,倾斜着躺在沟里,像是司机喝醉了酒才把车开成了这副样子。车前栅格上乱糟糟地缠着带刺的铁丝网。

他慢慢下到沟底,眼前的景象让她倒吸一口冷气:"我的天呐!"他对着11月晴朗的秋日喃喃自语道。方向盘后一个男人直挺挺地坐着,眼睛空洞地睁着,似乎在凝视着永恒。罗珀组织再也不会将他纳入总统选举的民意调查对象之中了。他的脸上都是血迹,身上还系着安全带。

司机一侧的车门已经变形,罗伊斯双手猛地用力才把车门打开。他侧身进车,解开了那人身上的安全带,想设法确认死者的身份。他伸手探入大衣内,注意到死者衬衣下有东西蠕动,就在皮带的上面,蠕动着,膨胀起来。斑斑点点的鲜血开始涌出,犹如邪恶的玫瑰绽放。

"什么东西!"他伸出手,捏住死者的衬衫,掀了起来。

罗伊斯看了一眼,便大声尖叫起来。

哈斯顿的肚脐上方被硬生生掏出了一个溃烂的洞。一张布满血迹的阴阳猫脸正从里向外看,怒目圆睁,寒光闪闪。

罗伊斯向后一个趔趄,大声尖叫,双手掩住脸。叫声惊动了附近田野上的一群乌鸦,它们呼啦啦地飞上天。

那只猫从里面挤了出来,猥亵地舒展了一下身体。

然后跳出窗外,罗伊斯看见它穿过高高的枯草消失得无影无踪。

他后来告诉当地报社的一名记者,那只猫似乎走得很急。

仿佛它还有未尽之事。

(方璐璐,汪源君 译;言声远,程 晨 校)

柽柳猎人

保罗·巴奇加卢皮

一株大型柽柳每年吸走 73000 加仑河水。洛洛整个冬天都以铲除柽柳为业，日薪 2.88 美元，外加供水补贴。

十年前，这倒是不错的活计。柽柳、棉白杨、沙枣和榆树遍布科罗拉多河各支流沿岸。十年前，在大章克申和莫阿布这样的镇子里，居民们都觉得能靠河流勉强度日。

洛洛站在峡谷边沿，骆驼玛吉是他唯一的同伴。他望着峡谷底部：有路直通谷底，爬下去得一小时。他把玛吉拴上刺柏，沿沟槽下滑。几片绿草已发芽，从雪中冒出，雪地上点缀着刺柏。正值晚冬，深谷开始有水涌出，河床冰盖正在消融。抬眼望去，白雪依旧笼着山峰。洛洛越过泥地，踩上碎石通道，继续滑行，农药罐在背上咚咚直响；铲子和撬杆不时撞击身旁的刺柏。这是一场远行。可话说回来，正因如此，才有了这片肥美的土地。下行的路很长，河岸多半深藏其中。

这是谋生的法子；其他人因旱灾逃离，他却留在这里。他是柽柳猎手，一只水虱，一株倔草。所有人都像蒲公英一样被吹离这片土地，向南或向东；多数人向北，因为那里河水偶尔丰沛；就算没有茂密蕨原和深水鱼群，至少还有活命的水。

总算滑到谷底。荫处寒气透骨，洛洛呼气成雾。

他掏出数码相机，拍摄工作证明。垦务局要求很严，命令柽柳猎手在各个角度拍摄柽柳，记录整个过程，准确定位，通过摄像机直接发送，一切在现场完成。他们还会偶尔到场，检查通过后才开闸发放供水补贴。

不过，无论他们多么严格，洛洛也有的是对策。他有条秘诀，可以永不失业。内政部及其下属垦务局对此一无所知。洛洛正偷偷播种柽柳，使其在已清理的区域再度繁殖。他悄悄将优质柳根沿河种植在荒僻难及的地带，防止其他柽柳猎手涌入这些地方。洛洛狡猾得很。眼前这棵柽柳，高约 400 米，根深叶茂，满是盐分，正是他的保底妙计。

记录完毕，他解开折锯、撬杆和铲子，把农药罐放在毫无生机的盐化河岸上，把折锯拉入柽柳根部。他每 30 秒一停，在切口倒上"盖灌能"除草剂，这样伤口恶化得更快，让柳树来不及自愈。不过，他会把最优质的柳树除根保留，以备日后之用。

日薪 2.88 美元，外加供水补贴。

颠簸摇晃一星期，玛吉才能把洛洛驮回农场。他们沿河行进，偶尔爬上平顶山，步入大漠，避开散乱的空城废墟。警卫队直升机在河上盘旋，如同恼怒的黄蜂群，排查私人水泵和私挖水渠。飞机呼啸而过，气流汹涌，机身之上，国民警卫队徽章闪闪发光。洛洛想起警卫队与河岸居民交火的情形，曳光弹和机枪在谷中交响；防空导弹穿过红岩大漠，在蓝色天空中划出一道弧形，嘶嘶作响，将一架盘旋的直升机就地摧毁。

但那是很久以前的事了。如今，警卫队在河上优哉游哉，无人胆敢侵扰。

洛洛爬上平顶山，凝视熟悉的荒镇：弯弯曲曲的大街小巷静沐在阳光里。在空城边缘，有一英亩农场，还有片5000平方英尺的豪华住宅区。高尔夫球场呈现风滚草一般的棕色，球场边缘立着死树和土丘，沙坑已不见踪影。

加州首次占据河流时，没人挂在心上。只不过一些城镇开始求水，几个新来的蠢货因无权用水而停止牧马，如此而已。几年后，人们开始减少洗澡时间；接着每周只洗一次澡；再然后开始用桶储水。从那时起，没人再拿"炎热"开玩笑。不管多热，也不算事。问题不在于缺水，也不在于炎热，而在于440万英亩—英尺的水全都流进了加州。水有的是，只是不给他们用。

他们活该像群傻猴一样，呆站在河边目送流水。

"洛洛？"

洛洛吓了一跳，还没拉住玛吉，玛吉就大惊失色，呻吟一声，奔向平顶山边缘，硕大的脚掌扬起漫天灰尘。洛洛手忙脚乱去拿猎枪，但枪挂在玛吉身侧枪套里。他骂骂咧咧地拽着玛吉转向，掏出一半猎枪，勉强抓住座位。

一张熟悉的脸探出刺槐丛。

"天杀的！"洛洛把猎枪塞回枪套，"哎呀呀，特拉维斯，你简直吓死我！"

特拉维斯咧嘴一笑，从刺槐那扎人的树皮里钻出来，一手握着灰帽，一手拉着缰绳，把骡子从树丛里拉出来，说："没想到吧？"

"我差点打死你！"

"别慌呀。这里就咱俩水虱而已。"

"我上次去下面抢东西时也这么以为。我给安妮弄了套新碟子，可到主干道的时候，有架超轻飞机停在当间，我们撞个正着，碟子全摔碎了。"

"吸冰毒的？"

"我挨了顿胖揍，但没打听到他们是谁。"

"妈的，他们肯定跟你一样惨。"

"他们差点儿弄死我。"

"我看他们没弄成。"

洛洛摇摇头，又骂了几句，但怒气已消。虽然遭遇不速之客，但他很高兴碰见特拉维斯。这里寂寥无人，洛洛离家太久，与玛吉聊天时都感到寂静。两位朋友仪式性地举壶小饮，一起扎营。他们聊到了垦务局；至于各自在何处铲除柳树则避而不谈。二人共览空城景象：蛇形的街道穿过死寂的房屋，河流尚无人迹，闪着波光。

夕阳西下，两人烤了喜鹊吃。直到这时，洛洛才提出盘算许久的问题。自打看到对方那张晒得乌黑的脸探出树丛，洛洛就有此疑惑。直接问呢，不太礼貌；不问呢，又忍不住。他剔掉牙缝里的肉丝，开口道："我以为你一直在下游工作呢。"

特拉维斯斜视着洛洛，面露疑色；洛洛看出来他日子不太好过。特拉维斯不像洛洛那么聪明，他没有栽培柽柳，没有保底之策；他也没有竞争意识，没想过职业终结的下场；如今才发现处境艰难。洛洛为他惋惜，因为特拉维斯人还不错。洛洛想告诉他种植柽柳的秘密，但他忍住了。这太危险。偷水乃是重罪，这事连老婆都没讲，怕她说漏嘴。和所有重罪一样，偷水只能悄悄干；洛洛这种罪名，去"大吸管"劳改都算轻的。

虽然洛洛侵犯了自己的隐私，特拉维斯还是平静下来，说："我养了几头奶牛到这里放,可惜弄丢了,大概被什么东西拐走了。"

"牧牛还要跑这么远的路啊。"

"确实,唉,一路上连灌木蒿都干死了。炎炎大旱把我的农场祸害不轻。"他咬紧嘴唇,若有所思地说,"但愿能找回牛群。"

"它们很可能顺流而下了。"

特拉维斯叹气道:"然后落入国民警卫队魔爪。"

"也许被直升机射杀,变成烤肉。"

"死加州佬。"

两人边说边咔了一口。太阳还在西沉,暗影静笼荒城,屋顶闪着红光,犹如一串红宝石点缀蓝色项链般的河流。

"你觉得城里还有值得一抢的货摊吗?"特拉维斯问道。

"你可以去看看。我去年已经抢得差不多了。在我之前肯定还有些人去过,所以,应该没啥了。"

"妈的!行吧,我可能会去一趟,说不定能搞点什么。"

"这次肯定没人拦你。"

警卫队直升机响彻静谧的夜空,似乎是表达反对意见。夜色沉沉,飞机只有黑点大,难以看清,很快又消失不见,行踪没在蟋蟀的唧唧鸣声里。

特拉维斯笑道:"还记得吗,有一次,警卫队说要驱逐所有掠夺者。我看电视上他们开着直升机和军车,说要保卫一切,直到恢复安定。"他又笑道,"还记得他们在街上开车横冲直撞吗?"

"记得呀。"

"我有时觉得,咱们是不是该多给他们点教训。"

"他们进攻哈瓦苏湖城时,安妮就在那里。你也看到了情况如何。"洛洛不由自主战栗了一下,"他们一旦炸了净水厂,就没什么好打的了。要是你家水阀断水,你也只能离开。"

"说的也对。我只是觉得,得反抗一把,出口气也行。"特拉维斯指着阴影下的城镇,说:"我记得当时下面的土地特别抢手,木材供应多快,建设就有多快。购物中心、停车场、住宅区,但凡能推平的地方,都布满建筑。"

"那时还没有'炎炎大旱'这个名字呢。"

"45000 人,没人知道发生了什么事。我那时还是个房产中介。"特拉维斯笑道,那是极短的自嘲之声;对洛洛而言,这更像是自怜之声。他们再次沉默,俯视这片荒城。

"我可能要去北方了。"特拉维斯终于说道。

洛洛转过头来,一脸惊讶。他忍不住想吐露秘密,但又忍住了,说:"去干什么?"

"可能摘水果吧。什么都行。毕竟那里有水。"

洛洛指着河说:"这儿就有水呀。"

"但不属于我们。"特拉维斯顿了下,说,"跟你坦白吧,我去过'大吸管'了。"

洛洛听了这莫名其妙的话,有些迷糊。这简直不可思议,但特拉维斯看起来一脸严肃。"大吸管?开玩笑吧?专门去那里?"

"没错。"特拉维斯耸耸肩,"反正我不找桎柳了。其实不远,比以前近。我花了一星期去铁路,跳上运煤火车,坐到州际公路搭顺风车。"

"那边怎么样?"

"空空荡荡。有个卡车司机说,加州政府和内政部列出计划,届时会封锁一些城市。"他意味深长地看着洛洛,"哈瓦苏事件后,他们发现计划要慢慢推进。他们研究出一种公式:在不出乱子的情况下,可以一次性覆灭多少城市和多少人口。反正就快完工,除了高速卡车、运煤火车和卡车站,什么也不剩了。"

"那你看见'大吸管'了吗?"

"当然了。就在州界的对面,老娘哎,大得吓人,根本爬不上去,活像条大漠银蛇,吧嗒吧嗒扑向加州。"他条件反射,啐口唾沫,"他们铺了水泥,防止渗漏;还搞来碳纤维,盖在河床上方,防止蒸发。河流就这么消失了。什么都没剩下,只有空谷一条,干巴巴的。到处都是直升机和军车,嗡嗡作响,跟个马蜂窝似的。他们不准我进入半英里内,怕极端环保分子炸它。那帮人也不喜欢这玩意。"

"你怎么看?"

"说不来。我就是觉得心慌。他们把咱们弄到这里,发一丁点供水补贴,明年却把所有的水都引到那大粗管里。我估计,加州佬正把咱们去年的供水补贴引到游泳池呢。"

蟋蟀在暗处唧唧响,一窝郊狼在远处开始呜呜叫。两人沉默片刻。终于,洛洛拍着朋友的肩膀,说:"唉,兄弟,这也算是它的最好归宿了。河水嘛,就不该在沙漠流。"

洛洛的农场是一片半盐碱地,面积有几英亩,离河很近。他爬上小丘眺望自家的地,安妮正在地里劳作。她挥挥手,继续挖坑,用丈夫挣来的"薪水"浇地种田。

洛洛停步,看着安妮劳作。热风肆虐,夹杂着鼠尾草和黏土的气息。邪门的风沙旋着安妮,掀翻她的头巾。洛洛微笑着看她拨弄头巾。她发现洛洛盯着自己,就挥手示意他别再晃悠。

他笑着和玛吉下山,依旧注视着安妮。他很感激妻子,无论自己何时铲柳归来,她都不离不弃。她十分坚定,比多数因旱灾离家的人都坚定,特拉维斯就是离乡者之一;她比洛洛认识的任何人都坚定,这一点毋庸置疑。有时她会做噩梦,受不了城镇或人群,或是半夜醒来呼唤无法见面的家人,她曾被驱离故土,所以洛洛更得播种怪柳,以便留在此地。

洛洛让玛吉屈膝,下地后牵它去饮水,水槽半满,尽是黏液和水虿。玛吉哼哼抱怨,洛洛提桶去了河边。农场本来有井,可惜他和大家一样没有采水权。水位降到最低可用储水线后,垦务局用速干水泥把井填掉。现在夫妻俩只能带桶到河里偷水,或者趁内政部不注意,踩着水泵把河水引入秘密水窖里,窖是《资源保护及使用指示》实行时挖的。

安妮把这份指示叫作"护示",这种叫法听起来像是在咳痰。水井被填还不算惨。更惨的是西班牙栎镇或羚羊谷或河滨镇等地:拉斯韦加斯和洛杉矶抢到水权后,这些城镇不管有钱没钱,其黄金地段都因丧失水权而沦为荒城。最惨的是"中央亚利桑那工程"关停后,亚利桑那州依旧从米德湖采水,上面就把他们的高架渠炸成碎片,居民只好逃离凤凰城(亚利桑那州首府)求生。还好,洛洛并未经历这种痛苦。

洛洛给水槽倒上清水,环顾四周,沙尘覆满农场,安妮独自劳作。洛洛觉得自己很幸运。他没有背井离乡,反而扎根此地。加州佬把他俩叫作水虱,可他们算个屁。如果没有他和安妮等人,加州佬早和其他人一样早死,随风远去。就算再多种些怪柳,那也是加州佬该遭的报应,毕竟他们害人不浅。

喂好玛吉,洛洛回屋,拿着滤壶倒了杯水。在土坯房阴下,水很清凉。头顶是刺槐木制成的横梁。洛洛坐下,拿出垦务局相机,连上屋顶的太阳能电池。相机电源灯闪着琥珀光。洛洛又喝了杯水。虽然早已习惯口渴,但今天却觉得喝不够。炎炎大旱扼住了他的喉咙。

安妮进屋,用晒黑的手臂擦拭额头,说:"别喝太多水。我没抽到水,附近有一帮警卫。"

"他们来干啥?我们连水阀都没开呀。"

"说是来找你的。"

洛洛闻言,差点握不住杯子。

事情败露了。

他们知道他在偷种柽柳;知道他挖掉优质柳根,沿河播种的事了。一周前他上传信息,说是在谷中发现柽柳,空前之大,价值约一英亩一英尺的供水补贴。现在警卫找上门了。

洛洛强忍颤抖,放好杯子,说:"他们有没有说要干吗?"声音竟未沙哑,他觉得很惊讶。

"只说要找你谈谈。"她想了想说,"他们还开了辆悍马,拿着枪。"

洛洛闭上眼,强忍着深呼吸一口气,"他们总是带着枪,应该没事。"

"我想起了哈瓦苏湖事件,他们把我们扫荡一空。那时他们关掉净水厂,大家都恨不得烧掉土地管理局。"

"应该没事。"他突然庆幸,没把柽柳妙计告诉她。怪罪不到她头上。要罚多少水呢?得几百英亩一英尺吧。大不了被抓,押到"大吸管"工作至死,偿还水债。他种了成百上千株柽柳,像赌桌上的老千,把树移来搬去,铲来除去,还得意扬扬地发送工作证明。

"应该没事。"他重复道。

"在哈瓦苏湖时大家不也这么说吗?"

洛洛朝着外面新耕的农场挥挥手。阳光正暴晒着那小片土地。"咱俩可不值得他们费心。"他强笑道,"也许和极端环保分子有关,他们总是想炸'大吸管'。他们可能逃到了这儿,应该是这样。"

安妮并不赞同,摇头说道:"不一定,为什么他们只找你问话,问我也一样呀。"

"也对,但我见多识广,所以他们才找我问话。他们只是在找极端环保分子。"

"嗯,也许是这样。"她若有所思地点了点头,像在努力说服自己似的,"极端环保分子,真是群疯子。人都没水喝了,他们却关心鱼啊鸟啊,要把河流让给它们。"

洛洛点头大笑道:"没错,一群傻瓜。"但他突然对极端环保分子有种兄弟般的同情,毕竟他们也和自己一样,被加州佬追捕。

洛洛彻夜未眠。直觉告诉他得逃,但他不敢告诉安妮真相,也不愿抛下她。他早上去猎树,但一无所获,一天下来,连一棵柽柳都没铲除。他本想饮弹自杀,枪管进嘴后,又心生怯意。活着就好,逃掉总比死掉强。最后,他盯着双筒枪,决定把真相告诉安妮,跟她说,自己盗水多年,必须逃向北方。她也许会一起逃,也许会改主意。他们会一起逃亡。至少可以这么干。

绝不能让这帮狗东西把自己押到劳营,在那里终老。

洛洛返回时,警卫已经在等他了。两个警卫蹲在军车阴影下聊天。洛洛爬上小丘顶时,一个警卫拍拍同伴的肩,指着洛洛。两人站了起来。安妮去农场垦土,不晓得有什么事情。洛洛拉住玛吉,观察警卫。他们倚着军车,盯着洛洛。

洛洛猛然想到了自己的下场,一幕幕如电影般闪在脑海,就像头顶的蓝天一样清晰。他手摸枪把,枪挂在玛吉身侧,警卫看不见。他调整玛吉身体角度遮挡枪管,骑着它下了山。

警卫朝他信步走来。车顶装着0.50口径机枪,警卫肩扛M-16S步枪。他们全套防弹武装,脸色发红,热得很。洛洛缓缓前来,打算当面击毙二人。汗水淌下肩胛,手心在枪把上打滑。

警卫镇定自若,步枪依然挂在肩上,任由洛洛继续靠近。其中一人还咧嘴冲洛洛笑了,大概40多岁,肤色黝黑。他出门有一会了,晒得不轻。另一人举手道:"嘿哟,洛洛!"

洛洛吃了一惊,手从枪把上松开。"难道是黑尔?"他认出了对方,是一起长大的朋友。他们一起玩过橄榄球,但那仿佛是100万年的事了。当时的球场绿草如茵,洒水器向天空喷射水珠。黑尔·珀金斯,原来是他。洛洛皱起眉头。他没法向黑尔开枪。

黑尔问道:"你还在这儿呀?"

"你他妈的怎么穿上了制服?和加州佬混在一起干什么?"

黑尔做个鬼脸,指着徽章,上面写着:犹他国民警卫队。

洛洛皱起眉头。犹他国民警卫队、科罗拉多国民警卫队、亚利桑那国民警卫队,没一个好东西。这些警卫都是外地雇佣兵。当地大部分警卫队员早早退伍,不忍屠杀自己人,也不想把亲朋好友赶出家园,更不愿把不舍离乡者就地处决。所以,不论是科罗拉多警卫,还是亚利桑那或犹他警卫,只要穿着制服,戴着高端夜视器,开着直升机巡河,就是不折不扣的加州佬。

也有少数像黑尔之类的人。

洛洛记得黑尔挺好相处,有次和他一起从麋鹿社偷了桶啤酒。洛洛盯着他问道:"你们的补助计划开展得怎样?"他瞥着另一个警卫,继续道:"是不是捞了不少?加州佬帮了大忙吧?"

黑尔眼含哀求道:"别这么说,洛洛。咱俩不一样,我得养家。我再干一年,他们就允许香农和孩子在加州附近落户。"

"还给你家后院修了泳池,对吧?"

"怎么可能,你不是不知道,那边也缺水呀。"

洛洛想奚落他,但已经没了心思,开始揣摩黑尔是否明智。想当初,加州在法院赢得水权,封锁城市,移民只能逐水而居,搬到加州。官僚们后知后觉,然后有精明人算了笔账,发现调水加移民解决不了缺水问题。于是,隔离墙建了起来。

不过,黑尔这种身份的人可以进入。

"你俩想干吗?"洛洛心想,既然他们没把自己拽下来,也没押走,不妨死撑到底。

警卫咧嘴笑道:"说不定,我们只是来看看水虱过得怎么样。"

洛洛怒目而视。这家伙,不妨一枪打死。他摸到枪把上,说:"垦务局给我设好了水阀,不劳你们大驾。"

警卫说:"哟,这儿有些印子呀,还挺大。"

洛洛僵笑着,他明白加州佬的意思。当初想拆水阀,用5种扳手强拧了很久,可还是放弃了。他急火攻心,抢扳手就砸;与此同时,自家的作物正在枯萎呢。从那以后,他只能带桶偷河水浇地,不再打水阀的主意。但那些扳手印痕还在,见证着他那时的疯狂。

"它照常运转呀,对吧?"

黑尔举手示意同伴闭嘴,说:"是,照常运转。可我们不为这个。"

"那为什么？你该不是专程开车扛枪，跟我说水阀凹痕的吧？"

黑尔叹口气，压住火，保持理智，说："你小子能不能从骆驼上下来，我们好好谈谈？"

洛洛打量着警卫，想了想在地面上的胜算，然后啐了口，说："妈的！行，我听你的。"他让玛吉跪下，爬下驼峰，说："安妮对此一无所知，别把她牵扯进来，都是我一个人干的。"

黑尔眉头紧锁，有点蒙，问道："你说什么呢？"

"你们不是来抓我的吗？"

黑尔身旁的加州佬笑道："为啥？就因为你从河里偷了几桶水？还是因为你偷挖水窖？"他又笑出声来，说："你们水虱都一个样，以为我们不知道这点破事吗？"

黑尔朝加州佬皱眉，转身对洛洛说："我们不是来抓你的。你知道'大吸管'的事吧？"

"当然。"洛洛一字一顿地回道。他欣喜若狂，心里的石头落地。他们不知道呀。他们连个屁都不知道。妙计就是妙计，妙得很呐。洛洛想憋住笑以听清黑尔的话，但他忍不住，心早像猴子一样上蹿下跳。他们还蒙在鼓里呢——

"等等，"洛洛举起手，"你刚说什么？"

黑尔重复道："加州停发供水补贴了。'大吸管'已经竣工，猎树计划没用了。他们封锁半数河流，和内政部达成协议，要把更多的资金投入到防渗漏防蒸发项目，这样才有利可图。所以，他们停止了供水补贴。"他顿了顿，说："对不住了，洛洛。"

洛洛眉头紧皱，说："但柽柳还在啊。凭什么让这些狗娘养的植物吸水？要是我铲除一棵柽柳，就算加州佬不要它偷走的水，也该把水给我啊。这水能养活很多人呀。"

黑尔看着洛洛，表示同情，说："法令不是我订的，我只负责执行。提醒你一句，你的水阀明年关停。就算你铲除再多的柽柳，也无济于事。"他环顾农场，耸了耸肩，说："反正再过几年，他们会把所有河流封入管道。没了水，柽柳自然活不长。"

"那我怎么办？"

黑尔从防弹背心口袋抽出小本，翻开一页说道："加州政府和垦务局会付给你前期买断金，算是补偿。"纸页在热风中翻动。他在本子上做了记号，撕下打孔支票，说："这买卖还不赖。"

洛洛接下支票，盯着它说："500 美元？"

黑尔落寞地耸肩道："他们就给这么多。这是纸印编码，上网确认后才有效。用垦务局相机拍摄即可。他们会给你转账，或者把钱存在信托机构，你去镇上取现。有土地管理局办公点就行。但得在 4 月 15 日前确认。大约换季前，垦务局会派人关你的水阀。"

"才 500 美元？"

"够你搬到北方了。明年出价会更低。"

"但这是我的农场呀。"

"只要炎炎大旱没结束，这土地就不属于你。对不住了，洛洛。"

"旱灾随时都会结束。为什么不多给我们几年时间？它随时都可能结束。"洛洛嘴上这么说，心里却没把握。要是在 10 年前，这还有可能。可现在不行了。炎炎大旱已经扎根。他攥紧支票，编码朝向胸口。

100 码外，河水正朝着加州奔流不息。

（姚海涛　译；李盼盼，秦梓林　校）

黑 猫

埃德加·爱伦·坡

  我即将要写的这个故事极其荒诞,但又极为平常。我并不指望人们相信。要是我盼着人们相信我所讲的,那我一定是疯了,因为连我自己心里都不相信这些。不过,我并没有疯,我也很肯定自己不是在做梦。但明天我就死到临头了,所以今天我要坦白一切,解放灵魂。我迫切希望把这一系列家庭琐事简明扼要、不加评论地公之于世。这些事件让我感到恐惧害怕、备受折磨、人生尽毁。但我并不想解释什么。这些事只让我感到恐惧,而对其他多数人来说,更不值一提,还不如巴洛克式建筑来得吓人。也许将来会有一些有识之士发现我的幻想不足为奇。这些有识之士比我更冷静、更讲逻辑,也不像我这样情绪化,那么我诚惶诚恐、详尽描述的这些东西,在他们看来只是一系列有着自然因果关系的小事罢了。

  我小时候性情温顺善良,远近皆知。心肠特别软,以至于成为同伴们的笑柄。我尤为喜欢小动物,父母对我百般纵容,因此我也能养各种各样的宠物。我大多数时间都跟它们待在一起,给它们喂食、爱抚它们是最快乐的时光。随着年龄的增长,这种特殊的癖性也随之增长,成年后,这也是我的一个主要的乐趣。有些人对忠诚聪明的狗疼爱有加,对他们来说,我几乎不必多费口舌说明个中趣味和满足。你要是常常感到人类的薄情寡义,那么动物身上的那种甘于牺牲的无私之爱便会直击心灵。

  我结婚比较早,幸运的是妻子与我也算志趣相投。她观察到我特别喜爱小宠物,因此只要一有机会,就去买那些最惹人喜爱的宠物。我们养了小鸟、金鱼、一条狗、几只兔子、一只小猴和一只猫。

  这只猫体格庞大、相貌美丽、通体漆黑,而且聪明得离奇。谈到这只猫的聪明才智,我那内心十分迷信的妻子就经常提起一个古老的传说,即所有黑猫都是经过伪装的女巫。我倒不是说我妻子对这一点极为认真,我提到这一点只是因为刚好想到而已。

  这只猫的名字叫普路托,它是我最喜欢的宠物和玩伴。我亲自喂养他,我在家里走到哪儿他就跟到哪儿。就连我过马路他也要跟着我,拦也拦不住。

  我们俩的友谊就这样持续了好几年,在此期间,因为酗酒无度,我的脾气和性格都变得越来越坏,一提到这我就感到无比羞愧。我一天天地变得越来越喜怒无常,烦躁易怒,丝毫不顾及他人的感受。我甚至对妻子粗语相向。最后,还对她拳脚相加。我的宠物们当然也能感受到我性格的变化。我不仅忽视了它们,而且还加以虐待。每当那些小兔子、小猴子,或是小狗碰巧或是出于亲热跑到我跟前来,我都会毫无顾忌地粗暴对待它们。但只有对待普路托,我仍然留有尊重,未曾下手。但我的病情愈发严重——世上哪有像酒精一样的病啊?——最后,就连日渐年迈、易怒的普路托也开始变成我的出气筒了。

  一天晚上,我醉醺醺地从镇上的一个常去的酒吧回到家,我觉得那只猫有意躲着我,于是一把抓住了它；他被我突如其来的暴行吓坏了，于是用牙齿在我手上轻轻咬了一口。我顿时感到自己被愤怒的恶魔所控制，不再清醒了。原来的灵魂似乎瞬间飞离了我的身体。喝下肚的杜松子酒让我如凶神恶煞一般，全身似乎都被点燃了。杜松子酒滋养着我的身体，使我的每一部分都激动不已。我从马甲口袋里掏出一把小刀，打开刀子，掐住那可怜的小畜生的喉咙，故意把它的一只眼睛从眼窝里挖了出来！当我写到这该死的暴行时，我面红耳赤，不寒而栗。

一夜酣睡，第二天早上我终于清醒了过来。我对自己犯下的罪行感到恐惧又悔恨；但这充其量只是一种微弱而模糊的感觉，我的灵魂仍然毫无触动。我再次沉溺于酒精当中，关于这件事的所有记忆也很快忘光了。

与此同时，猫的身体也在逐渐恢复。空洞的眼窝看上去果真可怕，但它看起来似乎不再感到任何痛苦了。他像往常一样在家里走来走去，但只要我一走近，它就不出所料地仓皇逃走了。毕竟我良心未泯，所以一开始，看到一个曾经如此爱我的畜生如今对我的厌恶毕露，我感到很难过。但这种难过很快就变成了恼怒。再然后，恶意似乎完全侵占了我的身心。这种恶念，哲学并不予以考虑。不过，我不确定我的灵魂是否活着，就像我也不确定恶念是不是人类内心的一种原始冲动，是人类的一种基本能力或情感，能够决定人类的性格。难道有谁不是明知不可的情况下依然屡次犯下卑鄙愚蠢的错误？难道我们有谁不是明知这样做犯法，却依然不顾自己的判断而为之吗？唉，正是这种恶念最终毁了我。正是内心这种深不可测的渴望，带来烦恼，违反本性，为错而错，使得我继续伤害这个无辜的畜生并害它最终丧了命。一天早上，我冷血地把它的脖子套上绳索，然后把它挂在树枝上，我的眼泪夺眶而出，痛苦与悔恨之情油然而生。我把它吊死是因为我知道它爱我，是因为我觉得它没有哪里冒犯了我，是因为我知道我这么做是在犯罪——这种罪行不可饶恕，会使得我不朽的灵魂永世不得超生——如果可能的话——甚至永不为最仁慈、最可敬的上帝所宽恕。

在这一暴行发生的那天晚上，我听到失火的叫声而从睡梦中惊醒。床上的帐子已经着了起来。整栋房子都在燃烧。我和我妻子，还有一个仆人从这场火灾中艰难逃生。这场大火烧得很彻底，我的一切财产都被大火吞没，自此我陷入了绝望之中。

但我也并非那么懦弱，试图将这场火灾和我的暴行建立起因果关系。但我要详细说说这一连串的事，希望不会落下任何一个环节。火灾的第二天，我重返了那片废墟。墙壁都坍塌了，只有一堵还立着。这是房间里的一堵隔墙，不算太厚，立于中央，我的床头就靠在这堵墙上。墙上的灰泥在很大程度上阻隔了大火，我认为这是最近刚刚粉刷过的缘故。一大帮人聚集在这堵墙周围，不少人都在聚精会神地检查这堵墙。不时传来的诸如"奇怪！"之类的词，让我也开始好奇。我走近，看到白墙上赫然刻着浮雕——是一只巨猫！刻得栩栩如生，令人惊奇。猫的脖子上还套着一根绳子。

我一看到这个幽灵，简直惊恐万分。但回过神来，我记起那只猫已经在房子旁边的花园里吊死了。火灾警报一响，花园就立刻挤满了人，一定是有人把绳子砍断把猫从树上放下来了，然后从一扇开着的窗户扔进了我房间里。这可能是为了叫醒我。其他几堵坍塌的墙壁把被残忍杀害的猫压在了刚刷好的灰泥里；在石灰、大火，加上尸体散发出的氨气这三者的共同作用下，这幅浮雕出现在了墙上。

我刚才细细讲来的事实，即使良心上不能自圆其说，倒也合乎情理，但它仍然给我留下了深刻的印象。几个月来,猫的幻影在我心中挥之不去;这段时间里,我又沉浸在一种伤感之情,但又算不上是悔恨。我甚至后悔害死这只猫,并在我经常去的那些下等场所周边试图找到外表相似的黑猫以作替代。

一天晚上,我醉醺醺地坐在一个下等酒馆里,突然注意到一个巨大的盛着杜松子酒或朗姆酒的黑桶,这是屋子里的主要物件,桶上面有一个黑色的家伙正在休息。我已经盯着桶顶看了好几分钟,奇怪的是,我竟然才察觉到上面的东西。我走过去用手摸了摸,是只黑色的猫——个头硕大——几乎和普路托一样大,除了一处之外,其他各个方面都跟它很像。普路托通体没有白色毛发;但这只猫的胸前有一片白斑,虽然模糊了点。

我一碰到它,它就立刻跳了起来,发出咕噜咕噜的声音,不停蹭我的手,我的关注似乎让它很高兴。而这正是我要找的猫。我立刻提出要从店主手里买下它;不料店主称这猫并不是他的——对这只猫一无所知——也从未见过它。

我继续抚摸着它,当我准备回家时,这只猫表现出了想要跟着我的意图;我让它跟着自己,在路上偶尔俯身拍拍它。它一到家里就十分温顺乖巧,不一会儿就成了我妻子的最爱。

至于我自己,没过多久我就发现自己对它开始感到厌恶;但我也搞不明白这是怎么回事,也不明白为什么它对我的喜爱如此明显,而我却感到厌恶和恼火。慢慢地,这种厌恶和恼火逐渐转变为仇恨。我开始躲着这只猫;一种羞愧感,加上对曾经我所犯暴行的记忆阻止了我对它实施虐待。几个星期以来,我没有对它动手,也没有以其他方式对它施暴;但渐渐地,我内心产生了一种难以言喻的厌恶之情,我一看到它的丑貌,就像躲避瘟疫一样默默逃走。

毫无疑问,我之所以恨它,是因为在我把它带回家的第二天早上,我发现了它和普路托一样,也被剜掉一只眼睛。然而,这使得我妻子对它更加疼爱,正如我之前所说,我妻子满怀仁慈,这曾经是我的特点之一,也使我感受到简单纯粹的幸福。

然而,尽管我对这只猫越发厌恶,它却反而对我越发偏爱,对我寸步不离,这对于读者来说一定难以理解。每当我坐着的时候,它就会趴在椅子下面,或者跳到我的膝盖上,对我百般示好,这实在令人厌恶。每当我站起来走路,它就会挤到我双脚之间,几乎要把我绊倒,又或者用它又长又锋利的爪子钩住我的衣服,爬到我胸前。在这种时候,虽然我迫切想要用一拳打死它,但我并未动手,一是因为我想起了我曾经所犯下的罪行,但主要还是因为——还是让我坦白吧——我对这只畜生的极度恐惧。

这种恐惧并不是害怕自己对它会施加什么暴力,我不知道该如何定义。即使身处死牢,我也羞于承认——没错,这只猫给我带来的惊惧,因一种纯粹的幻觉而加剧了。我妻子不止一次地提醒我注意猫身上的白斑,我之前也说过,这是这只奇怪的畜生和我杀死的那只畜生之间唯一明显的区别。想必读者还记得,这块斑虽然很大,但原本是很模糊的;不过,慢慢地,它竟不知不觉变得明显起来,最终呈现出了一种清晰的轮廓。我的理性好久以来一直都在努力拒绝承认这一点,把它当成一种幻想。现在,一提到它,我就感到不寒而栗。因此,我对它感到厌恶、恐惧,我要是敢的话,早就摆脱它了。要我说,它现在代表着一个极端丑陋、可怕的形象——一个绞刑架!——哦!多么可悲恐怖的刑具,它代表着恐怖和受罪——也代表着痛苦和死亡!

眼下,我忍受着人间不幸中的不幸。一只凶残畜生——我曾轻侮地杀死了它的同类——它对我这样一个按照上帝的模样创造出来的人,造成了难以忍受的痛苦!唉!无论白天还是黑夜,我都难得安宁了!在白天,这个畜生让我一刻都不能安静自己待会儿;在夜里,我不断从难以言喻的骇人噩梦中惊醒,感觉到它往我脸上呼出的热气,以及它压在我身上的庞大身躯——一个我无力摆脱的梦魇的具象——在我心头永远挥之不去!

在遭受这种折磨的重压之下,我内心仅剩的那点微弱的善意也消失殆尽了。邪念占据了我内心的全部——那些最黑暗、最邪恶的想法。我平日里就喜怒无常,如今更是对一切人和事都充满了仇恨;由于盲目放任自己,经常动不动就控制不住自己乱发脾气,唉!最经常遭罪但却对我最为忍耐的要数我妻子了。

因囊中羞涩,我们没钱置换,只能一直住在老房子里。一天,为了些家务事,它陪我一起下到地窖里。台阶很陡,就因为这只猫也跟着我们蹿下去,我差点儿被猫绊倒,一头栽下去。我怒不可遏,盛怒之下抄起一把斧子就朝它砍了下去,全然忽略内心深处对它的幼稚的恐惧。要是真如我所愿,一斧子下去,猫绝对一命呜呼了。谁知妻子伸手握住了我的手腕,拦下我的动作。这不拦还好,一拦我更是火冒三丈,抽回手,转而砍向她的头。她还没来得及哼唧两声,就命丧当场了。

干完这罪孽深重的残忍谋杀,我细细思索该如何处理尸体。我知道不论是白天还是晚上,只要搬尸体出房子,就难免可能被邻居看到。不少念头涌入脑海。我一会儿想分尸成小块儿烧毁,一会儿想在地窖里挖个坟,又想藏尸于集装箱,伪装成货物,雇个人从家里运出去抛尸井中。最后,我终于想出可谓是绝妙的天才计划,就是把尸体给砌进地窖墙里。据说中世纪的僧侣就是这样处理殉道者的。

这个地窖能派上这样的用场,实在是再好不过了。最近刚用粗灰泥刷过,地窖又潮,所以墙体还没干透,很好操作。而且有堵墙上原先是个假壁炉,现在也被填上刷泥了。我只要轻松地把这块撬开,挪进尸体,再照旧封好,肉眼根本看不出什么破绽。

果然一切如我所料。只用一根铁撬,我就撬开了砖墙,再仔仔细细地把尸体贴着内墙摆好,让她撑着不至于掉下来。接着,我弄来了石灰、黄沙、毛发,做足准备。还用和之前几乎一样的泥砌了一遍墙,几乎不费吹灰之力就把外墙恢复原样。等我整完,看到一切如常,才感到心满意足。整面墙完全没有整修痕迹,地上也收拾干净。我得意扬扬地自言自语道:"看看这,总算没有白忙活一场啊。"

接下来,我定要逮住那个害得我杀妻埋尸的畜生,把它大卸八块。要是它现在碰上我,真的就死定了。不过这滑头像是先前见我勃然大怒的样子,见势不妙就赶紧溜走了,不敢在我面前造次。这烦人精终于不在身边晃悠,我心头压着的石头也能落下了,那种隐秘而幽深的快感简直无法言说。到了晚上,它还是没出现。这是自它到我家来,我头回能睡一个太平安稳觉。尽管身负人命,我还是睡着了。

第两天过去了,第三天过去了,那只折磨人的畜生还是没有出现,我才终于能像个自由人一样呼吸。那家伙居然吓得从我家里逃走,再也不回来了!再也不用忍受它讨人厌的一切,我实在是太快乐了!我确实犯下了滔天罪行,内心却没怎么因此煎熬。也有人来例行调查过几次,甚至还来搜查过一次,都被我糊弄过去了,当然他们什么都没发现。我自以为高枕无忧了。

谁知到了第四天,来了一帮警察,把整个房子里里外外都仔细搜了个底朝天。我自恃准备万全,藏尸地极为隐蔽,那帮警察根本猜不到,因此丝毫不慌。那帮警察要求我陪同协助搜查,一个角落也不放过。搜了三四轮,他们终于走下地窖。我镇定自若。做了亏心事,也不怕鬼敲门。我双手抱臂,若无其事地在地窖里踱步。警察见状,也搜不出什么名堂,放了心,正要走。我喜不自胜,憋不住地想讲话,哪怕说一句,这样就更能证明自己的清白,好让他们放心。

等他们走上楼梯,我终于忍不住开口了。"警察同志,感谢你们相信我是无辜的。给你们请安了,祝您身体健康。同志,这房子可结实了。"我头脑发热,开始胡说八道,甚至都不知道自己在说什么。"这房子呀,真是造得太结实啦。这几面墙,要走了吗同志们?这几面墙很结实的。"言至此,我简直像失了智,拿起手里的一根棒子就朝藏着我爱妻尸身的那面墙砸去。

菩萨保佑,别让我再鬼上身了!敲击声还在地窖里回荡,就听见墓龛里传来了哭声,开始声音沉闷,时断时续,像小孩的哭声,继而转为冗长高亢的连声尖叫,不似人声。这是哀嚎,亦是悲鸣,半含恐怖,半含得意,像是地狱里鬼魂的痛苦惨叫和魔鬼的欢呼雀跃的合奏。

我当时的想法实在是愚蠢至极,羞于启齿。我脚步虚浮地走到另一面墙边。楼梯上的警察们瞬间惊惧交加,一动不动。不多时,他们反应了过来,十几个人手忙脚乱地拆墙。整面墙倒下,露出了直挺挺站着的腐烂不堪、血迹斑斑的尸体。尸体的头上赫然趴着那吓人的魔兽,张着血盆大口,独眼里冒着火、盛满了怒气。是它搞的鬼,先害我杀妻,再引来警察,置我于死地。原来我把这畜生砌进墙里了!

(张陈橙,方　菲　译;雷若岚,朱镜如　校)

我们的朋友朱迪斯

多丽丝·莱辛

自从一位加拿大妇女评价朱迪斯:"毋庸置疑,她就属于那种典型的英国老姑娘。"我便不再邀请她与人见面了。说话时她心满意足,热情洋溢,仿佛终于给一个世间罕见的标本贴上了标签。

几周前,一位美国社会学家从朱迪斯那里了解到她已40多岁,未婚,独居,他就问我:"她是不是就这样了?""什么就这样了?"我反问道。我们从此话不投机。

朱迪斯很少会受邀参加聚会。她是迫于压力才来的,不是为了帮别人的忙,而是为了纠正她自认为的性格缺陷。她有一次说:"我真的应该更喜欢结交新朋友才行。"我们又回到了早期的交友模式:偶尔晚上聚聚,偶尔去看场电影,偶尔她会打电话说:"我想去大英博物馆,正好路过你家附近。我还有20分钟的时间,来和我一起喝杯咖啡?"

由于朱迪斯的特立独行,其他人用"老处女"这个词对她疯狂臆测,认为她跟我两个姑妈差不多:70多岁,都未婚,一个是中国的前传教士,一个是伦敦一家著名医院的退休女护士长。这两位女士一起住在一个乡村小镇的大教堂下。她们会花很多时间为教会行善,与世界各地的朋友通信,照顾亲戚的孙辈和曾孙辈。然而,50年一成不变的生活并不意味着她们仍秉持着维多利亚时代晚期陈腐的观念。她们阅读了《观察家报》和《泰晤士报》评论的每一本书,以至于我最近收到了罗斯姑妈的一封信,问我是否认为《在路上》的作者也许有些小题大做了。她们对音乐很了解,还会写信鼓励那些她们觉得被忽视的年轻作曲家。"要知道,任何新的、原创的东西都需要时间被人们理解。"她们是消息灵通且持批评态度的托利党人,既可能向内政大臣写信以表支持,也可能发送抗议电报。我的这两位姑妈艾米丽和罗斯,当然就是名副其实的英国老处女。然而,一旦将她们与这个词联系起来,毫无疑问朱迪斯和她们在精神上即使不是姐妹,也算是表亲。因此,那些对寂寞独居的女人抱有怜悯与钦佩之心者,需要改变他们的态度吗?

当然,对此人们永远不会知道;而我现在觉得,我要是永远也不知道,就完全是我的错。在那件事发生之前,我和朱迪斯的友谊已经有5年多了。也许听上去有点不可思议,但那件事就像的确是我们目睹到了"朱迪斯的真面目"。

我和朱迪斯的朋友贝蒂拿到一件别人替换下来的迪奥连衣裙。她太矮了,撑不起来。她还说:"对于一个有3个娃,整天与锅碗瓢盆为伴的已婚妈妈来说,不适合穿这条裙子。也说不清为什么,就是不合适。"朱迪斯的身材倒是刚刚好。因此,一天晚上,我们约好带着那条裙子在朱迪斯的卧室见面。朱迪斯的美我们是知道的,我和贝蒂经常会在不经意间流露羡慕和嫉妒,尤其朱迪斯那高冷的面庞令我们羡慕不已。而朱迪斯穿上那件裙子后,我们愕然发现,朱迪斯的身材简直完美,不仅是我们俩,就是在大街上,任何女人在她面前都会黯然失色。

朱迪斯个子高高的,胸部小,身材苗条。她浅棕色的头发从中间分开,齐肩长短。高直的前额,笔挺的鼻子,饱满严肃的嘴唇,衬着她那引人注意的绿色大眼睛。她的眼睑洁白无瑕,在灯光下像是镶着金边,紧贴眼球,从侧面看,她的脸就像一个耀眼的镀金面具。这件裙子的布料是深绿色的,闪闪发光,剪裁得笔直,配上有点宽松的束腰上衣,只在喉咙处开领。这身打扮的朱迪斯不禁令人联想到古典主义的形象。也许是狩猎归来小憩的女神戴安娜?或是一个相当聪慧、选择在大英博物馆阅览室度过午后的森林圣女?诸如此类。贝蒂和我都一言不发,因为朱迪斯正对着一面长镜子审视自己,她一定知道自己看起来很漂亮。

她慢慢地脱下连衣裙,把它放在一边,又慢慢地穿上她之前脱下的旧灯芯绒裙和羊毛上衣。她一定捕捉到了我们懊丧的目光,因为她带着一丝嘲弄的微笑说道:"还是做自己更舒服些,不是吗?"她一字一句地补充道:"我必须承认,这条裙子让我光彩照人。"她的语气生硬,毕竟这种庸俗之语不应出自她口,倒似我们中的一人所言。

贝蒂大叫表示反对:"在看到你穿上它之后,我不能容忍其他任何人拥有它。我要把它收起来。"朱迪斯耸耸肩,有几分恼火。她穿着不成样式的裙子和衬衫,未施粉黛,站在那里对我们微笑,恐怕走在大街上四五十个人都不会多看她一眼。

不久后又发生了第二件小事,贝蒂打电话告诉我朱迪斯养了一只小猫。她问我是否知道朱迪斯喜欢猫。

"我不知道,但她当然会喜欢吧。"我说。

贝蒂和朱迪斯住在同一条街上,与她碰面的次数比我多。我通过贝蒂不断获知这只猫的成长历程、习性以及它对朱迪斯生活的影响。例如,她说她觉得有所牵挂和承担一些责任对朱迪斯来说是件好事。但这只猫长大后,邻居们就开始抱怨了。这是一只雄猫,没有做过绝育,每天晚上都发情乱叫。最后,房东说,除非她准备让人阉割这只猫,否则猫与朱迪斯只能留一个。朱迪斯在全英国寻找一个愿意领养这只猫的人,累得筋疲力尽。然而领养的条件是,此人必须签署一份书面声明,不让人阉割这只猫。当朱迪斯把猫送到兽医那里杀死时,贝蒂告诉我她哭了24小时。

"她没有想过要妥协吗?毕竟,如果让猫自己选择的话,它可能更愿意活下去。"

"我敢对朱迪斯说这么草率的话吗?发情期的公猫本性就是欲火焚身,因此朱迪斯认为只图自己方便而阉割这只猫是不道德的。"

"她是这么说的吗?"

"这不是明摆着的嘛。"

第三件小事发生在她去父母那里过圣诞期间,她把公寓借给她一个朋友的朋友,一名素昧平生、定居巴黎的年轻美国游客暂住。这个年轻人和他的朋友们在公寓里滥饮、纵欲、吸毒,快活了整整10天,等到朱迪斯回来她用了一周才把家里打扫干净,修好家具。她给那个美国小伙子打了两通电话,第一次是痛斥他的可憎,咒骂他如果识趣的话,能滚多远滚多远;第二次则为她的失态而道歉。"我要么选择让人住我的公寓,要么让它空着。而我既然已经把它交给了你,显然就没有理由再干涉你的自由,强求些什么。我真诚地请求你的原谅。"是非问题解决后,她又被他那些莫名其妙、谄媚而尴尬的道歉信惹恼了。

最让她生气的是道歉信中好奇、探究的口吻——他甚至有意前来进一步了解她。"你说他这是什么意思?"她这样问我,"他在我的公寓里住了10天之久。这难道还不够吗?"

至此，有关朱迪斯的一切，都已公开地、不加掩饰地、清楚地摆在有心了解它们的人面前；而在她看来，这些也已足够供能者来解读。

在过去 20 年，她一直住在伦敦西部一条繁忙街道上的一套两室小公寓中。这套公寓破旧不堪，且供暖不足。家具又旧又丑，现已明显摇摇晃晃、磨损破落。她的叔叔去世后，给她留下每年 200 英镑的遗产。她就靠着这笔钱和写诗的收入以及在夜校、大学校外班教授诗歌所得生活。

她不沾烟酒，所食甚少，并非出于自律，而是个人喜好。

她在牛津大学修的是诗歌与生物，成绩优异。

她是卡斯尔维尔家的人，一个中上阶层学院派家族的一员。在过去几百年，他们家族为英国持续培养了大量的卓越人才，都成为艺术与科学界的中坚力量。她与家人关系较为冷淡，家里尊重她，也不去打扰她。

她会独自一人在埃克斯缪尔或西苏格兰等地长途徒步旅行。

每三四年，她就出一本诗集。

她的公寓四壁都摆满了书。有科学、古典和历史读物，也有大量诗歌与一些戏剧，却没有一部小说。朱迪斯所说的"我当然不读小说"并不意味着小说在文学中没有一席之地或是微不足道，也不代表人们不应该读小说，而是说指望她读小说显然是不可能的。

我出入她的公寓多年才注意到一扇窗户下有两个长长的书架，每个书架上都分别放着一位作家的作品。说得好听点，这两位作家与朱迪斯走的完全不是一个路线。他们的风格是温和、怀旧、暧昧又充满遐想的。这些作品事实上都是典型的英国式纯文学，显然与她背道而驰。两个书架上的书没有一本被人读过；有些书页甚至还没裁开。然而，每本书都是题献给她的，写得动情，充满感激与欣赏，亦不乏见含情脉脉从中流露。简言之，明眼人只要仔细查看这两个书架，梳理上面作品的日期，就能发现朱迪斯从 15 岁到 25 岁与一位精通文学的老先生是忘年交，受其仰慕，25 岁至 35 岁期间则是另一位绅士的创作灵感。

在那段时间里，她也创作了自己的诗，不过可以很有把握地推断，她写的那种诗可能并不完全为她的两个爱慕者所欣赏。她的诗总是冷静而理智，而与这种形式相悖或相生的是其极为感性的内容。要想读懂这些诗，必须反复阅读。

关于这两位老相好的陈年旧事，我没有直接问过朱迪斯。不是因为她不会回答，也不是因为她会觉得这些问题不恰当，而是因为问这些显然没有必要。把这两书架她漠不关心的书摆在那里，本身就已经清楚地表明了她的态度。我能想象到她经过一番思索后，认为把书放在那里才是唯一可以说是公平或诚实的做法；尽管她其实根本不在乎别人用同样的方式对待她的作品。她对此嗤之以鼻，因为她定是看不起那些想要博取关注的人。

例如，一批新兴的"现代派"青年诗人常认为，在他们亦褒亦贬的前辈中，她是唯一一位"现代派"诗人。这是因为从她 15 岁开始写诗以来，她的诗歌就充满了科学、机械和化学意象。这就是她思考或感受世界的方式。

有一位年轻诗人不止一次跑到她的寓所，声称他们是同道中人，却发现她对"现代"、"新"、"当代"之类的字眼根本就无动于衷。她认为寻求公众的关注或批判都是可鄙的，这个观念已经根深蒂固，仿佛是下意识地，只需要轻蔑地耸一耸肩就可以表达出来，这让他勃然大怒，伤心不已。显而易见，她是不会在任何批评家身上浪费时间的。他气鼓鼓地离开了,将她的作品束之高阁,而她理所当然地认为就该这样,她的作品只有少数有鉴赏力的人才有资格阅读。

　　与此同时,她保持着自己的生活节奏,参与授课,一个人漫步伦敦,一个人作诗;有时我们会看到她和一位希腊语中年教授共赏音乐会或戏剧,这位教授有家室,两个孩子。

　　这位教授的出现引发了我和贝蒂的猜测:她是不是也会孤独? 难道她没有想过要结婚吗? 她是不是一个人夜里回到空荡荡的公寓时,也会感觉有些孤寂?!

　　最近,贝蒂的丈夫出差,孩子们也不在家,她无法忍受独守空闺,便请求朱迪斯收留她暂住,直到她的丈夫和孩子回来。

　　搬过去之后贝蒂打电话来告诉我:

　　"5个晚上其中4个晚上亚当斯教授是在十点左右过来的。"

　　"那朱迪斯会觉得尴尬吗?"

　　"你觉得她会吗?"

　　"那就算不觉得尴尬,至少也会觉得有点不妥吧?"

　　"不,丝毫没有。但我不得不说,我觉得他可配不上她。其实,他根本就不懂她,他竟然叫她'朱迪'!"

　　"我的妈呀,牙都酸掉了。"

　　"是哎。但我很好奇,想想看其他两个人可能也都叫她'朱迪'——'小朱迪'——这你能想象吗! 听起来多可怕? 不过这倒让我对朱迪斯多了点认识。"

　　"太令人动容了。"

　　"我想是的,但我觉得很尴尬——噢,并不是因为这种情况,而是因为想到她和他相处的方式。'朱迪,茶壶里的茶还够再倒一杯吗?'然后她相当乖巧贤惠地给他倒了一杯。"

　　"嗯。我懂你的感受。"

　　"有3个晚上,他俩一起去了朱迪斯的卧室——朱迪斯不在意这个,因为她一向如此,但到了早上亚当斯就不在她卧室里了,所以我问了问她。你知道当你问她一个问题时那是怎样一个场景,就好像你年年就那一个话题发表长篇大论,而她就只是接着之前结束的地方继续说,所以当她说出一些令人惊讶的话时,你就会觉得,要是自己还感到惊讶,岂不是个傻子了?"

　　"对。接着呢?"

　　"我问她是否遗憾没要个孩子,她说是的,但一个人总不能什么都有吧。"

　　"她是说一个人不能什么都有了吗?"

　　"是的。给人感觉她好像差一点就什么都有了。她说她觉得没孩子是人生的一大遗憾,因为如果有的话,她一定会把孩子教养得很好。"

　　"你会想这个问题,同样,她也会想。"

　　"我问过她关于婚姻的问题,但她说她似乎还是更适合做情妇。"

　　"你确信她用的是'情妇'这两个字?"

　　"你别说,这个词用得倒是挺准确。"

　　"确实。"

　　"接着她说,虽然她热衷于亲密关系、性事以及其他等等,但她希望早上醒来时是一个人,她享受那种感觉。"

"是的,当然的。"

"当然,不过她现在很烦恼,因为那个教授想娶她,或者说他觉得他应该要娶她。反正他特别负疚且执着于此。朱迪斯说她不明白教授为什么要离婚,毕竟这么多年来他那可怜的糟糠之妻想必过得十分艰辛,尤其她还含辛茹苦地拉扯大了两个孩子,把他们教养得很好。你知道吗,她谈起教授妻子时就好像那个女人是一个心地善良、任劳任怨的老妈子,而解雇这样一个老妈子是不公平的。不管三七二十一,朱迪斯马上就要动身去意大利了,她要找个地方缓缓,散散心。"

"她自己花钱去?"

"幸运的是,'第三套节目'组委托她做一些艺术项目。他们让她在万世英雄熙德和波吉亚家族两个主题中做选择。朱迪斯选择了后者。"

"波吉亚家族?"我很诧异,"朱迪斯吗?"

"是的,没错,我当时也觉得不可思议。她知道我为什么做此反应,于是表示前者这段史诗是她所感兴趣的,而对于后者,她则不太感冒。很明显文艺复兴不在她的研究范围内,毕竟文艺复兴处处充斥着辉煌、残酷和肮脏。当然啦,骑士精神、崇高的道德准则和那些近乎愚蠢的高尚行为才是她会感兴趣的东西。"

"经费是一样的吗?"

"一样。但你觉得钱能左右得了朱迪斯吗?"不,她说一个人总应选择尝试新东西,而不是简单地重复,这指的也就是文艺复兴了。当然了,她并没有这么说。

"她当然不会这么说啰。"

朱迪斯去了佛罗伦萨。几个月来,我们通过她寄来的明信片简要了解了她在那儿的所作所为。接着贝蒂决定她要独自去度假,因为她震惊地发现,只要她的丈夫离开一个晚上,她就无法入睡,她丈夫去澳大利亚的那3个星期,她感觉自己如行尸走肉,直到丈夫回来她才又活过来。她曾同她丈夫讲过这些,他表示认同,如果贝蒂真的感觉情况到了很严重的地步,他会安排贝蒂飞去意大利,如她自己所说,去找回她的自尊。

后来我收到了贝蒂寄来的这样一封信:

"根本没用,我现在要回家了。我早该知道的,就应该直面现实,一旦你真的结婚了,那可就什么也做不成了,如果你还记得我过去是个什么样!哎,可现在呢!我在米兰周边飙摩托,在威尼斯晒日光浴,然后我想我晒成棕褐色的肌肤肯定很有些能够发生什么魅力吧,就在我要与另一个孤独的灵魂坠入爱河的时候,我泄气了,我落荒而逃去了佛罗伦萨找朱迪斯,但她却不在那儿,她去了意大利里维埃拉。我不知道我还能做啥,所以就去那儿找她。当我看到那是个什么地方时我简直要笑出声了,那个地方可太'不朱迪斯'了,你知道吗,处处可见棕榈树、沙滩伞和不顾一切的欢乐氛围,还有一整片供游人观赏的蓝色大海,葡萄藤爬得到处都是。你真该见见她,她变漂亮了。在过去的15年里她似乎每个星期六早上都去苏荷区的一家意大利商店买食物。我当时肯定表现得很惊讶,因为她跟我说她喜欢苏荷区。我想正是所有那些令人生厌的恶习、裸体、妓女和那里的一切证明了她所言非虚?她告诉商店老板她要去意大利,他太太说,真巧呐,她也要回意大利,她特别希望能有一个像卡斯尔维尔小姐这样的老朋友能去那里看望她。朱迪斯对我说:'当她说出朋友这个词时,我不知道该说些什么,我们的关系没到那种程度,你懂我的意思吧?'她这样对我说。'当任何一个人把我称作朋友时,我总觉得对方有种自作多情,在过去的15年都是这样。'我对她说。'好吧。'我说,'你应该理解,你自己不也这样吗?''我是吗?'她说。'唔,你自己想想看。'我说。但其实我看得出来,她根本不打算去想这件事。不管怎样,她人就在这儿,我和她一起度过了一个星期。寡妇玛丽亚·里内里继承了她母亲的房子,所以她从苏荷区回自己家了。一楼是一家附近邻居经常光顾的逼仄的烤肉店,他们都是劳动人民,这个山上小城并不是个旅游区。寡妇和她年幼的儿子住在商店楼上,那是一个约莫10岁的令人讨厌的小屁孩。不管你怎么说,只有英国人知道该如何抚养孩子,我可不在乎这个观点是不是不被别人接受嘞。朱迪斯的房间在背面,没有阳台。她的房间下面是个理发店,理发师是寡妇的弟弟路易吉·里内里。是的,我要把他留到最后讲。他大约40岁,高大英俊而黝黑,就像一头大公牛,但更像是一头可爱的慈父般的公牛。他给朱迪斯剪了头发,看起来更轻盈了,现在就像戴了顶金头盔。朱迪斯的肤色是棕色的,寡妇里内里给她做了一条白色连衣裙和一条绿色连衣裙,这两条裙子令她焕然一新。当朱迪斯沿着街道走到下城区时,在场的意大利男人只要看一眼这个金色娇娃,便都拜倒在她的石榴裙下。

朱迪斯照单全收。她甚至偶尔会回应那些带着敬意的目光。然后她漫步走进海里,消失在浪花中。她每天游泳5英里,并且毫不费力。我并没有问朱迪斯情绪是否恢复了,因为看得出来她并没有。寡妇里内里在给朱迪斯做媒。我觉得这挺好笑的,但幸好没笑出来,因为朱迪斯问我:'你能想象我嫁给了一个意大利理发师吗?'她看上去是真心想知道。(她说这话时没有带着势利的口吻,只是在陈述她的想法。)'嗯,是的。'我说,'你是我认识的女人中,唯一一个我能想象得出嫁给意大利理发师的。'因为不管她嫁给谁,她永远都是她自己。'至少会保持一段时间。'我说。听了这话,她讥诮地说:'你应该说在英国可以保持一段时间,但在意大利却不行。'你什么时候感觉在英国,至少在伦敦,可以放纵不羁、享受自由或自由恋爱?没有。我没有。当然她才是对的。嫁给路易吉意味着要建立家庭,接触邻居、教堂和孩子。尽管如此,不管你信不信,她还是在考虑这件事。在这里,她像是完全变了个人,彻底地放松、自由随性。她渐渐被周围人们的关心关切打动了。这位寡妇就像她妈妈一样照顾她,给她煮咖啡,并听了她不少关于如何教育自己那个淘气小孩的金玉良言。不幸的是,她没有接受。路易吉为她疯狂。她去上城广场的餐厅用餐时,所有的工人都把她当作女神一样对待。嗯,宛如那儿的电影明星。

我对她说,你要是回英国,那真是疯了。首先,她的房租是每周10个先令,而吃意大利面、喝红酒直到破产也只用花一先令六便士。不,她说,留下来不为其他,只是自我放纵。为什么?我问。她说,她没有待在这儿的理由。她也想知道什么是值得她留下来的。所以她现在留下来只是因为那只猫。我忘了提到那只猫。这个小镇到处都是猫。这儿的意大利人喜欢猫。我曾想在餐桌上喂一只流浪猫,但服务员阻止了。午饭后,所有的服务员会把盘子用剩菜盛满,再端去给四处游荡的流浪猫们吃。天黑的时候,游客们都去餐馆吃饭了,海滩空无一人——你知道黄昏时海滩是多么的空旷和凄凉——那时,到处都能看见猫的身影。海滩似乎在移动,然后你才会发现其实是猫群在移动。

它们沿着大海边缘狭窄的灰色浅水湾悄悄前行,每走一步就会猛甩一下爪子,抓取死去的小鱼,抓到后用嘴叼起来抛到干沙上。然后它们疾跑着去抢鱼。你肯定没见过这样的场景——这么多的猫彼此嗥叫示威、撕扯打斗。黎明时分,当渔船驶进空旷的海滩时,猫成群结队地出现在那里。渔夫们把鱼切成片后扔给它们。猫们则又为了鱼咆哮和争斗。朱迪斯起得很早,她起来后便下楼去看这一场景。有时候路易吉也会去,他表现得很包容。因为他真正喜欢的是和朱迪斯挽着胳膊在上城广场上散步。(这里应该是向其他人炫耀朱迪斯)。你觉得朱迪斯会做这些事吗?但她确实这么做了,尽管有一丝丝勉强。但她微笑着享受她得到的关注,这是毫无疑问的。

她房间里有一只猫。实际上是一只小猫,但它怀孕了。朱迪斯说,在小猫下崽前,她不能离开。这只猫太小了,还没到生小猫的年纪。想象一下朱迪斯。在那间巨大石屋里,她坐在床上,脚丫子光着搁在石头地板上,看着那只猫,试图弄清楚为什么那样一只健康的、无拘无束的意大利猫,总是喂它吃最好的肉,竟会变得如此神经兮兮的。因为它确实是这么神经质的。当它看到朱迪斯看着它时,它会变得紧张,开始舔它的尾巴根部。但是朱迪斯一边继续观察它,一边谈起了意大利,英国人爱意大利人的原因是因为意大利人让英国人感觉优越。他们没有纪律。这是一个国家爱上另一个国家卑鄙的理由。

然后她谈到路易吉,说他没有愧疚感,但有罪恶感;而她恰恰相反,没有罪恶感,却怀有愧疚感。我没有问她这是不是一个无法逾越的障碍,因为从她的表情来看,这并不是。她说,她宁愿有一种罪恶感,因为罪是可以赎的。如果她理解罪恶,也许她会更了解文艺复兴。她说,路易吉很正常,不神经质。他当然是天主教徒。但他不介意她是个无神论者。他的母亲向他解释说,英国人都是异教徒,但内心善良。我想他认为只要朱迪斯与当地牧师进行几次充满智慧色彩的谈话,便能从此走上正轨。

与此同时,猫在房间里紧张地走动着,停下来舔尾巴,等到再也无法忍受朱迪斯再多看它一下时,它便在地板上翻滚起来,折起爪子,抬起眼睛,朱迪斯抓挠它那隆起的怀孕肚子,告诉它放松。她这个样子让我感到紧张,这不像她。我不知道为什么。然后路易吉的喊声从理发店传来。他走了过来,站在门口笑,朱迪斯也笑了。寡妇说:孩子们,玩得开心。之后他们走了,走到镇上吃冰激凌。猫跟着他们。它不会让朱迪斯离开它的视线,就像狗那样黏人。

朱迪斯游了几英里,看见这只猫躲在海滩小屋下,直到她回来才钻出来。然后她带着它走回山上,因为那个讨厌的小男孩在追它。我明天就要回家了,感谢上帝,回到我亲爱的老比尔身边,离开他快把我逼疯了。朱迪斯和意大利的一些事情让我很不安,我不知道是什么。关键是,朱迪斯和路易吉到底能谈些什么?没什么能谈的。他们怎么能(结婚呢)?当然,这并不重要。我看我是变成保守派了。下周见。"

轮到我享受一点阳光了,所以我没去见贝蒂。从罗马回来的路上,我在朱迪斯的度假地点小作驻足,穿过狭小的街道,便来到上城区。广场的拐角处有一座葡萄藤蔓掩映的餐馆,这家餐馆低矮的门槛上方挂着一块裂痕斑斑的木头牌子,上面用黑漆写着罗斯蒂克里亚。门上有一副红色珠子串起来的帘子,几只苍蝇落在这珠帘上歇脚。我伸手拨开珠帘,朝里望去，小屋黑黑的，有一个石制的柜台。一挂挂的萨拉米香肠吊在金属钩子上，玻璃罩盖着几盘熟肉，香肠和玻璃罩上也有一些苍蝇。木架上有几个罐头，再往四处看看，还有几条发白的面包，一些酒桶，还有一箱黏糊糊的、爬满果蝇的浅绿色葡萄，这些东西似乎是这里仅有的存货。角落里有一张木桌和两把椅子，两个工人坐在那吃着香肠和面包。一位妇人穿过餐馆后面的珠帘走了出来，她个子不高，身材微微发福，四肢修长，头发灰白。我问她卡斯尔维尔小姐在哪儿，她随即变了脸色，不悦地敷衍道："卡斯尔维尔小姐上周就走了。"说完她从柜台下拿出一块白布，赶走玻璃罩上的苍蝇。我说："我是她的朋友。""哦。"她应道，然后把双手放在柜台上，面无表情地看着我。两个工人起身，大口饮下最后一口酒，和女人点了点头就离开了。她和他们道完别，又看向我。见我没走，她叫道："路易吉！"后面的屋子里应了一声，珠帘发出细细簌簌的声音，一个瘦削的尖脸男孩和路易吉先后走了进来。路易吉个子高大、肩膀宽厚，黑色粗糙的头发像一顶帽子低垂在他的额头上。他看上去人不错，但此刻显得很不安。他姐姐和他说了一些什么，他站在她身边盟友一般坚定地说道，"卡斯尔维尔小姐已经不在这里了。"我正要放弃，这时一只瘦小的虎斑猫穿过那副遮住刺眼阳光的珠帘，缓缓走了出来。它的长相丑陋，后腿蜷缩在一起，走得很不舒服。小男孩突然龇起牙齿发出"嘶嘶"声，吓得猫不敢动弹。路易吉严厉地责备了男孩，又说了些鼓励猫的话。猫则就地而坐，目视前方，开始疯狂地舔舐起自己的胁腹。里内里夫人突然神态庄严道，"卡斯尔维尔小姐生我们的气了。有一天她很早就离开了这里，我们没想到她会走。"我解释道："也许她需要回家完成一些工作。"

里内里夫人耸了耸肩，叹了口气。然后，和她弟弟交换了一个眼神，神情十分凝重。显然，他俩已经讨论过这个话题了，而且决定以后对此绝口不提。

"我认识朱迪斯很久了。"我说道，试图找到一个合适的语气。"她是一位十分杰出的女性，一位诗人。"但他们对此并没有什么反应。与此同时，那个男孩龇牙咧嘴地笑着，眯起眼睛目不转睛地盯着那只猫，然后突然又发出"嘶嘶嘶嘶嘶"的声音，还大声尖叫了一下。猫向后一闪，撞到墙上，惊慌失措地想用爪子爬上墙去，惊魂甫定后，又坐了下来，开始急切地、无头苍蝇般地舔舐起自己的毛发。这次，路易吉打了男孩一掌，他结结实实地叫了起来，经过那只猫跑到了大街上。现在，这条道清开了，那只猫从地板窜到了柜台上，越过路易吉的肩膀，径直穿过珠帘进了理发店，砰的一声落在地上。

"朱迪斯离开我们时很难过，"里内里夫人犹疑地说，"她哭了。"

"我想她是哭了。"

"我知道的只有这些。"说完这最后一句话，里内里夫人放下手来，目光穿过我望着那副珠帘。谈话就此结束，路易吉简单地朝我点了点头，走到了后面。我和里内里夫人告别，然后走回下城区。在广场上，我看到了那个小男孩，餐厅外停着一辆卡车，他坐在卡车的脚蹬板上，光着脚丫子来回地蹭着尘土，眼睛茫然、不高兴地瞪着前方。

我得经过佛罗伦萨，所以我去了朱迪斯曾住过的地方。不，卡斯尔维尔小姐没有回来过。她的文件和书还在那儿，我要帮她带回英国吗？我装了一大箱子，把它们都带回了英国。

我打电话给朱迪斯，她说她之前已经写信让人把那些文件寄过来，但我竟然把它们都带了回来，这实在太好不过了。她还说，回佛罗伦萨似乎已经毫无意义。

"要我带到你家去吗？"

"当然，我会十分感谢的。"

朱迪斯的公寓很冷,她穿着一件灰绿色的羊毛长裙。她头发依旧那么柔软,金色头盔样式,脸色却是苍白的,甚至有些憔悴。她两腿岔开站着,背对着一个电热器——我要求她开的——双臂交叉,打量着我。

"我去过里内里她家了。"

"噢,是吗?"

"他们似乎很想念你。"她对此一言不发。

"我还看到了那只猫。"

"哦,我猜你和贝蒂已经讨论过这件事了,对吧?"她露出了一丝不太友好的笑容。

"嗯,朱迪斯,你一定知道我们很可能会这样做,对吧?"

她思忖了一会儿,开口说道:"我无法理解为什么人们喜欢讨论别人。哦,我不是在批评你。但是我不明白为什么你这么好奇,我不理解人类的行为,也不是很感兴趣。"

"我觉得你应该写封信给里内里他们一家。"

"当然,我已经写过信感谢他们了。"

"我不是那个意思。"

"你和贝蒂合起伙来商量的?"

"是的,我们讨论过这件事。并且觉得我们应该和你谈谈,让你写封信给他们一家。"

"为什么?"

"因为,他们都喜欢你。"

"喜欢。"她笑着说。

"朱迪斯,我这辈子从未感受到过那么失望的气氛。"

朱迪斯沉思了一会儿。"当发生的事情表明人与人在理解上确实存在不可逾越的鸿沟时,还有什么可说的呢?"

"理解上并不存在无法跨越的鸿沟。我想你要说我们在干涉你了?"

朱迪斯感到一丝不悦。"这话可真傻。这个想法也很傻。没有我的允许,谁都不可能干涉我。不,只是我很不理解人这个东西。我不理解你和贝蒂为什么要关心这件事,里内里一家为什么要关心这件事。"她补充道,脸上的微笑有些僵硬。

"朱迪斯!"

"如果你还要这样继续愚蠢下去,再聊也没有任何意义。你结束了这一切。"

"发生了什么? 是那只猫吗?"

"是,我想是的。但是这不重要。"她看着我讽刺的脸,说道:"那只小猫还太小了,不能生小猫。就是这样。"

"随你怎么说吧。但这显然不是事情的全部。"

"让我感到烦躁的是,我根本不明白当时为什么会那么难过。"

"发生什么了? 还是你不想谈论这件事情?"

"我可不在乎是否谈论这件事。你说这话真是再奇怪不过了,你和贝蒂都是。你要是想知道,我告诉你就是了。这有什么大不了的。"

"我当然想知道了。"

"也是!"她说道,"我要是你我可不会在乎这事儿。嗯,我觉得整件事情的关键在于,我对待那只猫的态度错了。猫本来是独立的动物,它们本应该自己找地方生小猫。但是那只猫不是这样的。有一天晚上,它爬到我的床上喵喵叫,想要吸引我的注意力。我不喜欢猫往我床上爬。第二天早上我看见它很痛苦,就陪它待了一整天。然后路易吉——他是里内里夫人的弟弟,你知道的。"

"没错。"

"贝蒂提过他吗?路易吉上楼来让我去游泳,他说猫应该自己照顾自己。我对此非常自责。这就是一个人完全迷恋另一人时,会发生的事情。/一个人完全迷恋上另一个人的话,就会变得完全不像自己。"

朱迪斯看向我的目光充满挑衅,身体也同时呈现出防御性和攻击性。"是啊,没错,我一直害怕这件事。待在那里的最后几周,我整个人都崩溃了,因为我让那件事发生了。"

"嗯,然后呢?"

"我把猫留在家里去游泳了。当时天很晚了,所以我只游了几分钟。我从海里出来的时候,那只猫跟着我,它已经在海滩上生了一只小猫。那个小畜生米歇尔——就是里内里夫人的儿子,你知道吗?他经常戏弄那可怜的小东西。有他在,那只母猫不敢接近小猫,不过小猫已经死了。我从海里出来时,米歇尔提着小猫的尾巴把它拎起来,朝我挥了挥。我让他把小猫埋了。他随手扒了一个两英寸深的沙坑,把它丢了进去——就在每天人来人往的海滩上。我找了个适合的地方,重新把那小猫埋了。米歇尔早就跑开了,他又去追那只可怜的母猫了。那猫受了惊,跑回了镇子里。我也跟着他们跑。追到米歇尔的时候,我气昏了头,动手打了他。我至今还不敢相信自己打了个孩子。从那之后我一直觉得自己禽兽不如。"

"你当时太生气了。"

"这不是借口。我本来永远也不敢相信自己竟然是做得出打小孩这种事的人。但事实是我下手很重,他哭着跑开了。那只可怜的母猫躲在一辆停在广场上的大卡车底下,叫声凄惨。之后,发生了一件出乎意料的事情。它刚叫了一声,大群猫便不知从哪里就冒出来,围在它身边。一分钟之前,还只有一只猫,一动不动地待在卡车下面,看着我那可怜的小母猫。"

"很感人啊。"我说道。

"为什么呢?"

"虽然没有明确的证据,"我回道,"但我觉得那些猫出现在那里,是因为担心它们身陷险境的朋友。"

"不可能。"她有些激动,"绝对不是这样,它们可能是出于好奇,或是其他什么原因。我们怎么可能猜得到。我爬到卡车下面,看到有两个小爪子从母猫的后面伸了出来。这只小猫胎位不正,卡住出不来了。我一只手按住母猫,另一只手把小猫拽了出来。母猫伸直了四肢,白色细长的爪子上满是褪色的伤疤和抓痕。它又咬又叫,不过刚刚出生的小猫还活着。母猫却丢下了小猫,穿过广场回到了房子里。紧接着,所有的猫都起身离开了。这是我见过的最古怪的事情。它们又消失了,一分钟之前它们还在那儿,不一会儿就全部不见了。我带着小猫,跟着母猫往回走。你不知道它是个多么可怜的小家伙,湿漉漉的毛发上沾满了灰尘。母猫爬到了我床上,又有一只小猫要出生了,不过这只也卡住了。所以母猫厉声尖叫的时候,我就把小猫拽出来了。两只小猫吮吸着乳汁,其中一只小黑猫体型较大,胖乎乎的,很可爱。小猫们喝奶的动作肯定是伤害到了母猫,它突然咬了小猫一口——突然就发狂了,你知道吗,就像是条件反射一样,咬住了小猫的后脑勺。小猫死了,就这样死了。太诡异了,不是吗?"她说着,用力地眨着眼睛,嘴唇颤抖。"它是小猫的妈妈,但它杀了小猫。随后,母猫从床上爬了下来,爬到了楼下小店的柜台下面。我叫来了路易吉,也就是里内里的弟弟。"

"嗯,我知道。"

"他说那只母猫还太小了,不仅受惊过度,还受了重伤。他把还有一口气的小猫放到它身边,母猫却起身走开了,它并不想要自己的小孩。之后,路易吉让我不要再看了,但我跟了过去。他拎起小猫的尾巴,冲着墙上猛地甩了两下,顺手把它扔到了垃圾堆里,又用脚拨开了一些垃圾,把小猫挪了进去,最后在它身上盖了些垃圾。之后路易吉说,那只母猫也应该被杀死,它已经身受重伤了,每生一只小猫都是对它的再次伤害。"

"他没有杀那只母猫,它还活着。不过它看向我的神情,倒让我觉得路易吉说的也没错。"

"是的。我也希望他是对的。"

"那是什么让你那么难过呢?是因为他杀了那只小猫吗?"

"噢,也不是,我知道就算他不那么做,小猫也会死的。但这不是重点,对吗?"

"那重点是什么呢?"

"我觉得我自己也不知道。"她之前语速很快,有些上气不接下气,这会儿放慢了语速:"这并不是是非对错的问题,对吧?为什么会跟对错扯上关系?这是关乎一个人的本质的问题。那天晚上,路易吉想和我一起散步,他对我很好,也是个好人,但我觉得浑身难受。"她的语气中有些挑衅。

"是的,他看起来是个好人。"

"那天晚上我难以入睡,我一直在自责。我一开始就不应该离开它去游泳。嗯,然后我就决定第二天就离开。我也确实这么做了。事情的原委就是这样。这整件事情就是一个错误,从头到尾,错得彻彻底底。"

"你指去意大利这件事吗?"

"噢,去度假本来是对的。"

"那你白做了这么多工作?你是说你不打算用这些东西做研究了?"

"不会了,这是个错误。"

"你为什么不先把这个研究项目搁置几个星期,到时候再看看情况怎么样?"

"为什么?"

"你可能会有不同的感觉。"

"这么说可真是奇怪。我为什么要那么做呢?哦,你的意思是,随着时间的流逝,伤口自会愈合——诸如此类的说法吗?这想法真是太奇怪了,我一直都觉得这种想法不可理喻。不是这样的,从一开始我就对这一整件事情感到不自在,这根本不是我自己。"

"你太不理性了,我不得不这么说。"

朱迪斯非常严肃地思考着这个问题,一边想一边皱起眉头,随后说道:"但是如果一个人不能相信自己的感觉,那他还能依靠什么呢?"

"当然是依靠人的想法了,我以为你会这么说。"

"你会这样吗?为什么呢?你们这些人真的很奇怪,真的。我真得不懂你们。"她关掉了电暖器,脸色也收了起来,她笑了笑,笑容友善,但又很显得很疏远,然后说道:"我真的觉得讨论这个问题毫无意义。"

1963 年

(薛琬荷,杨雨柔　译;宋佳文,言声远　校)

白猫米兰达

乔伊斯·卡罗尔·欧茨

有一位不差钱的绅士,在大约 56 岁的时候,对自己娇妻的白色波斯猫产生了一种强烈的憎恨。

他对这只猫的仇恨显得非常讽刺,也很令人费解,因为多年前明明是他亲手把这只小猫咪送给他新婚妻子的。他自己给她起了个名字叫米兰达,取自他最喜欢的莎士比亚剧中的女主人公。

同样讽刺的是,他向来不为情绪左右,除了妻子(他结婚结得有些晚了,这是他的头婚,而他妻子已经是二婚了),其他人他都不是特别的在乎,而且觉得憎恨其他人会有失身份。又有谁值得他那么在乎呢?作为一个不差钱的绅士,他的自主精神是大多数人难以企及的。

朱利斯·缪尔身材修长,有一双凹陷阴沉的眼睛,颜色惯常;头发稀疏灰白,像婴儿般细软;狭长的脸,布满皱纹,见过他的人们曾用精雕细琢这个形容词来描述这张脸,这并不纯粹是奉承。作为一个老美国血统的人,他丝毫没有受到时尚变迁和"身份"变换的影响:他知道自己是谁、祖先是谁,并对这个话题没有太大的兴趣。他在美国和国外的研究都是出于业余爱好,而不是出于学者的兴趣,因为他不想钻研太深。毕竟,生活才是一个人最重要的课题。

缪尔先生精通多种语言,他有一个习惯就是尤为在意自己的措辞,讲的话好像都是精心翻译过而变得通俗易懂的。他装出一副谨慎而又自觉的样子,既不虚荣,也不骄傲,但也不会无故谦逊。他是一个收藏家(主要收藏一些古书和硬币),但他又不是那种狂热的收藏家;他会带着一种莫名其妙的蔑视看待某些同伴的狂热。因此,当他对妻子那只美丽的白猫的仇恨迅速蔓延时,他感到非常惊讶,并一度觉得好笑。或者说,他被吓到了吗?他当然不知道这是怎么一回事!

他对白猫的敌意始于一种无缘无故的家庭恼怒。他隐约感觉到,在公共场合他都是高高在上的,被视作有头有脸的重要人物,在家里也理所应当地得到同样对待。并不是他天真地不知道猫在表达自己喜好的方式上不像人一样精妙和机敏。但是,随着猫越长越大,越来越娇惯,同时也越来越挑别,很明显,她不喜欢他。当然,艾丽莎才是她的最爱;然后是某个对她照料很多的人;但对于一个陌生人来说,第一次拜访就赢得或者似乎赢得米兰达反复无常的心并不罕见。"米兰达!过来!"缪尔先生有时会呼唤它——温和而有力,事实上对于动物来说,这是一种愚蠢的尊重——但在这种时候,米兰达很可能会冷漠地不眨眼地注视着他,也不朝他走过去。她似乎在说,追求一个对你漠不关心的人,真是个傻子!

如果他试图把她抱在怀里,抑或是如果他以一种嬉闹的方式想要制服她——那么她就会像面对一个陌生人一样,拼命地挣扎着让他放下。有一次,当她扭动着身体挣脱他的手时,不小心把缪尔先生的手背抓伤了,在他晚礼服的袖子上留下了淡淡的血点。"朱利斯,亲爱的,你受伤了吗?"艾丽莎问。"没有。"缪尔先生回答道,并用手帕轻轻地擦拭着伤痕。"我认为米兰达很兴奋,因为她有了伴。"艾丽莎说,"你知道的,她非常敏感。""的确如此。"缪尔先生温和地说,向客人们眨了眨眼。但是他的头上青筋突突地跳动着,他在想该如何徒手地掐死这只猫——他是那种会做出这种事的人吗?

更让人恼火的是日常中米兰达对他的厌恶之情。晚上,他和艾丽莎一起坐在沙发的两头看书,米兰达经常会不请自来地跳到艾丽莎的腿上——但在缪尔先生抚摸她时,她会小心翼翼地退缩。他声称受到了伤害,又自称非常有趣。"恐怕米兰达不喜欢我了。"他悲伤地说。(他也记不清米兰达自小是否做出过喜欢他的举动。或许当她还是一只小猫咪的时候,她的喜欢完全不讲道理?)艾丽莎笑了笑,抱歉地说:"她当然喜欢你啊,朱利斯。"猫在她的膝上发出了响亮而又悦耳的呼噜声,"但是——你知道猫是什么性子。"

"的确,我还在学习中。"缪尔先生僵硬地微笑道。

他觉得自己正在学,至于到底在学什么,他也说不清。

当初到底是什么让他对米兰达动了杀机,或者说实际上是起了这个念头,这个他是不会给别人说的。有一天,他看到米兰达在他妻子的一位导演朋友的脚踝上蹭来蹭去,看到她是如何肆无忌惮地向一小群赞赏她的客人展示她自己(即使是那些普遍厌恶猫的人也忍不住称赞米兰达——抚摸她,挠她的耳后,像白痴一样对着她咕哝),缪尔先生在想,当初是他自己决定把小猫咪带到自己家的,他为她花费了好多钱,理所当然地,她是他的,他想怎么处置她就怎么处置。诚然,这只血统纯正的波斯猫是这个家庭最珍贵的财产之一。缪尔的家产都是精挑细选、身价昂贵的。艾丽莎确实很喜爱她。但最终她是属于缪尔先生的。也只有他对她拥有生杀大权,不是吗?

"这个小猫咪太漂亮啦!公的还是母的?"

缪尔先生正在接待他的一位客人(事实上,是艾丽莎的一位客人;自从她回归了她的戏剧生涯之后,她建立起新的交际圈,交结的朋友广,鱼龙混杂),他一时想不出该如何回答。这个问题紧紧地萦绕在他的心头,仿佛是一个谜:是公的还是母的呢?

"当然是母的,"缪尔先生十分愉快地说道,"她的名字不是叫米兰达嘛。"

他在想,他是应该等到艾丽莎开始排练新剧的时候再开始,还是应该在他的决心消退之前开展"雷霆"行动?(艾丽莎是一位小演员,却备受尊重,9月份,她将在百老汇的首演中担任女主角的替补。)他该怎么做?他不能勒死这只猫——至少他自己不能表现出如此直接而又不加掩饰的残忍——他也不可能以意外的借口用汽车撞倒她。(尽管这确实是个意外。)在仲夏的一个夜晚,就在狡猾又丝滑的米兰达悄悄地趴在艾丽莎的新朋友奥尔本的大腿上时(奥尔本是一名演员、作家、导演;才华横溢),他们谈到了臭名昭著的谋杀案——用毒药去杀人——缪尔当然想得很简单。毒药,就它了。

第二天早上,他在园丁的棚子里翻来翻去,然后发现了剩下的一袋10磅重的白色粒状"啮齿动物"毒药。去年秋天,老鼠泛滥,园丁在阁楼和地下室都撒下了毒饵陷阱。(缪尔先生推测,结果令人非常满意。无论如何,老鼠没有了。)这种毒药的精妙之处就在于它能引起极度的口渴。因此，在吞下毒饵之后，中毒的生物就会主动去寻找水源，离开房子，在外面等死。这种毒药是否会"高抬贵手"，缪尔先生并不知道。

他可以在仆人周日晚上的休息时间下手，尽管艾丽莎的排练演出尚未开始，她在城里倒是要待几天。于是，缪尔先生亲自给米兰达喂饭，就在她经常吃饭的厨房角落里——在米兰达平时的食物中加入了一大勺的毒药。（这只猫简直就是被宠坏了！从一开始，米兰达还是一只7周大的猫咪时，就喂她一种含有特殊的高蛋白、高维生素的猫粮，加上切碎的生肝脏、鸡内脏，天知道还有一些其他什么东西，然而缪尔先生不得不沮丧地承认，把她宠坏了，他自己也有责任。）

米兰达像往常一样既挑剔又贪婪地吃着食物，完全没有意识到主人的存在，也毫无感激之意。给她喂饭的这人可能是一个仆人；也可能根本就无足轻重。如果她感觉到什么不同寻常之处——比如，她喝水的盘子被拿走了，而且没有归还——她不会做出任何表示，就像真正的贵族一样。就他所知，世上如此自以为是的生物，也就只有这只白色波斯猫了。

缪尔先生看着米兰达（按照他的计划）一步步走向死亡，他脸上的表情不是预期的那种愉悦，甚至也不是因为纠正错误，伸张正义（尽管是模棱两可的）而感到满足，而是一种深深的遗憾。毫无疑问，这个被宠坏的家伙活该被处死；毕竟，一只猫在一生中会对鸟类、老鼠和兔子做出多少难以想象的残酷行径啊！但是，他，朱利斯·缪尔——为她付出了那么多，实际上也为她感到骄傲——竟然发现自己必须去做刽子手，这使他感到悲哀。但是这是必须做的事，虽然他可能已经忘记了原因，但他知道，他，而且只有他，注定要做这件事。

另一个晚上，几个客人来吃饭，当他们坐在露台上时，米兰达不知从哪跳出来，如同一道白光一样，她沿着花园的墙行走，那羽毛状的尾巴竖着，环绕脖子的柔滑毛发飘摇在她高昂的头颅周围，金色的眼睛闪闪发光，正如艾丽莎所说的。"这是米兰达，来跟你们打招呼！她是不是很漂亮？"艾丽莎高兴地喊道。（她似乎从不厌倦评论她的猫有多美丽，缪尔先生认为这是一种天真的自恋。）客人们表达了惯有的赞美或奉承；意识到自己是众人注意的焦点，那只猫把自己舔舐干净，然后猛地优雅跳开，消失在通往河堤的陡峭石阶上。缪尔当时觉得自己明白了，为什么米兰达看起来会如此不同寻常地有趣：她代表了一种既无目的又有必要的美；一种完全是凭手段巧取而来（考虑到她的血统），但又完全理所当然的美（考虑到她是有血有肉的东西）：自然美。

然而，这种自然美总是一成不变地——自然吗？

现在，白猫已经饱餐一顿（像往常一样，盘子里还剩下四分之一），缪尔先生大声说："可惜，美不会救你。"他的语气中混杂着无限的遗憾和满足。

那只猫停下来，用她那平淡无波的眼睛一眨不眨地看着他。他感到一阵恐惧：她知道吗？她已经知道了吗？在他看来，她从来没有像现在这样漂亮过：她的皮毛洁白如丝；颈毛蓬松，仿佛刚刚打理过；总是摆出一副娇气而又蛮横的表情；胡须粗壮；精致的耳朵机灵地竖立着。当然，还有那双眼睛……

米兰达的眼睛总是让他着迷。那是一种黄褐色的金色调，因为它们有神秘的爆发力，似乎晚上可以理所当然、随心所欲地看到，无论透过月亮的倒影，或者缪尔回家驾驶的汽车前灯，它们都发出小束的柔光。"你觉得那是米兰达吗？"看看路边高高草丛中的两道闪光,艾丽莎问道。缪尔会说:"可能吧。""啊,她在等我们呢!她真是个小甜心!她在等我们回家呢!"艾丽莎会带着孩子般的兴奋喊道。缪尔先生什么也没说,他怀疑猫甚至没有意识到他们的离开,更不用说热切地等待他们回来了。

在缪尔看来,猫眼睛的另一个反常之处是:人类的眼球都一致是白色的,虹膜是彩色的,而猫的眼球是彩色的,虹膜是纯黑色的。整个眼球是绿色的、黄色的、灰色的,甚至蓝色的!对于光线或兴奋感的层次,虹膜反应如此神奇,会收缩成剃刀般细的裂缝,或者扩张的黑色几乎填满了整个眼睛……当她像现在这样抬头盯着他时,她的眼睛睁得大大的,但是却黯然失色。

"不,美救不了你。只有美还是不够的。"缪尔平静地说道。他用颤抖的手指打开纱门,让猫走进夜色中。当她从他身边走过的时候——真是个怪异的小东西!——她轻轻地在他的腿上蹭来蹭去,已经好几个月没有这样了。还是已经很多年了?

艾丽莎比缪尔小20岁,但看上去显得还要更年轻些:她身材娇小,有着一双非常漂亮的棕色大眼睛,齐肩的金发。她是个乐天派,有时又有些癫狂,天真得很老到。她坦言,自己是一个没多少事业心的小演员,毕竟专业的演出本身就是一项艰苦的工作,即便她已从残酷的竞争中脱身,仍免不了吃苦受累。

"当然,朱利斯把我照顾得很好,"她会这样说,同时挽着他的胳膊,或者把头靠在他的肩膀上休息一会儿。"在这里,我想要的一切都有了,真的……"她指的是缪尔先生结婚时给她在乡下买的房子。(当然,他们在曼哈顿也有公寓房,距离南边两小时车程的地方。但是缪尔先生逐渐对城市失去了兴趣——它就像猫的爪子在屏幕上磨来磨去一样磨着他的神经——所以他很少再来了。)艾丽莎在嫁给缪尔之前以她的娘家姓,霍斯,断断续续工作了8年;她的第一次婚姻——19岁时和一个著名的(臭名昭著的)好莱坞演员在一起了,自从两人不欢而散——简直就是一场灾难——她不愿谈论任何细节。(缪尔也不想问她那些年的事。对他来说,就好像它们根本就不存在过。)

在他们遇见彼此的时候,艾丽莎暂时结束了她的职业生涯。她在百老汇取得了一些成功,但还没有站稳脚跟。继续前进、继续尝试是否真的值得呢?季复一季,一轮轮的试镜,与新人的竞争,"前途光明"的影坛新星……她的第一次婚姻糟糕地结束了,她又谈过几段恋爱(具体几段,缪尔先生从不知道),现在也许是收心成家,找个好归宿的时候了。就在那时,朱利斯·缪尔出现了:虽然是中年大叔,也不是特别帅气,但家境富裕,温文尔雅,更重要的是,对她爱意浓浓,好像此生只为等她出现。

缪尔被她迷住了,而且他有大把的时间和金钱,比任何一个男人对她的追求都要猛烈。他似乎总是能在她身上看到别人看不到的品质;他的想象力丰富,活跃到狂热的程度,对于这样一个沉默寡言又克制的人来说,简直是一种奉承。他极力坚称,他爱她胜过她爱他,对此他毫不介意——尽管艾丽莎断言她也爱他——否则她会嫁给他吗?

婚后的几年,他们也聊到要个孩子,"组建家庭",但没有任何结果。艾丽莎要么太忙,要么身体不太好;或者他们在旅行;或是缪尔担心孩子会给他们的婚姻带来未知的影响。(艾丽莎留给他的时间肯定会变少吧?)随着时间的推移,他为自己死后没有继承人的想法而苦恼——也就是说,没有自己的孩子——但也无能为力。

他们社交生活丰富;他们都是非常忙碌的人。毕竟,他们还有漂亮的白色波斯猫。

"如果家里有个孩子,米兰达会伤心的,"艾丽莎说。"我们真的不能那样对她。"

"我们确实不能。"缪尔表示同意。

然后,艾丽莎突然决定重返演艺圈。她严肃地称之为"事业",好像是她久违的、一种不可抗拒的力量。缪尔先生为她感到高兴,非常高兴。他为妻子的事业心感到骄傲,他一点也不嫉妒她不断扩大的朋友、熟人和同事圈子。他不嫉妒她的男演员和女演员同事们——里卡、马里奥、罗宾、西比尔、埃米尔,以及现在黑瞳秋波潋滟、笑容灵黠甜美的奥尔本。他不介意她离家在外度过很多时间,也不介意在家里,她埋头在所谓的工作室里。随着她的日渐成熟,艾丽莎·霍斯的心态有所改变,对各种角色的接受度稳步提高,这给了她更多的舞台表现机会,即使必须降级扮演某些角色——无论如何,对于年长的女演员来说,这些角色是不可避免的,不管她们的外表漂亮与否。正如众人所言,她已成为一个更好的、演技派演员。

事实上,缪尔先生为她骄傲,也为她高兴。而如果说,他心中时不时也会有一份不能称为埋怨的埋怨——那也只是对于他们无法再并肩的些许遗憾。一位真正的绅士自然会将这些心思妥帖藏好的。

"米兰达在哪儿?今天看到米兰达了吗?"

已经中午了,4点钟了,天快黑了,米兰达都还没有回来。艾丽莎几乎一整天都在忙着打电话——电话似乎总是在响个不停——她逐渐意识到猫已经很久没出现了。她到外面去唤她;派仆人去找她。当然,缪尔先生也帮了忙,他在院子里徘徊,还在树林里走了一段,他双手拢在嘴边,颤抖地尖声呼唤着:"喵—喵—喵—喵—喵!喵—喵—喵!"这是多么可怜,多么愚蠢——多么徒劳!但他必须这样做,因为不知真相的人就会这样做。朱利斯·缪尔,那个最殷勤的丈夫,踏遍灌木丛就为了寻找他太太的波斯猫……

可怜的艾丽莎!他心里想。她会伤心几天,还是几周呢?

他也会想念米兰达的——至少,她是家庭成员之一。直到今年秋天,他们已经养她十年了。

那天的晚餐很沉闷而压抑。这不仅仅是因为米兰达失踪了(艾丽莎看起来真的很担心),还因为缪尔先生和他的妻子两人单独用餐;那张为两人准备的餐桌从美学角度看来格外失调。而且,餐桌上的气氛安静得多么不自然啊!缪尔先生试图和艾丽莎说话,但他的声音很快弱下去,陷入了内疚的沉默中。午饭时,艾丽莎站起来接了一个电话(当然是从曼哈顿打来的——她的经纪人,或者她的导演,或者奥尔本,又或是其他女性朋友——这是一个紧急电话,否则缪尔夫人不会为了接个电话打破这一亲密时刻),而缪尔先生在一旁垂头丧气。他恍惚着味同嚼蜡地吃完了这顿孤独的午餐。他回忆起前一晚——刺鼻的猫粮,颗粒状的白色毒药,那只精明动物抬头看他的样子;还有摩擦着他的腿的样子。那副磨磨蹭蹭的姿势是……爱?责备?还是嘲弄?他重新感到一阵内疚的刺痛,而五脏六腑也生疼起来。然后,他抬头一看,看到一个白色的东西正小心翼翼地沿着花园的墙头走来……

当然是米兰达回家了。

他震惊地看着,瞪着眼睛,说不出话——等着那个鬼魂消失。在眩晕中,他慢慢地站起身来。故作高兴地把这个消息告诉隔壁房间里的艾丽莎:"米兰达回来了!"

他喊道:"艾丽莎!亲爱的!米兰达回家了!"

米兰达的确在那,的确是米兰达。她在阳台上凝视着餐厅,眼睛闪着黄褐色的金光。缪尔先生颤抖着,但他的大脑迅速地接受了这个事实,并想通了其中的逻辑。她一定是把毒药吐了出来。一定是!或者,在园丁的棚子里度过了一个阴冷潮湿的冬夜后,毒药已经失去了效力。

他不得不强打起精神,赶紧推开门让白猫进来,声音激动得有些颤抖:"艾丽莎!好消息!米兰达回家了!"

艾丽莎则欣喜若狂地把猫抱在怀里,缪尔抚摸着米兰达的尾巴;艾丽莎是那么喜悦,缪尔先生也终于感到真正的释怀。回看自己曾经那么十分残忍和自私——当然这行为违背他的本心——考虑到米兰达既然从主人手里死里逃生。他也就不会再试第二次了。

在46岁结婚之前,朱利斯·缪尔和大多数从未结过婚的男男女女一样具有某种特质——性格内向、有点局促,更多是生活的观察者而非真正的参与者,并相信婚姻是无条件的;他认为夫妻一体并不仅仅是比喻意义上的。然而,他自己的婚姻感情显然在逐渐变淡。婚姻关系几乎已经断绝了,似乎也不可能再恢复了。毕竟,他很快就57岁了。(虽然有时他会想:这真的很老吗?)

在他们婚后的头两三年里(艾丽莎称自己的戏剧生涯日落西山),他们像所有已婚夫妇一样,共用一张双人床——或者说缪尔先生是这样认为的(因为他自己的婚姻并没有让他参透一般意义上的"婚姻")。然而,随着时间的流逝,艾丽莎开始轻声抱怨自己无法入睡,因为缪尔先生会在夜里"躁动"——抽搐、踢腿、翻腾、大声喊叫,有时甚至惊恐地大叫。被她吵醒后的片刻,他几乎不知道自己身在何处;然后他就会羞愧地连连道歉,而如果他还能睡得着的话,他就会蹑手蹑脚地溜到另一间卧室将就对付剩下的夜晚。尽管缪尔先生对这种情况很不满,他对艾丽莎是十分同情的;他有理由相信,这个可怜的女人(她的神经异常敏感)已经为他承受了许多个不眠之夜却没告诉他。她一直如此体贴,不愿意伤害别人的感情。

因此,他们养成了一种习惯,晚上休息时,缪尔先生会先与艾丽莎在床上待半小时左右,这样两人似乎都觉得更舒适;然后,为了尽量不打扰她,蹑手蹑脚地走进另一个房间,在那里他可以不受干扰地睡觉(他认为,如果说,偶尔的噩梦无法让他无法踏实入眠,那么那些无法让他惊醒的噩梦才最糟糕)。

然而近几年的情况就更糟了:艾丽莎养成了熬夜的习惯——要不就是躺在床上看书,要不就是看电视,甚至不时地打电话聊天,缪尔先生要上床和她一起睡似乎变得不大现实,晚上他只能吻她然后道声晚安,随后便去自己的卧室。有时在睡梦中,他会梦见艾丽莎在叫他回来——当他醒来时,他会急急忙忙冲到昏暗的走廊里,热切又满怀希望地在她的门口站一两分钟。在这种时候,他不敢抬高声音,只能近乎耳语:"艾丽莎?我最亲爱的艾丽莎?你叫我了吗?"

和缪尔先生的噩梦一样难以预测、反复无常的还有米兰达的夜间习惯,她有时会惬意地蜷缩在艾丽莎的床脚下,安然地睡到天亮,但有时又坚持要出去,不顾艾丽莎想要留她睡在自己床边。即使是幼稚的,但艾丽莎承认——知道这白色的波斯猫整夜都在那里,并且能在脚边感受到这只猫在缎被上温暖而坚实的重量,对她来说是一种安慰。

但当然，艾丽莎也承认，没有人能够强迫猫做任何违背它自己意愿的事。"这几乎是自然法则。"她郑重其事地说。

投毒未遂的几天后，缪尔先生在黄昏时分开车回家。在离家大约一英里远的地方，他看到了前面路上的那只白猫——一动不动地立在另一条车道上，仿佛被汽车的前灯冻住了。他不由自主地想到：这只是为了吓唬她——于是他转动方向盘，朝她的方向驶去。金色的眼睛里闪烁起茫然与惊讶的光芒——或许是恐惧，或许是了然——这只是为了平衡，缪尔先生边这样想边用力踩下油门，直接冲向白色波斯猫——在她开始向沟里跑的时候，他用车的左前轮撞到了她。砰的一声，猫咪发出了难以置信的尖叫——一切都结束了。

天哪！成了！

缪尔先生口干舌燥，浑身颤抖，他透过后视镜看到了被撞碎在路上的那团白色东西，看到它周围遍布着一摊深红色的液体。他本不想杀死米兰达，但这次他真的杀了她——没有预谋，因此也没有愧疚。

现在，这事永远地结束了。

"就算再懊悔也无济于事了。"他喃喃而又难以置信地说道。

缪尔先生开车是为了去村镇的药店给艾丽莎买药——她因为剧院的事情一直在城里忙活，很晚才挤着通勤火车回家，一到家就偏头痛发作，立刻躺倒在了床上。缪尔递给艾丽莎头痛片的时候，心怀愧疚，现在他觉得自己很虚伪、残忍：如果她知道自己做了什么，她的头会加倍痛。然而，他怎么能向她解释，他这次并不是要杀死米兰达，而是他的汽车方向盘仿佛不自觉地脱离了控制？缪尔先生于是想起了刚刚那场事故——事故后他飞速驶回家，到现在还是心惊肉跳，好似自己差点就要惨死。

他想起了那只猫可怕的惨叫声，在车撞上它的时候叫声几乎戛然而止——但又好像不是在一瞬间戛然而止。

那辆英国制造的豪华轿车的挡板上有凹痕吗？没有。

左前方的轮胎上有血迹吗？也没有。

那有任何事故迹象吗？就算是最轻微无害的那种？都没有。

"没证据！没证据！"缪尔先生兴高采烈地自言自语。他一步两台阶地上楼，走到艾丽莎的房间前。当他抬手敲门时，门内传来艾丽莎的声音，听得出来她显然感觉好多了，这也让他有些欣慰。她正在打电话，与某人热烈地交谈着，发出银铃般的轻快笑声，让他想起了和煦夏夜里的风铃。他的内心满怀爱与感激，"艾丽莎，亲爱的，从现在起，我们又会幸福如初！"

而接下来，令人难以置信的是，在睡觉的时候，那只白猫又出现了。它终究是没有死。

深夜，缪尔先生在艾丽莎的卧室里和她一同品尝白兰地，这时他第一个看到了米兰达：它爬上了屋顶——可能是通过花架爬上来的，它经常这样——现在它那张哈巴狗似的脸在窗户上冒出来，前几天晚上的场景噩梦般重现了。缪尔先生吓得浑身瘫软，而艾丽莎跳下床来，让猫进来了。

"米兰达！你在搞什么鬼！你在搞什么花样？"

实际上这只猫失踪的时间并未久到让人担忧，但艾丽莎却像很久没见到米兰达一样热情地迎接它。而缪尔先生不得不配合演好这出戏,他的心在胸口狂跳,对这只猫的厌恶让他的灵魂都抽搐。他希望艾丽莎不会注意到他眼中闪现的病态和恐惧。

他开车碾死的一定是另一只猫,不是米兰达……显然绝不可能是米兰达,不过是另一只有着黄褐色眼睛的白色波斯猫罢了,不可能是他的那一只。

艾丽莎对它嘘寒问暖,抚摸它,并允许它在床上过夜,但没过几分钟,米兰达就跳下来,抓着门缝要出去。它错过了晚餐,现在饿了;它已经享受够了女主人的宠爱。而缪尔先生正厌恶地盯着它,所以它看都没看它的主人一眼。他现在知道,他必须杀了它——就算只是为了证明他能做到这一点。

在那以后,这只猫机灵地避开了缪尔先生,不是像过去那样懒得理会他,而是它敏锐地察觉到他们之间的关系有些不同了。他知道,这只猫可能没有察觉到他曾试图杀死她的事实,但她一定感觉到了这一点。也许它那会儿一直躲在路边的灌木丛中,看到他开车对准那只与自己长相相似的猫,然后把它撞倒……

缪尔先生清楚,这不大可能,甚至可以说绝无可能。但那又怎么解释他在场时这只猫的行为举止呢?不管是示威还是模仿,难道是出于动物的恐惧?他一进房间,它就会跳到柜子上,仿佛是为了避开他的视线;或者跳到壁炉的壁架上(它似乎是故意把他的一个雕刻玉俑摔在了地上,碎成了十几块);它优雅地溜过某门口,它锋利的脚指甲敲打着硬木地板。有时他无意中在户外接近它时,它很可能会拼命地要爬上一个玫瑰花架,或葡萄架,或一棵树;或像个野生动物一样跑进灌木丛,动静很大。有时艾丽莎碰巧在场,她会对这只猫莫名其妙的行为感到惊讶。"你认为米兰达生病了吗?"她问。缪尔先生不安地回答:"我们应该带她去看兽医吗?"他不知道他们能否把它捉住去看兽医——至少,他没有把握。

他有想过向艾丽莎承认自己的罪行,或者说是他谋杀未遂的行为:他已经杀了那只惹人厌的猫——而她却没死。

8月底的一个晚上,缪尔先生梦见了一双炯炯有神却缥缈的眼睛。眼睛中央是黝黑的虹膜,就像老式的钥匙孔;这条缝隙一旦打开便通往虚空。他不能动弹,没法保护自己。这时,一个温暖的、毛茸茸的华丽重物压在他的胸口……使他的脸沾满绒毛!这只猫长着白色胡须的嘴紧贴着他的嘴,像一个毛骨悚然的吻,一瞬间,他的呼吸都被夺走了……

"哦,别!上帝!救救我吧!"

他的嘴被某种动物的口鼻堵住了,无法呼吸,可他不能动弹,不能把它甩开——他的胳膊仿佛灌了铅似的垂在身侧,口不能言,整个身体不能动弹……

"救我……救救我!"

他喊叫着,在被窝里惊慌失措地挣扎,自己惊醒过来。虽然他马上意识到这只是一个梦,但他仍然急促地喘息着,他的心脏剧烈跳动,他感觉自己要死了。他的医生一周前就严肃地说过,他很有可能患上心脏病和心脏衰竭。他的血压比以往任何时候都要高得多,这是多么不可思议啊……

缪尔先生从潮湿、凌乱的被褥上下来,手指颤抖地开了一盏灯。谢天谢地,他是一个人,艾丽莎没有看到他刚刚紧张的丑态!

"米兰达?"他低语,"你在吗?"

他打开了一盏顶灯,卧室里阴影闪烁,一瞬间他仿佛不认识这个房间了。

"米兰达……"

真是只阴险狡猾的猫!这坏心的畜生!尽管他冷静地告诉自己这只不过是一个梦,那只猫只是一个幻觉,米兰达根本不在他的房间,但是一想到那只猫碰了他的嘴唇,她还吃过老鼠——森林里最肮脏的东西它都吃,他就冲进浴室疯狂冲洗自己的嘴。

话虽如此,但那只猫确实把她温暖又毛茸茸的沉重身体压在了他的胸口上。它试图夺走他的呼吸,让他窒息,让他可怜的心脏停止跳动。它能做到。"只是一个梦。"缪尔先生大声说,对着镜子里的自己虚弱地笑着。(哦!想想看那个苍白而憔悴的鬼影确实是他……)缪尔先生提高了声音,用学者般严谨的语调说道,"一个愚蠢的梦,一个孩子的梦,一个女人的梦。"

回到房间后,他感觉有什么东西一闪而过——一个模糊的白色物体——在他的床下窜来窜去。但当他手脚并用地往床底看去时,还是什么也没有。

但是,他的的确确在长毛绒地毯里发现了一些洁白又僵硬的猫毛——一看就是米兰达留下的。啊,太明显了。"这就是证据!"他兴奋地说。还有些猫毛稀稀落落地散落在门边的地毯上,床边更多——好像那畜生在那里躺了一会儿,甚至可能滚来滚去(米兰达在阳台上晒太阳的时候经常这么做),优美地伸展四肢,愉快又悠闲。缪尔先生时常被她非凡的雍容美丽所打动:触摸那具肉体(还有她的皮毛)该多快乐啊!他无法想象。在他们的关系恶化之前,他甚至都有股冲动,想快步走到这只猫那里,用后脚跟狠狠踩在它暴露出来的浅粉色的柔软肚子上……

"米兰达,你在哪儿?你还在房间里吗?"缪尔先生呼唤道。他激动地喘不过气来。他蹲了好几分钟,想站起来的时候腿都酸了。

缪尔先生在房间里找了一圈,但那只白猫显然已经不在这里了。他走到外面的阳台上,靠着栏杆,眨着眼在昏暗的月光下搜寻米兰达的踪迹,但他什么都看不见——因为害怕,他忘记戴上眼镜了。好几分钟,他只是呼吸着夜间潮湿而几乎凝滞的空气,试图让自己冷静下来,但没过多久他就发现有点不对劲,隐隐约约有人在低声说话——是一个人还是许多人?

接着,他看见了:灌木丛中有一道像幽灵一样的白色身影。缪尔先生努力眨着眼,盯着那道白影看,但他现在的视力太差了。"米兰达?"然而上方传来什么东西窸窣跑过的声音,于是他转过身,看见另一个白色的身影正在斜斜的屋顶上奔跑,飞快翻过了屋顶。他一动不动地站着——说不清是出于恐惧还是狡黠。事实上,可能不止一只白猫,不止有一只白色波斯猫——不止一个米兰达!之前他从未这样想过。"但是或许这样就讲得通了。"他说。虽然受到了惊吓,他的头脑还是异常清醒,同往常一样。

时间还不是很晚,还不到凌晨一点。缪尔先生听到的那些低声细语是艾丽莎的声音,中间时不时夹杂着她轻快如银铃般的笑声。听到的人可能会以为卧室里另有他人陪着——但她当然只是在煲深夜电话粥而已,电话那头很可能是奥尔本——他们友好地谈天,也许在聊他们的男女演员同事,共同的好友和一些熟人,开一些关于他们的没有恶意的玩笑。艾丽莎阳台的窗户和缪尔先生的在同一侧,所以他能清楚地听到她的声音(又或者是几个人的声音?缪尔先生困惑地听着)。没有光线从她的房间里透出来;想必这通电话是摸黑打的。

缪尔先生又等了几分钟,但是灌木丛中的白色身影已经消失了。头顶上方的石质屋顶上空空荡荡,只有几片昏暗斑驳的月影。他形单影只,决定回去睡觉,在此之前他仔仔细细检查了一下房间里是否真的只有他一个人。他锁好了门和所有的窗户,开着灯睡——但他睡得很沉,无牵无挂。第二天早上艾丽莎的敲门声叫醒了他。"朱利斯?朱利斯?亲爱的,你没事吧?"她叫道。他惊讶地发现已经快中午了:比之前晚起了4个小时!

艾丽莎急匆匆地和他告了别。一辆豪华轿车要来接她进城;连续几个晚上她都会不在家;她很牵挂他,担心他的健康,希望不会出什么差错……"当然没事。"缪尔先生烦躁地说。这么晚才起床,他整个人都懒懒散散地,同时也感到困惑;睡这么久也还是萎靡不振。当艾丽莎和他吻别的时候,他一点儿也没有投入,更像是在受罪,她走了以后他强忍着才没有用手背擦嘴。"老天啊,救救我们吧!"他喃喃道。

因为寝食难安,缪尔先生对收藏也逐渐失去了兴趣。当一个古董书商把一本罕见的八开本的《宗教裁判指南》拿给他看的时候,他也只是稍微心动了一下,然后就把这本宝书拱手让给了和他竞争的另一位收藏家。几天后,书商提供机会让他竞拍四开本哥特版的马基雅弗利的《贝尔法人》,他更是兴致索然。"缪尔先生,您没事吧?"那个书商问道。(他们共事已经有25年了。)缪尔先生嘲讽地重复道:"您没事吧?!"接着挂断了电话。他从此和这个人断绝了来往。

缪尔先生对于金融事务更是完全失去了兴趣。他不再接华尔街那些为他理财的人打来的电话;对他来说,知道钱在那儿,而且会一直在那儿就足够了。至于其中的细节只会让他感到厌烦和粗俗。

9月的第3周,艾丽莎作为替补演员的戏剧开演了,好评如潮,这就意味着它将连续上演很长时间。尽管女主角身体非常健康,几乎不会缺席任何一场演出,但艾丽莎觉得有责任在城里再待久一点,有时候一待就是整整一周。(她在那里做了什么,日日夜夜在忙些什么,缪尔先生不知道,也放不下自尊心去问。)当她邀请他在城里共度周末时(为什么他不像过去一样高高兴兴地去拜访古董书商呢?),缪尔先生简洁地回道:"为什么要去城里?我在乡下应有尽有,过得很开心。"

自从那天晚上起了掐死米兰达的念头,缪尔先生和米兰达都更加关注彼此。他出现的时候,白猫不再逃避;相反,当他走进一个房间的时候,她就牢牢守住自己的地盘,似乎是在嘲笑他。如果他向她靠近,直到最后一刻,她才会躲开,然后紧贴着地板,像只蛇一样溜走。他咒骂她,她就龇牙咧嘴,喉咙里发出呜呜的声音。他大笑着,显得自己毫不在乎;她跳到他够不着的柜子顶部,蜷缩起身子幸福入睡。每天晚上艾丽莎都会按时打来电话;在她问候完米兰达之后,缪尔先生总会说:"还是那么的漂亮健康!你见不到她真是太可惜了!"

随着时间的流逝,米兰达胆子越来越大,也越来越放肆——也许是低估了主人的反应力。有时她会出现在脚底,他上楼或者出门的时候差点被绊倒;在他手里拿着可能伤人的利器时,比如切肉刀、火钳、皮面精装、厚重的图书之类的,她也敢靠近他。有一两次,缪尔先生独自进餐时正想着些有的没的,她甚至会跳到他的膝盖上,在餐桌上蹦蹦跳跳打翻那些杯盘。"魔鬼!"他尖声向她挥舞着拳头,"你到底想怎样!"

他想知道仆人们都在背后说些什么闲话。不知道这些闲话是否传到了城里艾丽莎那边。

但是有天晚上，米兰达犯了一个战术性错误，缪尔先生到底还是抓住了她。她溜进书房，而他正坐在灯下仔细查看收藏中的一些最为稀有、最有价值的钱币（美索不达米亚钱币，伊特鲁里亚钱币），显然她已经算计好可以从门口逃跑。但缪尔先生突然从椅子里跳起来，一脚关上了门，速度快到异乎寻常，几乎和猫一样敏捷。接着就是好一场追逐！好一顿挣扎！好一次疯狂的打闹！缪尔先生抓住了那只畜生，被她逃走，又抓住了她，被她挣脱；她狠狠地抓他的手背，抓他的脸；他又一次成功捉住了她，将她重重掼在墙上，血淋淋的手指圈紧她的喉咙。他挤啊，压啊！他终于抓到她了。真可谓天堂有路你不走，地狱无门你闯进来！那猫尖叫着，爪子在空中胡乱抓蹬，全身痉挛，奄奄一息，缪尔先生蹲着，眼睛鼓得和猫的眼睛一样大、一样疯狂，额头上青筋暴起。"这下好了！我这下抓住你了！这下好了！"他叫喊着。眼见那只白色波斯猫必死无疑的时候，缪尔先生书房的门突然打开了，一个仆人出现在门后，苍白的脸上满是不可置信的神色："缪尔先生？发生什么事了？我们听到……"这个蠢人说着。米兰达抓住缪尔先生松手的机会，瞬间从他的手中溜走，逃出了房间。

那件事情发生之后，缪尔先生似乎死了心，以后再没那样的机会除掉米兰达了。但他和米兰达之间的纠葛很快将会结束。

事情发生得实在突然，在11月的第2周，艾丽莎回家了。

她已经退出了那部戏，并且决定就此结束她的"演艺生涯"，甚至言辞激烈地告诉她的丈夫，她将有很长一段时间不想去纽约了。

他发觉她一直在哭，这令他感到惊讶。她的眼睛亮得不同寻常，并且看上去比他记忆中的小了些。她美丽的面孔正在枯萎，就好似有一张小了一号的更决绝的脸在她的面皮下涌动着，呼之欲出。可怜的艾丽莎！当初她离开时曾经是那么的满怀憧憬！但当缪尔先生走近她，想要抱住她、安慰她时，她躲开了。她的鼻孔皱起来，似乎连他的气味都令她反感。她避开他的目光，说道："拜托了，我觉得不太舒服。我现在最想的就是一个人待着，让我一个人静静吧。"

她回到自己的房间，躺在床上。连续几天，她的房门紧闭，只允许一个女佣进出。当然，倘若她挚爱的米兰达纤尊降贵，自然也是能进去的。（看到那只白猫并没有泄露出任何他们之间的怨仇的迹象，缪尔先生如释重负。他的双手和脸上被抓破的伤口在缓慢地愈合，但是艾丽莎沉浸在自己的悲痛中无法自拔，甚至都没注意到。）

艾丽莎房门紧锁，往纽约打了几通电话，她似乎经常在电话里哭泣。在这种特殊情况下，缪尔实在无奈，只能监听她的电话，但发现她的电话没有一通是打给奥尔本的。

这意味着……？说实话，他不知道这一切到底意味着什么，而且他也没法直接去问艾丽莎，因为这样会暴露出他在监听她的事实，这将进一步打击她本已脆弱的心。

缪尔先生往艾丽莎称病幽居的房间里送来小束秋天盛放的花朵，巧克力和糖果、精巧的诗集还有一条新的钻石手链。有好几次，他站在她的门外，如同一个热切的追求者，但是她只是解释道她还没做好见他的准备，至少目前还没有。她的声音尖锐，语气冷淡，缪尔先生之前从来没有听到过。

"你难道真的不爱我了吗,艾丽莎?"他突然痛哭流涕。

先是一阵短暂而令人尴尬的沉默,接着是:"我当然爱你,但你能不能离我远一点,让我一个人静静。"

为着艾丽莎,缪尔先生忧心忡忡,晚上连一到两个小时的安稳觉也睡不成。即使在他睡着的时间里,他也总是做着噩梦。那只白猫!她坐在他的脸上,这令人窒息的重量!他的嘴巴能尝到她的毛发!但是当他清醒时,他只是想着艾丽莎,想着为什么她虽然回了家,但事实上她的心并没有回到他这里。

他独自躺在那张孤零零的床上,睡在乱七八糟的床单中间,嘶哑地哭泣着。一天清晨,他摸摸下巴,感觉到了胡渣:他已经好几天没刮胡须了。

在阳台上,他碰巧看到一只白猫轻巧地跃上花园的围墙,这只猫比他印象里的白猫更大一些。她已经从那次袭击中完全康复了。(当然,她那时是否受伤都有待商榷,甚至这只是否就是那只冲进他书房的猫也存在疑问。)阳光下,她雪白的皮毛熠熠生辉,深嵌头骨的两颗黑色的瞳仁闪着金光。她雪白的皮毛在阳光下熠熠生辉,眼睛像是煤块一样镶嵌在头骨中,闪着金光。缪尔先生看着她,心想:天呐,她是造物主一件多么美的杰作!

尽管在下一刻,他意识到了她究竟是个什么东西。

11月末一个风雨交加的夜晚,缪尔先生开着车行驶在河道上方窄窄的黑色柏油路上,身旁的艾丽莎沉默不语。他想,在保持沉默这件事上,她是多么地执拗啊。她穿着一件黑色的克什米尔羊毛外袍,戴着一顶柔软的黑色毛帽,紧紧地裹着她的头,遮住了她大部分的头发。缪尔先生对这些时髦但又很低调的衣服一无所知,暗示着他们之间愈发的疏离。当他搀着她上车时,她小声地对他说道"谢谢",语气就像在质问:"哦!你一定非要碰我吗?"缪尔先生自嘲般向她一鞠躬,两手空空地站在雨中。

我曾经是那么爱你。

她一个字也不说,美丽的侧脸避开他,着迷般地看着窗外飘泼的大雨。车下的河流不安地涌动,在飘摇的风中,缪尔先生更用力地踩下那辆英国产汽车的油门。"这样更好,我亲爱的妻子。"缪尔先生小声说,"即便你并未爱上其他男人,但是令人心痛的是,你也并不爱我。"听着他这番庄严的话语,艾丽莎心头涌上几分愧疚,但是这还不足以使她转过身来面对他。"我最亲爱的?你明白吗?这是我们最好的结局——不用害怕。"缪尔先生越开越快,车身在疾风中猛烈地晃动。艾丽莎捂住嘴,似乎想要抑制住自己任何反抗的冲动。同缪尔先生一样,她呆若木鸡地盯着疾驶的人行道。

就在缪尔先生决绝地将车头转向路旁护栏时,她才做出反应打破僵局:她无声地尖叫着,拼命向后缩进座位里,但她既没有抓住他的胳膊也不去抢夺方向盘。在一瞬间,一切都结束了。汽车撞向护栏,在半空中翻转着,车身最终摔向石头遍地的半山腰,在火光中,一切归于平静。

他坐在带着轮子的椅子里——一辆轮椅!这对他来说是多么杰出的发明,他好奇这是哪个天才的创想。

尽管他没有能力自己推动轮椅,他几乎完全瘫痪了。

在失明之后,他什么也不想做主了!他对自己的处境感到满足,只要不需他费力做事情。(现在待着的这间屋子,他看不见,却总是感觉暖洋洋的,这都是妻子的照料。但也有时候难免会有不可预测的寒风吹进来。他目前的身体状况恐怕经受不住任何外界温度的改变。)

他忘记了许多事物的名字,但并不为此伤心。事实上,不知道名字,人们便不再执着于那些如鬼魅般萦绕心头却难以获得的事物。他的失明跟这有很大关系,他对此感激!感激不尽!

失明了,好像又不是完全看不见:因为他还是能看见(实际上看不见)有像水一样流动的、变化的白色,这些白色的溪流滴滴点点,令人惊叹,它们没有形体,没有线条,看不出形状,只是白色的而已,永无休止地在他脑中波动。

他显然经历过一些手术。到底几次,他不知道,也不想知道。最近几周,他们郑重地给他讲,他的脑部或许还要再开一次刀。如果他没理解错的话,这次手术的目的是恢复他左脚趾头的行动能力。如果他能笑的话,他一定会大笑,但是保持尊严的沉默也许更适宜。

艾丽莎甜美的声音和房间里其他的声音交相汇合,他们刻意压低的声音中难掩激动。但是据他所知,手术似乎从未发生,或者手术的确进行了,但成效甚微。他的左脚趾头,正如他身体的其他部分一样,显得那么遥不可及。

"你多走运啊,朱利斯,还好有辆车出现了! 不然,你早就死了!"

似乎在那场雷电交加的暴雨中,只有朱利斯·缪尔独自一人行驶在高悬于河堤的狭窄沿河道路上。不同寻常的是,他一直以高速行驶,最后车子失去控制,撞上了缺口的路边护栏,整辆车都翻过来……缪尔"奇迹般地"飞出车外,躲过了燃烧中车辆的残骸。他瘦削的身体里三分之二的骨头都碎了,头骨严重受挫,脊椎断裂,一扇肺叶被戳破……于是,关于朱利斯如何来到这个地方,他最后的归属地,这片乳白色的祥和之地的故事,就像被砸碎的挡风玻璃一样,在破碎和杂乱的碎片中浮现出来。

"朱利斯,亲爱的? 你醒着吗? 还是……?"熟悉而轻快的声音在迷雾中向他涌来,他试着把这个声音与一个名字联系起来,艾丽莎? 或者,不,是米兰达? 究竟是谁?

在谈论声中听到(有时他自己也能听到一点),总有一天他的视力能恢复一部分。但是朱利斯·缪尔很少听到,或者在意。那些日子里,他就这样活着,当某天他从昏迷中醒来,感觉到一个温暖的毛茸茸的身体在他的大腿上——"朱利斯,亲爱的,有个特别的访客来看你了!"柔软,但意料之外的沉重;温暖,但不是热得让人难受;起初它只是不停地扭动(就像一只猫必须反复扭动才能找到最舒服的休息姿势一样),但几分钟之内,它就奇迹般冷静下来,用她的爪子轻轻地揉踩着他的四肢,喉头呼噜呼噜,和他一起沉沉地进入梦乡。他很想透过他眼前微微发光的白翳,亲眼看到她独特的白色身躯;他当然也想用双手再次感受她的柔软,感受她那光滑的令人惊叹的皮毛。但他可以听到她喉头深处发出的极富韵律的呼噜声。在一定程度上,他能感到她温暖的身体里传来的脉搏跳动,她不可思议的生命活力,对此他永远感激不尽。

"我的爱啊!"

(曹文清,王文君 译;崔宪慧,雷若岚 校)

献给艾米丽的一朵玫瑰

威廉·福克纳

1

艾米丽·格里尔森小姐死的那天,全镇的人都来参加她的葬礼。男人大都带着一份崇敬和爱意,来瞻仰这座倒塌的丰碑;女人们则大多出于好奇,借此想对艾米丽小姐的房子一探究竟。这栋房子里只有一个年迈的男仆伺候,他既当园丁,又当厨子。至少已经10年没有外人进去过了。

这是栋四四方方的木屋,曾经涂了白色的漆,装点着70年代特有的圆顶、尖塔,以及带有涡卷装饰的阳台,既轻快明亮又透着沉重的历史气息。这儿曾经是镇上最繁华的街道。但后来,汽车间和轧花机一步步蚕食最后占领了这儿,连最令人敬畏的几个大家族都销声匿迹了。唯独艾米丽小姐的房子岿然独存于周围的棉花车、汽油泵中,日趋破败却仍在卖弄风情,很是碍眼。而如今,艾米丽小姐也加入那些庄严家族当中。在雪松环绕的墓地里,立着一排排无名墓碑,他们都是杰斐逊战役中阵亡的南北将士。这些大家族人和将士们一起长眠于此。

艾米丽小姐在世时一直是传统的化身,是全镇的一种责任和关注对象;她更代表着一种世袭的使命,这可以追溯至1894年的一天,镇长萨多里斯上校——正是他颁布法令规定黑人妇女不穿围裙不得上街——下令免除艾米丽小姐的税收,且这份特许从她父亲去世之日起永久有效。这并不是说艾米丽小姐甘受施舍,而是萨多里斯上校编造了一个复杂的故事,说艾米丽小姐的父亲曾借钱给镇上,镇上才以此为报。这种说辞只有萨多里斯上校那个年代、那种思想的人才会编得出来,也只有女人才会信以为真。

下一代人的想法更加前卫,等他们当上了镇长和议员时,这套做法引起了一些不满。元旦那天,他们给艾米丽邮寄了一封税收通知,但直到2月份都无人回应。于是他们又寄去一封公函,让她在方便之余去镇治安官那里一趟。一周后,镇长亲笔写信,表示愿意登门拜访,或是派车相接。作为回复,他收到一张古色古香的纸,字迹纤细流畅,墨迹有些许褪色,大意是说艾米丽小姐现如今足不出户。那份税收通知也随信附上,未作任何解释。

议员们召集全体参议院开了一场特别会议,派了一个代表团前去拜访艾米丽。他们叩响了大门,这扇门自八九年前艾米丽小姐不再教授瓷器彩绘之后便无人踏足过了。年迈的黑人管家接待他们到了昏暗的大厅,在那可以看见一道楼梯攀向更加阴暗之处。灰尘与废弃的味道扑面而来,像是封闭了太久,十分潮湿。随后,黑人管家带他们到了会客室,那里都是厚重的皮革家具。管家打开一扇百叶窗后,只见这些皮革早已满是裂痕。他们一坐下,大腿边便飘起一股细微的尘埃,在阳光照射下打着旋。壁炉前立着的镀金画架光泽不再,上面立着一幅炭笔肖像,画着艾米丽小姐的父亲。

艾米丽小姐一进屋,代表们便起身致意。她个头矮小,身材臃肿,穿着一身黑衣,一条细金链子垂至腰间,隐入腰带,手里拄着一根乌木拐杖,金属杖头的光泽已经消磨殆尽。她的骨架瘦小,也许正因如此,在别人身上看来仅是丰满,而在她身上却成了肥胖。她看上去就像一具浸泡在死水中的尸体,浮肿苍白。那双陷在堆积的脂肪中的眼睛就像陷在面团里的两颗小煤球。议员们向艾米丽说明来意时,这双眼睛就在他们之间来回打量。

她并未请他们就座,只是站在门口,静静地听着,直到那人结结巴巴地说完。言毕,一片死寂中只听到那块隐在金链子末端的怀表滴答作响。

她的声音干哑而冰冷:"我在杰斐逊无税可交。萨多里斯上校向我交代过。或许你们应该派一个人去查查政府档案,一查便知。"

"可我们查过了,艾米丽小姐,我们就是政府代表。想必您应当收到了治安官签署的通知吧?"

"我是收到一纸文书,"艾米丽小姐说,"也许他自认为是个治安官……我在杰斐逊无税可交。"

"但档案上并没说明这一点,您要知道,我们必须按照……"

"去找萨多里斯上校。我在杰斐逊无税可交。"

"但是,艾米丽小姐……"

"去找萨多里斯上校。"(萨多里斯上校死了快十年了。)"我在杰斐逊无需纳税。托比!"黑仆应声出现。"送客。"

2

就这样,他们铩羽而归,正如她在 30 年前"气味"一事上让他们的父辈无功而返。

事情发生在她父亲去世两年后,她的爱人也抛弃了她,虽然当时大家都以为他们会修成正果。父亲去世后,她就很少出门。在她的爱人走后,人们更是几乎就没见过她了。有几位女士壮着胆子去敲门,但都吃了闭门羹。整个宅子唯一的生命迹象是那个黑人,他当时还年轻,拎着采购的篮子进进出出。

"你能指望哪个男人会把厨房收拾得干干净净呢?"妇女们这样说道。因此当那股气味越来越刺鼻时,她们并不惊讶。这也算是喧闹的俗世与高高在上的格雷森家族间的一种特殊联系。

一位邻居家的妇女向 80 岁的市长兼法官史蒂文斯抱怨此事。

"但你到底要我怎么做呢,夫人?"他说。

"传话给她,让她把怪味散散,"妇人说,"法律是摆设吗?"

"没这个必要,"史蒂文斯法官说,"可能是那个黑鬼在院子里杀了条蛇或者老鼠。我会和他说说的。"

第二天,他又收到了两起申诉,其中一起来自一个男人,他踌躇地建议道:"真的不能再这样下去了,法官。我实在是不愿意打扰艾米丽小姐,但必须要采取措施了。"当晚市议会就召开了会议,3 位长者和 1 位青年晚辈一起商讨对策。

"很简单,"青年人说,"通知她,让她在限期内把自己家打扫干净,不然的话……"

"不行啊,先生,"史蒂文斯法官表示反对,"怎么能当面指责一位女士身上有怪味呢?"

于是第二天午夜过后,4 个男人穿过艾米丽小姐家的草坪,窃贼似的绕着房子潜行,在砖墙底部和地窖入口嗅来嗅去,其中一个男人时不时从肩上的麻袋里掏出些什么,像播种似的撒在地上。他们破开地窖门,在地窖和所有的外屋内都撒上石灰。当他们要再穿过草坪回去时,原先一扇暗着的窗户亮了起来。艾米丽小姐坐在那里,灯光在她身后,挺直的身体像雕像一般一动不动。他们蹑手蹑脚地穿过草坪,走进街道两边洋槐树的阴影中。一两周之后,气味不见了。

自那时起,人们才开始真正同情起她。我们镇上的人想起她的姑姥姥怀亚特老太太最后是怎样彻底疯掉的,都认为格里尔森一家有点自命不凡、自视甚高。没有一个年轻小伙能配得上艾米丽小姐这样的人。长久以来,我们都将格里尔森一家视作一幅活人画,艾米丽小姐身材瘦削,身着白色衣衫,她的父亲叉开双腿站在她前面,背对着她,手里握着一根马鞭,两人被框在向后开的前门中。所以当她快要30岁却仍然单身时,我们其实并不感到欣喜,反而觉得自己的想法被证实了:即使家族里有精神错乱的人,如果真有机会,她也不会全然放弃。

她的父亲死后,有传言说留给她的遗产只有那栋房子;从某种程度上说,人们很高兴。他们终于能可怜可怜艾米丽了。她现在孑然一身又身无分文,变得有人情味了。她终于能体会那种多一分钱便开心、少一分钱便沮丧的普通人的感受了。

在艾米丽父亲去世的第二天,镇上所有的女士都准备到他家拜访,一方面表达哀悼,另一方面也是去帮帮忙,这是我们的习俗。艾米丽小姐在门口迎接她们,穿着与往日无异,脸上也没有任何悲伤。她告诉他们她父亲没有死。一连3天,她都是这样,来拜访的牧师们和医生们都劝她让他们处理掉尸体。当他们要诉诸法律与武力时,艾米丽小姐崩溃了,他们便赶紧下葬了她的父亲。

那时我们并不觉得她疯了,只是认为她这样做是理所当然的。我们还记得她父亲赶走的那些年轻男人,我们知道她和其他人一样,当一无所有时,只能依靠那个夺走她一切的人。

3

她病了很长一段时间。再见到她时,她头发已经剪短了,看起来像个小姑娘,和教堂彩窗上的那些天使有几分相像,显得些许悲伤肃穆。

镇政府已订好合同,要铺设人行道,就在她父亲去世的那个夏天开始动工。建筑公司带着一批黑人、骡子和机器来了,工头是个北方佬,名叫荷马·巴伦。身形高大,皮肤黝黑,精明强干,声音洪亮,瞳色较浅。小男孩们经常成群结队地跟在他身后,听他咒骂黑人,听黑人们在镐头起落间有节奏地唱歌。没过多久,他就认识了镇上所有人。每当听到广场上哈哈大笑的声音,荷马·巴伦就一定会在人群中间。不久,每逢礼拜天的下午,我们都会看到他和艾米丽小姐同驾一辆黄轮轻便马车出行。那辆黄轮马车配上从马房中挑出的栗色马,十分相称。

一开始,我们都很高兴看到艾米丽小姐有了新的消遣对象,因为妇女们都说:"格里尔森家的人绝对不会看上一个北方佬,一个拿日工资的打工仔。"但是还有一些年纪稍大的人说,悲伤不会让一位真正的贵妇放下她矜贵身段的——尽管口头上不把它叫作"矜贵"。他们只是说:"可怜的艾米丽!她的亲属应该过来陪她。"艾米丽小姐在亚拉巴马是有一些亲戚的,但是多年前她父亲为了疯婆子怀亚特老太太的财产问题和他们闹翻了,两家就断绝了联系,甚至连葬礼他们都没出席。

老人们一说到"可怜的艾米丽",就开始窃窃私语。"你认为这是真的吗?"他们彼此说道,"当然是真的,不然还能怎么样……"他们用手捂着嘴,偷偷摸摸地说起来;在轻快驶去的马蹄嘚嘚声中,即便关上了遮挡周日午后阳光的百叶窗,还可听到绸缎的窸窣声:"可怜的艾米丽。"

她把头抬得高高的——甚至当我们深信她已经堕落了的时候也是如此,就好像她比以前任何时候都想要维系她身为格里尔森家族最后一名成员的尊严;就好像她需要与世俗接触才能证实她的百毒不侵。就比如说,那天她去买毒老鼠的砒霜。那是人们开始说"可怜的艾米丽"的一年后,也正逢她的两个堂姐妹来看望她。

"我要买点毒药,"她对药剂师说道。那时,她已经30多岁了,身材依旧纤细,却比以前更加清瘦了,一双黑色的眼睛清冷而又骄矜,脸上的肉在太阳穴和眼窝周围绷得紧紧的,宛如想象中的灯塔看守人应有的模样。"我要买点毒药。"她说道。

"好的,艾米丽小姐。您想要哪一种呢?是毒老鼠的那种吗?我建议……"

"我要你们店里最好的毒药。不管是什么种类。"

药剂师一连说了好几种:"这些毒药连大象都能毒死。但是你想要的是——"

"砒霜。"艾米丽小姐说道,"砒霜管不管用?"

"砒霜?好的,小姐。但是你想要的是……"

"我要的是砒霜。"

药剂师低头看了她一眼。她回视他,身体挺直,脸像一面绷紧的旗子。"当然有,"药剂师说道,"如果那是你想要的毒药。但是按照法律,你得告诉我你要拿它做什么。"

艾米丽小姐只是紧紧地盯着他,头向后仰了仰,以便正视他,直到他不得以移开目光,去拿了包砒霜,然后包好。黑人送货员把那包药送出来给她;药剂师却没有再露面。她回家之后打开药包,盒子上的骷髅头下注明:"毒老鼠专用。"

4

到了第二天,我们都说:"她要自寻短见。"这样最好不过了。第一次看到她和荷马·巴伦在一起的时候,我们都说,"她要嫁给他了。"后来又说,"她还得说服他呢。"因为荷马自己说他喜欢男人,大家都知道他和年轻男人们一起去麋鹿俱乐部喝酒——他不是那种会结婚的人。后来,每逢礼拜天下午,他们都会乘着漂亮的轻便马车经过,艾米丽小姐昂着头,荷马·巴伦歪戴着帽子,嘴里叼着雪茄,戴着黄手套的手握着缰绳和马鞭。我们躲在百叶窗背后不禁感慨道:"可怜的艾米丽。"

后来,有些女人开始说,这是小镇的耻辱,把年轻人带坏了。男人们都不想干涉这件事,但女人们最终迫使浸礼会牧师——艾米丽小姐一家人都是圣公会教徒——去拜访她。拜访经过他从未透露,但他再也不愿去第二次了。到了下个礼拜天,艾米丽和巴伦又驾着马车出现在街上。第二天,牧师妻子就写了封信给艾米丽在亚拉巴马州的亲戚。

于是,她家里又有了亲人造访。我们这些人就袖手旁观,关注着事态的发展。最开始无事发生。接着,我们确定他俩要结婚了。我们听说艾米丽小姐去过珠宝店,订了一套银质的男用盥洗用具,每件都印有"H. B."的字样。两天后,我们得知她买了全套男装,包括一件睡衣。这下我们就得出结论:"他俩结婚了。"我们真的很高兴。我们高兴是因为她的两位堂姐妹比艾米丽小姐更像格里尔森家的人。

所以,当荷马·巴伦离开的时候,我们一点也不惊讶,因为街道早就完工了。我们因为没有一场热闹的送别会而感到有点失望,但我们相信他是去为迎娶艾米丽小姐做准备了,或者是给她一个机会打发走堂姐妹们。(那时已经有一个阴谋集团,我们都是艾米丽小姐的盟友,帮她躲开堂姐妹。)果然,过了一个星期她们就走了。如我们所料,3天之内荷马·巴伦就回到了镇上。某天傍晚,一个邻居看见那个黑人在厨房门口让他进去了。

那是我们最后一次见到荷马·巴伦。艾米丽小姐也"消失"了一段时间。黑人提着菜篮子进进出出,但前门一直关着。偶尔我们会在窗边看到她,就像那天晚上男人们撒石灰时那样。但是几乎长达6个月,她都没有出现在街上。我们觉得这也在意料之中;就好像她父亲的性格给她的女性生活造成了很多麻烦,这种性格太过恶毒狂暴,难以根除。

当我们再次见到艾米丽小姐时,她身材发福,头发也开始花白。在接下来的几年里,艾米丽的头发变得越发灰白,直到它变成了椒盐般的铁灰色后,才不再变色。在她74岁去世的那天,她的头发仍然是那种充满活力的铁灰色,就像一个精力充沛的男人的头发一样。

从那时起,她家的前门就一直关着,只有在她40来岁时打开过六七年。那段时间里,她在教瓷器绘画。她在楼下的一个房间里布置了一个画室,和萨多里斯上校同时代的人们定期把女儿和孙女送到这里,就像他们自己每周日去教堂做礼拜,把25美分捐献给教堂一样。在此期间,艾米丽的税金都被免除了。

后来,新的一代人成了这个镇上的中坚力量和精神支柱。学绘画的学生们长大了,也渐渐离开了她,他们也不再让孩子们带着一盒盒颜料、单调的画笔和从女性杂志上剪下来的图片来找她学画。最后一个学生走了,前门就关上了,永远地关上了。当镇上实行免费邮递时,只有艾米丽小姐拒绝他们在她的大门上方钉上金属门牌号,并不允许他们在门上装信箱。无论别人怎么劝她也不听。

日复一日、年复一年,进进出出间提篮的黑仆在我们的眼前渐渐衰老下去,头发花白,弯腰驼背。征税通知单总是在每年的12月寄出,又总是在一周后原封不动地被邮局退回。偶尔,她的身影会出现在一楼某扇窗户里。她显然已将房子的顶楼完全封存了——她看上去像一尊壁龛里的雕像,目光似有若无地落在窗外,我们说不准她是否正在看着我们。屋外世代更迭,而屋内的她则永远高昂着头,不可忽视、不为所动、沉默寡言、固执己见。

她就这样死去了。在那座被灰尘和阴影吞噬的房子里,她的病床前只有一个步履蹒跚的老黑仆服侍。我们甚至不知道她病了,也早已放弃从那黑仆嘴里询问任何关于她的消息。

他不与任何人交谈,也许对她也不开口。多年的沉默似乎已使得他的嗓音变得粗哑尖锐。

楼下的某间房里,她在系着帘子的沉实的核桃木床上死去,满头灰发散落在因太久不见天日而发黄发霉的枕头上。

5

那黑仆立在前门,将第一批闻风而来的女人们迎进门内,妇人们窃窃私语,好奇地四处打量着。黑仆随即消失了,他径直穿过屋子,走出后门,从此再也没人见过他。

两位堂姐妹立刻就赶到了。全镇都出席了第二天她们主持的葬礼。他们看着艾米丽小姐安眠于花海之下,而蜡笔画像中她父亲的面容仍沉思于她棺木的上方。两旁的女士们唏嘘不已,暗叹死亡的可怕。而那些苍老的男人们,其中有些穿着精心打理过的邦联军制服,聚集在门廊和草坪上,谈起艾米丽小姐像是在怀念他们那个时代。他们相信艾米丽小姐与他们年龄相仿,自己曾有幸与她共舞,甚至向她求爱。老年人经常那样,他们不管时间是怎样有条不紊地向前推进的。在他们混乱的时间观里,过去不是一条越走越暗的道路,而是一块宽广无垠、长夏无冬的芳草地。唯一将他们与他们光辉的过去分隔开的,只有眼前近十年苍老的岁月所带来的困境。

楼上某间房已有40年没人看见过内里,这是我们都知道的。镇上的人等到艾米丽小姐体面下葬之后,才强行动用武力打开那间房。

冲开房门的力道震得整间屋子灰尘四起。窗边色调淡褪的玫瑰色短帘,隐在玫粉色灯罩里的吊灯,梳妆台,精心摆放的水晶饰品,男人盥洗用的镀银器皿。那银器已锈蚀得连首字母也看不清了。屋内的陈设与家具似乎是为一对新人准备的,而此刻却全都覆盖在由刺鼻的灰尘织成的一层薄薄的柩衣下。一只硬领同领带躺在其中,似乎刚刚从脖子上取下一般,可是一拿起来,就立刻在覆满灰尘的表面上留下一道新月状的凹痕。椅子上放着一件仔细叠好的西装,椅子下是两只高档皮鞋和随意丢弃的袜子。

而那男人躺在床上。

很长一段时间,我们只是站在那里,俯视着那带着意味深长的浅笑的骷髅头。这具身体显然曾摆出拥抱的姿态,然而那比爱更长久的死亡,那扭曲的爱也无力逆转的死亡夺走了他的生命。睡衣下他的肉体静静地腐烂、消逝,直到与身下的床融为一体,留在他的骨架与身旁的枕头上的,只剩残存的衣料和安静的浮灰。

我们发现床上的另一个枕头凹陷下去,是有人睡过的痕迹。我们中的一个倾身向前,从枕头上拈起什么。在似有若无却干涩刺鼻的浮尘中,我们看到了一根长长的铁灰色的头发。

(孙平平,李艳红　译;刘子煊,朱镜如　校)

苍　蝇

凯瑟琳·曼斯菲尔德

"你这儿挺舒服呀。"伍迪菲尔德老先生尖着嗓子说道,他窝在他的朋友——老板的办公桌旁,从那把巨大的绿皮革扶椅里往外看,就像婴儿车中的婴儿探头外窥一样。要聊的已经聊完了,他该走了。但他不愿离开。自从他退休,又罹患中风,妻子和女儿们就每天把他关在家里,除了周二。到了周二,他拾掇一番,穿戴整齐,被放回城里快活一天。至于他在那儿干了些什么,妻女不得而知。他是去朋友们那里捣乱了吧,她们这样猜想……也许如此。话说回来,人总是惜取最后的欢愉,好比树牢牢守住最后几片叶子。因此老伍迪菲尔德迟迟不走,一边坐着抽雪茄一边眼巴巴地盯着老板。老板坐在办公椅里前后摇晃,身材壮实,面色红润,比老伍迪菲尔德年长5岁,而身体依然强健,仍居掌舵者之位。这样老当益壮之人令见者感到欣悦。伍迪菲尔德苍老的声音满怀向往而又羡慕地补充道:"说真的,这里可真舒服啊!"

"没错,是舒坦极了。"老板表示赞同,手中的裁纸刀翻动着《金融时报》。事实上,他对自己的房间感到十分自豪,喜欢听到别人赞美它,尤其是来自老伍迪菲尔德的夸奖。安坐在房间中央,将那戴着围巾、垂垂老矣的虚弱身影尽收眼底,让他有一种深深的、实在的满足感。

"我可是刚翻新过这屋子。"老板说道,数周来他一直这样不厌其烦地介绍,如数家珍。"地毯是新的。"他指着大红的地毯,上有巨大的白色环状花纹。"家具也是新的。"他颔首示意大书柜与桌子,那桌腿的形状好像缠绕虬结在一起的糖浆。"还有电暖呐!"他兴奋地指向倾斜的铜盘上5根珍珠般闪闪发光的透明香肠。

说来说去,他却从未提及桌子上方的那张照片。照片上是一个军装少年,神色愀然,衬着照相馆里那种阴沉沉的乌云布景图。与房间里新添置的家具不同,这张旧照挂在那里已有6年之久。

老伍迪菲尔德开口道:"我想告诉你一件事来着,"他努力回忆,目光开始涣散,"是什么事呢?哎呀,今早出门时明明还想着的。"他双手哆嗦起来,两颊泛红。

可怜的老家伙,他快要不行了,老板想道。他朝老人善意地眨了眨眼,笑言:"告诉你,我这里有些喝的可以御寒,这可是老少皆宜的好东西。"他从表链上取下钥匙,打开办公桌下的橱柜,拿出一个宽扁的深色瓶子。"我说的灵丹妙药就是这个,"老板说,"供货的人悄悄跟我说,这玩意是温莎城堡地窖里的呢。"

老伍迪菲尔德瞠目结舌,惊讶程度不亚于看到老板从柜子里拎出一只兔子。

"这是威士忌?"他有气无力地尖声问道。

老板翻转过瓶子,好让他看商标。的确是威士忌。

"你知道吗,"老人仰视老板,目光惊疑不定,"在家里,她们从不让我喝酒。"他哭丧着脸。

"嘻,那是女人家不懂。"老板高声说道,从桌上的水瓶旁边一把抓过两只玻璃杯,各往里倒上一指深的酒。"喝下去,你就会好起来。可别掺水,那就是暴殄天物了。唔,好酒!"他一饮而尽,抽出手帕草草揩了揩嘴,望着正含着酒的老伍迪菲尔德。

老人咽下酒,沉默片刻,接着用微弱的声音说:"绝了呀!"

杯酒下肚,他的身子暖和了,僵化枯朽的大脑也活络起来,记起了他要说的事。

"是这样,"他从扶椅上吃力地撑起身子,"我估摸着这事你应该会关心。我家姑娘们上周去比利时给瑞吉扫墓,碰巧看到了你儿子的墓,靠得挺近。"

老人顿了顿,老板却并未回应。只有微颤了一下的眼皮表明他听见了。

"她们对墓地的条件很是满意,"老人继续说着,"打理得井井有条,周正极了。只是山长水远,诸多不便,如果葬在这儿就好了。你还没去那看过吧?"

"没,没去过。"由于种种原因,老板未曾跨越海峡前往。

"陵园可大了,"老人声音发颤,"干净齐整,像座花园。坟墓上鲜花丛丛,条条径路漂亮又宽阔。"言语中流露出他对那园内阔路的喜爱。

老人又顿住了,随后一下子眉飞色舞起来。

"我跟你说,那边的旅店居然一罐果酱卖10法郎!简直是抢钱啊。格特鲁德说那罐子很小,不过半克朗硬币那么大,才吃了一勺就让付钱。她气得把罐子都顺走了,干得好啊。这些黑心商人就是在利用我们的感情。他们明摆着是想宰客。"他转身走向门。

"干得好呀,干得好呀!"老板大声附和,嘴上这么说着心思却完全在别处。他绕过办公桌,跟随老人拖沓的步伐送他出门去。伍迪菲尔德离开了。

老板发着呆,许久不动。那头发灰白的收发员还在候命,东跑西跑,进进出出,像狗想要被牵出去遛弯似的。只听老板出声道:"麦西,半小时内我不想见客,明白吗,谁也不见。"

"是,先生。"

门关上了,老板迈着沉重有力的脚步再次走过鲜亮的地毯,肥胖的身躯猛一下瘫在弹簧椅上,倾身向前以手掩面。他心怀痛楚,打算好好哭上一场。

老伍迪菲尔德突然提到男孩的坟墓,这对他来说是个沉重打击。他仿佛看见墓地大开,他的儿子就躺在里面,而伍迪菲尔德家的女儿们站在周围俯视着他。说来也怪,虽然6年多过去了,但是老板从来没有想过这个男孩,唯一的印象是他身穿制服沉眠此地,完美无缺,永恒不变。"我的儿子!"老板呻吟道。然而他毫无泪意。在此之前,儿子死后的前几个月,甚至前几年里,只要说了这句话,他就会感到无比悲痛,只有大哭一场才能平静下来。他曾经宣称,而且逢人便说,时间无法治愈他的伤痛。别人也许会淡忘、恢复、会重整旗鼓,但他不会。这怎么可能呢?他的儿子可是独生子。从他出生起,老板就一直在为他经营这家公司;如果不是为了这个男孩,一切根本毫无意义。生活本身也失去了价值。要不是儿子会接替他的工作、继承他的事业,要不是有这个前景鼓舞着他,他怎么可能数年如一日地做牛做马、辛苦操劳呢?

这个前景曾经触手可及。战前,儿子在公司学习经营管理已经有一年了。他们每天早晨一起出发,晚上坐同一班火车回家。作为孩子的父亲,他收到了多少人的祝贺啊!也难怪他开始乐在其中。公司里上上下下,每个人都对他赞赏有加。他一点也没有被宠坏。不,他只是保持着他那开朗、自然的本性,与每个人交谈都言语得体,带着他那孩子气的神情和"实在太棒了!"的口头禅。

但这一切都完了,好像从来没有发生过一样。那天,麦西给了他一份电报,最终把他的一切毁得一干二净。"非常遗憾地通知你……"麦西离开后,办公室里只剩老板独自心碎,万念俱灰。

6年前,6年……光阴似箭啊! 事情好像发生在昨天一般。老板挪开了捂着脸的手;他感到疑惑。似乎有什么地方不对劲。身体感觉和心理期望并不相同。他决定站起来看看儿子的照片。但那不是他最喜欢的一张照片;上面的表情不自然。十分冷淡,甚至看起来很严厉。这孩子从来没有过这样的表情。

就在这时,老板注意到有只苍蝇掉进了他的大墨水瓶里,它正奋力试图爬出来,却无能为力。那挣扎的腿似乎在喊:救命! 救命! 可是墨水瓶的四周又湿又滑;它又掉回原地,开始游动。老板拿起一支钢笔,把苍蝇从墨水里挑出来,甩在一张吸墨纸上。大概有几分之一秒的时间,它静静地躺在身体周围渗出的墨迹上。然后,前腿挥动了几下,站稳了,撑起它那湿漉漉的小身体,开始了一项艰巨的任务——清理翅膀上的墨水。一条腿在翅膀上一遍又一遍地上下搓动,就像石头在镰刀上一遍又一遍地来回打磨一样。稍微歇了一会,苍蝇似乎踮起脚尖,试着先展开一只翅膀,然后再展开另一只翅膀。它最后成功了,接着便坐了下来,像一只小猫咪一样开始洗脸。现在想象一下,一只苍蝇在轻松、快乐地互相摩擦着两只小前腿。可怕的危险结束了;它逃出生天了;已经准备好迎接新生。

但就在这时,老板又有了一个主意。他把笔插回墨水里,粗壮的手腕搁在吸墨纸上。恰好就在苍蝇垂下翅膀时,一大滴墨水重重地落了下来。坏了! 这下它可怎么办? 可怜的小苍蝇似乎完全吓坏了,一动不动,害怕接下来会发生什么事。但是紧接着,它好像非常痛苦地一边挣扎一边向前爬。它的前腿不断挥动着,直到站稳了,这一次的动作慢了一些,新一轮的自救又开始了。

我可真是个魔鬼,老板心想。他对苍蝇的勇气感到由衷的钦佩。面对困难就该这样,精神可嘉! 永不言败,一切自有定数……但这只苍蝇又实现了艰难求生,老板正好来得及给钢笔添上墨水,又在苍蝇身上滴了一滴。这次又会如何呢? 等待结果的焦灼随之而来。但你看,它的前腿又在挥动了;老板如释重负。他俯身对苍蝇温柔地说:"你这个狡猾的小……"他想出了一个绝妙的主意,他可以帮忙把墨水吹干。尽管如此,它现在的努力还是有些胆怯和弱小,于是老板决定再来最后一次,他把笔深深地浸入墨水瓶中。

确实是最后一次。最后一滴墨落在浸湿了的吸墨纸上,那只湿透了的苍蝇躺在纸上不动了。后腿紧紧贴在身上;前腿被挡着,看不见。

"起来呀,"老板说,"快点!"他用钢笔戳了戳——毫无动静。什么也没有发生,也不太可能发生。那只苍蝇死了。

老板用裁纸刀把尸体挑起来,扔进了废纸篓。但是一种痛苦的感觉袭来,他感到格外害怕。他走上前,按铃叫麦西进来。

"给我拿些新的吸墨纸来,"他严厉地说,"动作麻利点。"麦西领命而去,老板一边慢慢地走着,一边开始琢磨自己之前一直在想些什么。是什么呢? 是……他掏出手帕,塞进了衣领里。他怎么也想不起来了。

(郝　悦,毛雪莹　译;张可欣,雷若岚　校)

归 航

拉尔夫·埃里森

　　托德醒过来了,看到两张脸悬挂在他头顶上。烈日灼灼,阳光刺眼,他分不清这两张脸是黑还是白。他尝试着动了动,感到一阵疼痛,仿佛整个身体都被阳光蒸烤着。刺眼的阳光直射进他的双眼。一时间,一种被白人触摸的昔日恐惧占据了他的心头。然后,剧烈的疼痛让他慢慢清醒。他隐约听到声音,他的确醒了。他们是谁?他心里嘀咕。不,他不是,我发誓他肯定是白人。然后他清楚地听到耳边传来的声音:

　　"你受伤了吗?"

　　他如释重负,这是个黑人的声音。

　　"他还没清醒呢。"他听见他们在交谈。

　　"给我点时间……喂,孩子,你伤得严重吗?"

　　他伤得很严重吗?他僵硬地躺在那里,身体的痛苦剧烈而可怕,听着他们的呼吸声,他试图感知他们的目的。他警惕地看着他们,思绪穿越了一段痛苦的距离回到了过去。像电影预告片一样,锯齿状的场景迅速浮现在他的脑海里,他看到自己驾驶着一架尾翼旋转的飞机降落,接着他从驾驶舱里爬出来并试图站起来。接着,就像在一片寂静中一样,他想起了骨头嘎吱嘎吱的声音。现在,他躺在一片田地里,身边站着一个黑人老头和一个孩子,一抬头就能看到他们焦灼的脸庞,这种记忆让他感到恶心,他不想再回忆下去了。

　　"孩子,你现在感觉怎么样?"

　　托德犹豫了一下,好像回答这个问题就等于承认了一个不可接受的弱点。然后他说:"我的脚踝。"

　　"哪只?"

　　"左脚。"

　　带着一种疏离感,他看着那个老头弯下腰,帮他脱下靴子,他瞬间感到脚上的压力缓解了。

　　"好点吗?"

　　"好多了。谢谢您。"

　　他有一种谈论别人的感觉,他关心的是一件更重要的事情,出于某种原因,他没有注意到。

　　"你伤得很重,"老人说。"我们得带你去医院。"

　　他觉得自己陷入了一片混乱。他看了看手表;他在这里躺了多久了?他知道世界上只有一件重要的事,那就是在他的长官生气之前把飞机送回战场。

　　"帮帮我,"他说,"扶我上飞机。"

　　"但你伤得很重……"

"把手给我!"

"但是孩子……"

他紧紧抓住老人的手臂,把自己拉了起来,没让左腿受力,看着那张皮革般光滑的脸逐渐与他自己处于同一高度,他心想:"我永远也不会让他明白。"

"现在,让我们看看。"

他听到一只鸟不断地叫唤,把老人推开。他摇摇晃晃,头晕目眩。无穷的黑暗笼罩着他。

"你最好坐下。"

"不,我没问题的。"

"但是你的伤会恶化的,孩子……"

他的内心一直都在极力否认这个事实,即使他的脚踝火辣辣地痛。他必须再试一次。

"你再乱动脚踝,他们会把你的脚截肢的。"他听到了说话的声音。

他屏住了呼吸,又开始尝试挪动。他的脚疼得厉害,他必须咬住嘴唇才不至于叫出声来。一阵绝望突然涌上了他的心头,他让那两个黑人把他抬了下来。

"你最好别着急。我们马上会给你找个医生的。"

他想,这最坏的运气如今竟叫我碰上了。热浪中弥漫着高辛烷汽油的浓烟味,这气味仿佛在讥笑着他。

"我们可以骑着老内德送他进城。"男孩说道。

内德? 他转头,看到男孩指着一排公牛,那些牛在埋着犁铧的犁沟尽头处啃食着草。一想到自己骑在一头公牛背上穿过城镇,经过满是白人的街巷,沿着机场的混凝土跑道一路向前,他的脑海里就迅速闪现出了屈辱的画面。他猛地一痛,想起了他女朋友写给他的最后一封信,"托德,"她在信中写道,"我不需要你写这些来告诉我你很会开飞机。我一直以来都知道,你和其他人一样勇敢。你写的信真让我生气。就因为你是黑人,托德,你就要一遍遍证明自己很勇敢又很有能力才满意是吗? 我觉得他们一直打那匹死马是因为他们不想告诉你们为什么你们还没有参与战斗。我真的很失望,托德。任何有头脑的人都可以学会开飞机,但是然后呢? 这种技能你要用在哪里? 又是为谁效力? 亲爱的,我希望你能好好想想,写写这方面的想法。我有时候觉得,他们在耍我们。这太屈辱了……"他揩了把脸上的冷汗,心想:她哪懂什么叫羞辱? 她从来没有下到南方来。现在,羞辱马上就要来了。那就是你必须接受他们对你的评判,知道他们永远也不会认为将你个人犯下的错算到你一个人头上,而是把这个错误归咎于你整个种族——这才叫羞辱。是的,羞辱就是你永远不只是你自己;羞辱就是你永远都要与这个无知老黑为伍。当然,他这人还不错,人好、和善又乐于助人。但是他不是你,好吧,在这一点上我可以免受羞辱。

"不,"他说道,"我有命令,决不能离开飞机……"

"哦,"那个老头沉吟,转头跟男孩说道,"泰迪,那你最好赶紧去找格雷夫斯先生,把他带过来……"

"不,等等!"在彻底意识到什么之前他大声抗议道。格雷夫斯可能是个白人。"请让他把消息传到飞行员训练场,他们会处理好剩下的事情的。"

他看到那个男孩跑着离开了。

"他过去要走多远?"

"可能一英里左右。"

他又躺了回去,盯着他那沾满灰尘的手表盘。他想,他们现在知道他出事儿了。飞机里有一台很好用的无线电联络机,但是这会儿它也没什么用了。这个老家伙肯定不会操作无线电。那只秃鹫把我撞回了100年前,他想。讽刺的声音在他脑子里无休止地盘旋着,就像是小飞虫绕着老头的头飞来飞去。我学了那么多,却还是要依赖这个"乡巴佬"对时空的感知。他的腿一阵阵地抽痛着。在飞机上,时间可不是通过不听使唤的腿上传来的阵痛来衡量的,只要看一眼仪器表,立马知道了。他用手肘撑着,扭过身,看见飞机机身上落满了灰尘。他感到如鲠在喉,每当他想到飞行时,总有这种感觉。飞机伏在那儿,他想,真像是蝗虫蜕下的外壳。失去了飞机,我就是赤身裸体的。它对我来说不是一台机器,而是一套穿在身上的衣服。他突然尴尬而惊诧起来,喃喃自语道:"它是我仅存的尊严了……"

他看到那个老头正看着自己,他那件破旧的工作服在高温下软趴趴地贴在他身上。他突然特别想对老头倾诉他的感受,但那丝毫没什么意义。如果我试图解释我为什么一定要飞回去,他只会觉得我害怕那些白人长官,但是这不仅仅是出于害怕……极度的痛苦,就像是脸上黏腻的汗水一样,紧紧地裹挟着他。他看向老头,老头正在欣赏飞机,嘴中断断续续地哼着调子。他心中突然暗暗生出一种憎恨之感。像他这样的老头经常跑到训练场来,像不经事的孩子般用新奇的目光注视着他们这些飞行员。起初,这让他感到自豪,这些人为他这段新的人生经历带去了意义是这段新经历中有意义的一部分。但是很快他就意识到了,这些人根本不懂他的成就,正如来自白痴的赞美只会招人厌恶一样,他们的到来让他觉得耻辱与尴尬。

那么,关于飞行的一部分意义就因此消失了,而他再也无力挽回。假如我是一名职业拳击手,我会活得更像个人吧,他想。不再被当作会耍点把戏的猴子,而是一个真正的人。他们仅仅是因为他是一个会开飞机的黑人而高兴,而这对于他来说远不够。他感到自己与他们之间割裂开了,因为年龄,因为迥异的理解与感知,因为所掌握的技术,因为他需要借助别人的赞赏来映照衡量自己。不知怎么地,他感到自己遭受了背叛,正如他小时候某天发现父亲已经死了时的那种感觉。对于他来说,现在任何他所认为的真正的赞赏都来自他的白人长官,而那些来自黑人们的赞赏,他无法肯定其真假。夹困在无知无识的黑人与居高临下的白人之间,他的飞行航线似乎是由那些不起眼且不自然的地标所标记,在一些使用越来越专业而神秘的术语表达的机密命令下,他的航路疾转过黑人老头所象征的耻辱与白人长官所代表的阴霾。他盲目地飞行着,只知道有一个着陆点,在那里他将展翅翱翔。到那时,连敌人都会赞赏他的技艺之高超,而他也将展现他最深刻的价值,他不由悲从中来,这价值既不是来自那些趾高气扬的人,也不是来自那些不理解却还要赞赏他的人,而是体现在让那些敌人为他的气概与能力咬牙切齿。

他叹了口气,看着公牛在干燥的棕色大地上刻下奇形怪状、古老苍凉的身影。

"放轻松点,孩子,"老头安慰道,"那个男孩不会去很长时间的,他对飞机可着迷了。"

"我可以等。"他说。

"你这是什么飞机?"

"一架高级教练机。"他说,看到老头露出了微笑,手指触摸着低垂的机翼,在金属的映衬下像是扭曲而粗糙的深色木头。

"那它能飞多快呀？"

"每小时 200 多英里。"

"天哪！这也太快了，我敢打赌飞起来就像是根本没动似的！"

托德挺直身子，敞开了飞行服，阴凉瞬间消散了，他感觉自己仿佛躺在一个火球里。

"你介意我进去看看吗？我一直好奇想看看……"

"请自便吧，只是别碰任何东西。"

他听到老头哼哧哼哧地爬上金属机翼。老头现在就要问问题了，好吧，一定都是些不用思考就能作答的问题……

他看到老头望向驾驶舱，眼睛像孩子一样亮了起来。

"你一定非常了解这些东西都是怎么操作的吧。"

他没有作声，看着老头走下来，屈膝跪在他身边。

"孩子，你怎么会想着要飞上天的呀？"

因为这是世界上最有意义的行为……因为这能让我与你有别，他想。

但他说的却是："我猜是因为我喜欢它吧，在我看来这是战斗与死亡的最好方式。"

"是吗？或许你说的对，"老头说，"可是你觉得还要等多久他们才会让你上战场？"

他心下一紧。这是所有的黑人都会问的问题，他们开口询问时总是流露出卑微而胆怯希冀与渴盼，每每听见托德都感到内心无比空虚，比他第一次开完飞机下舱时所感受到的还要强烈。他感到头晕目眩。突然他意识到，他们的谈话在朝着危险的方向进行，那是他不愿驶向的不安全的未知领域。如果放任谈话进行下去他只会受到侮辱，他要让这个试图帮助他的老头闭嘴！

"我拜托你个事儿……"

"什么？"

"你刚才冲下来的那幕真的吓到我了。"

他没有回答，而老头宛如循着迹的狗般似乎从中嗅出了他的恐惧以及他心底冒泡升腾的怒火。

"你简直吓坏我了。当我看到你开着那玩意儿在空中旋转跳跃，像匹刹不住的马一样俯冲下来时，我还以为你要没救了。我差点吓到中风！"

他看到老头咧嘴一笑，"今天早上这里发生了一些事儿，猜猜看。"

"什么事儿？"他问。

"好吧，我知道的第一件事儿就是，这里来了两个白人小伙儿，寻找鲁道夫先生，也就是格雷夫斯先生的表弟。一听说这事儿我就来劲儿了……"

"为什么？"

"为什么？因为他从疯人院破门逃走了，这就是原因，他很可能杀了人，"他说，"不过，他们现在应该抓到他了。然后你来了，一开始我以为你是其中一个白人小伙子。真他妈的，要不是你掉在那里。我的老天，我确实听说过你们这些孩子，但我可从没见过你们中的任何一个。你都不知道当我看到一个长得像我的人在驾驶飞机时是什么感觉！"

老人不停说着，声音在托德的思绪中流动着，就像空气在飞机机身上流过。他不由觉得自己真是个傻瓜。他回想起飞机旋冲前太阳是如此闪耀，衬得镇外的广告牌无比亮堂；又想起男孩轻轻拽着的蓝色风筝在阳光下有多么舒展，在机身下飞得多么欢畅，宛如一朵奇形怪状的花在风中绽放。他曾经也放过这样的风筝,并试着在目光难以触及的绳子末端找到那个男孩。但是他飞得太高太快了。他驾着陡直攀升的飞机驶离,内心狂喜。他想,太陡了。他最先学的规则之一是,如果推力角太陡,飞机就会旋冲。然后,他没能把飞机往上拉,因为一只秃鹰吓了他一跳,于是任由飞机俯冲向下。一只讨厌的秃鹰!

"孩子,玻璃上的血是怎么来的?"

"一只秃鹰的。"他说,回忆起血和羽毛是如何溅到舱门上的。他仿佛闯进了一场鲜血淋漓的黑暗风暴之中。

"哦,我知道的!这附近有很多秃鹰。它们不吃任何活物,就爱围着死了的东西转。"

"差一点它就可以把我当饭吃了。"托德冷冷地说。

"说它是'霉运'一点不错。泰迪给它们起了个名字,叫它们'吉姆·克劳们'。"老人笑着说。

"这名字真是贴切得要命啊。"

"它们是最可恶恶心的鸟。有一次我看到一匹马四仰八叉直挺挺地躺着,好像生了病,你知道那是什么样吧。所以我大喊,'从那里爬起来,伙计!'只是想确认下它是不是真病了!结果,该死的,孩子,我居然看到两只秃鹰从马肚子里飞出来!是的!当时阳光照在它们身上,这些鸟像吃了顿烧烤似的,油腻极了!"

托德觉得他要吐了,他的胃在颤抖。

"那是你编的,"他说。

"不!我看见那匹马就像看见你一样,真真切切。"

"好吧,我很高兴碰到我的是你。"

"孩子,这陆地上能看到很多有趣的东西。"

"不,我要让你亲眼看看。"他说。

"对了,这里的白人不喜欢看到你们在天上飞。他们曾经打扰过你们吗?"

"没有。"

"嗯,但他们有这个想法。"

"总有人想打扰别人,"托德说,"你怎么知道?"

"我就是知道。"

"好吧,"他反驳道,"没有人打扰过我们。"

托德眺望天空时,血流在他的耳朵里鼓动着。看到天空中有一个黑点,他紧张起来,努力辨认这个他看不太清的东西。

"你觉得那像什么?"他兴奋地问。

"不过又是一只'霉运'罢了,孩子。"

然后他便失落地看着秃鹰扇动的翅膀。它展开翅膀,平稳地低飞,尾羽拖着气流,迅速地消失在绿色的树幕后面。他想象中这儿的鸟就是这样的,来去无踪,只剩下倾斜的松枝刺向苍白的天空。他躺在那里,屏息盯着它消失的地方,陷入了一阵厌恶与钦佩之中。为什么老天让它们生得如此恶心,却又教它们飞得如此好?"感觉我像飞升到了天堂。"他兀地听到这句话。

老人轻声笑着,摩挲着他那长着胡茬的下巴。

"你说什么?"

"嘘,我死后上天堂……也许等我讲完这件事的时候,他们就会来找你了。"

"我希望如此。"他疲惫地说。

"你们这些小家伙们有没有坐在一起撒过谎?"

"不经常。这算是一次吗?"

"好吧,我不太确定,因为这件事发生在我死的时候。"

老人停顿了一下,"不过,关于秃鹰的事,那可不是谎话。"

"好吧。"他说。

"你想听天堂的故事吗?"

"请讲。"他回答,把头靠在胳膊上。

"我去了天堂,背后马上就生出了翅膀。是一对6英尺长的翅膀。就像白色天使的翅膀一样。我简直不敢相信。我靠自己的翅膀飞上了几朵云,并挨个把它们飞了个遍,真是开心。你知道,因为我不想一开始就出丑……"

托德想,这是个老故事了,有人在多年之前和我讲过,虽然我现在已经不记得了,但是至少能让老人不谈秃鹫。

他闭上双眼将就听着。

"……我做的第一件事就是攀上一朵低矮的云丛,然后往下跳。该死啊,孩子,如果这些翅膀没用该如何是好!刚开始,我试着拍打右翅,接着拍打左翅,最后我尝试着拍打双翅。上帝啊,我开始在人们头顶飞翔,他们的目光都汇集在我身上……"

他看着老人比画着双臂做出飞行的姿势,听到老人提及想象中的人群时,他的脸上浮现出一丝嘲弄的骄傲,他想,我这个样子会上报纸的,接着,他听到老人说,"我继续飞啊,直到我遇到了几个黑人天使。——不知道为什么,之前还不相信我成了天使,现在看到真的黑人天使,我信了!我真的是一个天使!——但是他们让我最好下来,因为我们这些黑家伙需要套上一种特制的束具才能飞行,这就是他们没有飞行的原因。哦,当然了,如果你是黑人,你得比一般人更强大才能戴得动这种束具飞行……"

这不是我听过的那个故事,托德沉思,他到底想讲什么?

"但是我对着自己说,我不应该为没带束具而感到困扰!才不要!'因为上帝让你长出双翼,你就不应该让任何人为你套上束缚阻碍你飞行。'所以,管他呢,我开始飞翔了,孩子。"他咯咯直笑,眨巴眨巴眼睛,"你知道吗,我得让所有人都知道我老杰弗逊能和其他人飞得一样好。而且我可以飞得和鸟儿一样灵活!我甚至能在空中翻跟斗——但是我可要小心不要让我的黑脚踝从白袍子里露出来……"

托德很不安。这个笑话逗得他想笑,但是身体现在不服他管束。他回想起小时候嚼完母亲给的糖衣药片后,母亲总是嘲笑他徒劳地想要去除嘴里药片的难闻气味。

"哈……"他继续听老人讲述,"我飞得可好了,加速又加速,快得都能吹起一阵猛烈的风。我能做各种各样的飞行特技,在星群中上下遨游,向月亮飞去。嘿,我把白天使中的恶魔都吓得要死,好一番闹腾。孩子,我没什么恶意。我很畅快,我为最终获得自由而感到畅快。无意之中,我磕下了星星的一些边角,他们告诉我一场风暴由此而起,这将造成梅肯县好几起死亡——不过我发誓,我才不信他们的鬼话。"

托德生气地想,他在编排我,觉得我是个笑话。老人朝我咧着嘴笑……喉头干涩。托德看了一眼手表,他们怎么还不来?既然他们一定会来救他,那为什么还没有人来?曾经我也是他们中的一员,翱翔天际,托德想,现在我陷入了什么境地了呢,就像约拿进了鲸鱼的肚子。

"我只是尽情飞呀,任凭羽毛掉落在人们脸上。一个圣彼得召见了我。他说,'杰弗逊,告诉我两件事,为什么你不套上束具就飞行呢?你怎么飞得这样快?'我一五一十地告诉他,我没穿束具是因为它碍手碍脚,但是我并没有飞得像他形容的那么快,因为我只用了一只翅膀。圣彼得说,'你只用了一只翅膀飞行?'我说,'是啊,'害怕他责怪我。然后他说,'嗯,既然你的翅膀生得这样非凡,那么就暂时放下你的束具吧。但是从现在开始不准再用一只翅膀飞了,''因为你他妈的飞得太快了!'"

托德想,真是狗嘴里吐不出象牙来。为什么当时我不让他和那个男孩一块走呢?他躺在坚硬的地面上身体隐隐疼痛,可要翻身的时候,他把脚踝扭伤了,忍不住疼得叫出了声,又为此而感到痛恨。

"伤势更严重了吗?"

"我……我把脚踝扭了。"他忍着疼说。

"孩子,尝试着转移注意力不要想它。是我就会这么做。"

他紧咬嘴唇,通过承受另一种疼痛——忍耐杰弗逊讲故事时有节奏的嗡嗡声,来抵抗身体上的疼痛。杰弗逊似乎沉浸在自己的创作中不亦乐乎。

"……在经历了那么多的麻烦之后,我慢悠悠地漂浮在天堂里。但我忘记了黑人只能用单翼飞翔这件事,于是我不得不重新展开一只翅膀。这一次,我靠着我那折断的手臂,飞得快到让魔鬼都感到自愧不如。我飞得太快了,上帝啊,我又一次被老圣彼得叫住了。他说,'杰夫,我不是警告过你不要超速吗?''是的,'我说,'这只是一个意外。'他悲伤地看着我,摇了摇头,我知道我得离开了。他说:'杰夫,你还有你飞行的速度对天堂来说是一个威胁。如果我让你继续飞翔,天堂将会是一片喧嚣。杰夫,你该离开了!'孩子,我和那个白人老人争论,恳求他,但这一点用都没有。他们直接冲向了我,把我直接扔到了天堂之门外,然丢给了我一个降落伞和一张亚拉巴马州的地图……"

托德听着他大笑,几乎说不出话来,他们之间仿佛出现了一道屏障,他的耻辱映在屏障上像火一样闪闪发光。

"也许你最好停一会儿。"他说道,声音缥缈。

"没什么。"杰弗逊笑着说道,"当他们给我降落伞时,老圣彼得问我在走之前是否想说几句。我感觉糟透了,看都不想看他一眼,尤其是有这么多白人天使站在我身边。然后有人笑了,把我气疯了。所以我告诉他:'好吧,你确实抓住了我的把柄。你把我赶出来。你是掌控者,所以我对此无能为力。但你必须得承认:我在这里的时候,是有史以来天堂里最会飞的天使!'"

杰弗逊突然爆笑起来,托德感到了巨大的羞耻,似乎只有用暴怒才能将其洗去。这笑声令他翻江倒海,激起强烈的羞耻感,久久无法平静,即便是能驾驭精细的飞机也无法让他感到欣慰,他听到自己在尖叫:"为什么你要这样嘲笑我?"

那一刻他恨透了自己,但他已经失去了控制。他看到杰弗逊不知不觉张大了嘴,"什么——?"

"回答我!"

他的脉搏砰砰作响,好像奔腾的血液随时会冲破他的太阳穴,他试图接近老人,但摔倒了,他尖叫道:"他们不会让我们飞的,我能做些什么?也许我们是一群以死马为食的秃鹰,但我们可以希望成为老鹰,不是吗?不是吗?"

他筋疲力尽地向后倒去,脚踝重重地摔回地面。他嘴里的口水像稻草一样。如果他还有力气,他会掐死这个老人。这个笑嘻嘻的年老的小丑让他觉得像在战场上被白人军官注视着一样。然而这位老人既没有权力、威望和军衔,也没有什么技术。没有什么东西能让他摆脱这种可怕的感觉。他看着杰弗逊,看着他的脸挣扎着流露出一种混乱的情感。

"孩子,你这是什么意思?你在说什么……"

"滚开。去把你的故事说给白人听去。"

"但是,我没有那种意思……我……我没有想伤害你的感情……"

"求求你。离我远一点!"

"我没有,孩子。我完全没有别的意思。"

托德冷得发颤,想从杰弗逊脸上找到他刚刚看到的嘲弄。但是现在那张脸变得阴沉、疲惫、苍老。他感到十分不解。他不能确定是否就是这张脸上曾经露出过嘲笑,也不确定杰弗逊一生中是否真的笑过。他看到杰弗逊伸出手来抚摸他,然后缩了回去,他想知道除了疼痛之外,还有什么是真的,现在疼痛让他的视线变得模糊了。也许这一切都是他想象出来的。

"别因此沮丧,孩子。"他沉思着说道。

他听到杰弗逊疲惫地叹了口气,仿佛有口难言。他的愤怒消退了,只留下了痛苦。

"我很抱歉。"他咕哝道。

"你只是因为疼痛而筋疲力尽,只是……"

他透过一片模糊,微笑着看着他。有一瞬间,他感到他们因误解而尴尬地沉默着。

"孩子,你在这一带上空做什么呢?难道你不怕他们把你当作乌鸦而开枪打你吗?"

托德紧张起来。他是又被嘲笑了吗?但他还没来得及想明白,疼痛又让他颤抖起来,他另一部分身体则没有感觉到如此疼痛,这让他回忆起第一次看到飞机的情景。在他记忆中,空军基地里似乎有无数个机库被震得半开半掩,每一个机库中都会有一架飞机飞出,就像是从蜂房里飞出的小蜜蜂一样。

我第一次见到飞机的时候年纪还小,飞机还不常见。当时我 4 岁半,唯一见过的飞机就是在博览会上悬挂在汽车展览区天花板上的一架模型机。那时候我还不知道那只是个模型,我不知道真正的飞机有多大多贵。对我而言,那架飞机模型是个迷人的玩具,但零部件却很齐全,我母亲说只有有钱人家的白人小男孩才能拥有它。我固执地站在那儿,满怀羡慕,头向后仰望着那灰色的小飞机在汽车闪闪发光的车顶上方划出弧形。我发誓,不管未来有没有钱,总有一天我会拥有它。我妈妈硬拽着我出了这个展区,之后就连旋转木马、摩天轮和赛马也无法吸引我的注意力。我沉迷于用嘴唇模仿飞机微小的嗡嗡声,用手模仿它在飞行中快速盘旋的动作。

在那之后,我不再用堆在后院的木材做手推车或汽车了,而是开始制作飞机。我用几块告示牌当机翼,小箱子当作机身,再用一块木材当方向舵,就这样制造出了双翼飞机。博览会给我小小的世界带来一些新的启发,我一遍遍问母亲下一次博览会是什么时候。我想躺在草地上,望着天空,看着嬉戏的鸟儿变成翱翔天际的飞机。要是能再次看到飞机,我愿意一年都乖乖听话。我不厌其烦地向每个人询问飞机的事,但家中长辈也知之甚少,他们没什么能告诉我的。只有我叔叔了解一点,更棒的是,他还会用木片雕刻出螺旋桨,它能在空中飞速旋转,在涂了油的钉子上发出嘈杂的颤音。

我对飞机的渴望超越了其他任何事物;比如带有橡胶轮胎的红货车,再比如能在轨道上行驶的火车。我反复问母亲:

"妈妈?"

"你想要什么呢,孩子?"她回答我。

"妈妈,如果我说了你会生气吗?"我说。

"你想要什么,我没时间应付你这些愚蠢的问题。你到底想要什么?"

"妈妈,你能不能给我一个……?"我想问。

"给你什么?"她说。

"你知道的,妈妈;我一直想向你要……"

"孩子,"她说,"你要是不快点说你要什么的话,我就得打你屁股了,我还要做事呢。"

"哦,妈妈,你知道……"

"我刚刚跟你说什么了?"她说。

"就是你什么时候能给我买个飞机呢。"

"飞机!你疯了吧?我跟你讲多少次了,不要有这种愚蠢的想法。我告诉过你,飞机太贵了,我敢说如果你再为这些事烦我,我就要把你揍得半死!"

但这番话并没有打消我的念头,几天后,我可能会再说一次。

某天,发生了一件奇怪的事。那时是春天,我却整个早上都莫名其妙地感觉又热又烦。我在后院赤脚踢球时,记得四周景色很美。多刺的刺槐树上挂满了花,像一串串芬芳的白葡萄。阳光下,几只蝴蝶在萌芽而潮湿的新草上飞舞。我进屋去拿黄油面包,出来时听到一种陌生的低沉的声音。这和我以前听过的任何声音都不一样。我试着确定声音的位置,但是没用。这种感觉就像我在房间里找我父亲的手表时,听到了看不见的滴答声。这让我觉得好像我忘记了完成妈妈布置的任务……找啊找,我最终在头顶上空找到了声音来源。在天空中,只见一架飞机飞得很低,大约在100码外!它飞行得太慢,看起来像没有移动一样。我张大了嘴;面包和黄油掉进了泥土里。我想手舞足蹈,欢欣鼓舞。我突然想到一点,兴奋地颤抖起来:"一些白人小男孩的飞机飞走了,只要我能将它抓在手里,那这架飞机就是我的了!"这架小飞机和博览会上的一样,飞得只有屋檐那么高。我看着它稳稳地向前飞行,心中充满希冀,心头火热。我打开屏风,爬过去,在那里等着。当飞机飞过来的时候,我就一把抓住,然后快速地冲下来,在别人看到之前跑进屋里。这样就没人能来认领它了。飞机嗡嗡的声音越来越近,当它像蓝色的银十字架一样悬挂在我正上方时,我伸出手试图抓住了它,就像用手指戳破肥皂泡一样。但飞机继续飞行,就好像我只是在它后面呼了一口气。我又抓了一次,疯狂地想抓住它的尾巴,却抓了个空,失望之情在我的喉咙里涌动。我绝望地最后一次出手,奋力向前,手指从屏风上扯了下来。我坠落下来,猛地摔在地上。我用脚跟蹬了蹬地,平复呼吸,躺在地上放声痛哭。

我妈妈冲了进来。

"怎么了孩子!发生什么事了?"

"它飞走了!它飞走了!"

"什么飞走了?"

"飞机……"

"飞机?"

"是的,就像博览会上的那个……我……我试着让它停下,但是它还是直接飞走了……"

"什么时候?"

"就在刚刚。"我痛哭流涕。

"它朝哪儿飞了,孩子,哪个方向?"

"那边,朝那儿飞的……"

我指向那架渐行渐远的飞机,她双手叉腰扫视着天空,格子围裙在空中飘动。末了她低头看向我,缓缓摇了摇头。

"真的不见了!不见了!"我哭喊道。

"儿子,你是蠢吗?"她说道,"难道你没看出那是架真飞机,不是那种玩具模型吗?"

"真的……?"我忘记了哭泣。"真的飞机?"

"是,真的飞机。你知不知道你伸手去抓的东西比一辆汽车还大?你还试着在这儿抓住它,我打赌它正在比屋顶高200多英里的地方飞呢。"她觉得我很丢人。"在别人发现你做了什么蠢事之前赶紧给我进屋,你是不是觉得你那小胳膊很长……"

我被带进屋里脱了衣服上床,妈妈叫了医生过来。我哭得很惨;疼痛和失望各占一半,失望是因为我发现飞机离我实在是太远了。

医生来了之后,我听见妈妈告诉了他飞机的事情,还问他我是不是脑子有什么问题。他解释说我之前已经发了好几个小时的烧。但是我在床上躺了一个星期,时不时还会在睡梦里看见那架飞机就在我的指尖上面飞行,飞得很慢很慢,几乎像是没动。每次我都会伸手去抓它,但怎么都抓不到,每一个这样的梦里,我都会听到奶奶的警告:

"年轻人,年轻人
你的手臂还太短
无法与上帝抗衡……"

"嘿,孩子!"

起初他并不知道自己身在何处,他看着眼前正指点着什么的老人,视线模糊。

"那是不是你们的飞机,来找你的?"

眼前逐渐清晰起来,他看见远处田野上空有一个小小的黑色物体在热浪中翱翔。但他不能确定,身体也痛得要命,那个自己被螺旋桨的旋转叶片劈成两半的可怕幻想反复出现,他生怕这变成现实。

"你觉得他看到我们了吗?"他听到老人问他。

"看到我们？我希望如此。"

"他像一只从地狱里飞出来的蝙蝠！"

他费劲集中精神，然后听到了微弱的马达声，他希望这一切能尽快结束。

"你现在感觉怎么样？"

"像一场噩梦。"他说。

"嘿！他从别的路绕回来了！"

"可能他看见我们了，"他说。"也许他是去派遣救护车和地勤人员了。"也或许，他绝望地想着，他根本就没有看到我们。

"你让那男孩儿去哪了？"

"去格雷夫斯先生那儿，"杰弗逊说道，"他是这片地的主人。"

"你觉得他会打电话让人过来帮忙吗？"

杰弗逊迅速地看了他一眼。

"噢，是的。达布尼·格雷夫斯因为杀人事件名声不好，但他会打电话给……"

"杀人事件？"

"那5个人……你没听说吗？"他惊讶道。

"没有。"

"每个人都知道达布尼·格雷夫斯的事，尤其是黑人。他杀的人已经够多了。"

托德又有种天黑后被困在白人社区的感觉。

"他们都做了什么？"他问

"也许他们是人类本身就是错误吧，"杰弗逊说。"他欠了一些人的钱，就像他欠我一样……"

"那你为什么留在这？"

"因为我们是黑人，孩子。"

"我知道，但是……"

"我们免不了跟白人讨生活？"

他从杰弗逊的眼睛上移开目光，感到有些安慰，又有点心虚。他绝望地想，我很快沦落到和他们一样了。他闭上眼睛，眼皮在阳光下烧得血红，耳边是杰弗逊的说话声。

"我无处可去，"杰弗逊说，"如果我跑了，他们会来找我。但达布尼·格雷夫斯是个疯疯癫癫的家伙，他无时无刻不在开玩笑。他可以卑鄙至极，也有可能掉头来支持黑人。我见过他这样做。但我恨透了他。因为一旦他帮一个人帮倦了，他就不会再管那个人了。然后，其他白人就变本加厉地报复他帮助过的人。对他来说，这只是一个笑话。他对任何人都不屑一顾，除了他自己……"

托德听出老人声音中的一丝冷漠。就好像他要跟自己说的话撇清关系，免得惹火上身。

"他只是帮你一个忙，然后就自顾自离开，留你一个人坐立难安。我离他远远地，在这你必须这样。"

他想，如果脚踝的疼痛能缓一缓就好了。飞机旋转着下坠，离地面越来越近，我与平庸的黑人们的差距也越缩越小了，这话在他脑海中闪过。汗水涌入了他的眼睛，他确信如果他的脑海中仍是一片天旋地转，他将永远无法看到飞机。他试图看向杰弗逊，杰弗逊手里拿的是什么？那是一个小黑人,另一个杰弗逊！一个小黑人杰弗逊在捧腹大笑,另一个则冷眼旁观。然后,杰弗逊抬起头来,转身要说话,但托德的思绪已经飘远了。托德回到了他早已遗忘的一天,在炎热干燥的土地上寻找天空中的飞机。他和母亲隐秘地穿过空荡荡的街道,黑色的面孔从拉上的窗帘后探出头来,有人在拍打窗户,他回头看到一张张黑色的脸从紧闭的百叶窗后窥视着。而他母亲看着空荡荡的街道,摇着头催促他前进,起初闪过一道光,飞机引擎嗡嗡作响,透过太阳光他看到它在盘旋时闪着银光,看到一阵阵白烟,听到他母亲的喊声。来这,孩子！他第二次看到这样的景象了,飞机飞得很高,突然爆炸并慢慢坠落。他看着,被催促着离开,空气中到处都是快速旋转的白色卡片,这些卡片在风中飞舞,散落在屋顶上,跌进水沟里,一个女人跑过来,抓起一张卡片尖叫着读起来。他冲进卡片雨里,从空中抓住飞洒下来的卡片,就像他在冬天接住飘落的雪花一样,来吧,孩子！来吧,我说！他看着她把卡片拿走,看到她的脸变得困惑和紧绷,她颤抖着说:"黑鬼不能投票。"接着他看见卡片上印着的白色头套,头套上挖着两个黑魆魆的空洞,一时吓得要死,惊惧地哀叫了一声,然后看到飞机优雅地旋转着,在阳光下像一柄炽热的剑般闪闪发光。看着飞机翱翔,他被巨大的恐慌和迷恋攫住了。

烈日高悬,他听见杰弗逊喊着什么,渐渐地他看见3个人影在被热浪炙烤地变形了的田野上移动。

"看起来好像是医生来了,全都穿着一身白。"杰弗逊说。

他们终于来了,托德暗想。这个想法让他舒了一口气,紧绷着的弦一消失,他觉得自己要昏过去了。但是他一闭上眼睛,身体就被钳制住,那3名白人男子抱着他的臂膀,强迫他穿上某种外套。他挣扎着,但是终于败下阵来,他的臂膀被牢牢束在身侧。疼痛火焰般舔过他的眼皮,他突然明白自己是被捆在了一件紧身衣里。这是什么下流的恶作剧?

"这个应该能捆得住他,格雷夫斯先生。"他听见有人这么说。

他全身的能量似乎都集中在他的眼睛里,死死地盯住那些人的脸。那是格雷夫斯和另外两个穿着医院制服的男子。叫格雷夫斯的那人说的一番话使他在恐惧和仇恨两种极端情绪间摇摆着。

"穿上紧身衣之后,他看上去是个挺可爱的小东西,是不是,哥几个？你们能来,我很高兴。"

"这个小伙子没疯,格雷夫斯先生。"另外两人中的一个说道,"他需要一个医生,不是我们。不明白你为什么领着我俩到这来。你可能觉得这是个好玩的恶作剧,但是你的表亲鲁道夫杀了人。不管是白人还是黑人,只要疯了,对我们来说都没区别……"

托德看着那男人面色愠红,接着格雷夫斯居高临下地看着他,笑了起来。

"这个黑鬼也该待在精神病院里,哥几个。我知道杰夫家的小鬼头说着什么'黑鬼飞行员'。我们都知道不能让一个黑鬼飞得那么高,他会发疯的。黑鬼的脑子适应不了高海拔……"

托德看着那张无精打采涨红的面皮,感觉到他曾经能想象的所有无名的恐怖和猥琐都在眼前变成现实。

"咱们走吧。"一个侍从说着。

托德看着另一个人向他伸出手,才察觉到自己躺在一具担架上。

他吼道:"把你的手拿开！"

他们缩回手,一脸惊讶。

"黑鬼你说什么?"格雷夫斯问他。

他默不作声,感觉格雷夫斯的脚对准了他的头。他的胸腔被击中了,他几乎不能呼吸。他无助地咳嗽着,看到格雷夫斯的嘴唇紧紧咧开,挂在一嘴黄牙上。他试着转过头。他同时感觉到一只苍蝇拖着半死的身体缓缓爬过他的脸,而他的体内一枚炮弹刚刚炸裂。热烈、歇斯底里的笑声从他的胸腔里炸开,使得他眼球鼓起,他觉得他脖子上冒起的青筋一定要爆开了。这时,一部分的他脱离出来,站在这一切混乱之后,目视着格雷夫斯那张红脸上的惊异,见证着他自己的发狂。他以为这一切永远不会结束了,他会就这样大笑到死去。杰弗逊的笑声在他的耳边大响,他寻找着他的身影,将视线急切地投到他的脸上,似乎在这个由愤怒和羞辱造就的疯狂的世界里,杰弗逊就是他唯一的拯救者。杰弗逊的存在让他一定程度上感到安心。他突然感觉到虽然他的身体依旧以不自然的姿态被禁锢在紧身衣里,但是这件事不再如炸雷般在他的脑海里回响,而是变成远远的回音。他心怀感激地听着杰弗逊的声音。

"格雷夫斯先生,军队确实跟他讲过让他不要离开他的飞机。"

"黑鬼,我才不管什么军队不军队的,你给我滚出我的地盘。飞机就算了,毕竟是我们纳税人交的钱买的。但是你,不行。是死也好,是活也好,我不想要黑鬼在我的土地上。"

托德现在什么也感知不到了,他迷失在疼痛里。

格雷夫斯吩咐着:"杰夫,你和泰迪过来抓着担架,我想让你们把这只黑鹰送回那个黑鬼飞行营地里去,把他扔在那儿。"

杰弗逊和男孩沉默地向他走来。他转过头,在意识到的同时也立刻起了疑心,也许只有这两个人可以将他从那令人窒息的孤立状态中解放出来。

他们弯腰提起担架。一个侍从走向泰迪。

"小子,你觉得自己抬得动吗?"

"我觉得我行,先生。"泰迪回道。

"好吧,那你到后面来吧,让你老爸抬前面,这样他的腿就能抬高起来了。"

他看着那些白人男子走在前面,然后是杰弗逊和男孩抬着他沉默地跟随着。然后他们停了下来,他感觉到有一只手抹过了他的脸,然后队伍又前进了起来。他感觉自己似乎从那种孤立无援中被抬出来,被一个人的世界重新接纳。一股暗流在杰弗逊、男孩和他之间无言地涌动着。他们抬着他的动作很轻柔。远远地,他听见知更鸟清脆的一声啼叫。他抬眼,看见一只秃鹫静止般地停留在空中。在那一刻,整个下午在此刻停滞,他等待着那熟悉的恐惧再度覆没他。但是,他只听见男孩轻声哼着一支歌,歌声萦绕在他的脑海,他看见那只黑鸟向着太阳的方向滑翔,包裹在一团金光中,熊熊燃烧。

(曹文清,魏梦洁 译;言声远,朱镜如 校)

致　谢

　　一本书从酝酿到成书往往历经多年，本教材亦是如此。该教材是随着南京航空航天大学英语文学教学改革的不断深入和英语专业建设的不断推进而产生并日渐成熟的。自南京航空航天大学英语专业作为省重点专业建设起，编写该书的想法便已萌生。2021年南京航空航天大学英语专业被教育部批准为国家级一流专业建设点，为了将"新文科"建设推向深入，并使课程思政教学改革落地生根，该教材出版时机已经成熟。

　　感谢南京航空航天大学教务处和研究生院，为本书的立项、研究、编写和出版提供了资金支持，同时也感谢外国语学院教材基地的大力支持。感谢外国语学院院长范祥涛教授，石云龙教授，教务处副处长刘长江教授，我有幸分别作为主编或参与《当代中国》《英语文学阅读与欣赏》和《民航英语口语》等教材的编写，积累了宝贵经验。

　　感谢本书选篇所涉及的各位作家、理论家、思想家。所涉及的作品，或为经典，或为新作，都为呈现大千世界插上了想象的翅膀。所涉及的理论家，或为自然科学，抑或人文社科领域的思想家，提出的重要理论或概念都凝聚了人类智慧的光芒，为文学解读和欣赏提供了锐利的思想武器，为诘问世间百态、人生万象提供了无穷的思想资源。我们联系到大部分原作者或代理公司，他们都欣然同意我们节选他们的作品供中国的学者和学生赏读，但是由于种种原因，有的实在未能取得联系，我们也希望借此机会请看到这本书的原作者与我们联系，商讨版权使用事宜。

　　感谢外国语学院研究生同学的参与和本科生同学的建议。在本书编写过程中，英美文学课程的多位研究生参与了部分工作，主要是对相关作品进行翻译和校对，翻译、校译的过程也是教学相长、师生同游的过程。本教材的编写同本科生对课程的建设性建议密不可分。同学们的期待和鞭策是将教改推向深入的不竭动力。正是同学们对知识的渴求,使我认识到在教学内容上需篇篇有看点、节节有重点,这推动了我对教学的更多探索。

感谢南京大学出版社领导的大力支持,尤其是荣卫红老师的敦促和孙辉老师的编辑工作,使本教材能如期付梓。由于编者水平有限,教材中难免有不足之处,恳请广大读者批评指正。